Learn Java for Web Development

Vishal Layka

Apress®

Learn Java for Web Development

ISBN-13 (pbk): 978-1-4302-5983-1

ISBN-13 (electronic): 978-1-4302-5984-8

President and Publisher: Paul Manning
Lead Editor: Steve Anglin
Development Editor: Matthew Moodie, Chris Nelson, Tom Welsh
Technical Reviewer: Boris Minkin
Editorial Board: Steve Anglin, Mark Beckner, Ewan Buckingham, Gary Cornell, Louise Corrigan, James T. DeWolf, Jonathan Gennick, Jonathan Hassell, Robert Hutchinson, Michelle Lowman, James Markham, Matthew Moodie, Jeff Olson, Jeffrey Pepper, Douglas Pundick, Ben Renow-Clarke, Dominic Shakeshaft, Gwenan Spearing, Matt Wade, Steve Weiss
Coordinating Editor: Anamika Panchoo
Copy Editor: Kim Wimpsett
Compositor: SPi Global
Indexer: SPi Global
Artist: SPi Global
Cover Designer: Anna Ishchenko

Distributed to the book trade worldwide by Springer Science+Business Media New York, 233 Spring Street, 6th Floor, New York, NY 10013. Phone 1-800-SPRINGER, fax (201) 348-4505, e-mail `orders-ny@springer-sbm.com`, or visit `www.springeronline.com`. Apress Media, LLC is a California LLC and the sole member (owner) is Springer Science + Business Media Finance Inc (SSBM Finance Inc). SSBM Finance Inc is a Delaware corporation.

For information on translations, please e-mail `rights@apress.com`, or visit `www.apress.com`.

Apress and friends of ED books may be purchased in bulk for academic, corporate, or promotional use. eBook versions and licenses are also available for most titles. For more information, reference our Special Bulk Sales–eBook Licensing web page at `www.apress.com/bulk-sales`.

Any source code or other supplementary materials referenced by the author in this text is available to readers at `www.apress.com`. For detailed information about how to locate your book's source code, go to `www.apress.com/source-code/`.

To the four stars in my universe: my parents, Shobha and Madan, and my brothers, Deepak and Nishant.

Contents at a Glance

Contents

About the Author

Vishal Layka is the chief technology officer of Star Protocol. He is involved in the architecture, design, and implementation of distributed business systems, and his focus is on consulting and training with the JVM languages. His language proficiencies include Java, Groovy, Scala, and Haskell. Vishal is also the lead author of *Beginning Groovy, Grails, and Griffon* (Apress, 2012). When he needs a break from technology, Vishal reads eclectically from calculus to star formation.

About the Technical Reviewer

Boris Minkin is a senior technical architect at a major financial corporation. He has more than 20 years of experience working in various areas of information technology and financial services. Boris obtained his master's degree in information systems at Stevens Institute of Technology in New Jersey. His professional interests are in Internet technology, service-oriented architecture, enterprise application architecture and development, cloud computing, distributed caching, Java, and grid and high-performance computing. You can contact Boris at `bm@panix.com`.

Introduction

This book is for a large cross section of modern Java web developers, with various levels of experience.

Learning the Java programming language is a noble cause, but learning merely the Java language is not enough in the real world. Java developers have to learn Java EE, a collection of related server-side technologies, to put their Java skills to any real use.

But learning Java EE is not enough either. The Java language along with Java EE may suffice to develop web applications for projects in the same organization, as a means to reusability, but the diverse landscape of Java on the Web is permeated with several web frameworks, such as Spring Web MVC, that make development much easier; thus, a Java web developer has to have the knowledge of these web frameworks.

But this is not enough still. In the very first line of this introduction, I mentioned that this book is for a modern Java web developer. Modern Java is more than just a language; it is now a fully optimized platform because several other languages such as Groovy and Scala, called the *JVM languages*, now run on the Java Virtual Machine (JVM). All such JVM languages, especially Groovy, have a close association with Java, and you will come across web applications before long where Java and these other JVM languages work in tandem. The most ambitious projects will require you to build web applications using these JVM languages.

This book addresses all the needs of a modern Java web developer. It is designed for beginners up to intermediate developers and explains the specifics of Java on the Web. For example, this book is perfect for developers who are aware of technologies like MVC but do not yet understand how and why they have changed the way web applications are built.

This book is also for developers who want to learn frameworks other than JSF 2 (which is bundled with Java EE). This book covers four types of web frameworks: request based, component based, rapid, and reactive. Among these four types, the book covers five proven web frameworks: Struts 2, Spring Web MVC, JSF 2, Grails 2, and Play 2.

In addition, this book is for developers who have no experience in the Java, Groovy, and Scala programming languages but who yearn to create web applications. This book provides the essentials of these three languages in the appendixes.

Instead of simply pronouncing one web framework the best, *Learn Java for Web Development* shows the strengths of the most popular web frameworks by means of a real-world bookstore application. Developing a complete real application necessitates a seamless collaboration of dynamic functionalities, and the code for building such components is contrived and too involved. Instead of focusing on developing such moving parts, this book confines its attention on leveraging the strengths of each web framework.

How the Book Is Structured

The book consists of eight chapters, which I'll describe next, plus the three previously mentioned appendixes that introduce the Java, Groovy, and Scala languages.

Chapter 1: Introducing Java Web Development

Chapter 1 explains the main objective that shapes this book and highlights what appears in the subsequent chapters. This chapter begins with a discussion of a significant change in the Java landscape, its implication, and what Java exactly means today. The chapter then discusses the three key players that join forces in building modern Java web applications: the JVM languages, Java EE, and the Java web frameworks.

This chapter introduces the key features of a modern Java web application such as Ajax and REST, WebSocket for real-time web application, the Typesafe stack for a reactive web application, and client-side MVC frameworks for responsive and single-page web applications. Finally, the chapter introduces some important aspects of modern web development that are beyond the scope of this book, such as Java information retrieval on the Web, and briefly introduces the central component of Web 3.0, which is still an open subject of research, the Semantic Web.

Chapter 2: Building Web Applications Using Servlets and JSP

Chapter 2 begins with a discussion of the evolution and architecture of web applications. The chapter then highlights how to use the standard web API. The first pass at the sample application uses only servlets and JSP. Then the chapter shows you how to build the same application as a Model 2 application.

Chapter 3: Best Practices in Java EE Web Development

Chapter 3 examines the chain of causality that leads to the need for following best practices. The chapter explains the need to evolve projects and introduces Expression Language and JSTL. The chapter then discusses the Java EE web tier patterns.

Chapter 4: Building a Web Application Using Struts 2

In Chapter 4, you'll learn about Struts 2. Not as popular as it used to be, Struts 2 is introduced in this book for developers who have to maintain legacy applications. This chapter first introduces the key architectural components of Struts 2. Then you will learn to develop your first application using Struts 2 and Maven 4. Moving forward, you will learn to develop the bookstore application and integrate with Tiles 3.

Chapter 5: Building Java Web Applications with Spring Web MVC

Chapter 5 explains three key objectives of the Spring Framework: loose coupling using dependency injection, dealing with cross-cutting concerns using AOP, and removing boilerplate code using Spring templates. Elucidating how Spring 3 works, the chapter introduces the Spring Web MVC architecture. Then you will learn to build your first web application using Spring 3 Web MVC. This chapter also shows you how to build the bookstore application. You will learn to use the latest version of the SpringSource tool suite.

Chapter 6: Component-Based Web Development Using JSF

Chapter 6 introduces you to a component-based framework called JSF 2 that is bundled with Java EE. After you have familiarized yourself with the request-based framework presented in Chapter 4 and Chapter 5, understanding JSF 2 will be much easier. This chapter shows you how JSF 2 represents a paradigm shift in web development and introduces you to key components of the JSF 2 architecture. After you have a firm grasp of the architecture components, this chapter shows you how to develop your first JSF 2 application, and along with this you will learn the life-cycle phases of a JSF 2 application. Then the chapter shows you how to integrate JSF 2 with the Spring Framework so that you can access the database via Spring templates from the JSF 2 web layer. Finally, the chapter shows you how to develop the bookstore application.

Chapter 7: Rapid Web Development with Grails

Grails is a rapid application development framework that lets you create web applications in record time. Chapter 7 introduces you to two techniques of generating web applications with Grails: static and dynamic scaffolding. The chapter then takes you through the code generated and explains step-by-step how the code works. Having presented the code generated, this chapter shows you how to develop the bookstore application with Grails 2. This chapter also covers unit testing, an oft-neglected task in application development. This chapter shows you how to build tests for your web applications using the JUnit testing framework. Then this chapter shows you how to use the in-memory database H2. In this chapter, you will also learn to use the latest version of the Groovy-Grails tool suite.

Chapter 8: Play with Java and Scala

Chapter 8 introduces the key web player of the Typesafe stack, the Play 2 framework, and explains how the Typesafe stack provides an alternative to Java EE to build Java- and Scala-based applications. First you will learn to develop a Java-based web application using Play 2. Then you will learn to develop a Scala-based web application using Play 2. Subsequently, this chapter shows how to use the model and access a database in Play 2.

Chapter 1

Introducing Java Web Development

The mind, once stretched by a new idea, never returns to its original dimensions.

—Ralph Waldo Emerson

An intelligent machine is that which extends the very imagination with which it was built. An example of this is the instruction called `invokeDynamic`,[1] which was introduced with Java 7 to optimize the performance of dynamically typed languages on the Java Virtual Machine (JVM). The JVM, originally intended for Java, can now host a myriad of programming languages, including Groovy[2] and Scala.[3] This has led to a renaissance of Java web development. This new paradigm of cross-pollination and diverse, well-founded options carves out a number of niches in the Java ecosystem, resulting in a richer web landscape than ever before.

The open source community has capitalized on the multiparadigm capabilities offered by the languages that run on the JVM, by means of web frameworks, to dramatically enhance the productivity in web development. Java EE[4] advanced this momentum, pioneered by Java frameworks such as Spring,[5] by standardizing and improving the API and runtime environment. Further, functional programming constructs, in the form of lambdas, have been added to Java 8. As a result, Java is on the rebound to become an übersolution.

This chapter sets the stage for the book by introducing the three key players that join forces in building modern Java web applications: the JVM languages, Java EE, and the Java web frameworks.

---

[1]`http://cr.openjdk.java.net/~jrose/pres/200910-VMIL.pdf`
[2]`http://groovy.codehaus.org/`
[3]`www.scala-lang.org/`
[4]`www.oracle.com/technetwork/java/javaee/overview/index.html`
[5]`http://spring.io/`

> **Note** The JVM languages represent a new category of languages that run on the JVM. With the latest version, Java 8, Java is no longer a privileged JVM language and is now simply one of the many languages that run on the JVM.

The chapter begins by introducing the JVM languages and then introduces Java EE. The Java EE platform is the set of API specifications that act as the building blocks for developing web applications. The chapter then highlights the Java web frameworks, which will be the subject of the book from Chapter 4 onward.

JVM Languages

The JVM is the runtime environment that provides you with the ability to use different programming languages for building web applications. The JVM languages can be largely classified into two types: languages that are designed for the JVM and existing languages that are ported to JVM.

Languages Designed for the JVM

Plenty of languages are specifically designed for the JVM; Table 1-1 describes a few of them. All but Clojure are discussed in this book.

***Table 1-1.** Languages Designed for the JVM*

Language Designed for JVM	Description
Clojure[6]	Clojure is a dynamically typed, functional language.
Groovy	Groovy is a dynamic, compiled language with syntax similar to Java but is more flexible.
Java	Java is a statically typed, imperative language. The latest release of Java, Java 8, supports aspects of functional programming.
Scala	Scala is a statically typed, compiled language that supports aspects of functional programming and performs a large amount of type inference, much like a dynamic language.

Here are some important definitions:

- *Dynamic typing*: Dynamic typing keeps track of information about what sort of values the variables contain by carrying the type information on the values held in variables.
- *Static typing*: In static typing, the type information is all about the variables, not the values in them.

---

[6]`http://clojure.org/`

- *Imperative languages*: These are languages in which the state can be mutated by the instructions in the language.
- *Functional languages*: In functional languages, the functions operate on values as in procedural languages, but instead of mutating the state, the functions are purely mathematical functions that return new values.

Figure 1-1 shows where Java 8, Groovy, Scala, and Clojure fall on the functional language continuum. Java 8 introduces lambdas, which makes it slightly functional, Groovy has had functional constructs since its inception and is even more functional with Groovy 2.0, and Scala is the most functional of the three object-oriented (OO) languages. Clojure, on the other hand, is a purely functional, non-OO language.

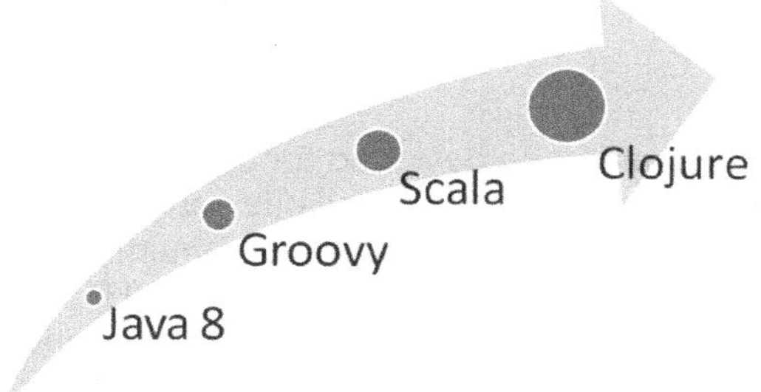

***Figure 1-1.** Functional gradation of JVM languages*

> **Note** In Figure 1-1, no version number is mentioned for Groovy, Scala, and Clojure because Java supports aspects of functional programming starting from Java 8 only.

Languages Ported to the JVM

JRuby, Jython, and Rhino are a few of the mainstream JVM implementations of existing languages. Table 1-2 describes them.

Table 1-2. Languages Ported to the JVM

Languages Ported to JVM	Description
JRuby[7]	JRuby is a JVM reimplementation of the Ruby programming language. Ruby is a dynamically typed OO language with some functional features.
Jython[8]	Jython is a reimplementation of Python on the JVM, so it is a dynamic language.
Rhino[9]	Rhino provides an implementation of JavaScript on the JVM. JavaScript is a dynamically typed OO language.

This book is based on some of the mainstream object-oriented JVM languages that were specifically designed for the JVM, namely, Java, Groovy, and Scala.

Java EE

Java began life as a programming language designed for building stand-alone applications and grew rapidly into other spheres. A large part of Java's popularity can be attributed to its usage in creating web applications. A web application consists of static and dynamic (interactive) web pages. *Static* web pages contain various types of markup languages (HTML, XHTML, and so on) and are used, in general, to provide information; *dynamic* web pages, on the other hand, are capable of generating content with the aid of additional web components (covered in Chapter 2). Thus, a *web application* is a collection of web pages and is capable of generating dynamic content in response to requests. Unlike a web page used merely to provide information, a web application lets you perform some activity and save the result. Developing a web application, however, is fundamentally different from building stand-alone applications and requires you to understand the following three key elements:

- *The Java EE platform*: This is the set of API specifications that are the building blocks of the web application.
- *The web container*: The web container implements the API specifications of the Java EE platform. Specifically, the web container provides the services for managing and executing web components such as servlets, JSPs, filters, listeners, and render responses to the client. The web containers are covered in Chapter 2.

> **Note** There are several types of containers, but this book will focus on the web container primarily used for web applications. You have to choose the container based on the kind of application you want to develop.

- *Web components*: These are hosted by the container. These web components, such as servlets, JSPs, filters, and listeners, are covered in Chapter 2.

[7]http://jruby.org/
[8]www.jython.org/
[9]https://developer.mozilla.org/en-US/docs/Rhino_documentation

The Java EE Platform

The Java EE platform is driven by the following two goals:

- Providing the API specifications that are the building blocks of the web application.
- Standardizing and reducing the complexity of enterprise application development. It does this by providing an application model that defines an architecture for implementing services as multitiered applications.

Figure 1-2 summarizes the evolution of Java EE and, for the sake of brevity, shows only the new specifications added with each release.

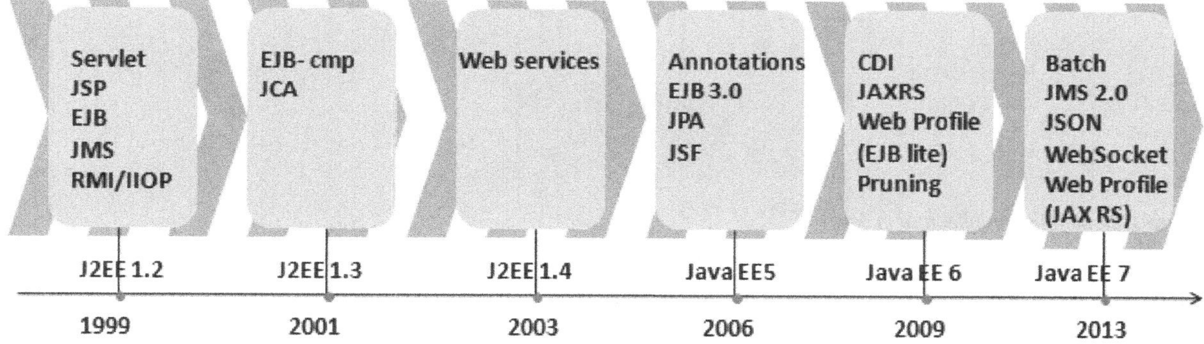

Figure 1-2. The evolution of Java EE

> **Note** *Pruning* (also known as *marked for deletion*) consists of a list of proposed features for possible removal in the next Java EE release in order to reduce the size of the platform or to keep it from bloating.
>
> The goal of Web Profile is to allow developers to create web applications with the appropriate set of technologies.

The Java EE platform is aimed at standardizing and reducing the complexity of enterprise application development by providing an application model that defines an architecture for implementing services as multitiered applications. In a multitiered application, the functionality of the application is separated into distinct functional areas, called *tiers*. Figure 1-3 illustrates the typical multitiered architecture in a Java EE application model.

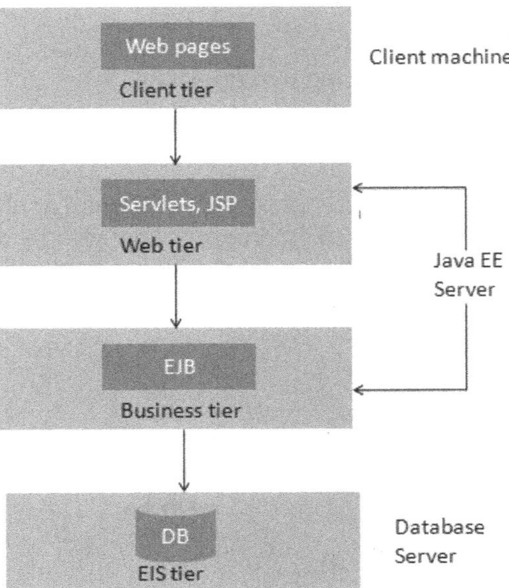

***Figure 1-3.** Multitier architecture in Java*

The Client Tier

The client tier is the top tier in a multitiered Java EE architecture; it consists of application clients that make requests to the Java EE server, which is often located on a different machine. The server processes the requests and returns a response to the client. An example of a client is a web browser or a stand-alone application.

The Web Tier

The web tier consists of components that handle the interaction between clients and the business tier. After receiving a request from the client, the web tier does the following:

1. Collects input from the client
2. Controls the flow of screens or pages on the client
3. Maintains the state of data for a user's session
4. Obtains results from the components in the business tier
5. Generates dynamic content in various formats to the client

As shown in Figure 1-2, a new Web Profile specification has been added in Java EE 7.[10] Table 1-3 lists technologies included in the Web Profile specification. As mentioned earlier, the goal of Web Profile is to allow developers to create web applications with the appropriate set of technologies.

[10]`www.oracle.com/technetwork/java/javaee/tech/index.html`

Table 1-3. Web Profile 7 Specification

Specification	Version	URL
JSF	2.2	`http://jcp.org/en/jsr/detail?id=344`
JSP	2.3	`http://jcp.org/en/jsr/detail?id=245`
JSTL	1.2	`http://jcp.org/en/jsr/detail?id=52`
Servlet	3.1	`http://jcp.org/en/jsr/detail?id=340`
WebSocket	1.0	`http://jcp.org/en/jsr/detail?id=356`
Expression Language	3.0	`http://jcp.org/en/jsr/detail?id=341`
EJB Lite	3.2	`http://jcp.org/en/jsr/detail?id=345`
JPA	2.1	`http://jcp.org/en/jsr/detail?id=338`
JTA	1.2	`http://jcp.org/en/jsr/detail?id=907`
Bean Validation	1.1	`http://jcp.org/en/jsr/detail?id=349`
Managed Beans	1.0	`http://jcp.org/en/jsr/detail?id=316`
Interceptors	1.2	`http://jcp.org/en/jsr/detail?id=318`
Contexts and Dependency Injection	1.1	`http://jcp.org/en/jsr/detail?id=346`
Dependency Injection for Java	1.0	`http://jcp.org/en/jsr/detail?id=330`
Debugging Support for Other Languages	1.0	`http://jcp.org/en/jsr/detail?id=45`
JAX-RS	2.0	`http://jcp.org/en/jsr/detail?id=339`
JSON-P	1.0	`http://jcp.org/en/jsr/detail?id=353`

Regarding the Web Profile specifications listed in Table 1-3:

- In Java EE 7, no changes were made to JSP and JSTL because these specifications have not been updated.
- Expression Language has been removed from JSP and now has its own JSR (341).
- Servlets and JSF have both been updated.
- WebSocket 1.0 was introduced in Java EE 7.

This book concentrates on the web tier of Java EE; we will dive deep into the web tier in Chapter 2.

The multitier architecture of Java EE has a tremendous impact on the development of Java enterprise applications. A *Java enterprise application* can be defined as a Java application that utilizes the enterprise services offered by Java EE. In fact, a web application can be classified as an enterprise application if it utilizes Java EE services in the form of components packed in the web tier. Java EE isolates these services functionally into separate tiers, as illustrated in Figure 1-3, by providing an application model on which the Java enterprise applications should be built. As a consequence, the Java enterprise application mirrors the multitier architecture of Java EE. Figure 1-4 illustrates a generalized view of the layers of a typical web application.

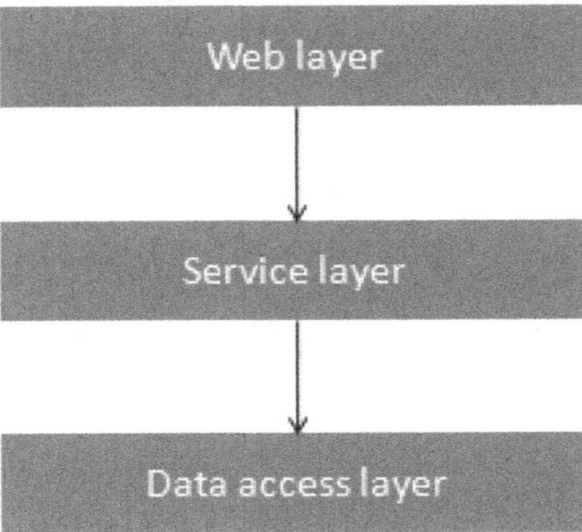

***Figure 1-4.** A generalized view of layers in an enterprise application*

Each layer in Figure 1-4 is an area of *concern*, for the application. For instance, the web layer deals only with employing the web tier components of Java EE. Having different layers in an application results in what is called a *separation of concerns*. In terms of implementation, this separation of concerns is achieved using coarse-grained interfaces.

The concern is the feature, functionality or business functions with which the application's developer needs to be concerned. Crosscutting such concerns is inherent in complex systems and leads to *code scattering*, which is when code for one concern spans many modules, and *code tangling*, which is when code in one module concentrates on addressing multiple concerns. Code scattering and code tangling lead to a lack of clarity, redundancy, rigidity, and continuous refactoring. Figure 1-5 illustrates how the system services of logging, transaction, and security crosscut the business functions of the application.

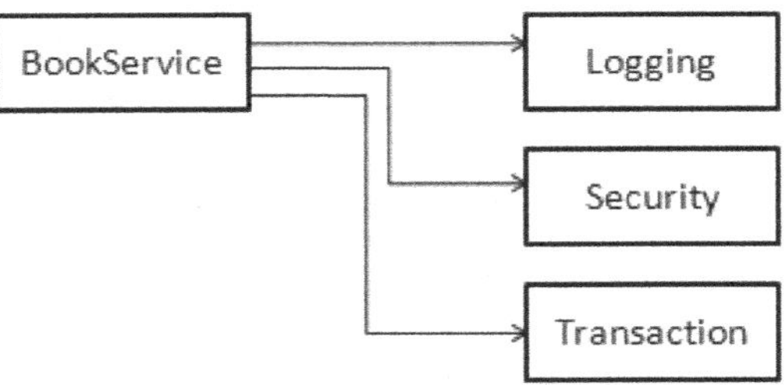

***Figure 1-5.** BookService involved with system services*

`BookService` in Figure 1-5 is too involved with the system services. Each object knows and is responsible for logging, security, and transaction. A method, for example, to purchase a book in `BookService` should be concerned only with how to purchase the book and not with whether it is secure or transactional. Separation of concerns, one of the main goals of software engineering, lets you handle each service on its own and thereby does the following:

- Promotes traceability within and across the artifacts in the system, throughout the life cycle of the system
- Controls the impact caused by the change, thereby providing scope for evolution and noninvasive adaptation
- Promotes development of cohesive units, thereby facilitating reuse

SEPARATION OF CONCERNS

The term *separation of concerns* (SoC) was coined by Edsger W. Dijkstra in his paper "On the role of scientific thought."[11] Dijkstra explains in in the following terms:

> *Let me try to explain to you, what to my taste is characteristic for all intelligent thinking. It is, that one is willing to study in depth an aspect of one's subject matter in isolation for the sake of its own consistency, all the time knowing that one is occupying oneself only with one of the aspects. We know that a program must be correct and we can study it from that viewpoint only; we also know that it should be efficient and we can study its efficiency on another day, so to speak. In another mood we may ask ourselves whether, and if so: why, the program is desirable. But nothing is gained—on the contrary!—by tackling these various aspects simultaneously. It is what I sometimes have called "the separation of concerns," which, even if not perfectly possible, is yet the only available technique for effective ordering of one's thoughts, that I know of. This is what I mean by "focusing one's attention upon some aspect": it does not mean ignoring the other aspects, it is just doing justice to the fact that from this aspect's point of view, the other is irrelevant. It is being one- and multiple-track minded simultaneously.*

Web Layer

The web layer of a web application consists of the web tier components of Java EE such as servlets and JSP. The web layer can access the service layer, but there should not be a tight coupling between the web layer and the service layer. That is, changing the service layer should not impact the web layer.

[11] www.cs.utexas.edu/users/EWD/transcriptions/EWD04xx/EWD447.html

Service Layer

The service layer consists of the business tier components of Java EE such as Enterprise JavaBeans (EJBs). The service layer can access the data access layer, but there should be no tight coupling between the service layer and the data access layer. In fact, the service layer should not know anything about the web or data access layer. The service layer provides a coarse-grained interface for the web layer.

Data Access Layer

The data access layer consists of the data tier components of Java EE such as JDBC and JPA. This layer should not contain any business logic. This layer abstracts the actual persistence mechanism (in other words, JDBC or JPA) from the service layer by providing the coarse-grained interface to the service layer.

> **Note** The call flow in this architecture is always from the top layer to the bottom layer. In other words, the service layer should be able to call the data access layer but not vice versa.

In this chapter, you will build the data access layer of the bookstore application and query it via a stand-alone Java application. In Chapter 2, you will replace this stand-alone Java application with a web layer using the web tier components of Java EE (specifically, servlets and JSPs). You will use this data access layer throughout this book, and from Chapter 4 onward you will build a web application repeatedly by rebuilding the web layer using different web frameworks.

Oracle and the Java Community Process (JCP) provide standardized enterprise components, and if successful enterprise applications can be built using these components, then why do we need web frameworks? What are web frameworks for? The next section answers these questions.

Java Web Frameworks

While Java EE does a great job of standardizing the enterprise infrastructure, providing an application model, and providing components adequate to develop web applications, two major problems are associated with it.

- Interacting directly with the Java EE components often results in massive boilerplate code and even code redundancy.
- Creating an enterprise application using the Java EE infrastructure is a nontrivial task that requires a great deal of expertise. The team members usually involved in creating an enterprise Java EE application act in varied roles, and all of them may not have the level of expertise that meets the Java EE criteria.

Frameworks address these two major problems (and several other concerns discussed in detail in Chapter 3). Table 1-4 describes the web frameworks you will learn about in this book.

Table 1-4. JVM-Based Web Frameworks

Web Frameworks	Language	Download From
Struts 2	Java	`http://struts.apache.org/download.cgi#struts2314`
Spring Web MVC	Java	`www.springsource.org/spring-community-download`
JSF 2	Java	`www.oracle.com/technetwork/java/javaee/downloads/index.html`
Grails 2	Groovy	`www.grails.org/download`
Play 2	Java and Scala	`www.playframework.com/download`

Now that you have looked at the three key players that join forces in building modern Java web applications (the JVM languages, Java EE, and the Java web frameworks), it is time to delve into some specifics about Java.

The following section introduces Java so you can build your first stand-alone Java application. Since this book is centered on web development using Java and is not about Java as a programming language, the introduction to Java is brief—it's just enough to help newcomers to the language follow the subsequent chapters.

Getting Started with Java

A *Java application* is a computer program that executes when you use the `java` command to launch the JVM. In the Java programming language, all source code is first written in plain-text files (in Notepad, for instance, or in any text editor) with the `.java` extension. The source files are compiled by the `javac` compiler into `.class` files that contain bytecode instructions. The JVM reads these bytecode instructions and translates them into the machine-language operations that each computer executes. By making the JVM available on many platforms, Sun transformed Java into a cross-platform language. As shown in Figure 1-6, the very same bytecode can run on any operating system for which a JVM has been developed.

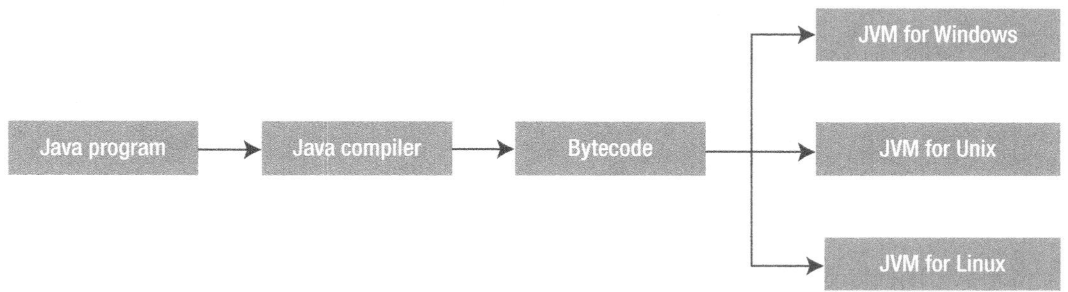

***Figure 1-6.** Cross-platform Java*

Because the JVM is available on many different operating systems, the same `.class` files are capable of running on Windows, Unix, Linux, or Mac OS. In the section that follows, I will show you how to compile and run your first Java application. But first you need to set up the development environment.

Setting Up the Development Environment

The Java software is available in two distributions.

- The Java Runtime Environment (JRE)
- The Java Development Kit (JDK)

The JRE includes a JVM and the core libraries; it is essentially just an environment for running bytecode. The JDK includes the JRE, a Java compiler (javac), and other tools—the basic software you need to write and compile Java programs.

Before you can start compiling and running Java programs, you need to download and install the JDK and configure some system environment variables.

Most of the code in this book requires Java 7, but some of the code is based on Java 8, so you should install Java 8. To get the latest version of the JDK)), follow these steps:

1. Open `www.oracle.com/technetwork/java/javase/downloads/index.html` in a web browser.
2. Click the Download JDK button.
3. Follow the instructions provided by the web site.
4. Run the installer and accept any defaults.

To confirm you have installed the JDK correctly, type `javac` on the command line from any directory on your machine. If you see instructions on how to run `javac` correctly, then you have installed it successfully.

Creating and Running Your First Java Application

This section demonstrates how to create, compile, and execute a simple Java application on Windows. Every Java application has one class that is the program's starting point (often called an *entry point*). Listing 1-1 illustrates a `HelloWorld` entry-point class.

***Listing 1-1.** A HelloWorld Java Application*

```
1.    public class HelloWorld {
2.    public static void main(String[] args) {
3.    System.out.println("Hello World.");
4.     }
5.    }
```

- *Line 2*: The `main` method in line 2 makes this class an entry-point class. This method accepts inputs and starts the program.

The name of the Java application should be the name of the entry-point class, and the file that holds a Java class must have the same name as the class. Therefore, the `HelloWorld` class in Listing 1-1 must be stored in a file named `HelloWorld.java`.

> **Note** Every Java application has only one main method.

You use the javac program in the bin directory of your JDK installation directory to compile Java programs. Assuming you have edited the PATH environment variable on your computer, you should be able to invoke javac from any directory. To compile the HelloWorld class in Listing 1-1, do the following:

1. Open a command prompt and change to the directory where the HelloWorld.java file is saved.
2. Type the following command:

```
javac HelloWorld.java
```

If everything goes well, javac will create a file named HelloWorld.class in your working directory.

Running Your Java Application

To run your Java application, you have to use the java program that is part of the JDK with the command java <class name>. Again, having added the PATH environment variable, you should be able to invoke java from any directory. From your working directory, type the following:

```
java  HelloWorld
```

Note that you do not include the .class extension when running a Java application. You will see the following on your console:

```
Hello World.
```

Developing Java Applications with an IDE

In this book you will use the Eclipse *Kepler* integrated development environment (IDE). To download it, follow these steps:

1. Open www.eclipse.org/downloads/ in a web browser.
2. Follow the instructions provided by the web site.
3. Run the installer and accept any defaults.

Creating Your First Project in the IDE

After you've started Eclipse, you can make a new project as follows:

1. From the File menu, select New, and then select Project. The New Project window appears.
2. In the New Project window, double-click Java Project. The New Java Project window appears, as illustrated in Figure 1-7.

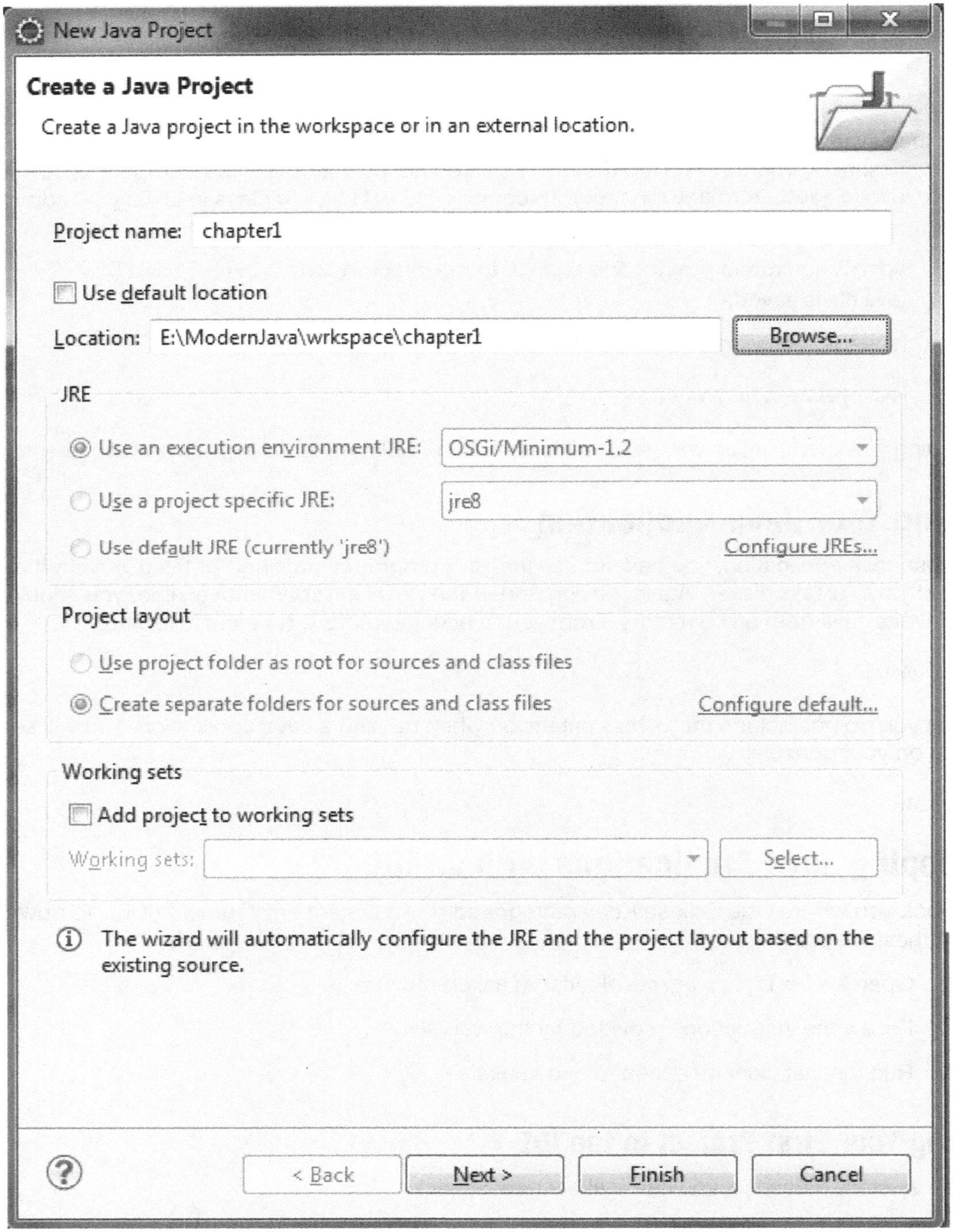

Figure 1-7. Creating a Java project

3. Type **chapter1** in the "Project name" field.
4. Click Finish. You can change a number of other options here. However, for our purposes, the default settings work just fine.

Creating the Application

To create a class with a `main` method for your first program, follow these steps:

1. Right-click the chapter1 project in the Eclipse Package Explorer, choose New, and then choose Class. The New Java Class window displays, as shown in Figure 1-8.

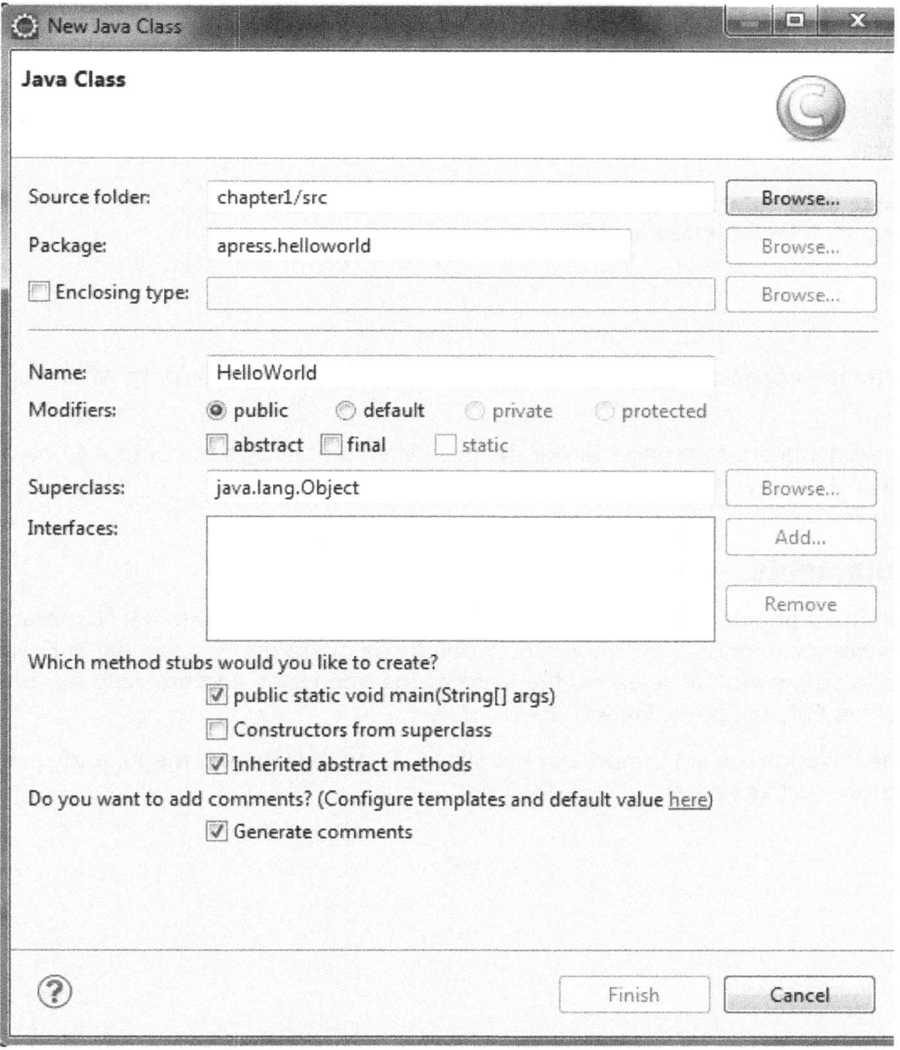

Figure 1-8. Creating a Java class

A *package* groups classes together. In the Name field, you can type the name of the class, which is `HelloWorld`. Select the check box that gives you a `main` method (`public static void main (String args[])`). When you're done, you should have a class similar to the one in Listing 1-2.

2. Click "Generate comments." This will be explained soon.

Listing 1-2. A Simple Java Application

```
packageapress.helloworld;

/**
 * A Hello World Java application
 * @author Vishal Layka
 *
 */
public class HelloWorld {

    /**
     * Entry point
     * @paramargs
     */
    public static void main(String[] args){
        System.out.println("Hello World");
    }

}
```

You can now run the application by clicking the Run button in the toolbar or by choosing Run from the Run menu.

Eclipse then displays a console panel under the code area that shows the output of your program. In this case, it says "Hello World."

Javadoc Comments

A Javadoc comment begins with the /** character sequence and ends with the */ character sequence. The compiler ignores everything between these character sequences. In Eclipse, you can add the Javadoc comments by selecting the class or method name and pressing Alt+Shift+J. To see all the shortcuts in Eclipse, press Ctrl+Shift+L.

To generate the Javadoc, select the project in Eclipse, select the Project menu, and click Generate Javadoc, as shown in Figure 1-9.

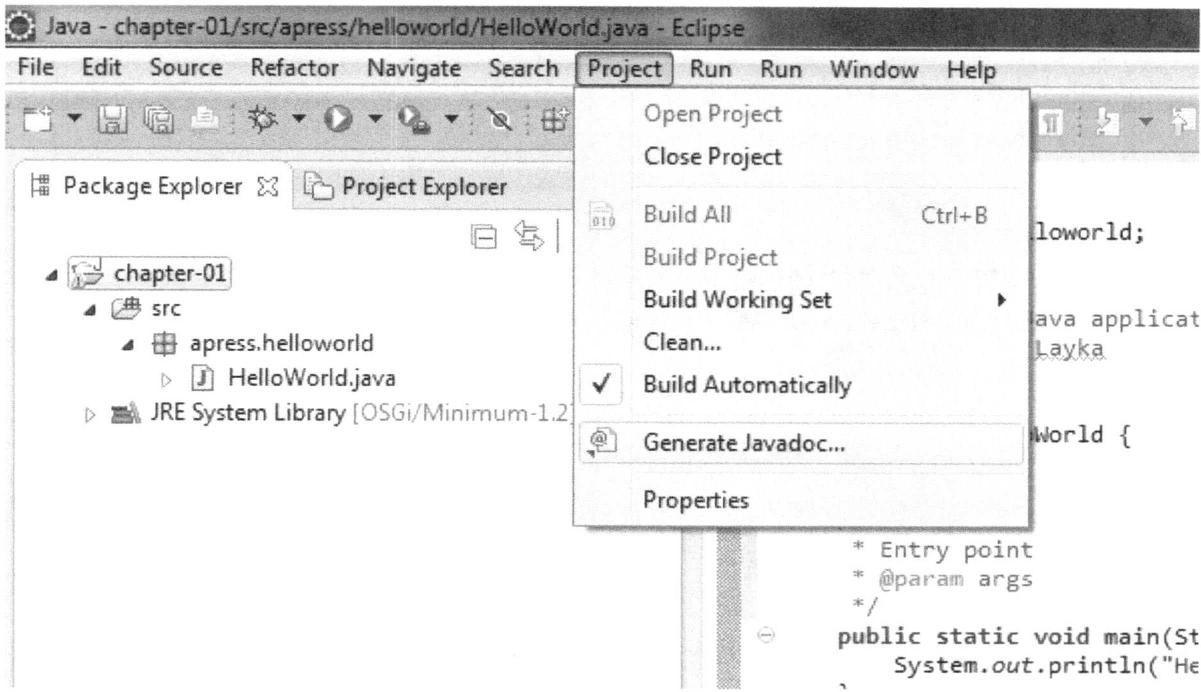

Figure 1-9. Generating a Javadoc

A window will open (Figure 1-10) where you can select Java projects or their underlying resources for which a Javadoc needs to be generated. Several other options are also available; you can select whether to generate a Javadoc for public/private APIs, and so on. For now, configure the `javadoc.exe` file in the "Javadoc command" field and browse to and select the target folder where the Javadoc should be generated.

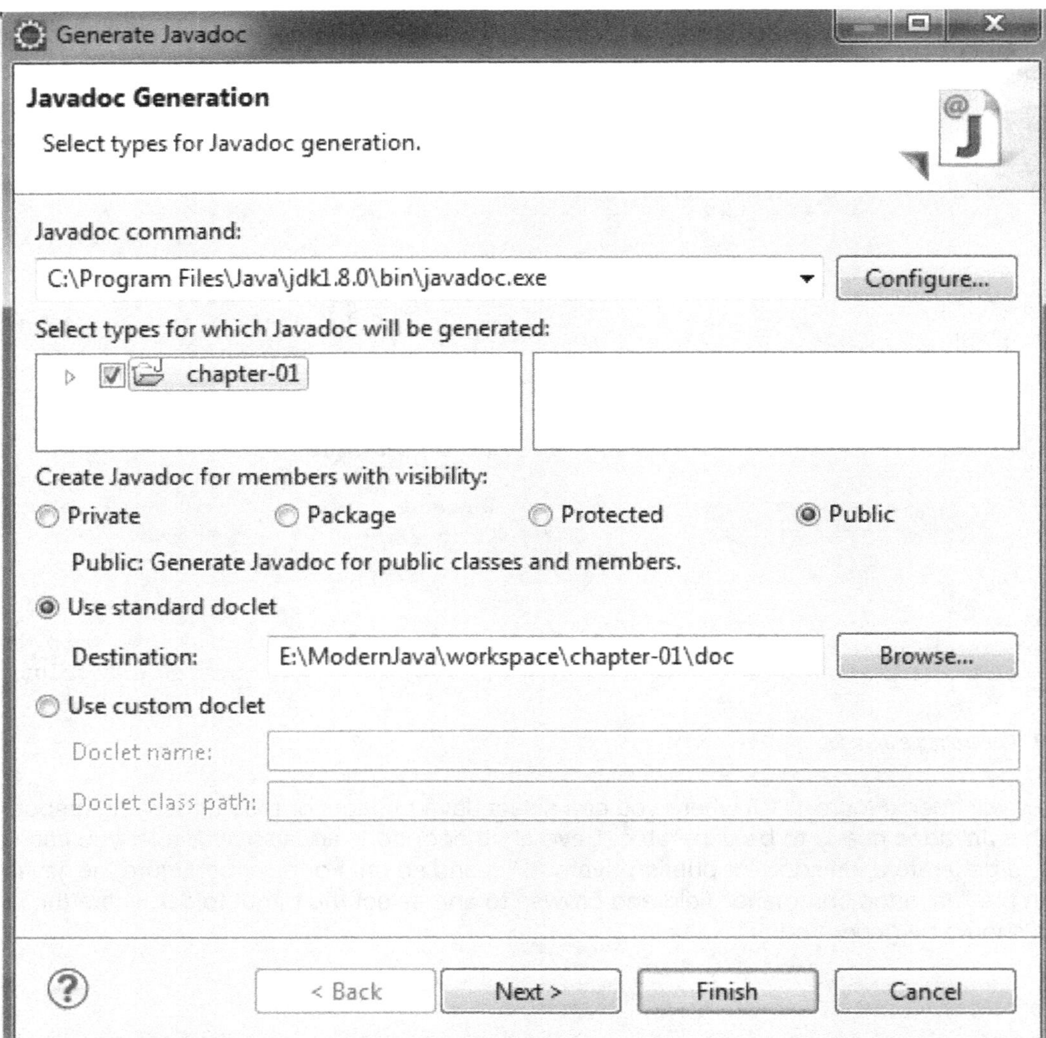

Figure 1-10. Generating a Javadoc

Click Finish. On the console you can see the progress of the Javadoc generation. Figure 1-11 shows the generated Javadoc.

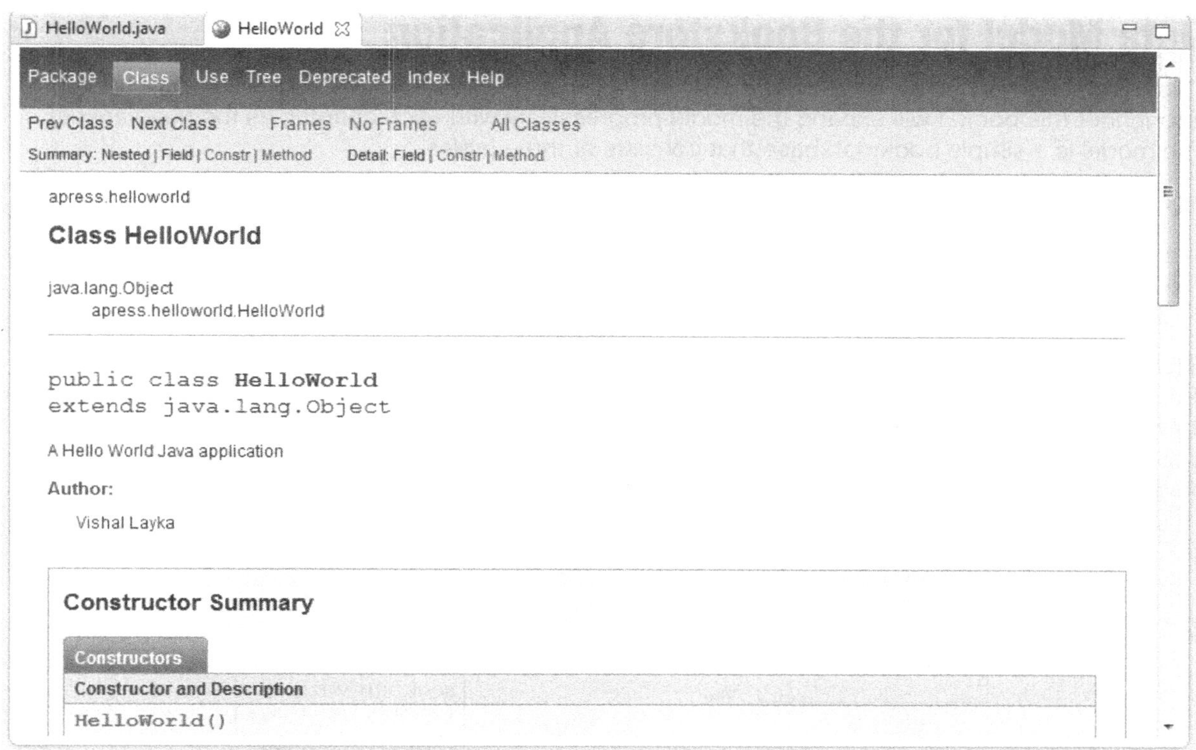

Figure 1-11. Javadoc for the HelloWorld class

Now you will learn how to create a simple but functional version of the stand-alone bookstore application that you'll work on throughout this book.

The Bookstore Application

Instead of simply declaring one web framework as the best, this book intends to show the strengths of the most popular web frameworks by means of a real-world bookstore application. Developing a complete real application necessitates a seamless collaboration of dynamic functionalities, and the code for building such components is contrived and too involved. Instead of focusing on developing such moving parts, this book confines its attention on leveraging the strengths of each web framework. Throughout the book, you will learn how to use Java EE and the Java web frameworks to build the bookstore web application. In this chapter, you will take the first step by building a traditional stand-alone Java bookstore application. In Chapter 2, you will transform the stand-alone application into a web application.

Throughout this book, I will use a single web application case study to demonstrate how to write a web application using servlets and JSPs and the different web frameworks such as JSF, Struts 2, Spring Web MVC, and rapid web development frameworks such as Grails and Play. The application allows users to view books and search for them by keyword, usually by the first name or last name of the author and the title of the book.

Data Model for the Bookstore Application

This section introduces a simple data model that will be used for the bookstore web application throughout this book. I will expand the model progressively with each chapter, as the need arises. The model is a simple book database that consists of three tables.

- The Category table stores the different categories of books; categories include Java, Scala, and so on.
- The Book table stores the book details such as titles.
- The Author table stores the details of the authors.

Each category can have zero or more books. For instance, there could be zero or more books in the Java category in the bookstore. In other words, there is a one-to-many relationship between the Category and Book tables. Similarly, each book can have one or more authors. In other words, there is a one-to-many relationship between the Book and Author tables. The entity-relationship (ER) diagram in Figure 1-12 illustrates this relationship.

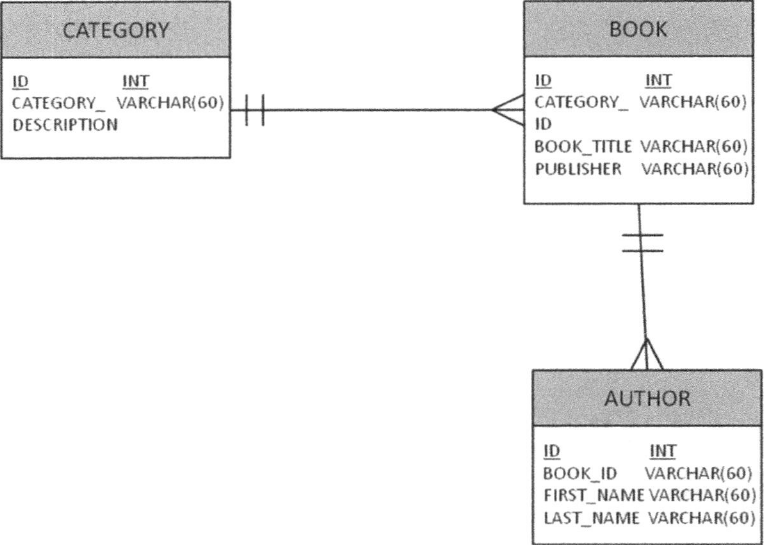

***Figure 1-12.** Entity-relationship diagram of the data model*

This data model is not production-ready because you can have a many-to-many relationship between Category and Book, and you can have a many-to-many relationship between Book and Author. I have kept the data model simple so that the complexity of the data model does not get in the way of learning the mechanics of building a web application. However, you can, for example, model a many-to-many relationship between Book and Author, as illustrated in Figure 1-13.

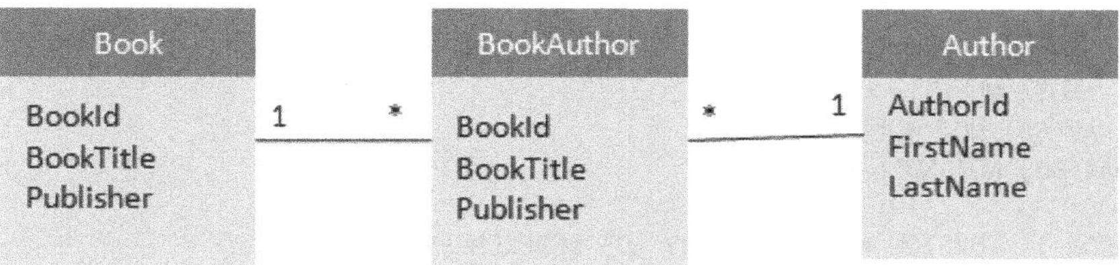

Figure 1-13. Many-to-many relationship between Book and Author

The sole purpose of the BookAuthor table is to provide a many-to-many relationship between Book and Author.

> **Note** As shown in Figure 1-13, there is a one-to-many relationship between Book and BookAuthor, and there is a one-to-many relationship between Author and BookAuthor. In fact, the sole purpose of the BookAuthor table is to provide a many-to-many relationship between Book and Author—in other words, an author can write many books, and a book can have many authors.

Because of the profusion of web applications across several domains, many relational and nonrelational databases such as NoSQL[12] have emerged. In this book, I'll use MySQL[13] because it is the most widely used free database management system (DBMS). To install MySQL, go to `http://dev.mysql.com/downloads/` and click Download. You can download MySQL Server 5.5 or newer. You can see the instructions for installing MySQL at `http://dev.mysql.com/doc/refman/5.5/en/installing.html`.

To create the books database, use the following command:

```
create database books;
```

You need to instruct MySQL to create tables in the books database by using the following command:

```
use books;
```

Now you can create the tables using the statements illustrated in Listing 1-3.

Listing 1-3. Creating Tables for the Bookstore

```
CREATE  TABLE CATEGORY (
ID  INT NOT NULL  AUTO_INCREMENT ,
CATEGORY_DESCRIPTION  VARCHAR(20)  NOT NULL ,
PRIMARY KEY (ID)
);
```

---

[12]http://nosql-database.org/
[13]www.mysql.com/

```
CREATE  TABLE BOOK (
ID  INT NOT  NULL AUTO_INCREMENT,
CATEGORY_ID  INT  NOT  NULL ,
BOOK_TITLE  VARCHAR(60) NOT NULL,
PUBLISHER  VARCHAR(60) NOT NULL ,
PRIMARY KEY (ID) ,
CONSTRAINT  FK_BOOK_1  FOREIGN KEY (CATEGORY_ID) REFERENCES CATEGORY(ID)

);

CREATE  TABLE  AUTHOR (
ID  INT  NOT NULL AUTO_INCREMENT ,
BOOK_ID  INT  NOT  NULL ,
FIRST_NAME  VARCHAR(20)  NOT NULL ,
LAST_NAME  VARCHAR(20)  NOT NULL ,
PRIMARY KEY (ID) ,
CONSTRAINT FK_AUTHOR_1 FOREIGN KEY (BOOK_ID) REFERENCES BOOK (ID)
);
```

You can verify the created tables using the `show tables` command, as illustrated in Figure 1-14.

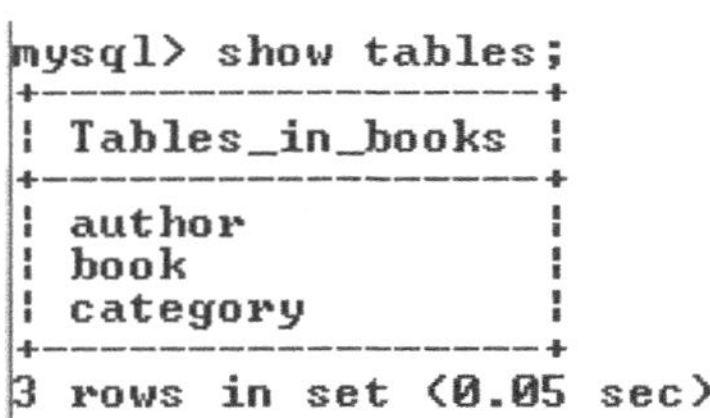

***Figure 1-14.** All tables in the database*

You can also check the structure of the tables using the command `describe <table-name>` or `desc<table-name>`, as illustrated in Figure 1-15.

```
mysql> DESC CATEGORY;
+----------------------+-------------+------+-----+---------+----------------+
| Field                | Type        | Null | Key | Default | Extra          |
+----------------------+-------------+------+-----+---------+----------------+
| ID                   | int(11)     | NO   | PRI | NULL    | auto_increment |
| CATEGORY_DESCRIPTION | varchar(20) | NO   |     | NULL    |                |
+----------------------+-------------+------+-----+---------+----------------+
2 rows in set (0.01 sec)

mysql> DESC BOOK;
+-------------+-------------+------+-----+---------+----------------+
| Field       | Type        | Null | Key | Default | Extra          |
+-------------+-------------+------+-----+---------+----------------+
| ID          | int(11)     | NO   | PRI | NULL    | auto_increment |
| CATEGORY_ID | int(11)     | NO   | MUL | NULL    |                |
| BOOK_TITLE  | varchar(60) | NO   |     | NULL    |                |
| PUBLISHER   | varchar(60) | NO   |     | NULL    |                |
+-------------+-------------+------+-----+---------+----------------+
4 rows in set (0.01 sec)

mysql> DESC AUTHOR;
+------------+-------------+------+-----+---------+----------------+
| Field      | Type        | Null | Key | Default | Extra          |
+------------+-------------+------+-----+---------+----------------+
| ID         | int(11)     | NO   | PRI | NULL    | auto_increment |
| BOOK_ID    | int(11)     | NO   | MUL | NULL    |                |
| FIRST_NAME | varchar(20) | NO   |     | NULL    |                |
| LAST_NAME  | varchar(20) | NO   |     | NULL    |                |
+------------+-------------+------+-----+---------+----------------+
4 rows in set (0.00 sec)
```

***Figure 1-15.** Structure of the tables*

Now populate the tables using the insert statements, as follows:

```
insert into category (category_description) values ('Clojure');
insert into category (category_description) values ('Groovy');
insert into category (category_description) values ('Java');
insert into category (category_description) values ('Scala');
```

You can verify the populated Category table as illustrated in Figure 1-16.

```
mysql> select * from category;
+----+----------------------+
| ID | CATEGORY_DESCRIPTION |
+----+----------------------+
|  1 | Clojure              |
|  2 | Groovy               |
|  3 | Java                 |
|  4 | Scala                |
+----+----------------------+
4 rows in set (0.00 sec)
```

***Figure 1-16.** All categories in the Category table*

```
insert into Book (CATEGORY_ID, BOOK_TITLE, PUBLISHER) values (1, 'Practical Clojure', 'Apress');
insert into Book (CATEGORY_ID, BOOK_TITLE, PUBLISHER) values (2, 'Beginning Groovy, Grails and
Griffon', 'Apress');
insert into Book (CATEGORY_ID, BOOK_TITLE, PUBLISHER) values (2, 'Definitive Guide to Grails 2',
'Apress');
insert into Book (CATEGORY_ID, BOOK_TITLE, PUBLISHER) values (2, 'Groovy and Grails Recipes',
'Apress');
insert into Book (CATEGORY_ID, BOOK_TITLE, PUBLISHER) values (3, 'Modern Java Web Development',
'Apress');
insert into Book (CATEGORY_ID, BOOK_TITLE, PUBLISHER) values (3, 'Java 7 Recipes', 'Apress');
insert into Book (CATEGORY_ID, BOOK_TITLE, PUBLISHER) values (3, 'Java EE 7 Recipes', 'Apress');
insert into Book (CATEGORY_ID, BOOK_TITLE, PUBLISHER) values (3, 'Beginning Java 7 ', 'Apress');
insert into Book (CATEGORY_ID, BOOK_TITLE, PUBLISHER) values (3, 'Pro Java 7 NIO.2', 'Apress');
insert into Book (CATEGORY_ID, BOOK_TITLE, PUBLISHER) values (3, 'Java 7 for Absolute Beginners',
'Apress');
insert into Book (CATEGORY_ID, BOOK_TITLE, PUBLISHER) values (3, 'Oracle Certified Java Enterprise
Architect Java EE7', 'Apress');
insert into Book (CATEGORY_ID, BOOK_TITLE, PUBLISHER) values (4, 'Beginning Scala', 'Apress');
```

You can verify the populated Book table as illustrated in Figure 1-17.

```
mysql> select * from book;
+----+-------------+------------------------------------------------------+-----------+
| ID | CATEGORY_ID | BOOK_TITLE                                           | PUBLISHER |
+----+-------------+------------------------------------------------------+-----------+
|  1 |           1 | Practical Clojure                                    | Apress    |
|  2 |           2 | Beginning Groovy, Grails and Griffon                 | Apress    |
|  3 |           2 | Definitive Guide to Grails 2                         | Apress    |
|  4 |           2 | Groovy and Grails Recipes                            | Apress    |
|  5 |           3 | Modern Java Web Development                          | Apress    |
|  6 |           3 | Java 7 Recipes                                       | Apress    |
|  7 |           3 | Java EE 7 Recipes                                    | Apress    |
|  8 |           3 | Beginning Java 7                                     | Apress    |
|  9 |           3 | Pro Java 7 NIO.2                                     | Apress    |
| 10 |           3 | Java 7 for Absolute Beginners                        | Apress    |
| 11 |           3 | Oracle Certified Java Enterprise Architect Java EE7  | Apress    |
| 12 |           4 | Beginning Scala                                      | Apress    |
+----+-------------+------------------------------------------------------+-----------+
12 rows in set (0.00 sec)
```

***Figure 1-17.** All books in the Book table*

```
insert into Author (BOOK_ID, FIRST_NAME, LAST_NAME) values (1, 'Luke', 'VanderHart');
insert into Author (BOOK_ID, FIRST_NAME, LAST_NAME) values (2, 'Vishal', 'Layka');
insert into Author (BOOK_ID, FIRST_NAME, LAST_NAME) values (3, 'Jeff', 'Brown');
insert into Author (BOOK_ID, FIRST_NAME, LAST_NAME) values (4, 'Bashar', 'Jawad');
insert into Author (BOOK_ID, FIRST_NAME, LAST_NAME) values (5, 'Vishal', 'Layka');
insert into Author (BOOK_ID, FIRST_NAME, LAST_NAME) values (6, 'Josh',  'Juneau');
insert into Author (BOOK_ID, FIRST_NAME, LAST_NAME) values (7, 'Josh', 'Juneau');
insert into Author (BOOK_ID, FIRST_NAME, LAST_NAME) values (8, 'Jeff', 'Friesen');
insert into Author (BOOK_ID, FIRST_NAME, LAST_NAME) values (9, 'Anghel', 'Leonard');
insert into Author (BOOK_ID, FIRST_NAME, LAST_NAME) values (10, 'Jay',  'Bryant');
insert into Author (BOOK_ID, FIRST_NAME, LAST_NAME) values (11, 'B V', 'Kumar');
insert into Author (BOOK_ID, FIRST_NAME, LAST_NAME) values (12, 'David', 'Pollak');
```

You can verify the populated Author table as illustrated in Figure 1-18.

```
mysql> select * from author;
+----+---------+------------+------------+
| ID | BOOK_ID | FIRST_NAME | LAST_NAME  |
+----+---------+------------+------------+
|  1 |       1 | Luke       | VanderHart |
|  2 |       2 | Vishal     | Layka      |
|  3 |       3 | Jeff       | Brown      |
|  4 |       4 | Bashar     | Jawad      |
|  5 |       5 | Vishal     | Layka      |
|  6 |       6 | Josh       | Juneau     |
|  7 |       7 | Josh       | Juneau     |
|  8 |       8 | Jeff       | Friesen    |
|  9 |       9 | Anghel     | Leonard    |
| 10 |      10 | Jay        | Bryant     |
| 11 |      11 | B V        | Kumar      |
| 12 |      12 | David      | Pollak     |
+----+---------+------------+------------+
12 rows in set (0.00 sec)
```

***Figure 1-18.** All authors in the Author table*

Data Access Layer for the Bookstore Application

Now that the database is ready, you will build the data access layer for application. The data access layer will retrieve the data via JDBC from the database and directly map the result set into Java objects. These Java objects are the domain objects in the application that are the Java representation of the tables in the database. The data access layer is responsible for interfacing with the underlying persistence mechanism in a transparent way in order to store and retrieve objects from the database. This transparency means that the data access layer can switch the persistence mechanism from plain JDBC[14] to ORM[15] persistence technologies such as Hibernate,[16] JPA,[17] and so on, without affecting the client of the data access layer. This transparency is achieved via the data access object (DAO) pattern, as illustrated in Figure 1-19. The `DAO` object provides an interface to the database or the underlying persistence mechanism, thus abstracting the underlying implementation from the client.

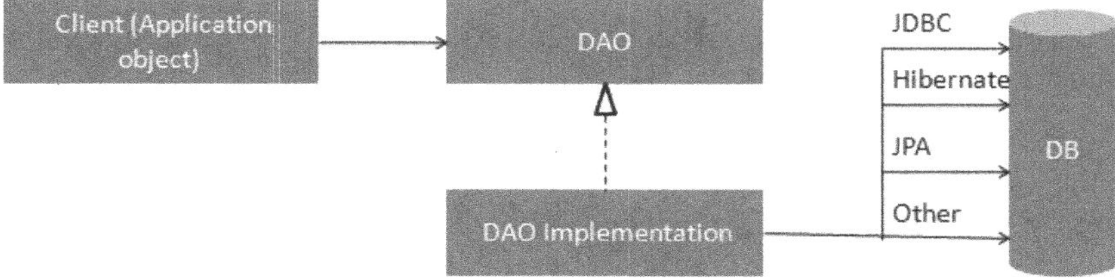

***Figure 1-19.** DAO pattern*

[14]www.oracle.com/technetwork/java/overview-141217.html
[15]http://en.wikipedia.org/wiki/Object-relational_mapping
[16]www.hibernate.org/
[17]www.oracle.com/technetwork/java/javaee/tech/persistence-jsp-140049.html

The DAO maps application calls to the persistence mechanism and provides specific data operations without exposing details of the database. The DAO interface abstracts the implementation details of accessing the data from the client (application object) and provides the domain-specific objects that the client (application object) needs.

First you need to create the domain-specific classes for the Java object representations of the database tables. Listings 1-4, 1-5, and 1-6 show the `Book`, `Author`, and `Category` domain classes, respectively.

Listing 1-4. Model: Category

```
package com.apress.books.model;

public class Category {
    private Long id;
    private String categoryDescription;

    public Long getId() {
        return id;
    }

    public void setId(Long id) {
        this.id = id;
    }

    public String getCategoryDescription() {
        returncategoryDescription;
    }

    public void setCategoryDescription(String categoryDescription) {
        this.categoryDescription = categoryDescription;
    }

    public String toString() {
        return "Category - Id: " + id + ", Category Description: "
                + categoryDescription;
    }

}
```

Listing 1-5. Model: Book

```
package com.apress.books.model;

import java.util.List;
import com.apress.books.model.Author;

public class Book {
    private Long id;
    private Long categoryId;
    private String bookTitle;
```

```
    private List<Author> authors;
    private String publisherName;

    public Long getId() {
        return id;
    }

    public void setId(Long id) {
        this.id = id;
    }

    public Long getCategoryId() {
        return categoryId;
    }

    public void setCategoryId(Long categoryId) {
        this.categoryId = categoryId;
    }

    public String getBookTitle() {
        return bookTitle;
    }

    public void setBookTitle(String bookTitle) {
        this.bookTitle = bookTitle;
    }

    public List<Author> getAuthors() {
        return authors;
    }

    public void setAuthors(List272103_1_En authors) {
        this.authors = authors;
    }

    public String getPublisherName() {
        return publisherName;
    }

    public void setPublisherName(String publisherName) {
        this.publisherName = publisherName;
    }

    public String toString() {
        return "Book - Id: " + id + ", Book Title: " + bookTitle;
    }

}
```

Listing 1-6. Model: Author

```
package com.apress.books.model;

public class Author {
    private Long id;
    private Long bookId;
    private String firstName;
    private String lastName;

    public Long getId() {
        return id;
    }

    public void setId(Long id) {
        this.id = id;
    }

    public Long getBookId() {
        return bookId;
    }

    public void setBookId(Long bookId) {
        this.bookId = bookId;
    }

    public String getFirstName() {
        return firstName;
    }

    public void setFirstName(String firstName) {
        this.firstName = firstName;
    }

    public String getLastName() {
        return lastName;
    }

    public void setLastName(String lastName) {
        this.lastName = lastName;
    }

    public String toString() {
        return "Author - Id: " + id + ", Book id: " + bookId + ", First Name: "
                + firstName + ", Last Name: " +lastName;
    }

}
```

Now let's start with a simple interface for BookDAO that encapsulates all the data access by your web application. Listing 1-7 shows the BookDAO interface.

Listing 1-7. BookDAO Interface

```
1.  package com.apress.books.dao;
2.
3.  import java.util.List;
4.
5.  import com.apress.books.model.Book;
6.  import com.apress.books.model.Category;
7.
8.  public interface BookDAO {
9.      public List<Book>findAllBooks();
10.
11.     public List<Book>searchBooksByKeyword(String keyWord);
12.
13.     public List<Category>findAllCategories();
14.
15.     public void insert(Book book);
16.
17.     public void update(Book book);
18.
19.     public void delete(Long bookId);
20.
21. }
```

- *Line 9*: This is the `findAllBooks()` method for listing all the books from the database.
- *Line 11*: `SearchBooksByKeyword(String keyWord)` allows the user to search books by keyword in the title of the book or by the first and last names of the author.
- *Line 13*: `findAllCategories()` is required by the application to provide a categorized listing of books.

The methods in this interface correspond to the CRUD terms (in other words, create, read, update, and delete) of the application. Listing 1-8 illustrates the implementation of the `BookDAO` interface.

Listing 1-8. Implementation of the BookDAO Interface

```
package com.apress.books.dao;

import java.sql.Connection;
import java.sql.DriverManager;
import java.sql.PreparedStatement;
import java.sql.ResultSet;
import java.sql.SQLException;
import java.sql.Statement;
import java.util.ArrayList;
import java.util.List;

import java.apress.books.model.Author;
import java.apress.books.model.Book;
```

```
import java.apress.books.model.Category;

public class BookDAOImpl implements BookDAO {

    static {
        try {
            Class.forName("com.mysql.jdbc.Driver");
        } catch (ClassNotFoundException ex) {
        }
    }

    private Connection getConnection() throws SQLException {
        return DriverManager.getConnection("jdbc:mysql://localhost:3306/books",
                "root", "password");
    }

    private void closeConnection(Connection connection) {
        if (connection == null)
            return;
        try {
            connection.close();
        } catch (SQLException ex) {
        }
    }

    public List<Book> findAllBooks() {
        List<Book> result = new ArrayList<>();
        List<Author> authorList = new ArrayList<>();

        String sql = "select * from book inner join author on book.id = author.book_id";

        Connection connection = null;
        try {
            connection = getConnection();
            PreparedStatement statement = connection.prepareStatement(sql);
            ResultSet resultSet = statement.executeQuery();
            while (resultSet.next()) {
                Book book = new Book();
                Author author = new Author();
                book.setId(resultSet.getLong("id"));
                book.setBookTitle(resultSet.getString("book_title"));
                book.setCategoryId(resultSet.getLong("category_id"));
                author.setBookId(resultSet.getLong("book_Id"));
                author.setFirstName(resultSet.getString("first_name"));
                author.setLastName(resultSet.getString("last_name"));
                authorList.add(author);
                book.setAuthors(authorList);
                book.setPublisherName(resultSet.getString("publisher"));
                result.add(book);
            }
        } catch (SQLException ex) {
            ex.printStackTrace();
```

```
        } finally {
            closeConnection(connection);
        }
        return result;
    }


    public List<Book> searchBooksByKeyword(String keyWord) {
        List<Book> result = new ArrayList<>();
        List<Author> authorList = new ArrayList<>();

        String sql = "select * from book inner join author on book.id = author.book_id"
                + " where book_title like '%"
                + keyWord.trim()
                + "%'"
                + " or first_name like '%"
                + keyWord.trim()
                + "%'"
                + " or last_name like '%" + keyWord.trim() + "%'";

        Connection connection = null;
        try {

            connection = getConnection();
            PreparedStatement statement = connection.prepareStatement(sql);
            ResultSet resultSet = statement.executeQuery();
            while (resultSet.next()) {
                Book book = new Book();
                Author author = new Author();
                book.setId(resultSet.getLong("id"));
                book.setBookTitle(resultSet.getString("book_title"));
                book.setPublisherName(resultSet.getString("publisher"));
                author.setFirstName(resultSet.getString("first_name"));
                author.setLastName(resultSet.getString("last_name"));
                author.setBookId(resultSet.getLong("book_id"));
                authorList.add(author);
                book.setAuthors(authorList);
                result.add(book);
            }
        } catch (SQLException ex) {
            ex.printStackTrace();
        } finally {
            closeConnection(connection);
        }

        return result;
    }

    public List<Category> findAllCategories() {
        List<Category> result = new ArrayList<>();
        String sql = "select * from category";
```

```
118.            Connection connection = null;
119.            try {
120.                connection = getConnection();
121.                PreparedStatement statement = connection.prepareStatement(sql);
122.                ResultSet resultSet = statement.executeQuery();
123.                while (resultSet.next()) {
124.                    Category category = new Category();
125.                    category.setId(resultSet.getLong("id"));
126.                    category.setCategoryDescription(resultSet
127.                            .getString("category_description"));
128.                    result.add(category);
129.                }
130.            } catch (SQLException ex) {
131.                ex.printStackTrace();
132.            } finally {
133.                closeConnection(connection);
134.            }
135.            return result;
136.        }
137.
138.        public void insert(Book book) {
139.        }
140.
141.        public void update(Book book) {
142.        }
143.
144.        public void delete(Long bookId) {
145.
146.        }
147.    }
```

Listing 1-8 is an implementation of the BookDao interface for interacting with; this interaction includes connecting to the database and selecting, deleting, and updating data via pure JDBC. JDBC provides the driver that is specific to each database and that allows Java code the database.

- *Lines 18 to 37*: These lines show the code required for managing a JDBC connection.
- *Line 26*: The `getConnection()` method returns a driver-implemented `java.sql.Connection` interface. This interface allows you to run SQL statements against the database. For this to work, you need to provide a MySQL Connector/J JAR file. A MySQL Connector/J is a native Java driver that converts JDBC calls into a network protocol the MySQL database can understand. The `DriverManager` manages drivers and provides static methods for establishing connections to the database.

> **Note** You can download the MySQL Connector/J from `http://dev.mysql.com/downloads/connector/j/`. Place this connector JAR in the classpath of the project.

- *Lines 30 to 37*: The connections need to be closed because connections are expensive when it comes to the performance of the application.
- *Lines 39 to 144*: These lines are implementations of CRUD services in the BookDAO interface.
- *Lines 67, 108, and 133*: You created a connection for each statement in the CRUD services. You need to close these connections; keeping them open will result in the poor performance of the application.

Client for the Data Access Layer

Now that your data access layer is ready, you will query it with a stand-alone Java application. In Chapter 2, you will replace this Java app with a web application. Listing 1-9 illustrates the Java application.

Listing 1-9. Stand-Alone Bookstore Java App

```
package com.apress.books.client;
import java.util.List;

import com.apress.books.dao.BookDAO;
import com.apress.books.dao.BookDAOImpl;
import com.apress.books.model.Book;

public class BookApp {
    private static BookDAO bookDao = new BookDAOImpl();

    public static void main(String[] args) {
        // List all books
        System.err.println("Listing all Books:");
        findAllBooks();
        System.out.println();
        // search book by keyword
        System.err.println("Search book by keyword  in book title : Groovy:");

        searchBooks("Groovy");
        System.out.println();

        System.err.println("Search book by keyword  in author's name  : Josh:");

        searchBooks("Josh");


    }

    private static void findAllBooks() {
        List<Book> books = bookDao.findAllBooks();
        for (Book book : books) {
            System.out.println(book);
        }
    }
    private static void searchBooks(String keyWord) {
```

```
        List<Book> books = bookDao.searchBooksByKeyword(keyWord);
        for (Book book : books) {
            System.out.println(book);
        }
    }
}
```

Figure 1-20 illustrates the directory structure of the stand-alone application.

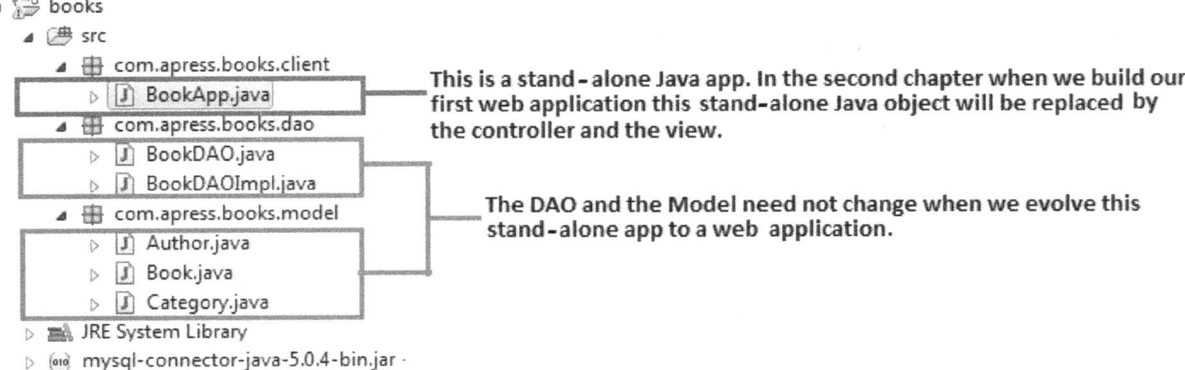

***Figure 1-20.** Directory structure of the stand-alone bookstore application*

Running this application gives the following output:

```
Listing all Books:
Book - Id: 1, Book Title: Practical Clojure
Book - Id: 2, Book Title: Beginning Groovy, Grails and Griffon
Book - Id: 3, Book Title: Definitive Guide to Grails 2
Book - Id: 4, Book Title: Groovy and Grails Recipes
Book - Id: 5, Book Title: Modern Java Web Development
Book - Id: 6, Book Title: Java 7 Recipes
Book - Id: 7, Book Title: Java EE 7 Recipes
Book - Id: 8, Book Title: Beginning Java 7
Book - Id: 9, Book Title: Pro Java 7 NIO.2
Book - Id: 10, Book Title: Java 7 for Absolute Beginners
Book - Id: 11, Book Title: Oracle Certified Java Enterprise Architect Java EE7
Book - Id: 12, Book Title: Beginning Scala

Search book by keyword  in book title : Groovy:
Book - Id: 2, Book Title: Beginning Groovy, Grails and Griffon
Book - Id: 4, Book Title: Groovy and Grails Recipes

Search book by keyword  in author's name  : Josh:
Book - Id: 6, Book Title: Java 7 Recipes
Book - Id: 7, Book Title: Java EE 7 Recipes
```

In the next chapter, you will develop the web layer that will replace this client and that will call the data access layer in the bookstore web application.

Trends and Technologies in the Java Web Landscape

Now it is time to delve into the trends and technologies in today's Java web landscape. This may seem daunting to a newcomer to Java, but the goal is to familiarize you with the tools, technologies, and trends in Java web application development in order to give you a glimpse of the modern Java landscape. When you learn to develop web applications using rapid web frameworks such as Grails 2 and Play 2, you will see that most of these tools and technologies are provided out of the box.

As mentioned throughout the chapter, the JVM, originally intended for Java, can now host a myriad of programming languages, including Groovy and Scala. As a consequence of this emerging multiprogramming paradigm, modern web applications are often characterized in one or more of the following ways:

- Responsive web applications
- Single-page web applications
- Real-time web applications
- Reactive web applications
- Mashups and web services

Responsive Web Applications

One of the greatest strengths of the Web is that it is flexible. This flexibility, however, is also its greatest weakness. This weakness manifests itself when a web application tested on one browser is viewed on the different browser and doesn't perform properly. This cross-browser compatibility problem has only grown with the advent of smartphones. As shown in Figure 1-21, as of the end of 2013, there are 6.8 billion mobile subscriptions worldwide, and that number is poised to grow to 8 billion by 2016 (`www.itu.int/ITU-D/ict/facts/index.html`).

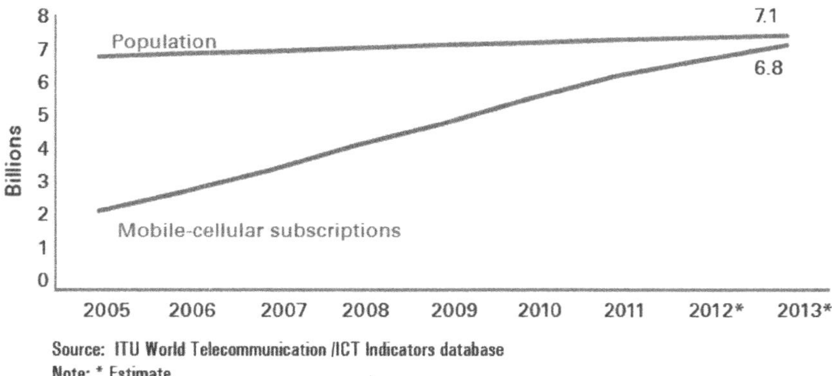

Figure 1-21. Mobile subscriptions

Web applications are expected to run on smartphones as well as on the desktop, but creating separate web applications for the desktop and the smartphone has significant overhead for development as well as maintenance. In May 2010, Ethan Marcotte wrote an article for A List

Apart titled "Responsive Web Design" (`http://d.alistapart.com/responsive-web-design/ex/ex-site-flexible.html`) that defined a groundbreaking approach. He used existing tools (which will be explained later in this section) to create a site that displays beautifully on different devices, as illustrated in Figure 1-22 and Figure 1-23.

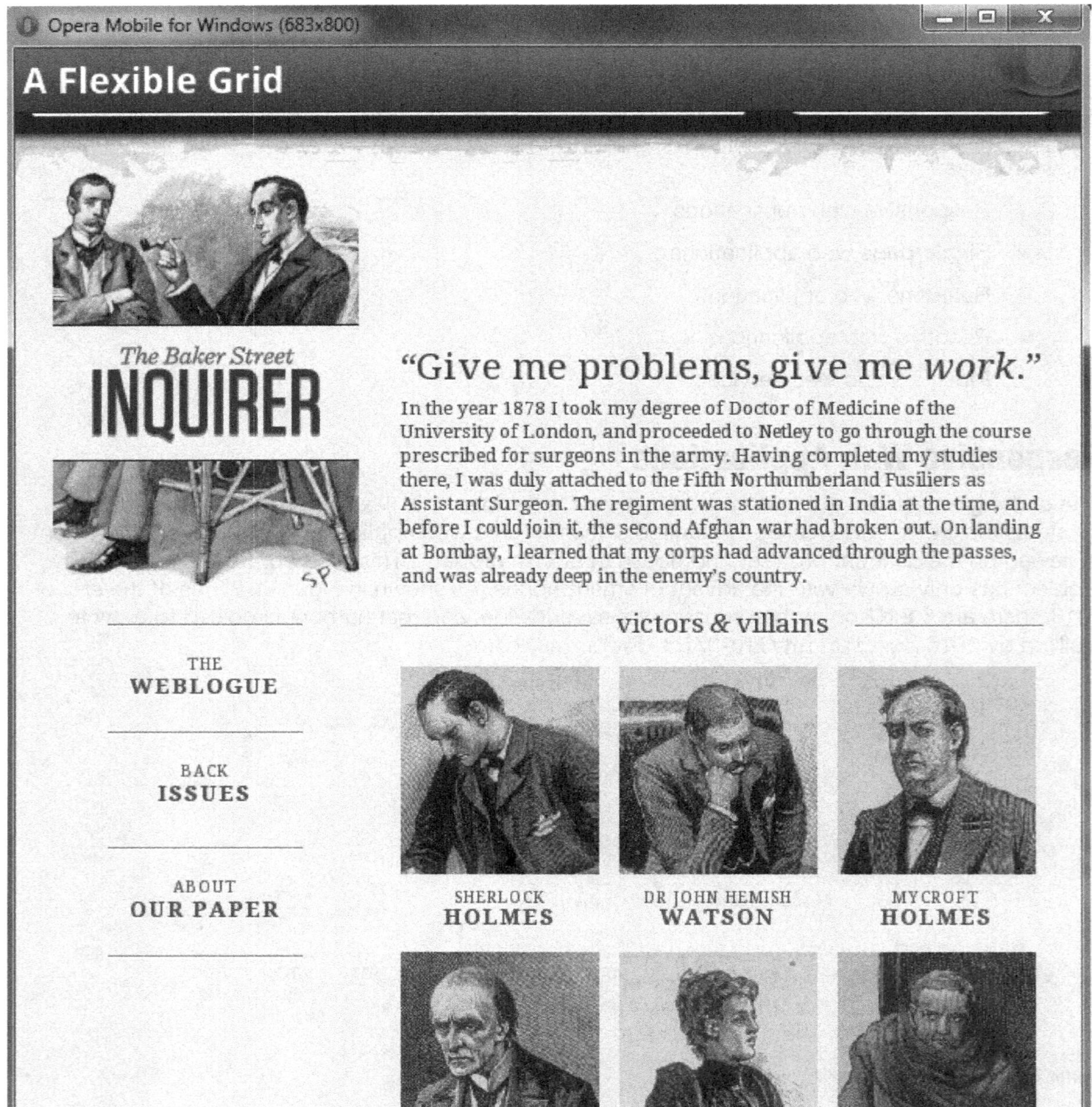

Figure 1-22. Responsive web site by Ethan Marcotte

***Figure 1-23.** The same responsive site on a smartphone*

Responsive web applications are device-agnostic, in that they adapt themselves to the device on which they are run. The technique goes as far as rethinking the way page layouts are designed. You can go one step further by designing the web application with the smallest screen (smartphones) in mind and then progressively enhance the application to run on desktop screens. This technique is known as *mobile-first* design. The philosophy of a mobile-first design is that if you design the interface and the web components to run with acceptable performance on a smartphone, the performance on desktop screens will be blazing fast. In addition, using the smartphone real estate wisely will also be applied to the desktop screens, which will result in better usability of the application.

The core technologies employed in developing responsive web applications are CSS3,[18] jQuery[19] and jQuery plug-ins,[20] LESS,[21] CoffeeScript,[22] and front-end frameworks such as Bootstrap,[23] Polyfills, and Modernizr.

[18]www.w3.org/Style/CSS/current-work.en.html
[19]http://jquery.com/
[20]http://plugins.jquery.com/
[21]http://lesscss.org/
[22]http://coffeescript.org/
[23]http://getbootstrap.com/

Here are some important definitions in the responsive world:

- *Unobtrusive JavaScript*[24]: Unobtrusive JavaScript is a means of separation of concerns, that is, separating the look and feel from behavior concerns. This results in a pure markup, and the JavaScript (behavior) works unobtrusively across different browsers and devices. jQuery is a popular library that helps in writing unobtrusive JavaScript. CoffeeScript compiles into JavaScript. It is used as an alternative to JavaScript and considerably reduces code.
- *CSS3 media queries*: Media queries are the primary means of making web applications responsive. Media queries use media features such as device-width, device-height, orientation, and device-aspect-ratio in a CSS file to develop a responsive web application.
- *LESS*: LESS is the CSS preprocessor that is used when a CSS3 stylesheet gets unmanageable. LESS extends CSS with dynamic behavior such as mixins and functions.
- *Polyfills*: Polyfills are JavaScript, used to make a browser HTML5-enabled. The polyfills provide missing functionality in the browser and provide a fallback.
- *Modernizr*: Modernizr is a JavaScript library that detects HTML5 and CSS3 features in the browser and conditionally loads polyfills.

Single-Page Web Application (SPA)

Another trend in web application development is a *single-page web application* (SPA).

- The client-side code—such as HTML, JavaScript, and CSS—is retrieved with a single page load; the page does not reload at any point in the process, and the control is not transferred to another page.
- The resources, such as images, are dynamically loaded and added to the page in response to events.

SPAs are built using Node.js[25] as the web server. AngularJS is a full-featured SPA framework.

Real-Time Web Application

A *real-time* web application delivers responses to events in a measurable and acceptable time period, depending on the nature of the event, by means of asynchronous, bidirectional communication between the client and the server. WebSocket is the core technology employed for developing real-time web applications. WebSocket provides a full-duplex and bidirectional communication protocol over a single TCP connection. That is, a client and a server can send messages to each other and independent of each other.

---

[24] www.w3.org/wiki/The_principles_of_unobtrusive_JavaScript
[25] http://nodejs.org/

A few examples of the applications that require real-time functionality are chat applications, multiplayer online games, stock trading applications, and so on.

> **Note** The Java API for WebSocket is defined as JSR 356; see Table 1-3.

Reactive Web Application

Reactive applications are a new class of applications that are fundamentally different from traditional web-based applications and are driven by the Typesafe[26] Reactive Platform. The Typesafe Reactive Platform is a suite of integrated products consisting of the Play 2 framework, Akka,[27] and Scala, along with the Typesafe Console for command and control. Reactive programming is becoming crucial because of multicore processors and because it advocates asynchronous and event-based programming. The Play framework is an alternative to the enterprise Java stacks. Play is built for the needs of modern web and mobile applications, leveraging technologies such as REST, JSON, and WebSocket, to name a few. These technologies allow the creation of rich, highly interactive user interfaces rendered via any modern browser, while at the same time making it easier to render portions of the page in parallel and to do partial-page updates or progressive enhancements.

Mashups and Web Services

A *mashup* is a web application that uses content from more than one source to create a new service displayed in a single graphical interface. With mashups you can develop powerful applications by combining web services. You can find popular APIs for mashups at `www.programmableweb.com/apis/directory/1?sort=mashups`. This section will focus on web services and then touch on a fascinating trend, which is still an area of research: the Semantic Web.

A *web service* is a software component stored on one machine that can be accessed over the network by an application (or other software component) on another machine. The machine on which a web service resides is referred to as a *web service host*. The client application sends a request over a network to the web service host, which processes the request and returns the response. Making a web service available to receive client requests is known as *publishing* a web service; using a web service from a client application is known as *consuming* a web service.

Web services use technologies such as XML and JSON[28] for data interchange.

JavaScript Object Notation

JavaScript Object Notation (JSON) is used for representing data as an alternative to XML. JSON reduces the payload of web requests, improving the overall performance of a web application. JSON is a text-based data-interchange format used to represent objects in JavaScript as collections of name-value pairs represented as Strings.

---

[26] `http://typesafe.com/`
[27] `http://akka.io/`
[28] `www.json.org/`

Note JSON Processing is defined as the Java API for JSON Processing in JSR 353; see Table 1-3.

Two Java APIs facilitate web services:

- *JAX-WS*: This is based on the Simple Object Access Protocol (SOAP),[29] which is an XML-based protocol that allows web services and clients to communicate, even if the client and the web service are written in different languages.
- *JAX-RS*: This uses Representational State Transfer (REST), which is a network architecture that uses the Web's traditional request-response mechanisms such as GET and POST requests.

Simple Object Access Protocol

The Simple Object Access Protocol (SOAP) is a platform-independent protocol that uses XML to interact with web services, typically over HTTP. Each request and response is packaged in a SOAP message, which is XML markup containing the information that a web service requires to process the message. A SOAP web service works as follows:

1. When a method of a SOAP web service is invoked, the request is packaged in a SOAP message enclosed in a SOAP envelope and sent to the server on which the web service resides.
2. When the SOAP)web service receives this message, it parses the XML representing the message and then processes the message's contents.
3. Then, the web service, after processing the request, sends the response to the client in another SOAP message.
4. The client parses the response.

Representational State Transfer

The term *representational state transfer* (REST) was introduced and defined in 2000 by Roy Fielding in his doctoral dissertation[30] at UC Irvine. REST refers to an architectural style for implementing web services called RESTful web services. Each method in a RESTful web service is identified by a unique URL.

Note RESTful web services are defined as JSR 339, as shown in Table 1-3.

---

[29] `www.w3.org/TR/soap/`

[30] `www.ics.uci.edu/~fielding/pubs/dissertation/rest_arch_style.htm`

Unlike SOAP, REST does the following:

- Identifies a resource as a URI
- Uses a well-defined set of HTTP methods to access the resource
- Works with multiple representation formats of a resource

Semantic Web (Web 3.0)

Web 2.0 began to take shape in 2004. It was pioneered by Google and followed by social applications such as video sharing, social networking, microblogging, photo sharing, Wikipedia, and virtual worlds such as Second Life. Mashups played a major role in the evolution of social applications and Web 2.0.

The term *Semantic Web* refers to the W3C's vision of the Web of linked data. The Semantic Web can be viewed as a set of standards that allow machines to understand the *meaning* of information on the Web. The Web as it is today constitutes data that has no meaning in itself, and the meaning has to be constituted manually after gathering the data from the Web. Semantic Web technologies enable you to create data stores on the Web, build vocabularies, and write rules for handling data. Linked data are empowered by technologies such as RDF,[31] SPARQL,[32] and OWL.[33] The Semantic Web is the future of the Web and is a subject of ongoing research. I recommend Aaron Swartz's *A Programmable Web: An Unfinished Work*[34] as an excellent resource on the Semantic Web. You can also follow the latest news on the Semantic Web.

Summary

This chapter introduced the Java language and then took you on a whirlwind tour through the Java landscape. The diverse landscape of the Java world consists of several web frameworks (such as Struts 2, Spring Web MVC, JSF 2, Grails 2 and Play 2) that make development much easier; thus, as a Java web developer, you need to be familiar with these web frameworks. Modern Java is more than just a language; it is now a fully optimized platform for several other industry-strength languages such as Groovy, Clojure, and Scala. All these languages, especially Groovy, have a close association with Java, and you will come across web applications before long where Java and these alternative JVM languages will work in tandem.

The subsequent chapters will address all these needs of a modern Java web developer. Specifically, in the next chapter, you will create a Hello World web application that utilizes the basic building blocks of a web application, namely, servlets and Java Server Pages. From there, you will then transform the stand-alone application into your first full-blown web application: a bookstore application using servlets and JSP.

---

[31] www.w3.org/RDF/

[32] www.w3.org/TR/rdf-sparql-query/

[33] www.w3.org/TR/owl-features/

[34] www.morganclaypool.com/doi/pdf/10.2200/S00481ED1V01Y201302WBE005

Chapter 2

Building Web Applications Using Servlets and JSP

Protocol is everything.

—François Giuliani

The core Internet protocols substantiate and sustain the Web, so understanding these protocols is fundamental to understanding how web applications are developed.

The Internet is a colossal network of networks, and in general, all of the machines on the Internet can be classified into two types: the server and the client. The *client* is the machine requesting some information, and the *server* is the machine that provides that information. The information data that flows from the information provider (that is, the server) to the information requester (that is, the client) is bound by a definite rule that governs the marshaling of the information to be transmitted by the server and the unmarshaling of the information to be translated or read by the client. This rule is called the *protocol*. The web browser (that is, the client), the web server (that is, the server), and the web application all converse with each other through the Hypertext Transfer Protocol (HTTP). The clients send HTTP requests to the web servers, and the web servers return the requested data in the form of HTTP responses. The HTTP clients and the HTTP servers are the bricks and mortar that lay the foundation of the World Wide Web, and HTTP is the *lingua franca* of the Web.

HTTP is a request-response stateless protocol, the corollary of which is that, from the web server's view, any request is the first request from the web browser. When a client makes a request for the resource, the request also encloses the identification of the resource being requested, in the form of a Uniform Resource Locator (URL). URLs are described in RFC 3986[1] as a uniform way of uniquely identifying a resource. URLs are designed to implicitly provide a means of locating a resource by describing its "location" on a network.

---

[1]www.ietf.org/rfc/rfc3986.txt

> **Note** A URL is a concrete form of Uniform Resource Identifier (URI), which is a mechanism to distinguish entities. But URIs in themselves are abstract. There are two concrete forms of URI: URL and Uniform Resource Name (URN). URN is still experimental and not widely adopted.

A generic URL is a hierarchical sequence of components, structured as `scheme://hostName:portNumber/path/resource?query string`.

To identify the parts of a URL, consider a URL that lists the details of a book on your bookstore web site, as shown here:

```
http://www.yourbookstore.com/bookstore/bookServlet?action=bookDetails
```

Figure 2-1 illustrates the parts of this URL.

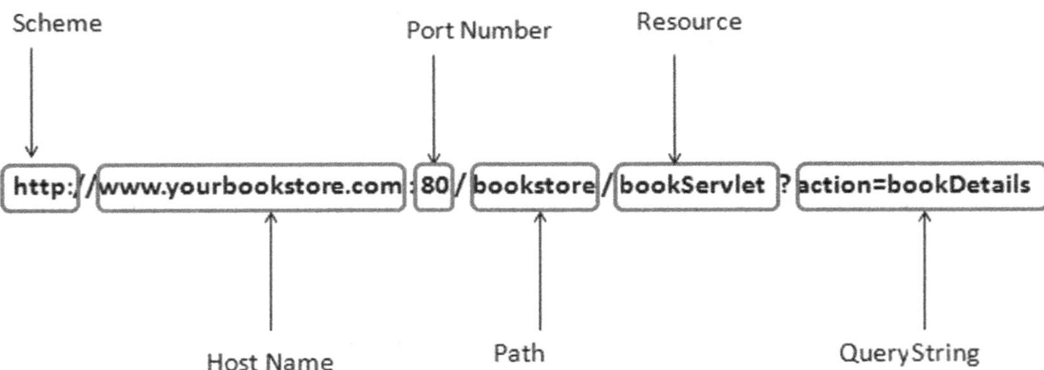

***Figure 2-1.** Anatomy of a URL*

The host name and port number together are termed an *authority*. By default, a web server such as Tomcat, as explained later, listens for incoming requests on port 8080. Some parts of the URL shown in Figure 2-1 are optional, including the port number (which defaults to the well-known ports 80 and 443 for the HTTP and HTTPS schemes, respectively) and the query string.

> **Note** HTTPS is HTTP over Secure Sockets Layer (SSL); it allows secure, encrypted communications.

When present, a query string is a series of name-value pairs preceded with a question mark (?) and with an ampersand (&) separating the pairs.

Note Query strings are supported only for the GET method. There are other HTTP protocol methods, such as POST, DELETE, and PUT.

A web application is a collection of web components that work together to provide a specific functionality on the Web. In the Java EE specification, a web component is defined to be either a Servlet or a Java Server Page (JSP) page.

Note Other than servlets and JSP pages, a web application may also comprise static resources such as HTML documents, images, and the metadata or configuration files that define properties of the web application; however, these are not considered to be web components.

The web application and its constituent components are managed and executed inside the web container, also called a *servlet container*, which provides additional features to the web application such as security. When the web server gets a request for specific functionality that a particular web component (such as a servlet or a JSP page) can provide, the web server forwards the request to the servlet container in which the web component resides. All requests for the dynamic content (that is, all requests to the web component that is responsible for generating the dynamic content) are mediated by the servlet container, as shown in Figure 2-2.

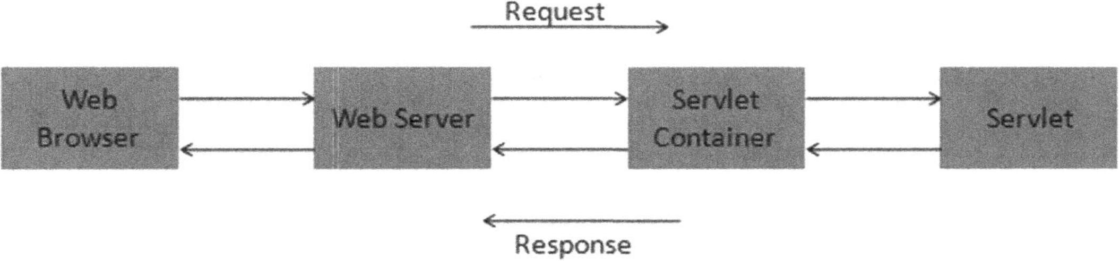

***Figure 2-2.** Request for dynamic content*

The Java EE Servlet and JSP specifications describe the service contract that a servlet container must provide and specify how a servlet should use those services. In terms of implementation, a *servlet* is a Java class that acts as a dynamic web resource.

Servlets

Servlets are the central processing unit of a Java web application and are responsible for most of the processing required by a web application. Specifically, a servlet is a Java class that implements the `javax.servlet.Servlet` interface. The `Servlet` interface defines the methods that all servlets must implement. "One ring to rule them all!" This interface, along with other methods, defines key life-cycle methods such as `init()`, `service()`, and `destroy()` to initialize a servlet, to service requests, and to remove a servlet from the server, respectively. Table 2-1 describes all the methods of the `javax.servlet.Servlet` interface.

Table 2-1. *The Life-Cycle and Non-Life-Cycle Methods of the Servlet Interface*

Modifier and Type	Method
`void`	`init(ServletConfig config)`
`void`	`service(ServletRequest req, ServletResponse res)`
`void`	`destroy()`
`ServletConfig`	`getServletConfig()`
`String`	`getServletInfo()`

The life-cycle methods are invoked by the container at appropriate instants in a servlet's life in the following sequence:

1. The servlet is constructed and then initialized with the `init` method.
2. Any calls from clients to the service method are handled.
3. The servlet is then destroyed with the `destroy` method, garbage collected, and finalized.

The `Servlet` interface methods illustrated in Table 2-1 are explained here:

- `init(ServletConfig)`: Called by the servlet container exactly once after instantiating the servlet. This method must complete successfully before the servlet is a candidate to receive any requests.
- `service()`: Called by the servlet container, after the servlet's `init()` method has completed successfully, to allow the servlet to respond to a request.
- `destroy()`: Called by the container to destroy the servlet and serves as a method in which the servlet must release acquired resources before it is destroyed.
- `getServletConfig()`: Allows the servlet to get start-up information in the form of a `ServletConfig` object returned by this method. The `ServletConfig` object contains initialization and start-up parameters for the servlet.
- `getServletInfo()`: Allows the servlet to return its own information such as the servlet's author and version.

Your First Web Application Using a Servlet

In Chapter 1, you installed the Eclipse Kepler IDE. You will develop your first web application in Eclipse in this section. Specifically, you will use Tomcat 7 both as the HTTP server and as the servlet container. You can install Tomcat 7 by downloading the source distribution of Tomcat as a ZIP file from `http://tomcat.apache.org/download-70.cgi`.

Start Eclipse and select the Window ➤ Preferences menu option to display the Preferences dialog, as illustrated in Figure 2-3.

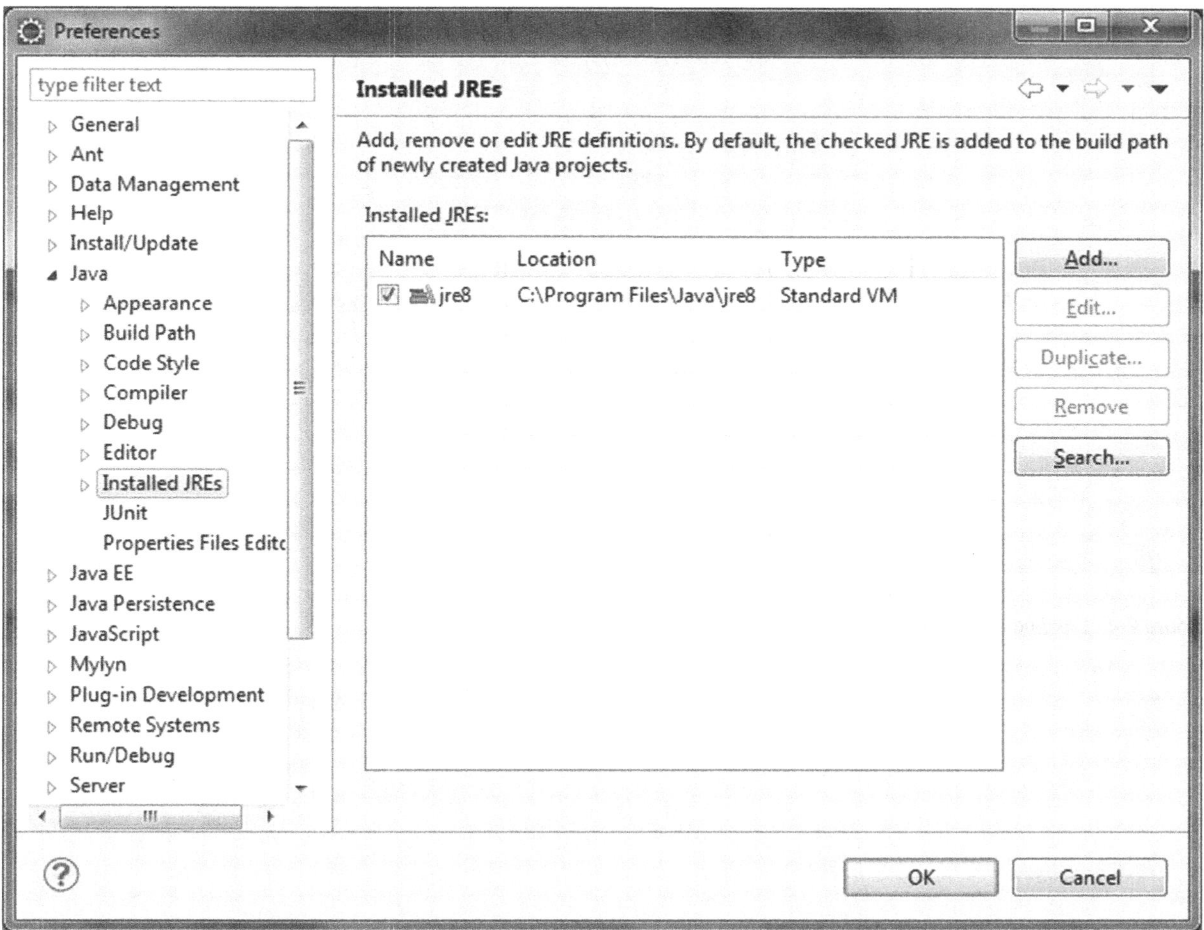

Figure 2-3. Preferencesdialog, verifying installed JRE

In the left pane of this dialog, drill down to Java ➤ Installed JREs and verify that your previously installed version of JRE8/JDK 8 shows up. If it doesn't, click the Add button to add a reference to your JDK. Create a Dynamic Web Project by selecting File ➤ New ➤ Dynamic Web Project, as shown in Figure 2-4. Name the project **helloworld**, as shown in Figure 2-5.

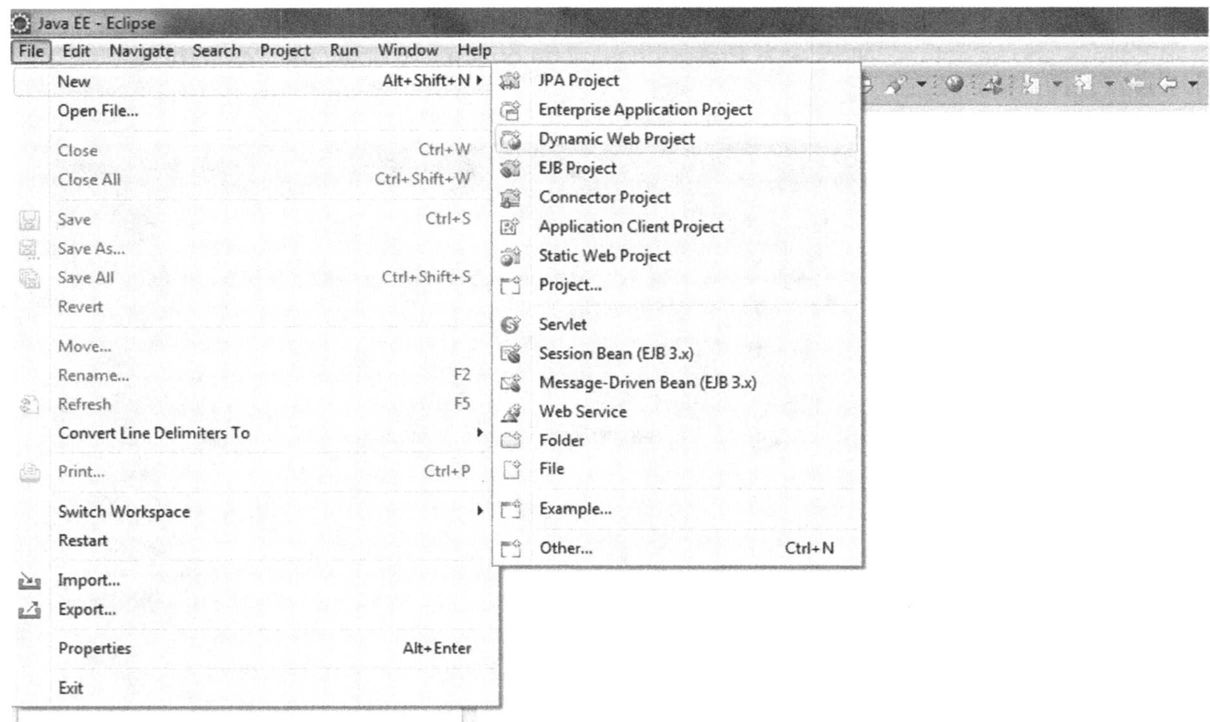

Figure 2-4. Creating a new project

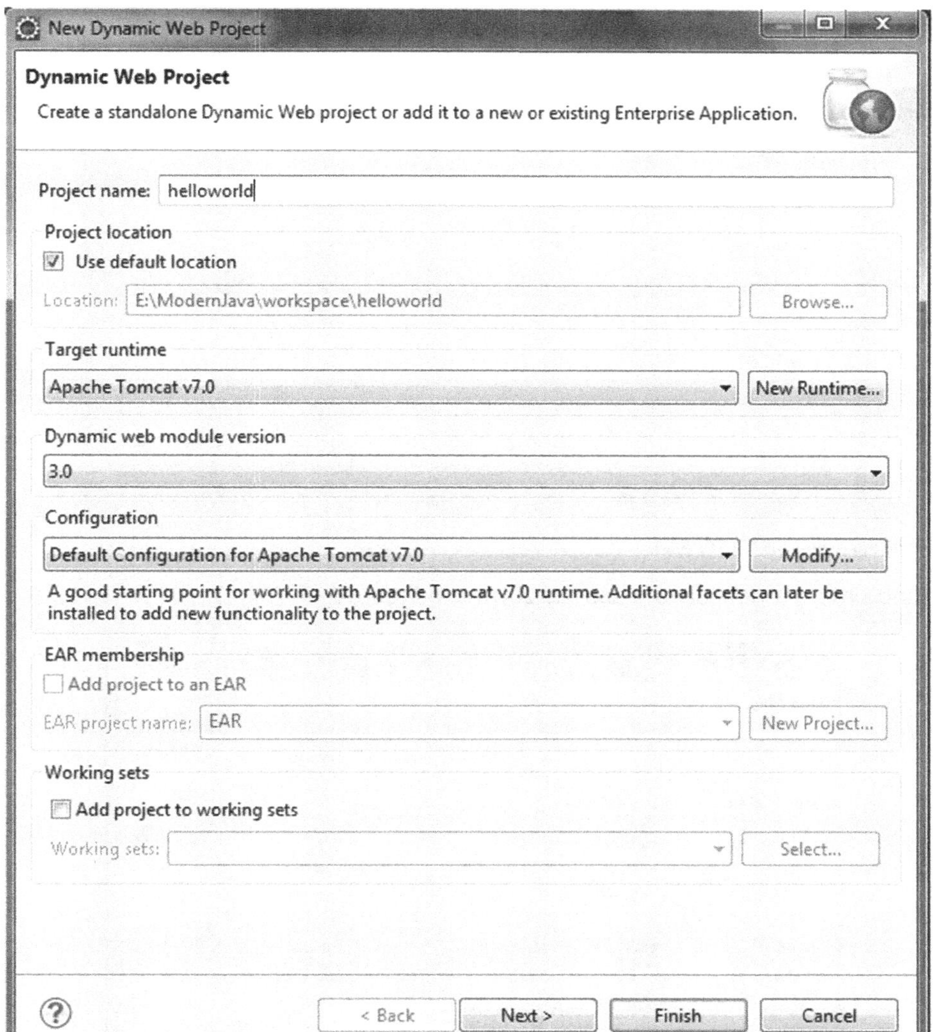

***Figure 2-5.** Creating the helloworld project*

Click Next, and check "Generate web.xml deployment descriptor," as shown in Figure 2-6. Later we will see how it is possible to configure the web module without `web.xml`.

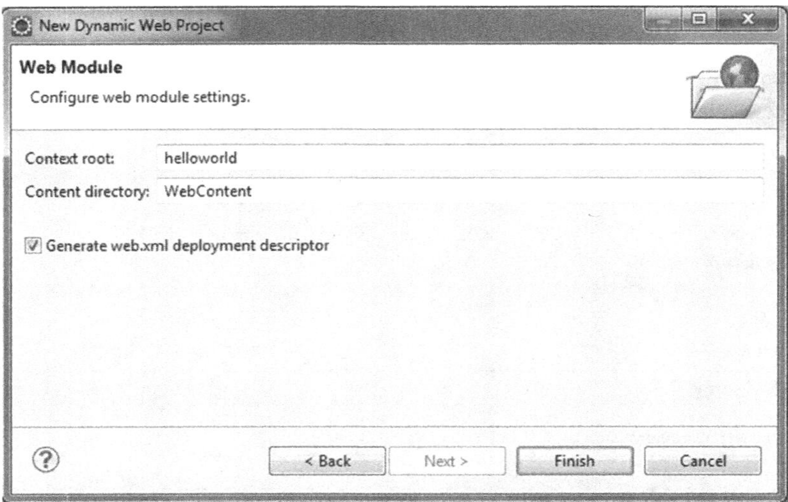

Figure 2-6. Configuring web module settings

Click Finish, and create a new Java class, as shown in Figure 2-7.

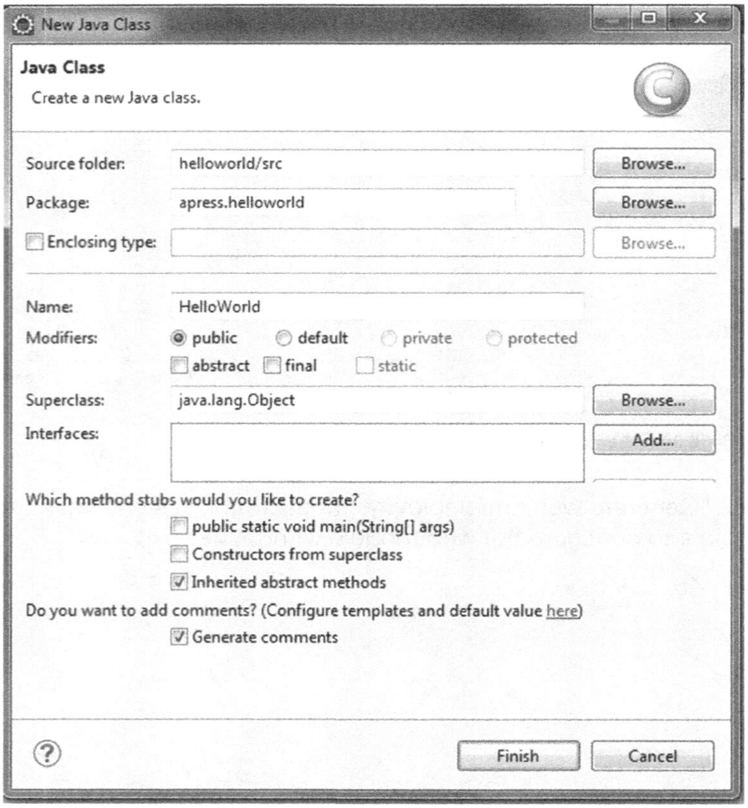

Figure 2-7. Creating a Java class: the servlet

Modify the generated `HelloWorld` class with the code in Listing 2-1.

***Listing 2-1.** HelloWorld Servlet*

```
package apress.helloworld;

import java.io.IOException;
import java.io.PrintWriter;

import javax.servlet.http.HttpServlet;
import javax.servlet.http.HttpServletRequest;
import javax.servlet.http.HttpServletResponse;

public class HelloWorld extends HttpServlet{

protected void doGet(HttpServletRequest request,
HttpServletResponse response)
{
try
{
response.setContentType("text/html");
PrintWriter printWriter = response.getWriter();
printWriter.println("<h2>");
printWriter.println("Hello World");
printWriter.println("</h2>");
}
catch (IOException ioException)
{
ioException.printStackTrace();
}
}

}
```

Modify the `web.xml` file with the code in Listing 2-2.

***Listing 2-2.** Web.xml: Deployment Descriptor*

```
<?xml version="1.0" encoding="UTF-8"?>
<web-app xmlns:xsi="http://www.w3.org/2001/XMLSchema-instance"
xmlns="http://java.sun.com/xml/ns/javaee"
xmlns:web="http://java.sun.com/xml/ns/javaee/web-app_2_5.xsd"
xsi:schemaLocation="http://java.sun.com/xml/ns/javaee
http://java.sun.com/xml/ns/javaee/web-app_3_0.xsd"
id="WebApp_ID" version="3.0">
<display-name>helloworld</display-name>
<servlet>
<servlet-name>HelloWorld</servlet-name>
<servlet-class>apress.helloworld.HelloWorld</servlet-class>
</servlet>
<servlet-mapping>
<servlet-name>HelloWorld</servlet-name>
```

```
<url-pattern>/hello</url-pattern>
</servlet-mapping>
<welcome-file-list>
<welcome-file>index.html</welcome-file>
<welcome-file>index.htm</welcome-file>
<welcome-file>index.jsp</welcome-file>
<welcome-file>default.html</welcome-file>
<welcome-file>default.htm</welcome-file>
<welcome-file>default.jsp</welcome-file>
</welcome-file-list>
</web-app>
```

Now we need to configure `HelloWorld servlet` as a web module in Tomcat. SelectWindow ➤ Show View ➤ Servers in the menu bar of Eclipse, as illustrated in Figure 2-8.

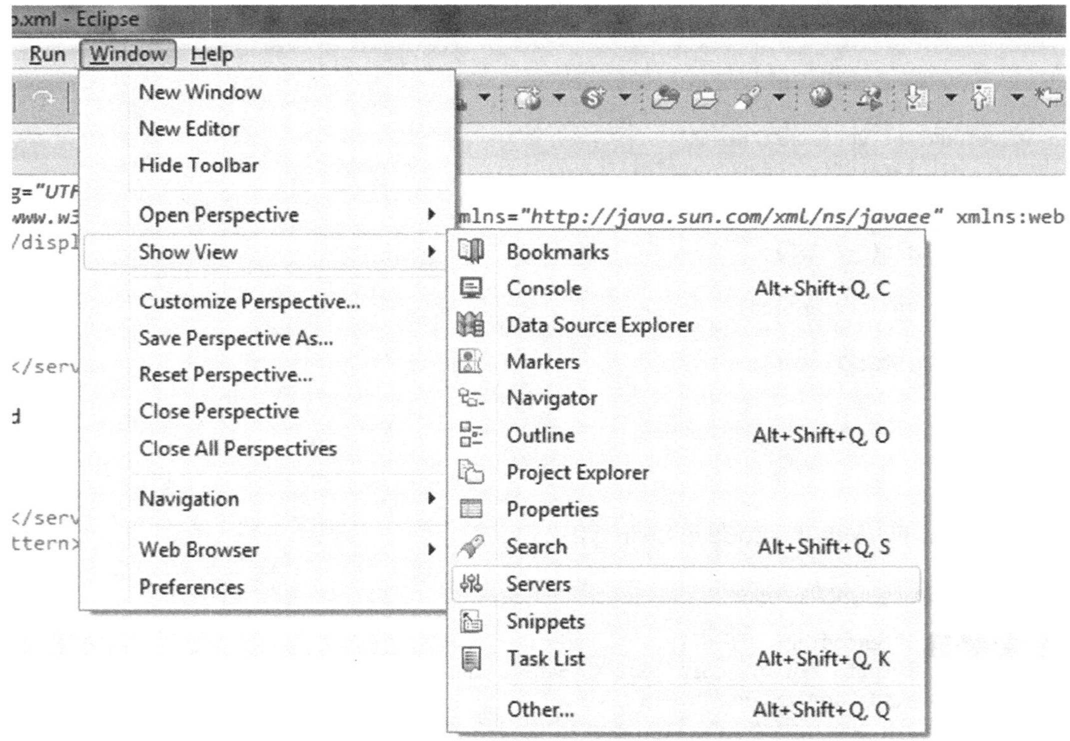

Figure 2-8. Adding the server

On the Servers tab, right-click and add Tomcat 7 as the new server, as shown in Figure 2-9.

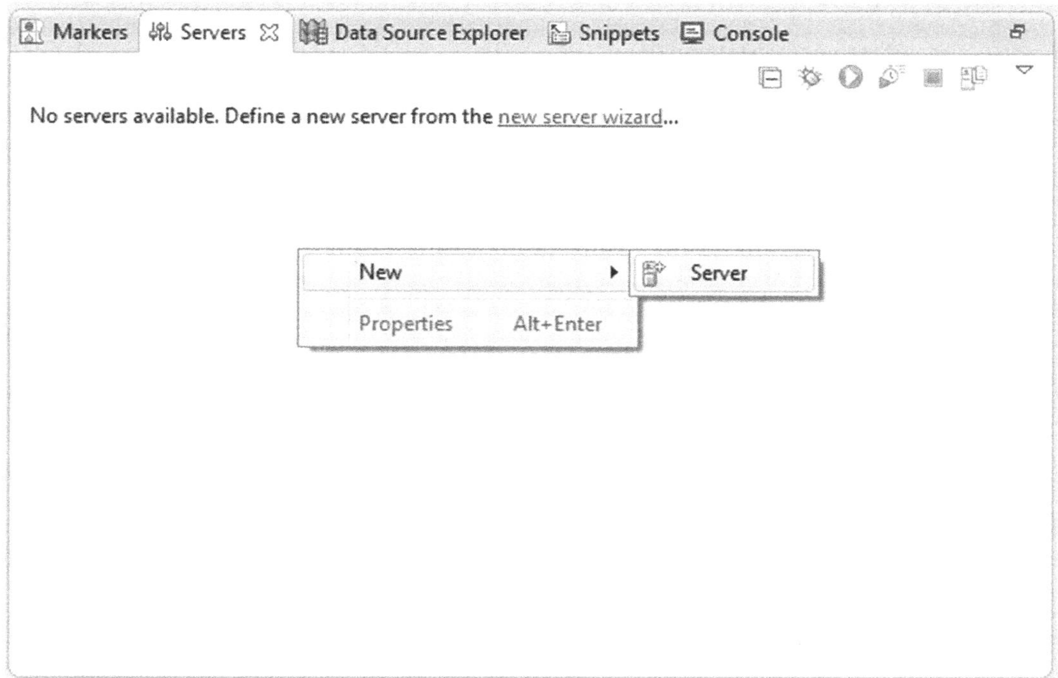

Figure 2-9. Defining the server

Next you will have to define a new server, as illustrated in Figure 2-10.

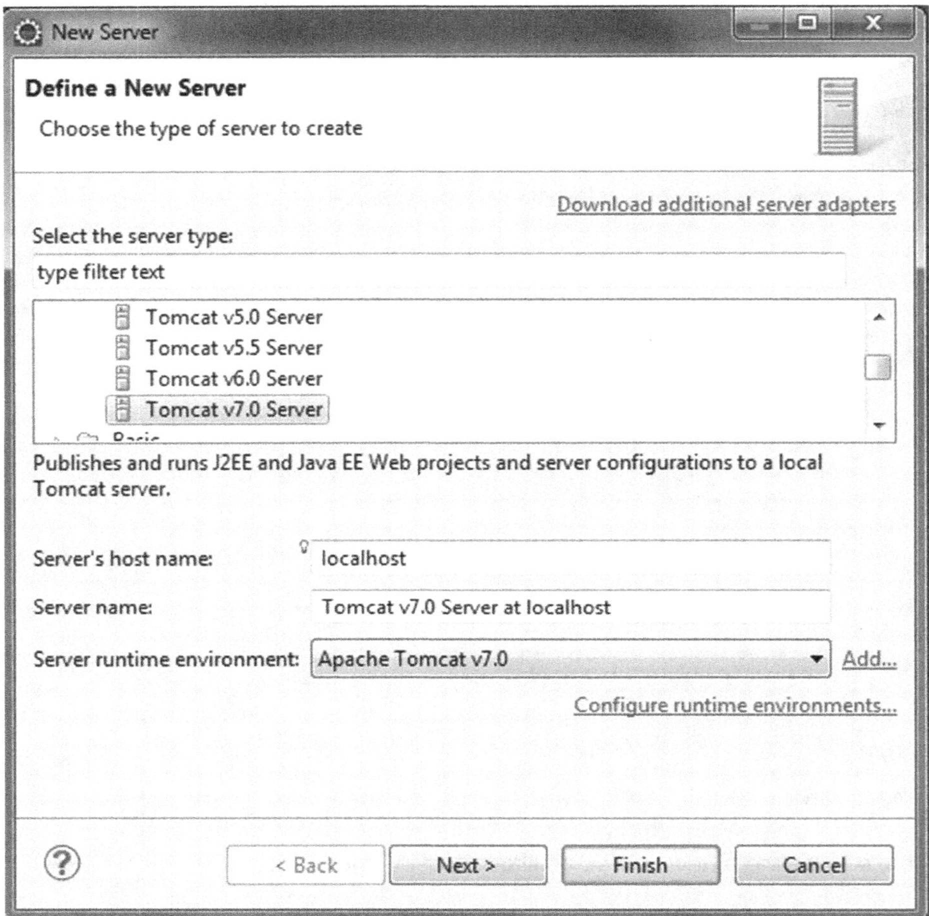

Figure 2-10. Defining the Tomcat server

Now configure the helloworld project by moving the resources to the right in the configured section, as shown in Figure 2-11.

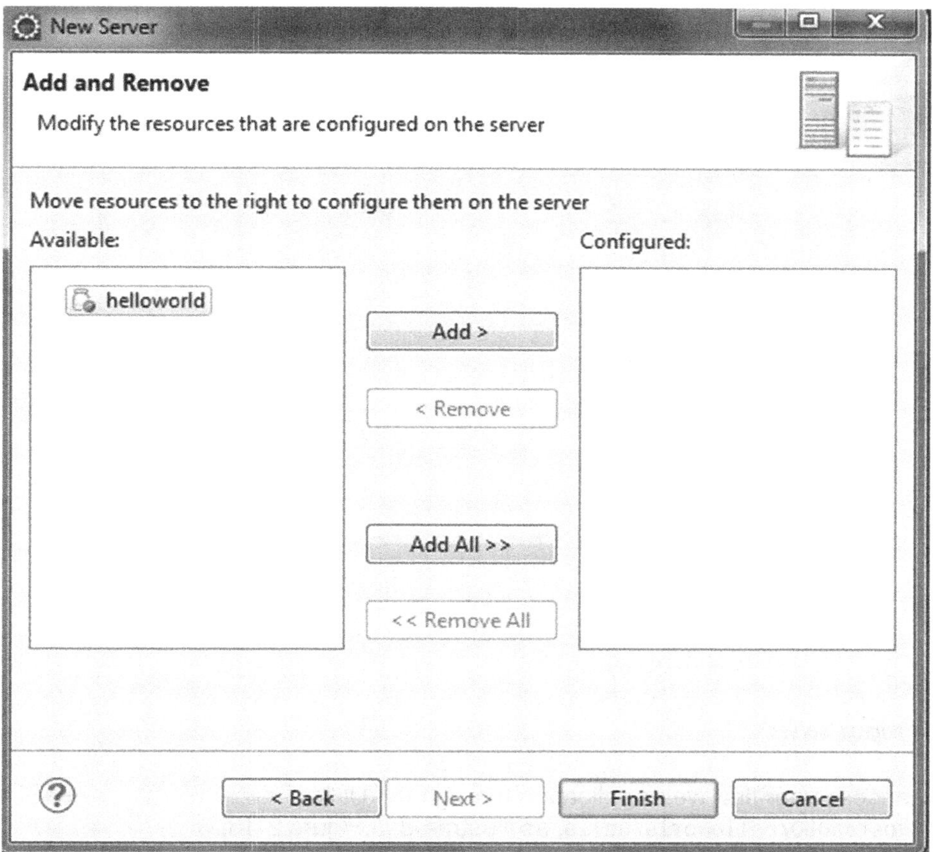

Figure 2-11. Configuring the resource on the server

Click Add, and the resource will be configured on the server. Then click Finish. Start the server and access the application using the URL shown in Figure 2-12.

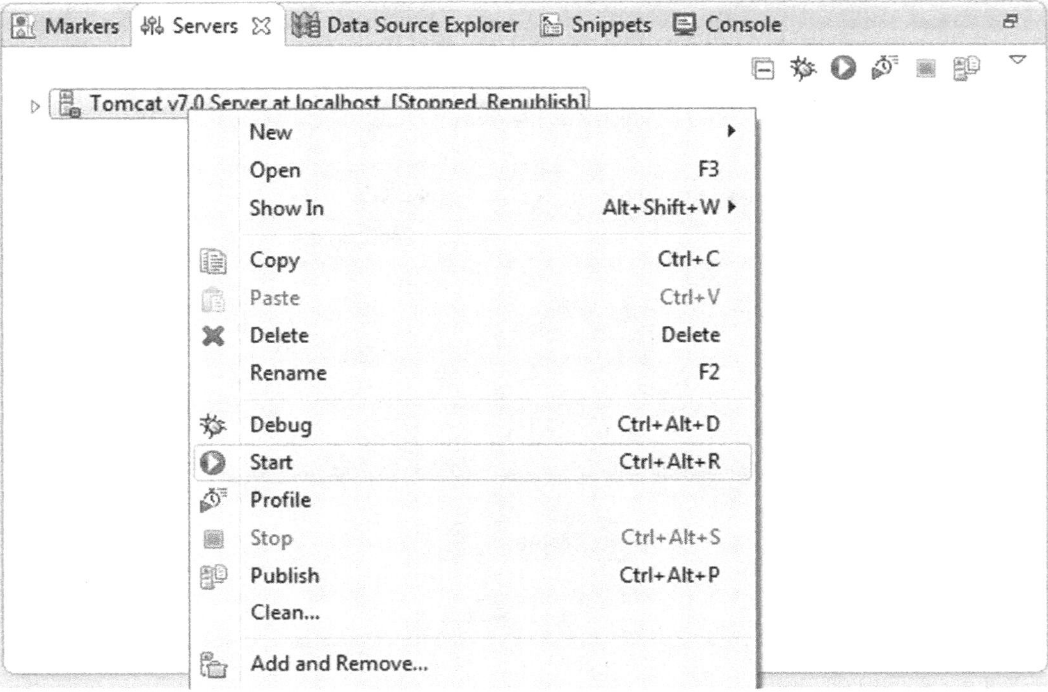

Figure 2-12. Starting the server

You can now access your first web application through the URL `http://localhost:8080/helloworld/hello`, as illustrated in Figure 2-13.

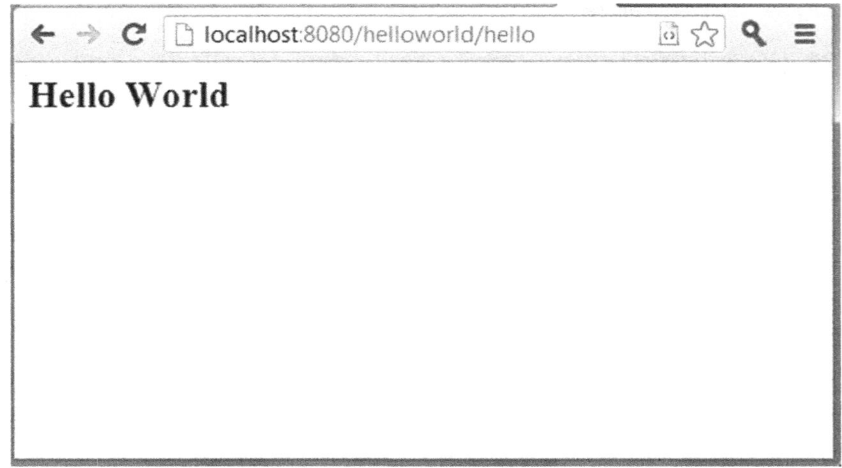

Figure 2-13. Running the helloworld web application

In the following section, you will learn how the request flows through the application and how the container finds the servlet in the helloworld application you developed. Then you will use the `HelloWorld` servlet to understand the life-cycle methods of the servlet.

Request Flow for the HelloWorld Servlet

The request originating from the web browser flows through the web server and the servlet container before the `HelloWorld` servlet can generate the response, as explained in following sections.

HTTP Request Message

The URL used to access the helloworld web application is `http://localhost:8080/helloworld/hello`. When the user accesses the web application through this URL, the web browser creates the HTTP request, as illustrated in Listing 2-3.

Listing 2-3. HttpRequest Message

```
1.GET /helloworld/hello HTTP/1.1
2.Host: localhost:8080
3.User-Agent: Mozilla/5.0 (Windows NT 6.1) AppleWebKit/537.31 (KHTML, like Gecko)
Chrome/26.0.1410.43 Safari/537.31
```

- *Line 3*: This line describes the specific user agent (web browser) that initiated communication by making a request for a specific resource using HTTP, described in line 1.
- *Line 1*: The request made by the user agent is of the form shown in Figure 2-14.

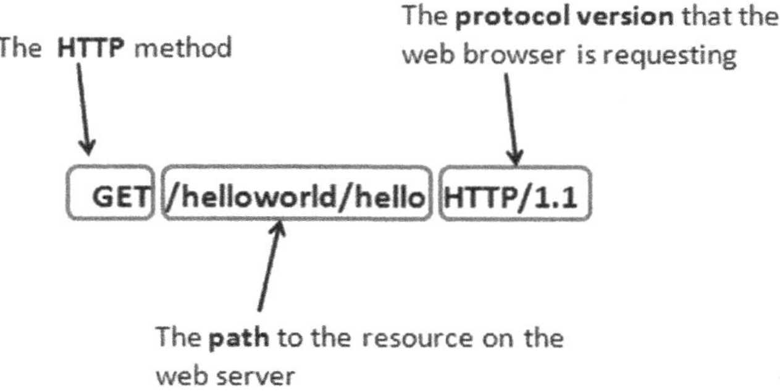

***Figure 2-14.** Anatomy of HTTP request message*

- *Line 2*: This machine (your machine) that is running a web server is a server machine. `Localhost` is specified where you would otherwise use the host name of a computer. For example, directing a browser installed on a system running an HTTP server to `http://localhost` will display the home page of the web site installed on that system, as illustrated in Figure 2-15.

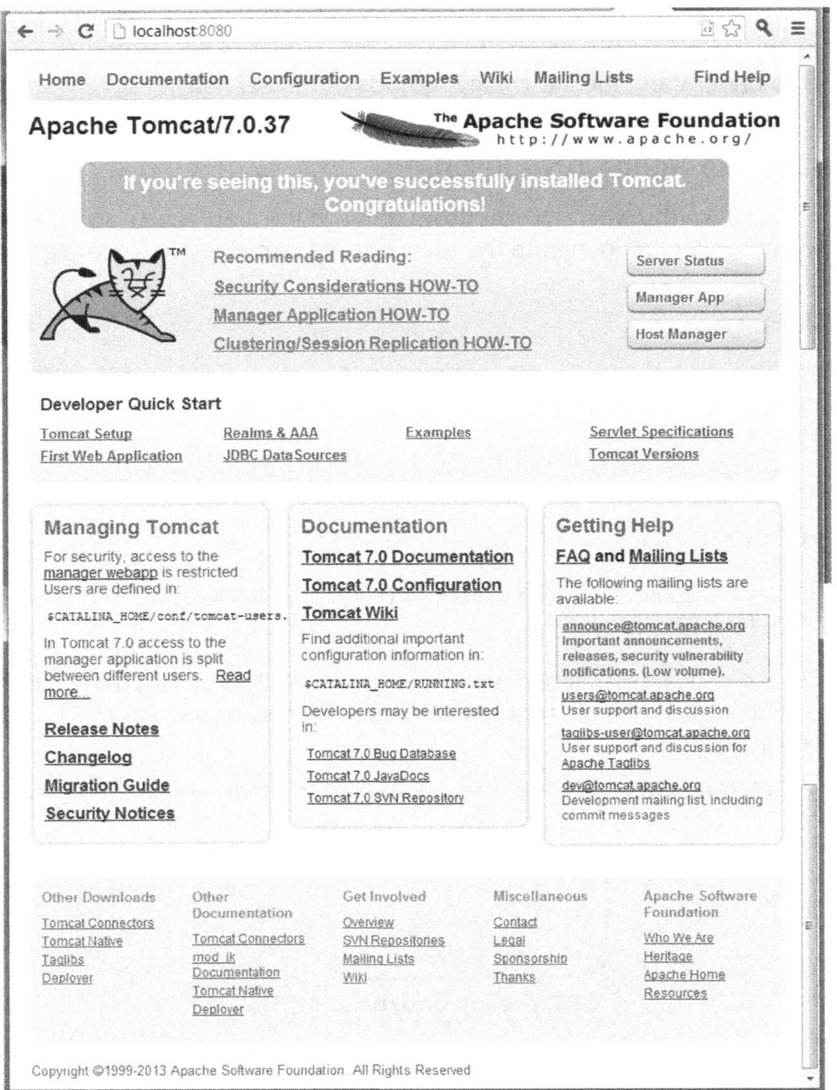

***Figure 2-15.** Home page of the web server*

Figure 2-15 shows the homepage of Tomcat that you will see when you start Tomcat on your machine by running `startup.bat` in the `bin` directory of Tomcat. A server machine makes its services available to the Internet using numbered ports, one for each service that is available on the server. For example, if a server machine is running a web server, the web server would typically be available on port 80, or 8080 in the case of Tomcat.

Examining the Request

When the client (web browser) makes a request (a GET request in this case), the web server (Tomcat) sees the resource path /helloworld/hello in the request in line 1 and determines that the resource requested by the user is not a static page (for example a .html file) and so forwards the request to the web container (Tomcat). Astute readers will notice that Tomcat serves the role of the web server and the web container.

Locating the Servlet

The resource path in the request (line 1 in Listing 2-3) is mapped to the HelloWorld servlet through the web.xml file written in Listing 2-2. This web.xml file is called a *deployment descriptor* because it describes the deployed servlet to the web container. Through the deployment descriptor, the web container determines the servlet that needs to be called to serve the original HTTP request that the web browser initiated. For the sake of reader's convenience, the web.xml is shown again here in Listing 2-4.

Listing 2-4. web.xml

```
1.<?xml version="1.0" encoding="UTF-8"?>
2.<web-app xmlns="http://java.sun.com/xml/ns/javaee" xmlns:xsi="http://www.w3.org/2001/XMLSchema-instance"
xsi:schemaLocation="http://java.sun.com/xml/ns/javaee
http://java.sun.com/xml/ns/javaee/web-app_3_0.xsd" version="3.0">
3.<servlet>
4.<servlet-name>HelloWorld </servlet-name>
5.<servlet-class>
6.apress.helloworld.HelloWorld
7.</servlet-class>
8.</servlet>
9.<servlet-mapping>
10.<servlet-name>HelloWorld</servlet-name>
11.<url-pattern>/hello </url-pattern>
12.</servlet-mapping>
13.</web-app>
```

- *Lines 1 to 2*: These lines contain boilerplate XML stating the version, encoding, and schema used for the XML file.
- *Lines 3 to 8*: The <servlet> tag is used to configure our servlet. It contains two nested tags: <servlet-name> defines a logical name for the servlet, and <servlet-class> indicates the Java class defining the servlet.
- *Lines 9 to 12*: The <servlet-mapping> XML tag is used to configure our servlet. It contains two nested tags: <servlet-name> matches the value set in the <servlet> tag, and <url-pattern> sets the URL pattern for which the servlet will execute.

Java EE web applications run from within a context root. The context root is the first string in the URL after the server name and port. For example, in the URL http://localhost:8080/ helloworld/hello, the string helloworld is the context root. The value for <url-pattern> is relative to the application's context root. A Java EE `web.xml` file can contain many additional XML tags. Besides mapping URLs to actual servlets, you can use the deployment descriptor to customize other aspects of your web application such as security roles, error pages, tag libraries, and initial configuration information. However, these additional tags are not needed for this helloworld application. The web container loads the `HelloWorld` servlet class and instantiates it. Only a single instance of the `HelloWorld` servlet is created, and concurrent requests to the `HelloWorld servlet` are executed on that same instance. Every client request generates a new pair of request and response objects. The container runs multiple threads to process multiple requests to a single instance of the `HelloWorld` servlet.

> **Note** In a distributed web app, there is one instance of a particular servlet per JVM, but each JVM still has only a single instance of that servlet.

The Life-Cycle Methods

The life cycle of an object describes the sequence of steps an object must go through during its existence. The life of a servlet is different from a normal Java class because a servlet has to execute inside the web container. Figure 2-16 shows the hierarchy of the `HelloWorld servlet`.

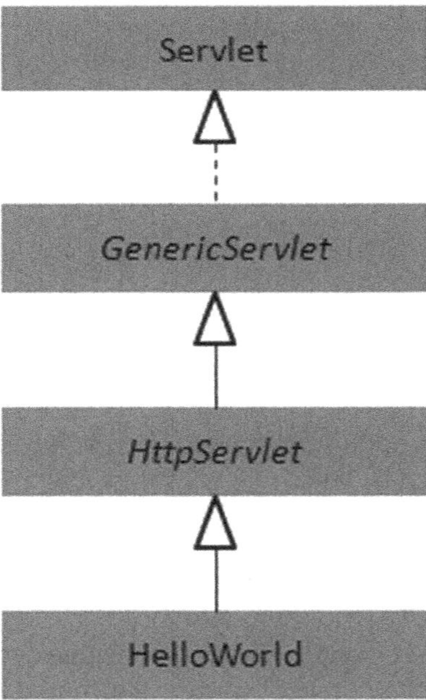

***Figure 2-16.** Hierarchy of HelloWorld servlet*

GenericServlet

Most servlets provide similar basic functionality through an abstract `javax.servlet.GenericServlet` class provided by the Servlet API. The `GenericServlet` class implementation is protocol-independent, so it does not matter if it has to respond to HTTP or FTP requests. The `GenericServlet` abstract class defines an `init()` method that is called by the default `init(ServletConfig)` method to execute any application-specific servlet initialization.

HttpServlet

In a web application, lack of any protocol-dependent processing in a `GenericServlet` class signifies that the developer has to write the code for this processing in any subclass she creates. Since HTTP is the most well-known and widely used protocol on the Web, the Servlet API also includes one more abstract subclass of `GenericServlet`: `javax.servlet.http.HttpServlet`. The `service()` method is implemented by `HttpServlet`, which inspects the incoming HTTP method and invokes the appropriate method for that request type.

> **Note** HTTP/1.1 defines seven request methods. The `HttpServlet` class provides default implementations for each of these methods that you can override in your servlets. However, most web application comprise servlets that override only the `doGet()` and `doPost()` methods.

An HTTP request to an `HttpServlet` subclass goes through a number of steps:

1. A call to the public `service (ServletRequest, ServletResponse)` method by the container.
2. Delegation of this call to `HttpServlet`'s protected `service (HttpServletRequest, HttpServletResponse)` method.
3. The protected `service (HttpServletRequest, HttpServletResponse)` method then delegates to the appropriate `doXxx` method, depending on the HTTP method used for the request.

HelloWorld Servlet

As mentioned in the previous section, the superclass of your servlet includes two versions of `init()`, one that takes a `ServletConfig` and one that's a no-arg. The `init(ServletConfig)` method calls the no-arg `init()`, so you need to override only the no-arg version.

init()

The container calls `init()`on the servlet instance. You can override it in order to get database connections registered with other objects. Otherwise, the `init()` method from the `Genericservlet` runs.

1. When a servlet instance is created, its `init()` method is invoked. The `init()` method allows a servlet to initialize itself before the first request is processed. You can specify `init()` parameters to the servlet in the `web.xml` file or via annotations.
2. The web container calls the `init()` method of the servlet (only once in the servlet's life), and the `init()` method must complete before the container can call `service()` method.

service()

The container calls the `service()` method of the servlet. This method looks at the request, determines the type of HTTP method, and invokes the matching `doGet()` or `doPost()` on the servlet. You never override it. Your job is to override `doGet()` or `doPost()` and let the service implementation from `HTTPServlet` worry about calling the right one.

- When the `service()` method is called on your servlet, it will be handed references to `HttpServletRequest` and `HttpServletResponse` objects that implement the `HttpServletRequest` and `HttpServletResponse` interfaces. The container implements these interfaces.
- For every request received to the servlet, the servlet's `service()` method is called. For `HttpServlet` subclasses, one of the `doGet()`, `doPost()`, and so on, methods is typically called. The container creates two objects: `HTTPServletRequest` and `HttpServletResponse`.
- The `service()` method can be called multiple times as long as the servlet is active in the servlet container.
- The `service()` methods call `doGet()/doPost()`. You always override at least one of them in your servlet.

destroy()

The servlet container calls the `destroy()` method on the servlet, and this method is called only once. This method provides the servlet with an opportunity to release acquired resources before it is destroyed.

ServletContext and ServletConfig

After the `init()` method is called, the servlet gets one `ServletConfig` object per servlet and one `ServletContext` per web application. In a distributed environment, you will have one `ServletContext` per JVM. A `ServletContext` is a means by which a servlet can connect with both the container and the other parts of the web application. In the servlet, the only time you have to go through the `ServletConfig` to get the `ServletContext` is if your servlet is not an `HttpServlet` or a `GenericServlet`.

The ServletConfig object can be used to do the following:

- Pass deploy-time information to the servlet (such as a database or enterprise bean lookup name) that you do not want to hard-code into the servlet. This deploy-time information is called the *servlet init parameters*. The servlet init parameters will be discussed in the next section.
- Access the ServletContext.

The ServletContext object can be used to do the following:

- Access the web application parameters
- Set attributes that all components of the application can access
- Get server information, including the name and version of the container and the version of the API that is supported

A servlet can have three types of parameters:

- Request parameters
- Initialization (init) parameters
- Context-initialization (context-init) parameters

Initialization Parameters

The initialization parameters are defined in the web.xml file, as illustrated in Listing 2-5.

Listing 2-5. Defining Initialization Parameters

```
<servlet>
<init-param>
<param-name>email </param-name>
<param-value>vishalway@.gmail.com</param-value>
</init-param>
</servlet>
```

You cannot use init-parameters until the servlet is initialized. Your servlet inherits getServletConfig(), so you can call that from any method in your servlet to get a reference to a ServletConfig. Once you have a ServletConfig reference, you can call getInitParam().

When the container initializes a servlet, the following happens:

1. The container makes a unique ServletConfig for the servlet.
2. The container reads the init parameters from the deployment descriptor and sets them in the ServletConfig object.
3. The container then passes the ServletConfig to the servlet's init (servletConfig) method.

> **Note** Once the container sets the init params in `ServletConfig`, the container never reads init param from the deployment descriptor again, unless the servlet is redeployed.

Context-Init Parameters

Context-init parameters are similar to init parameters. The main difference between the context-init parameters and init params is that context parameters are available to the entire web app while the init parameters are available to just the servlet. Listing 2-6 illustrates the context-init parameters in the `web.xml` file.

Listing 2-6. Defining Context-Initialization Parameters

```
<context-param>
<param-name>email </param-name>
<param-value>vishalway@gmail.com</param-value>
</context-param>
```

The `<context-param>` element is not nested inside the `<servlet>` element.

Listing 2-7 illustrates how to get the context-init parameters from your servlet.

Listing 2-7. Getting Context-Initialization Parameters

```
out.println(getServletContext().getInitParameter("email");
```

Every servlet inherits a `getServletContext()` method. The `getServletContext()` method returns a `ServletContext` object.

RequestDispatcher

In a web application, there are two ways to alter the request flow.

- *Redirecting the request*: The request is redirected to a completely different URL. The redirect can be done by calling `sendRedirect()` on the response object. The redirect is done by the browser.
- *Dispatching the request*: The request is dispatched to another component in the web app, typically a JSP page. A request dispatch is different from a redirect in that it does the work on the server side. A `RequestDispatcher` is called on the request, and a redirect is called on the response.

Figure 2-17 shows the methods in the `RequestDispatcher` interface.

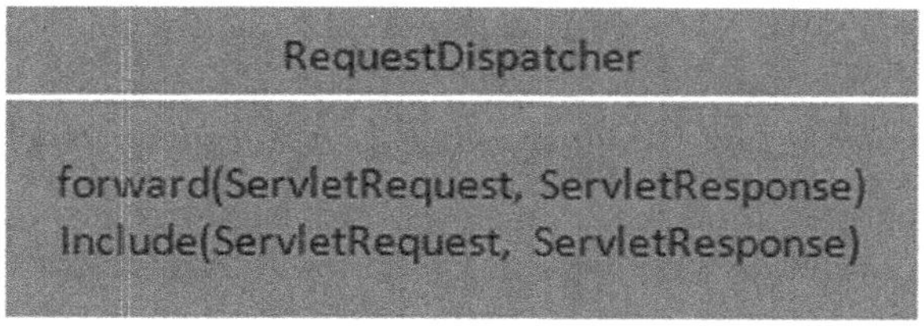

RequestDispatcher

forward(ServletRequest, ServletResponse)
Include(ServletRequest, ServletResponse)

Figure 2-17. RequestDispatcher interface

You can get a `RequestDispatcher` in two ways.

- Getting a `RequestDispatcher` from a `ServletRequest`
- Getting a `RequestDispatcher` from a `ServletContext`

Getting a RequestDispatcher from a ServletRequest

```
RequestDispatcher view = request.getRequestDispatcher("bookDetails.jsp");
```

The `getRequestDispatcher()` method in `ServletRequest` takes a path for the resource to which the request is being forwarded. If the path begins with a forward slash (/), it is considered by the container to be starting from the root of the web application. If the path does not begin with the forward slash, the container considers it relative to the original request.

Getting a RequestDispatcher from a ServletContext

```
RequestDispatcher view = getServletContext().getRequestDispatcher("/bookDetails.jsp");
```

The `getRequestDispatcher()` method takes a `String` path for the resource to which you are forwarding the request. The `RequestDispatcher`, thus obtained from the context or request, can be used to forward to the resource because the `RequestDispatcher` knows the resource you are forwarding to, in other words, the resource that was passed as the argument to the `getRequestDispatcher()`. Listing 2-8 illustrates calling forward on a `RequestDispatcher`.

Listing 2-8. Calling forward on RequestDispatcher

```
RequestDispatcher view = request.getRequestDispatcher("bookDetails.jsp");
view.forward(request, response);
```

Filters

A *filter* is a reusable Java component that can transform the content of HTTP requests, responses, and header information. Filters are used for the following:

- Accessing static or dynamic content or modifying the request headers before invoking a request
- Intercepting the invocation of a web component after the call is invoked

- Providing actions on web components by using a chain of filters in a specific order
- Modifying the response headers and response data before they are rendered

A filter is created by implementing the `javax.servlet.Filter` interface and providing a no-arg constructor. A filter is configured in a web application either in the deployment descriptor using the `<filter>` element or in the `@WebFilter`annotation (introduced in the section that follows). In the `<filter>` element, you must declare the following:

- `<filter-name>`: Used to map the filter to a servlet or URL
- `<filter-class>`: Used by the container to identify the filter type

> **Note** You can also declare the initialization parameters for a filter.

Listing 2-9 illustrates the filter declaration.

Listing 2-9. Declaring the Filter

```
<filter>
<filter-name>ResponseFilter</filter-name>
<filter-class>com.apress.ResponseServlet</filter-class>
</filter>
```

Filters can be associated with a servlet using the `<servlet-name>` element. Listing 2-10 maps the `Response Filter` filter to the `ResponseServlet` servlet.

Listing 2-10. Mapping the Filter to the Servlet

```
<filter-mapping>
<filter-name>Response Filter</filter-name>
<servlet-name>ResponseServlet</servlet-name>
</filter-mapping>
```

Filters can be associated with groups of servlets using `<urlpattern>`, as illustrated in Listing 2-11.

Listing 2-11. Associating a Filter with a Group of Servlets

```
<filter-mapping>
<filter-name>Response Filter</filter-name>
<url-pattern>/*</url-pattern>
</filter-mapping>
```

In Listing 2-11 the response filter is applied to all the servlets in the web application.

A web application typically comprises the following filtering components:

- Authentication filters
- Caching filters

- Data compression filters
- Encryption filters
- Image conversion filters
- Logging and auditing filters

Configuring Servlet via Annotations

From Servlet 3.0 onward, servlets can be configured either via `web.xml` or using annotations or both. Table 2-2 describes the annotations supported by a Servlet 3.0–compliant web container.

Table 2-2. Annotations for Configuring the Servlet

Annotation	Description
`@WebFilter`	Defines a filter in a web application
`@WebInitParam`	Specifies init parameters to be passed to the servlet or the filter
`@WebListener`	Annotates a listener to get events
`@WebServlet`	Defines a component in a web application
`@MultipartConfig`	Indicates that the request is of type `mime/multipart`

In the section that follows, you will develop a helloworld project in which you will configure the servlet via annotations. Right-click the project helloworld, create a new servlet class, and give the class name as HelloWorld, as shown in Figure 2-18. Click Next.

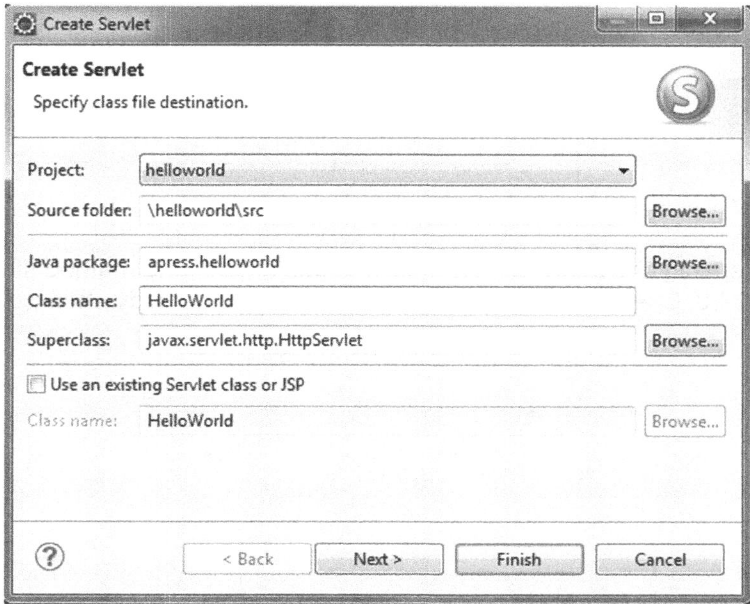

Figure 2-18. Creating a servlet

On the next screen, you can fill in the information pertaining to the deployment descriptor such as the initialization parameters and URL mappings, as illustrated in Figure 2-19. For the HelloWorld application, you do not have to fill in the values for initialization parameters. The default value of the URL mapping, in this case `/HelloWorld`, is just fine. This value in the "URL mappings" field is the servlet path of the URL, as explained in the previous section. Click Next.

Figure 2-19. URL mapping

On the next screen, specify the modifiers, interfaces to implement, and method stubs to generate, as illustrated in Figure 2-20. Check doGet and doPost if they are not already checked. Then click Finish.

Figure 2-20. Specifying methods

The IDE generates the `HelloWorld` servlet illustrated in Listing 2-12.

Listing 2-12. HelloWorld Servlet Using Annotations

```
package apress.helloworld;

import java.io.IOException;
import javax.servlet.ServletException;
import javax.servlet.annotation.WebServlet;
import javax.servlet.http.HttpServlet;
import javax.servlet.http.HttpServletRequest;
import javax.servlet.http.HttpServletResponse;

/**
 * Servlet implementation class HelloWorld
 */
@WebServlet(urlPatterns = { "/HelloWorld" }, description = "A hello world servlet")
public class HelloWorld extends HttpServlet {
```

```
15.private static final long serialVersionUID = 1L;
16.
17.    /**
18.     * @see HttpServlet#HttpServlet()
19.     */
20.    public HelloWorld() {
21.        super();
22.        // TODO Auto-generated constructor stub
23.    }
24.
25./**
26. * @see HttpServlet#doGet(HttpServletRequest request, HttpServletResponse response)
27. */
28.protected void doGet(HttpServletRequest request, HttpServletResponse response) throws
ServletException, IOException {
29.// TODO Auto-generated method stub
30.}
31.
32./**
33. * @see HttpServlet#doPost(HttpServletRequest request, HttpServletResponse response)
34. */
35.protected void doPost(HttpServletRequest request, HttpServletResponse response) throws
ServletException, IOException {
36.// TODO Auto-generated method stub
37.}
38.
39.}
```

- *Line 13*: This line shows the usage of the @WebServlet annotation. The HelloWorld servlet is decorated with the @WebServlet annotation to specify the name, URL pattern, initialization parameters, and other configuration items usually specified in the web.xml deployment descriptor.
- *Line 14*: This line shows that the HelloWorld servlet extends the HTTPServlet.
- *Lines 28 to 37*: These lines show the doGet and doPost methods generated by the IDE.

Add the code in Listing 2-13 to the doGet method of the HelloWorld servlet.

***Listing 2-13.** Printing "Hello World"*

```
PrintWriter out = response.getWriter();
out.println("<h2>Hello World !</h2>");
```

You will have to import java.io.Printwriter. You can do this in Eclipse by selecting Source ➤ Add Import or by pressing Ctrl+Shift+M; now you can run the application on the server. Right-click HelloWorld.java in the helloworld project in Eclipse and then select Run As ➤ Run on Server. The server you are using in this case is Tomcat 7.0. Then use the following URL to access the application:

```
http://localhost:8080/helloworld/HelloWorld
```

Figure 2-21 shows the output.

***Figure 2-21.** Accessing the application*

For more information on the Java Servlet technology, refer to the Java Servlet 3.1 specification[2] and the Java Servlet web site.[3]

Java Server Pages

Servlets enable the web server to generate dynamic content. However, servlets have one major disadvantage in that the HTML code is required to be hardwired in the Java code. To eliminate this cross-cutting of concerns, the Java Server Pages (JSP) technology was created. JSP uses a combination of static HTML content and dynamic content to generate web pages, thus separating the concern of embedding HTML content in Java code.

Your First Web Application Using JSP

Now you will create a "Hello World" application using JSP. Since you created a project with this name earlier, make sure to delete or rename the old project first. Then right-click in the project explorer and select Dynamic Web Project, as shown in Figure 2-22. Name the project **helloworld**.

[2]http://jcp.org/en/jsr/detail?id=340
[3]www.oracle.com/technetwork/java/index-jsp-135475.html

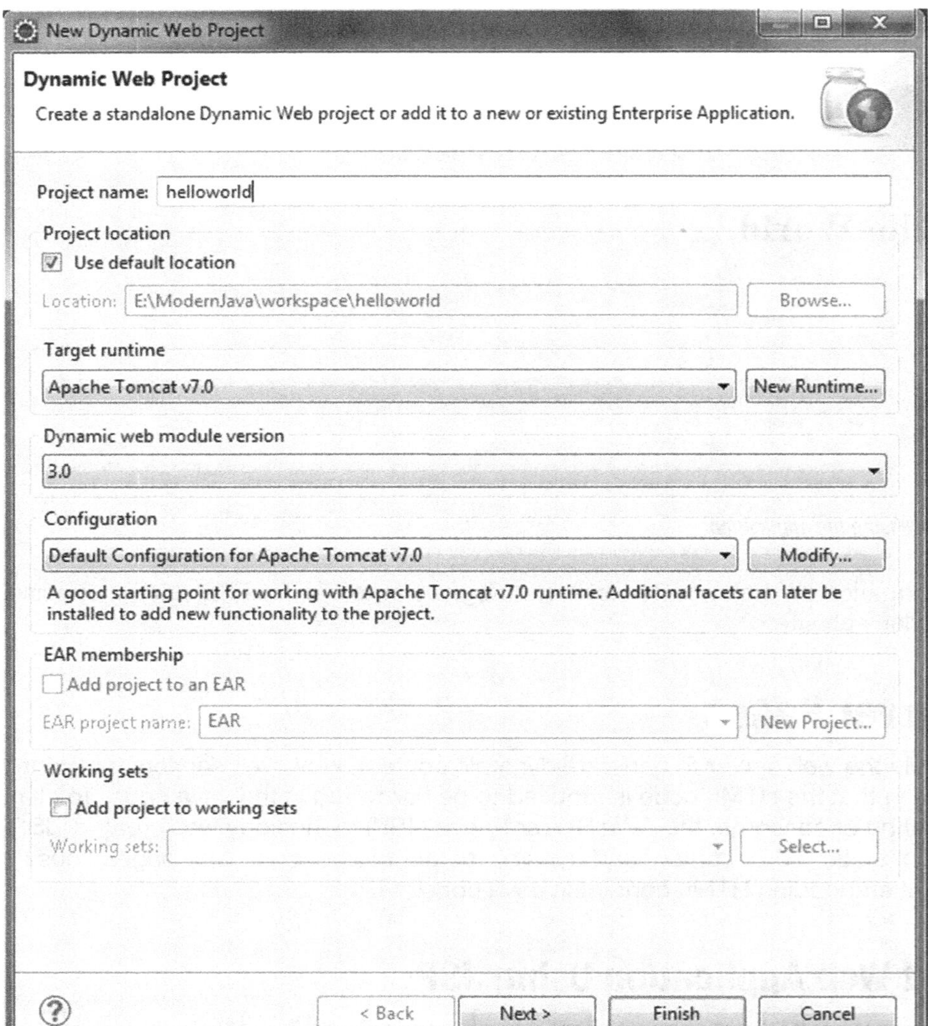

***Figure 2-22.** Creating the helloworld project*

Right-click the project helloworld, create a new JSP file, and give the name as **helloworld.jsp**. Click Next. Click Finish on the next screen.

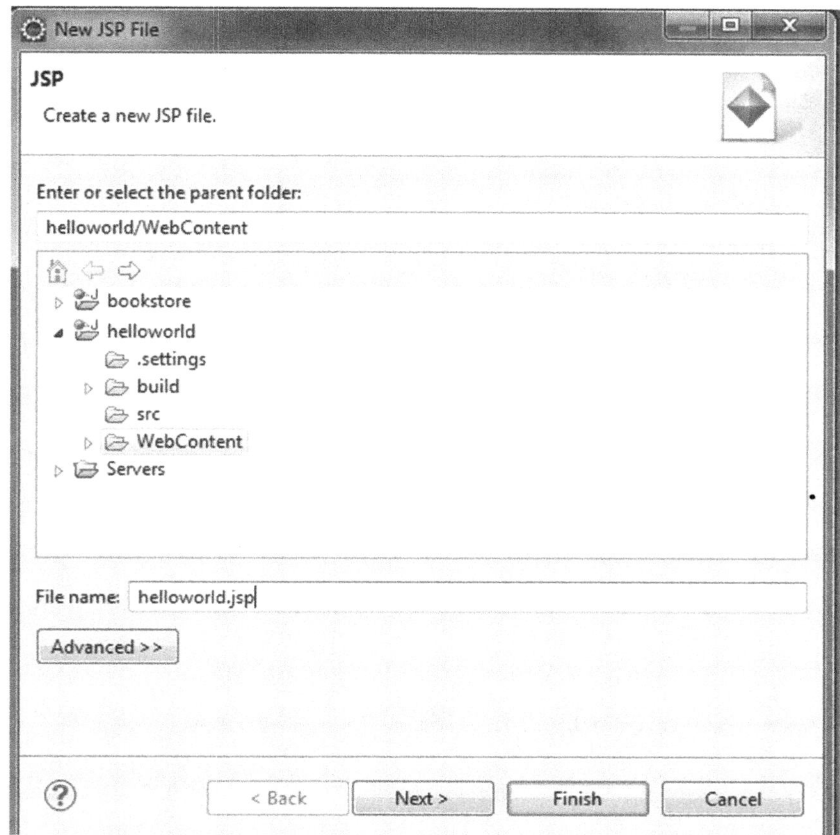

***Figure 2-23.** Creating the JSP file*

Modify the code of `helloworld.jsp` as illustrated in Listing 2-14.

***Listing 2-14.** helloworld.jsp*

```
<!DOCTYPE html >
<html>
<head>
<meta http-equiv="Content-Type" content="text/html; charset=ISO-8859-1">
<title>Hello World</title>
</head>
<body>
Hello World!
</body>
</html>
```

Deploy the application on the server, as shown in Figure 2-24.

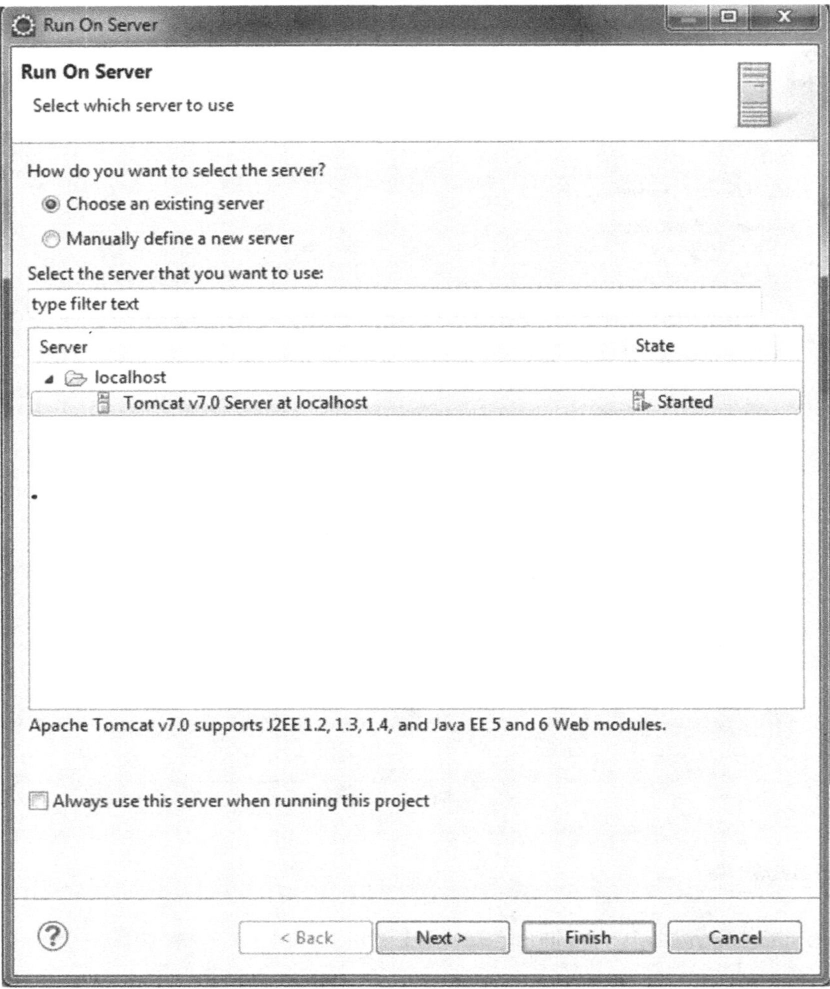

***Figure 2-24.** Running the application on the server*

Launch the application using `http://localhost:8080/HelloWorld/hello.jsp`.

Figure 2-25 shows the output.

Figure 2-25. Accessing the JSP

JSP Basics

This section will cover the fundamental JSP constructs. A sound understanding of the classic approach is essential for understanding its limitations and to appreciate the power of more advanced techniques such as Expression Language, which is a subject of the next chapter. Before Expression Language was added to the JSP specification, a billion JSP pages were written using the classic approach, and you may still have to maintain them or refactor them. This need for backward compatibility is one reason why the JSP specification still covers the classic components. But when you have to write new JSPs in your application, you should not write backward-compatible code; instead, you should use the best-practice approach, which will be explained in the next chapter. When JSP 1.0 was added to the JSP specification in 1999, it was meant to produce dynamic, web-based content by embedding business-logic code in the template data. To that end, the following JSP elements were provided to be used within a JSP page to manipulate Java objects and perform operations upon them, thereby enabling the generation of dynamic content:

- Directives
- Declarations
- Expressions
- Scriptlets
- Implicit objects
- Standard actions

JSP Directives

JSP directives are instructions to the JSP container that are processed during the page translation process. Directives provide a mechanism for making page-level information available to the JSP engine. The directives are declared between <%@ and %> directive delimiters and take the following form:

```
<%@ directive {attribute="value"}* %>
```

Page Directive

The page directive is used to provide instructions about a specific JSP page to be used by the container to generate the underlying servlet. The following is the basic syntax of the page directive:

```
<%@ page attribute="value" %>
```

Table 2-3 describes the attributes associated with the page directive.

***Table 2-3.** Attributes of the Page Directive*

Attribute	Purpose
`autoFlush`	Controls the behavior of the servlet output buffer. It indicates whether the buffer should be automatically written when it is full.
`buffer`	Specifies the buffering model for the servlet output stream. It indicates the size of the buffer.
`contentType`	Specifies the MIME type and character encoding scheme for the response.
`errorPage`	Specifies the URL of a JSP that handles the error conditions and reports the runtime exceptions.
`extends`	Indicates a superclass that the generated servlet must extend.
`import`	Specifies the classes for use in the JSP page similar to the `import` statement in Java.
`info`	Specifies a string for servlet's `getServletInfo()` method.
`isELIgnored?` `isELEnabled`	Specifies whether the EL expression is allowed in the JSP page.
`isErrorPage`	Specifies whether this JSP page is meant to handle error conditions and report runtime exceptions.
`isScriptingEnabled`	Specifies whether scripting elements are allowed in the JSP page.
`isThreadSafe`	Indicates whether the JSP page can handle concurrent requests.
`language`	Indicates the scripting language that is used in the JSP page.
`session`	Specifies whether the JSP page participates in the HTTP session.

Include Directive

The `include` directive is used to specify static resources that should be included within the current JSP page translation unit. The `include` directive has an attribute called `file` that specifies the URL for the resource that should be included. The general form of this directive is as follows:

```
<%@ include file="relative url" >
```

The following example demonstrates using the `include` directive to include a standard JSP header and footer in the current translation unit (Listing 2-15). You can create a project like your first web application, helloworld, and replace `helloworld.jsp` with `main.jsp`. Listing 2-15 illustrates `main.jsp`.

Listing 2-15. main.jsp

```
1.<%@ include file="header.jsp" %>
2.
3.<p>content</p>
4.
5.<%@ include file="footer.jsp" %>
```

- *Line 1*: This line includes `header.jsp` in the `main.jsp` file at translation time.
- *Line 5*: This line includes `footer.jsp` in the `main.jsp` file at translation time.

Listing 2-16 illustrates `header.jsp`.

Listing 2-16. header.jsp

```
1.<html>
2.<head></head>
3.<body>
4.<%out.print("header"); %>
```

- *Line 4*: This line uses an implicit object `out`. Implicit objects will be introduced later in this chapter. The implicit `out` object represents an instance of the `JspWriter` class and is used to write character data to the response stream.

Listing 2-17 illustrates `footer.jsp`.

Listing 2-17. footer.jsp

```
1.<%out.print("footer"); %>
2.</body>
3.</html>
```

Figure 2-26 illustrates the output.

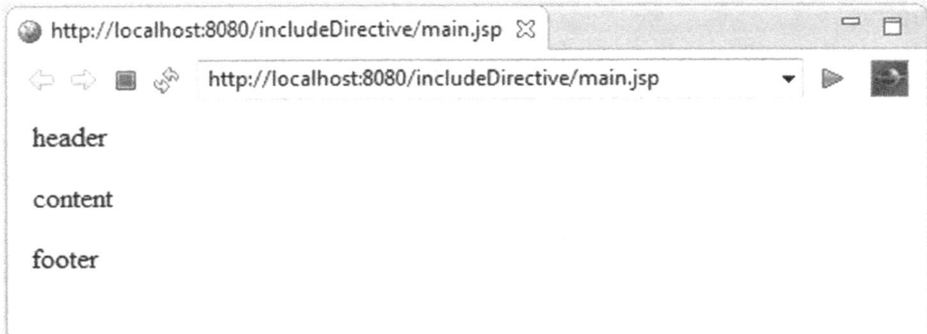

Figure 2-26. Using the include directive

Taglib Directive

The Java Server Pages API provides standard actions, covered in the next section, that encapsulate functionality. The JSP API also allows you to define custom actions that implement custom behavior. Several such custom actions, also called *custom tags*, are assembled in a library called a *tag library*. The `taglib` directive is used to define a prefix and location for a tag library in the current JSP page. The `taglib` directive uses the following syntax:

```
<%@ taglib uri="uri" prefix="tagPrefix" >
```

The `uri` attribute value is an absolute or relative path that specifies the location of the tag library, and the `prefix` attribute specifies the custom action to be used in the current JSP. Listing 2-18 illustrates the usage of the `taglib` directive for an example tag library called `helloTagLib`, which comprises a tag called `hello` that prints a "Hello World" message.

Listing 2-18. Usage of the Taglib Directive

```
1.<%@ taglib uri="/ helloTagLib" prefix="helloTag" %>
2.<html>
3.<body>
4.<helloTag:hello/>
5.</body>
6.</html>
```

- *Line1*: The URI to the library `helloTagLib` and prefix `helloTag`
- *Line 4*: Using the `hello` tag via the prefix

Declarations

Using declarations, JSP allows you to declare methods and variables in JSP pages. Once they are in a JSP page, they are available to scriptlets and expressions throughout the page. JSP declarations are placed between `<%!` and `%>` declaration delimiters. Since declarations are used with expressions and scriptlets, I will introduce expressions and scriptlets in the following sections, and then I will show you how declarations, scriptlets, and expressions are used in a JSP page.

Expressions

Expressions are similar to scriptlets, but they evaluate a regular Java expression and return a result, which is a `String` or something convertible to a `String`, to the client as part of the response. The general syntax is as follows:

```
<%= expression %>
```

Scriptlets

Scriptlets are blocks of Java code surrounded within the <% and %> delimiters to create dynamic content. Listing 2-19 illustrates the usage of a declaration with a scriptlet and expression.

Listing 2-19. Usage of Declaration, Scriptlet, and Expression

```
1.<%!
2.public String hello() {
3.String msg = "Hello World";
4.return msg;
5.}
6.%>
7.Message from <b>Scriptlet</b>: <%hello();%><br/>
8.Message from <b>Expression</b>: <%=hello() %>
```

- *Lines 1 to 6*: These lines contain a JSP declaration that declares a `hello()` method. Line 1 is the start tag, and line 6 is the end tag of the declaration.
- *Line 7*: The `hello()` method declared in lines 1 to 6 is used in an expression on line 7.

Figure 2-27 illustrates the usage of declaration, scriptlets and expression.

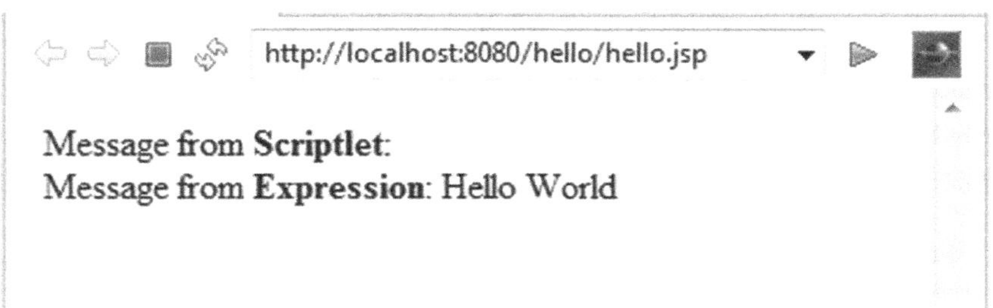

***Figure 2-27.** Using the declaration, scriptlet, and expression*

Implicit Objects

In a web application, multiple web components collaborate with each other and share information by means of objects that are maintained as attributes of four scope objects. You access these attributes by using the `getAttribute` and `setAttribute` methods of the class representing the scope. Table 2-4 lists the scope objects.

Table 2-4. Scope Objects

Scope Objects	Servlet API	Accessible From...
Application/web context	javax.servlet.ServletContext	Web components across the application
Request	Subtype of javax.servlet.ServletRequest	Web components that handle the request
Session	javax.servlet.http.HttpSession	Web components in a session
Page	javax.servlet.jsp.JspContext	The JSP page that creates the object

> **Note** In addition to the standard servlet request, session, and application scopes, JSP adds a fourth scope called *page scope*.

A JSP page can access some specific objects through scripting variables. These objects are provided by the JSP container and are called *implicit objects*. These implicit objects can be accessed in scriptlets, in expressions, or as part of the EL expressions. (The EL expressions are introduced in Chapter 3.) Table 2-5 lists the nine implicit objects with the corresponding API.

Table 2-5. Implicit Objects

Implicit Object	Usage	API
application	Accesses application-level objects	ServletContext
config	Provides configuration information	ServletConfig
exception	Accesses error status	JSPException
out	Accesses the JSP output stream	JSPWriter
page	Provides a reference to the current JSP	Object
pageContext	Accesses the JSP container	PageContext
request	Provides access to the client request	ServletRequest
response	Provides access to the JSP response	ServletResponse
session	Shares information across client requests	HttpSession

These implicit objects are described in more detail in the following sections.

application

The implicit `application` object provides a reference to the `javax.servlet.ServletContext` interface. The `ServletContext` interface is used to provide access to any context-initialization parameters that have been configured for the JSP page via the deployment descriptor of the web application. The `ServletContext` object and parameters stored in them by the web container are available to the entire web application. The `application` object provides the developer of the JSP page with access to the `ServletContext` object.

config

Similar to the application object, the config object provides a reference to the ServletConfig interface of the web application. The ServletConfig interface is used to provide access to any initialization parameters that have been configured for the JSP page via the deployment descriptor of the web application. The config object provides the JSP developer with access to the ServletConfig object.

exception

The implicit exception object is available to JSP to handle the error conditions and report the runtime exceptions using the errorPage page directive.

out

The implicit out object represents an instance of the JspWriter class that is used to write character data to the response stream.

page

The JSP implicit page object is an instance of the Object class and represents the current JSP page.

pageContext

A pageContext provides context information by providing access to all the namespaces associated with a JSP page and to several page attributes. Also, it contains the reference to implicit objects.

request

The request object is an instance of the javax.servlet.http.HttpServletRequest interface. It represents the client request. The request implicit object is generally used to get request parameters, request attributes, header information, and query string values.

response

The implicit response object is an instance of the javax.servlet.http.HttpServletResponse interface and represents the response to be given to the client. The implicit response object is generally used to set the response content type, add cookies, and redirect the response.

session

The JSP implicit session object is an instance of a Java class that implements the javax.servlet.http.HttpSession interface. It is used to store session state for a client.

Listing 2-20 illustrates the usage of the often-used implicit objects. First it shows the common task of setting a book attribute in the request, session, and application scopes in a servlet. Then it shows their JSP equivalents.

Listing 2-20. Usage of Common Implicit Objects

```
1.getServletContext().setAttribute("book", book);
2.request.setAttribute("book", book);
3.request.getSession().setAttribute("book", book);
4.application.setAttribute("book" book);
5.request.setAttribute("book" book);
6.session.setAttribute("book" book);
7.pageContext.setAttribute("book" book);
```

- *Line 1*: This sets the book attribute in a ServletContext without using implicit objects.
- *Line 2*: This sets the book attribute in a request object. The request object is also an implicit object in JSP. Hence, setting the attribute in a servlet is similar to setting the attribute in a JSP page.
- *Line 3*: This sets the book attribute in the session without using implicit objects.
- *Line 4*: This sets the book attribute in the ServletContext using the application implicit object.
- *Line 5*: This sets the book attribute in a request object. request is also an implicit object in JSP. Hence, setting the attribute in JSP is similar to setting the attribute in a servlet.
- *Line 6*: This sets the book attribute in the session using a session implicit object.
- *Line 7*: This sets the book attribute in PageContext using a pageContext implicit object. There is no equivalent of pageContext in a servlet. A PageContext instance provides access to all the namespaces associated with a JSP page, provides access to several page attributes, and provides a layer above the implementation details. Implicit objects are added to the pageContext automatically.

Standard Actions

The JSP standard actions provide a way to do the following:

- Manipulate JavaBeans
- Dynamically include files
- Perform URL forwarding

The <jsp:include> Action

The <jsp:include> action provides a way to include at runtime the directive for including the contents of a separate web component in the declaring JSP page. The syntax for using the standard include action is as follows:

```
<jsp:include page="relativeURL" flush="true"/>
```

We will create two JSPs, shown in Listing 2-21 and Listing 2-22, to illustrate the use of the `<jsp:include>` action.

Listing 2-21. main.jsp

```
1.<html>
2.<head>
3.</head>
4.<body>
5.<%out.print("Inside main.jsp"); %><br/>
6.<jsp:include page="sub.jsp"/>
7.</body>
8.</html>
```

- *Line 6*: Uses the `<jsp:include>` to include the target JSP page (`sub.jsp`)

Listing 2-22. sub.jsp

```
<html>
<head>
</head>
<body>
<%out.print("Inside sub.jsp"); %><br/>
</body>
</html>
```

Figure 2-28 shows the output when `main.jsp` is accessed.

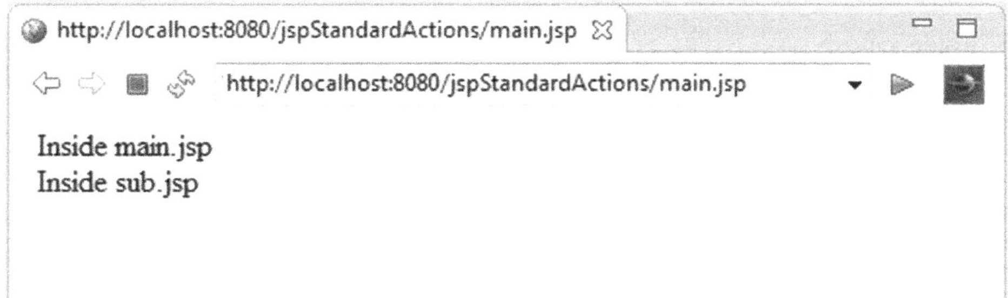

***Figure 2-28.** Using the <jsp:include> action*

The <jsp:forward> Action

The `<jsp:forward>` action is used to forward the current request to another resource such as a static page, a JSP page, or a servlet. The syntax for the action is as follows:

```
<jsp:forward page="relativeURL" />
```

We will use the two JSPs created in the previous section to illustrate the use of the `<jsp:forward>` action as illustrated in the Listing 2-23 and 2-24.

Listing 2-23. Using the Forward Action in main.jsp

```
1.<html>
2.<head>
3.</head>
4.<body>
5.<%out.print("Inside main.jsp"); %><br/>
6.<jsp:forward page="sub.jsp"/>
7.</body>
8.</html>
```

- *Line 6*: Uses `<jsp:forward>` to forward to the target JSP page (`sub.jsp`).

Listing 2-24. sub.jsp

```
<html>
<head>
</head>
<body>
<%out.print("Inside sub.jsp"); %><br/>
</body>
</html>
```

Figure 2-29 shows the output when `main.jsp` is accessed.

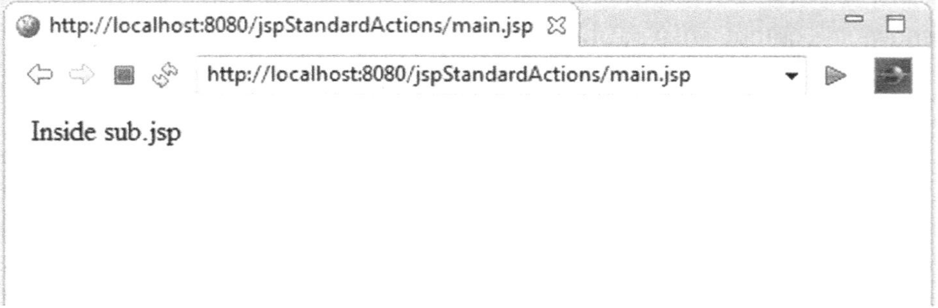

***Figure 2-29.** Usage of the forward action*

To understand the difference between the include action and the forward action, compare Listing 2-21 with Listing 2-23 and compare Figure 2-28 with Figure 2-29. In Listing 2-23, we use the forward action in `main.jsp`, instead of the include action. The forward action transfers the control to `sub.jsp`, just like the include action. But when `sub.jsp` completes, unlike the include action, control does not go back to `main.jsp`.

The <jsp:useBean>, <jsp:getProperty>, and <jsp:setProperty> Actions

These three standard actions can eliminate a great deal of scripting code including declarations, scriptlets, and expressions.

The useBean action is used to declare and initialize the bean object. Once the bean is initialized, you can use the jsp:setProperty and jsp:getProperty actions to set and get bean properties

The <jsp:useBean> action has the following syntax:

```
<jsp:useBean id="someId" class="SomeClass" />
```

The <jsp:setProperty> action sets the properties of a bean.

The <jsp:setProperty> action has the following syntax where someId is the ID of the useBean:

```
<jsp:setProperty name="someId" property="someProperty" .../>
```

The <jsp: getProperty> action, as the name suggests, gets the value of a given property. If the property is not a string, it converts it to a string.

The <jsp: getProperty> action has the following syntax where someId is the ID of the useBean:

```
<jsp:getProperty name="someId" property="someProperty" .../>
```

Listing 2-25 shows how to create a user bean, and Listing 2-26 shows the usage of these three actions in a JSP page.

Listing 2-25. User Bean

```
package com.apress.jspactions;

public class User {

private String name;

public String getName() {
return name;
}

public void setName(String name) {
this.name = name;
}

}
```

The user bean in Listing 2-25 will be used in user.jsp, which is shown in Listing 2-26.

Listing 2-26. user.jsp

```
<html>
<head>
</head>
<body>
<jsp:useBean id="user" class="com.apress.jspactions.User" />
<jsp:setProperty name="user" property="name" value="vishal" />
Hello <jsp:getProperty name="user" property="name" />
</body>
</html>
```

Figure 2-30 shows the output when `user.jsp` is accessed.

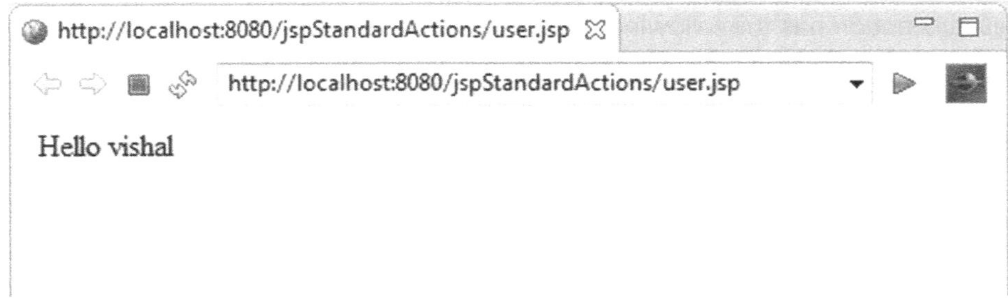

***Figure 2-30.** Usage of useBean, getProperty, and setProperty actions*

The MVC Pattern

The motivation for the Model-View-Controller (MVC) pattern has been around since the conception of object-oriented programming. Prior to MVC, the browser directly accessed JSP pages. In other words, JSP pages handled user requests directly. This was called a Model-1 architecture, as illustrated in Figure 2-31. A Model-1 architecture exhibited decentralized application control, which led to a tightly coupled and brittle presentation tier.

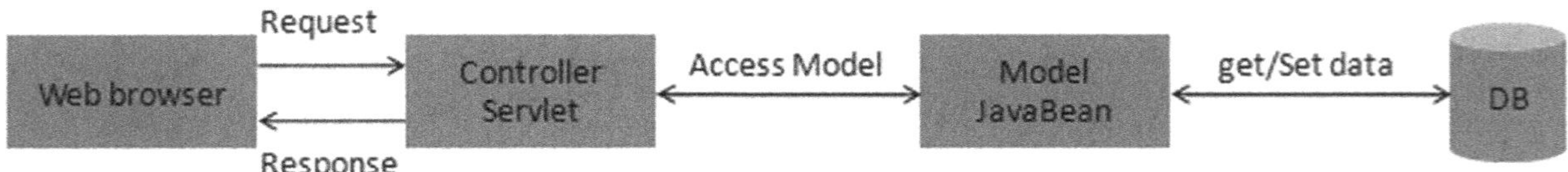

***Figure 2-31.** Model-1 architecture*

A Model-2 architecture for designing JSP pages is in actuality the MVC pattern applied to web applications. MVC originated in Smalltalk and has since made its way to Java community. Figure 2-32 shows the Model-2 (in other words, MVC) architecture. In Model-2, a controller handles the user request instead of another JSP page. The controller is implemented as a servlet. The following steps are executed when the user submits the request:

1. The controller servlet handles the user's request.
2. The controller servlet instantiates the appropriate JavaBeans based on the request.
3. The controller servlet communicates with the middle tier or directly to the database to retrieve the required data.
4. The controller sets the JavaBeans in one of the following contexts: request, session, or application.
5. The controller dispatches the request to the next view based on the request URL.
6. The view uses the JavaBeans from step 4 to display data.

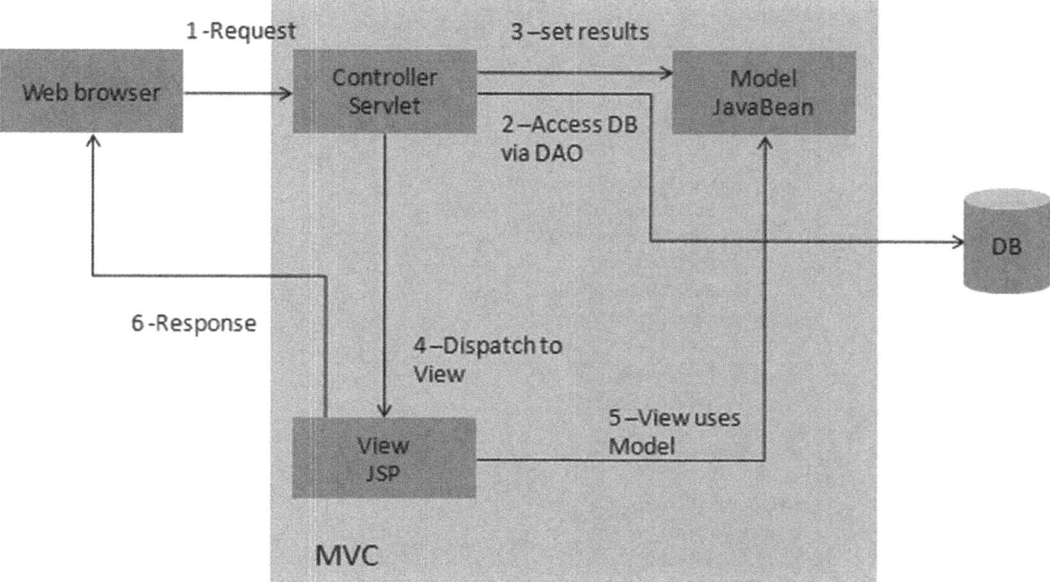

Figure 2-32. Model-2 architecture

Bookstore Application

In the previous chapter, we developed the data-access layer for the bookstore application and queried it with a stand-alone Java application. In this chapter, we will replace the stand-alone Java layer with a presentation layer. The data-access layer at the bottom will remain the same, as illustrated in Figure 2-33.

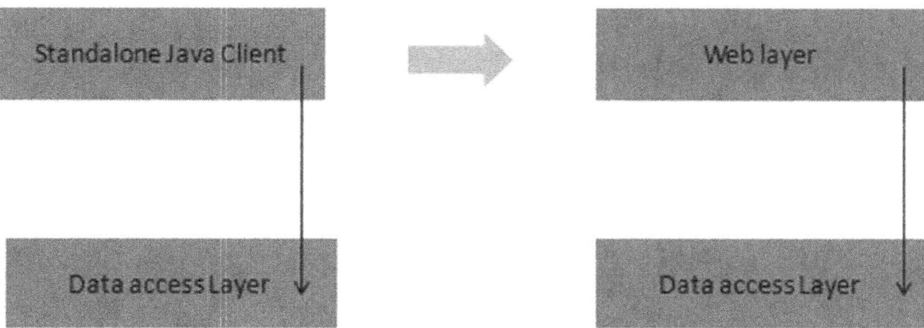

Figure 2-33. Replacing the stand-alone Java client with a presentation layer

In a production-ready application, you should also add a service layer to handle the database exception. As the application grows, a partitioned application keeps the separation of concerns clean. Figure 2-34 shows the directory structure of the bookstore application.

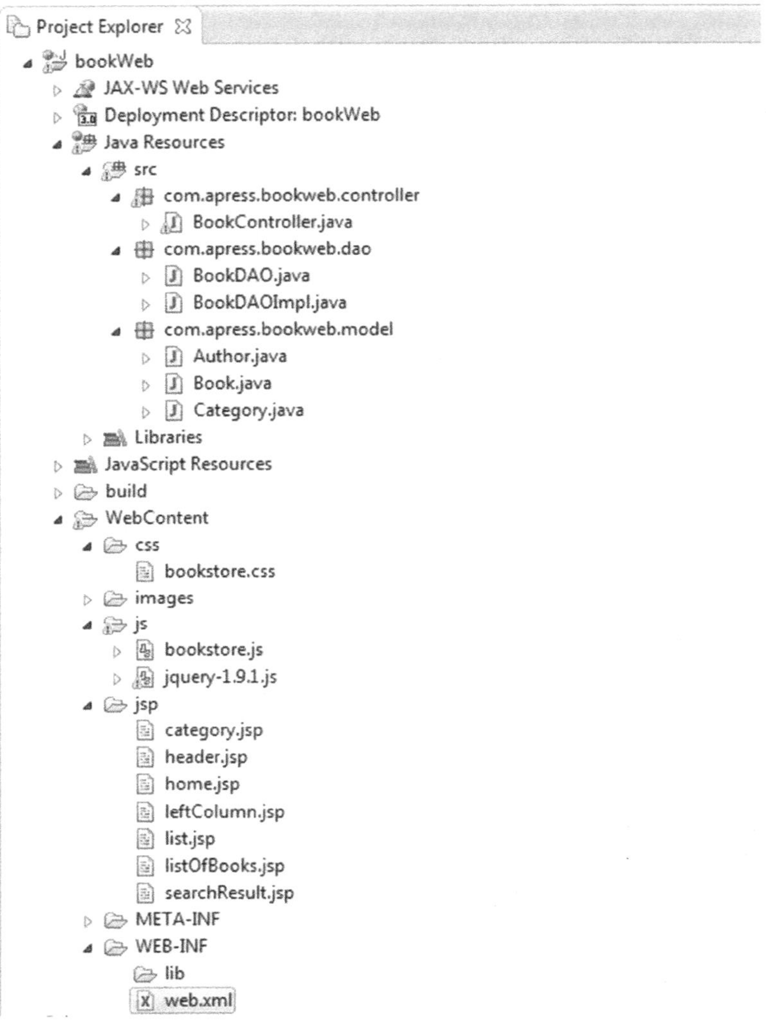

***Figure 2-34.** Directory structure of the bookstore application*

Home Page

Figure 2-35 shows the home page of the application. On entering the URL (`http://localhost:8080/bookWeb/books`), the home page displays the menu, which consists of the categories of the books available in the bookstore database.

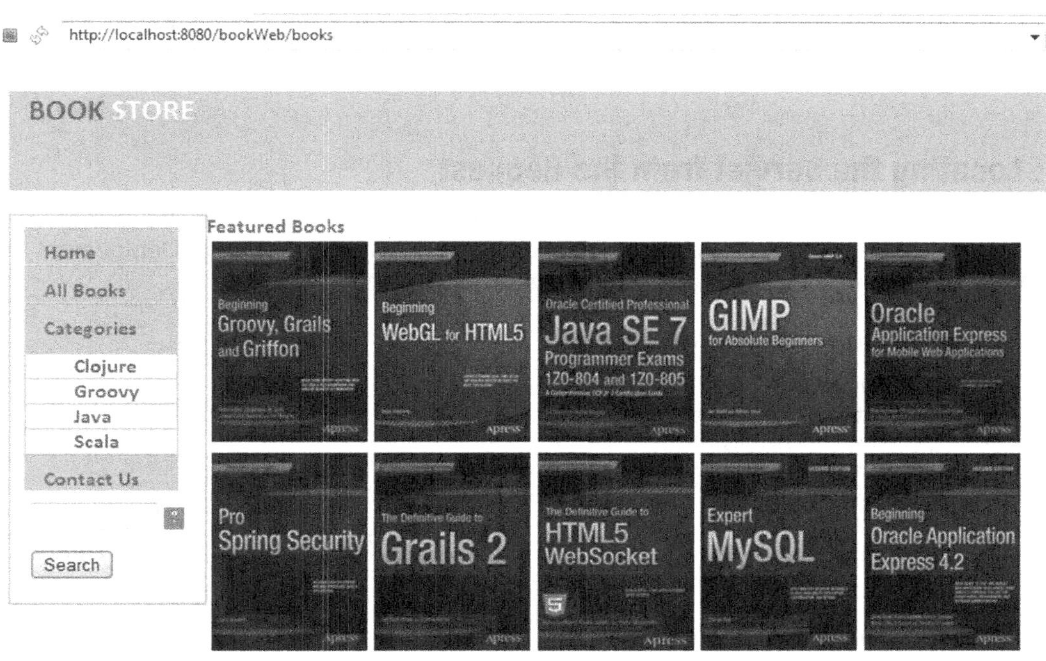

Figure 2-35. Home page of the bookstore application

Figure 2-36 shows the MVC architecture of the bookstore application. For the sake of brevity and understanding how the categories are displayed on the home page, only the components related to the home page and categories are shown in the figure.

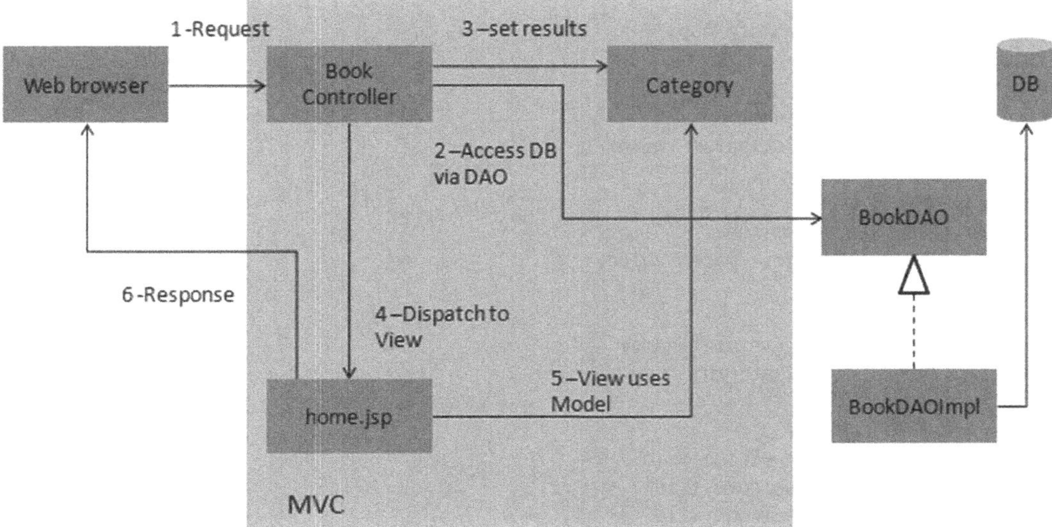

Figure 2-36. MVC in bookstore application

In the MVC architecture shown in Figure 2-36, *M* stands for Category, *V* stands for `home.jsp`, and *C* stands for `BookController`. The application flow comprises six steps, as discussed in the following sections.

Step 1: Locating the Servlet from the Request

The URL (`http://localhost:8080/bookWeb/books`) is for the dynamic content, so the web server forwards the request to the servlet container (Tomcat). Listing 2-27 illustrates the Deployment Descriptor.

Listing 2-27. Deployment Descriptor of the BookstoreWeb App

```
<?xml version="1.0" encoding="UTF-8"?>
<web-app xmlns:xsi="http://www.w3.org/2001/XMLSchema-instance"
xmlns="http://java.sun.com/xml/ns/javaee"
xmlns:web="http://java.sun.com/xml/ns/javaee/web-app_2_5.xsd"
xsi:schemaLocation="http://java.sun.com/xml/ns/javaee
http://java.sun.com/xml/ns/javaee/web-app_3_0.xsd"
id="WebApp_ID" version="3.0">
<display-name>bookWeb</display-name>
<servlet>
<servlet-name>BookServlet</servlet-name>
<servlet-class>com.apress.bookweb.controller.BookController</servlet-class>
<init-param>
<param-name>base</param-name>
<param-value>/bookWeb/books</param-value>
</init-param>
<init-param>
<param-name>imageURL</param-name>
<param-value>/bookWeb/images</param-value>
</init-param>
<load-on-startup>1</load-on-startup>
</servlet>
<context-param>
<param-name>param1</param-name>
<param-value>/bookWeb/books</param-value>
</context-param>
<context-param>
<param-name>imageURL</param-name>
<param-value>/bookWeb/images</param-value>
</context-param>
<servlet-mapping>
<servlet-name>BookServlet</servlet-name>
<url-pattern>/books </url-pattern>
</servlet-mapping>
<welcome-file-list>
<welcome-file>index.html</welcome-file>
<welcome-file>index.htm</welcome-file>
<welcome-file>index.jsp</welcome-file>
<welcome-file>default.html</welcome-file>
```

```
37.<welcome-file>default.htm</welcome-file>
38.<welcome-file>default.jsp</welcome-file>
39.</welcome-file-list>
40.</web-app>
```

- *Line 30*: `url-pattern/books` is mapped to the `BookServlet` in the `<servlet-mapping>` element, which is mapped to the servlet class `BookController` on line 9.
- *Lines 20 to 27*: We specify context parameters to the servlet in the `web.xml` file, since context parameters are available to the entire web app. When a servlet instance is created, its `init()` method is called by the servlet container. The `init()` method allows a servlet to initialize itself before the first request is processed. We override the `init(ServletConfig config)`method in the `BookController` for getting the categories from the bookstore database. These categories will be available to the entire application. The overridden `init(ServletConfig config)` in the `BookController` is illustrated in Listing 2-28.

Step 2 and Step 3: Accessing DB via DAO to Get the Categories from the Database and Setting the Categories in the Model

Listing 2-28 shows the `BookController`.

***Listing 2-28.** init() Method in BookController*

```
1.public void init(ServletConfig config) throws ServletException {
2.super.init(config);
3.BookDAO bookDao = new BookDAOImpl();
4.// calling DAO method to retrieve bookList from Database
5.List<Category> categoryList = bookDao.findAllCategories();
6.ServletContext context = config.getServletContext();
7.context.setAttribute("categoryList", categoryList);
8.}
```

- *Line 5*: This list of categories is obtained from the database by calling `findAllCategories()` on the bookDao object.
- *Line7*: The list of categories is set in the `ServletContext` so that the list is available to the entire webapp.

Step 4: Dispatching to the View

As the `init()` method is completed in the previous step, the container calls the `service()` method of the servlet (discussed in life-cycle methods of servlet). This method looks at the request, determines the HTTP method, and invokes the matching `doget()` or `dopost()` on the servlet. Listing 2-29 illustrates the `doGet()` and `doPost()` methods of the servlet.

Listing 2-29. doGet() and doPost() in BookController

```
1.protected void doGet(HttpServletRequest request,
2.HttpServletResponse response) throws ServletException, IOException {
3.doPost(request, response);
4.}
5.
6.protected void doPost(HttpServletRequest request,
7.HttpServletResponse response) throws ServletException, IOException {
8.String base = "/jsp/";
9.String url = base + "home.jsp";
10.String action = request.getParameter("action");
11.String category = request.getParameter("category");
12.String keyWord = request.getParameter("keyWord");
13.if (action != null) {
14.switch (action) {
15.case "allBooks":
16.findAllBooks(request, response);
17.url = base + "listOfBooks.jsp";
18.break;
19.case "category":
20.findAllBooks(request, response);
21.url = base + "category.jsp?category=" + category;
22.break;
23.case "search":
24.searchBooks(request, response, keyWord);
25.url = base + "searchResult.jsp";
26.break;
27.
28.}
29.}
30.RequestDispatcher requestDispatcher = getServletContext()
31..getRequestDispatcher(url);
32.requestDispatcher.forward(request, response);
33.}
```

- *Line 3*: The `doPost()` method is called from the `doGet()` method.
- *Line 9*: This line constructs the URL that points to the home page view (`home.jsp`).
- *Line 10*: This line gets the action parameter from the request. But since this is a home page, there is no associated action parameter, so the variable action is `null`.
- *Lines 13 to29*: The code block from lines 13 to 29 is skipped as the action is `null`. If the action was not `null`, the URL would have been reconstructed to point at a different view depending on whether the action value is `allBooks` or `category` or `search`.
- *Line 32*: The `RequestDispatcher` forwards to the view name in the URL on line 31.

Step 5: Accessing the Model from the View

In the previous step, the controller forwards to the view `home.jsp` using the `RequestDispatcher`.

Listing 2-30 illustrates a fragment of `home.jsp`, which includes `leftColumn.jsp`. The `leftColumn.jsp` file uses the model `Category` to display categories on the left menu of the home page.

***Listing 2-30.** Including leftColumn.jsp in home.jsp*

```
1.<body>
2.<div id="centered">
3.
4.<jsp:include page="header.jsp" flush="true" />
5.<br />
6.<jsp:include page="leftColumn.jsp" flush="true" />
7.<span class="label">Featured Books</span>
8...........
9.</div>
10.</body>
```

- *Line 6*: The `<jsp:include>` tag is used to include `leftColumn.jsp`. This is done because the left-side bar of the application (the menu) is common to all screens in the application, but instead of writing the left-side bar in all screens, we write it in one JSP page and include it wherever required as a means to reusability. (In the next few chapters on web frameworks, we will see more advanced techniques for reusing JSPs.)

Listing 2-31 illustrates the code fragment related to categories in `leftColumn.jsp` where the `Category` is accessed.

***Listing 2-31.** Accessing the Category Model in leftColumn.jsp*

```
1.<li><div><span class="label" style="margin-left: 15px;">Categories</span></div>
2.<ul>
3.<%
4.List<Category> categoryList1 = (List<Category>) application.getAttribute("categoryList");
5.Iterator<Category> iterator1 = categoryList1.iterator();
6.while (iterator1.hasNext()) {
7.Category category1 = (Category) iterator1.next();%>
8.<li><a class="label"href="<%=param1%>?action=category&categoryId=<%=category1.
getId()%>&category=<%=category1.getCategoryDescription()%>"><spanclass="label" style="margin-left:
30px;"><%=category1.getCategoryDescription()%></span></a>
9.</li>
10.<%}%>
11.</ul></li>
```

- *Line 4*: In this line, the category list is obtained from the `ServletContext`. We had saved the category list in the `ServletContext` obtained from the database in step 2.
- *Line 6 to 10*: The category details are displayed in the markup, such as the category description that you see on the home page.

> **Note** The JSP page in Listing 2-31 uses scriptlets and expressions to obtain the categories and display them. Using scriptlets and expressions are bad practices and should be avoided as much as possible. This is the subject of the next chapter, which will show you how to replace scriptlets and expressions with JSTL and EL.

Step 6: Sending the Response

The view constructed in the previous step is delivered to the browser.

Listing All the Books

When the user clicks All Books on the menu, the list of all books is displayed, as illustrated in Figure 2-37.

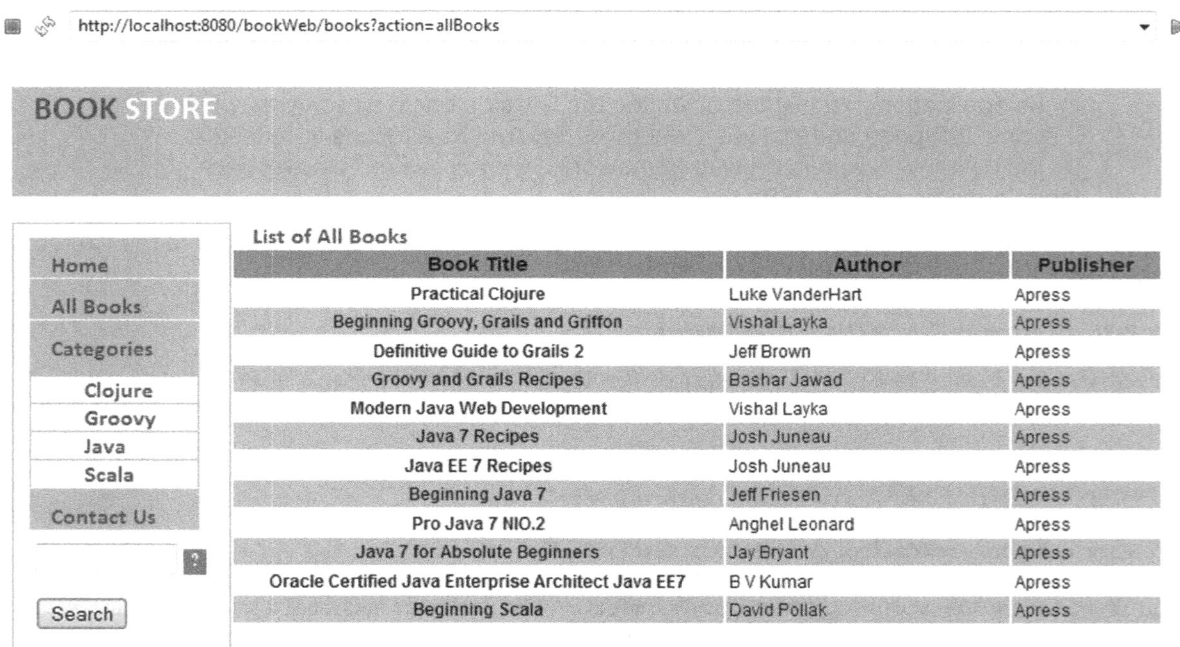

***Figure 2-37.** Listing all books*

The All Books link is in the `leftColumn.jsp` file. Listing 2-32 illustrates the code fragment for the All Books link on the menu.

Listing 2-32. All Books Link in leftColumn.jsp

```
1.<li><div>
2.<a class="link1" href="<%=param1%>?action=allBooks"><span
3.style="margin-left: 15px;" class="label">All Books</span></a>
4.</div></li>
```

- *Line 2*: This line is the All Books link displayed in the menu. When this link is clicked, the value of `action-allBooks` is added to the URL as the parameter, as shown in the URL:

  `http:localhost:8080/bookWeb/books?action=allBooks`

Step 2, which is locating the servlet from the request, is executed, but this time the action is not `null` and has a value `allBooks`. So, the code block in the `doPost()` method in the `BookController`, shown in Listing 2-33, is executed.

Listing 2-33. All Books in the doPost() in BookController

```
1.protected void doPost(HttpServletRequest request,
2.HttpServletResponse response) throws ServletException, IOException {
3.String base = "/jsp/";
4.String url = base + "home.jsp";
5.String action = request.getParameter("action");
6.String category = request.getParameter("category");
7.String keyWord = request.getParameter("keyWord");
8.if (action != null) {
9.switch (action) {
10.case "allBooks":
11.findAllBooks(request, response);
12.url = base + "listOfBooks.jsp";
13.break;
14.case "category":
15.findAllBooks(request, response);
16.url = base + "category.jsp?category=" + category;
17.break;
18.case "search":
19.searchBooks(request, response, keyWord);
20.url = base + "searchResult.jsp";
21.break;
22.
23.}
24.}
25.RequestDispatcher requestDispatcher = getServletContext()
26..getRequestDispatcher(url);
27.requestDispatcher.forward(request, response);
28.}
```

- *Line 8*: The action is not `null`, and the value of the action is `allBooks`.
- *Lines 10 to 12*: The helper method `findAllBooks(request, response)` is invoked, the URL is reconstructed to point to `listOfBooks.jsp`, and `RequestDispatcher` forwards to the view provided to the `RequestDispatcher` in the form of a URL.

Listing 2-34 shows the helper method `findAllBooks(request, response)` in the `BookController`.

Listing 2-34. findAllBooks() in BookController

```
1.private void findAllBooks(HttpServletRequest request,
2.HttpServletResponse response) throws ServletException, IOException {
3.try {
4.BookDAO bookDao = new BookDAOImpl();
5.List<Book> bookList = bookDao.findAllBooks();
6.request.setAttribute("bookList", bookList);
7.
8.} catch (Exception e) {
9.System.out.println(e);
10.}
11.}
```

- *Lines 5 to 6*: This list of all books is obtained from the database using the `findAllBooks()` method on the DAO and is set as an attribute in the request.

Searching the Books by Category

When the user clicks a specific category on the menu, the list of books in that category is displayed, as illustrated in Figure 2-38.

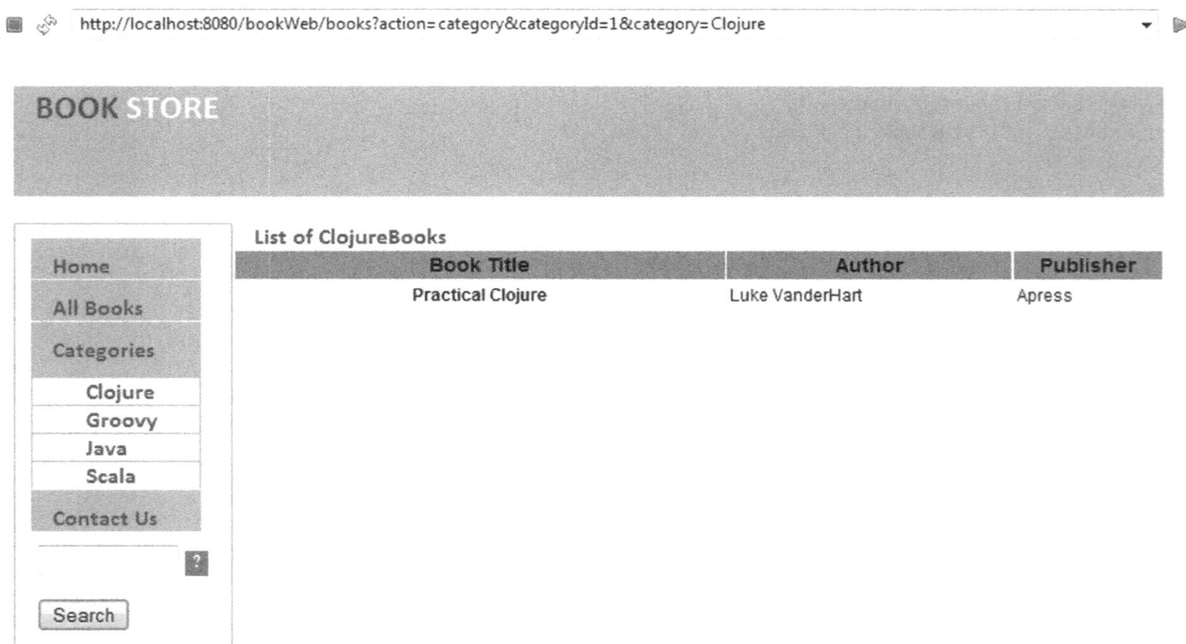

Figure 2-38. Searching the book by category

We saw in the previous section that the categories are in `leftColumn.jsp`. Listing 2-35 illustrates the code fragment for the category.

Listing 2-35. Categories Link on the Menu (leftColumn.jsp)

```
1.<li>
2.<a class="label" href="<%=param1%>?action=category&categoryId=<%=category1.
  getId()%>&category=<%=category1.getCategoryDescription()%>"><span class="label"
  style="margin-left: 30px;"><%=category1.getCategoryDescription()%></span></a>
3.</li>
```

- *Line 2*: This is the link of the category displayed in the menu. When this link is clicked, the ID of the category and description and the name of the action category is added to the URL as the parameter, as shown in the following URL:

  `http:localhost:8080/bookWeb/books?action=category&categoryId=1&category=clojure`

Again, step 2, which is locating the servlet from the request, is executed, and this time the action is not `null` and has a value category. So, the code block in the `doPost()` method in the `BookController`, shown in Listing 2-36, is executed.

Listing 2-36. doPost() in BookController

```
protected void doPost(HttpServletRequest request,
HttpServletResponse response) throws ServletException, IOException {
String base = "/jsp/";
String url = base + "home.jsp";
String action = request.getParameter("action");
String category = request.getParameter("category");
String keyWord = request.getParameter("keyWord");
if (action != null) {
switch (action) {
case "allBooks":
findAllBooks(request, response);
url = base + "listOfBooks.jsp";
break;
case "category":
findAllBooks(request, response);
url = base + "category.jsp?category=" + category;
break;
case "search":
searchBooks(request, response, keyWord);
url = base + "searchResult.jsp";
break;

}
}
RequestDispatcher requestDispatcher = getServletContext()
.getRequestDispatcher(url);
requestDispatcher.forward(request, response);
}
```

- *Line 8*: The action is not null, and the value of the action is category.
- *Lines 15 to16*: The helper method findAllBooks(request, response) is invoked, the URL is reconstructed to point to listOfBooks.jsp, and RequestDispatcher forwards to the view provided to the RequestDispatcher in the form of a URL.

Listing 2-37 shows the helper method findAllBooks(request, response) in the BookController.

Listing 2-37. findAllBooks() in BookController

```
1.private void findAllBooks(HttpServletRequest request,
2.HttpServletResponse response) throws ServletException, IOException {
3.try {
4.BookDAO bookDao = new BookDAOImpl();
5.List<Book> bookList = bookDao.findAllBooks();
6.request.setAttribute("bookList", bookList);
7.
8.} catch (Exception e) {
9.System.out.println(e);
10.}
11.}
```

- *Lines 5 to 6*: A list of all books is obtained from the database using the findAllBooks() method on the DAO and is set as an attribute in the request.

Searching the Books by Keyword

You can search the books by the author's name or a keyword in the book's title, as illustrated in Figure 2-39.

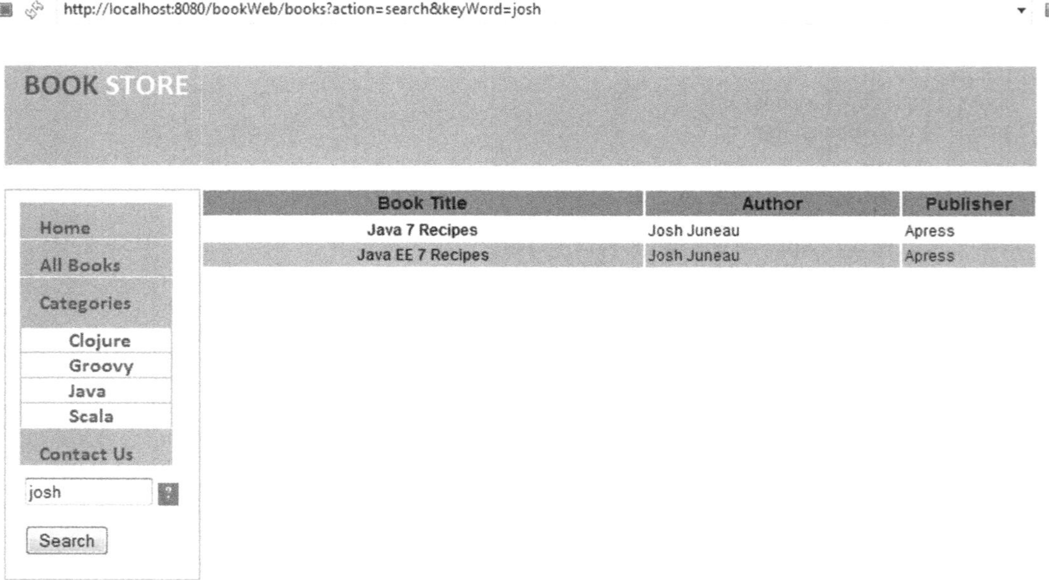

Figure 2-39. Searching books by keyword

Before we talk about how the search by keyword works, let's first take a look at one usability aspect of search. There is a question mark next to the search field, which serves to help the user. In other words, on mouse-hover, a tooltip is shown that indicates search parameters to be used, as illustrated in Figure 2-40.

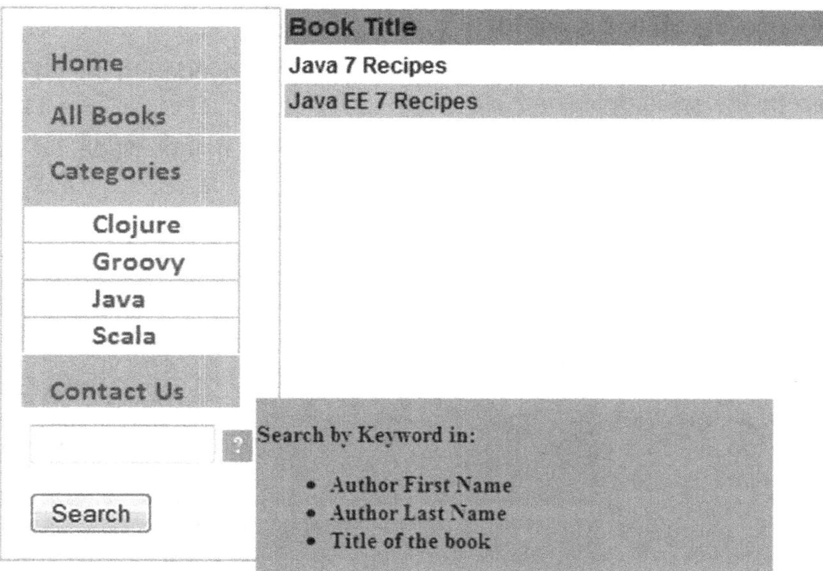

***Figure 2-40.** Tooltip for the search parameters*

To understand how the tooltip works, take a look at the markup of the search field, which is in `leftColumn.jsp`, as illustrated in Listing 2-38.

***Listing 2-38.** Search Field Markup*

```
1.<form class="search">
2.<input type="hidden" name="action" value="search" />
3.<input id="text"type="text" name="keyWord" size="12" />
4.<spanclass="tooltip_message">?</span>
5.<p />
6.<input id="submit" type="submit" value="Search" />
7.</form>
```

- *Line 4*: This has a class `tooltip_message`. The tooltip works using jQuery and CSS on this class.

Listing 2-39 illustrates the jQuery code.

***Listing 2-39.** jQuery for the Tooltip*

```
$(document).ready(function () {
$("span.tooltip_message").hover(function () {
$(this).append('<div class="message"><p>Search by Keyword in:<ul><li>Author First Name </li>
<li>Author Last Name <li>Title of the book </li></ul></p></div>');
```

```
4.},function () {
5.$("div.message").remove();
6.});
7.});
```

- *Line 2*: The class `tooltip_message` and the `<span>` tag are used as a selector on which the hover function is called.
- *Line 3*: The message to be displayed in the tooltip is appended to the object returned by the selector in line 2.

In the similar manner, a tooltip can be added to the images on the home screen, as illustrated in Figure 2-41. Listing 2-40 illustrates the jQuery function used.

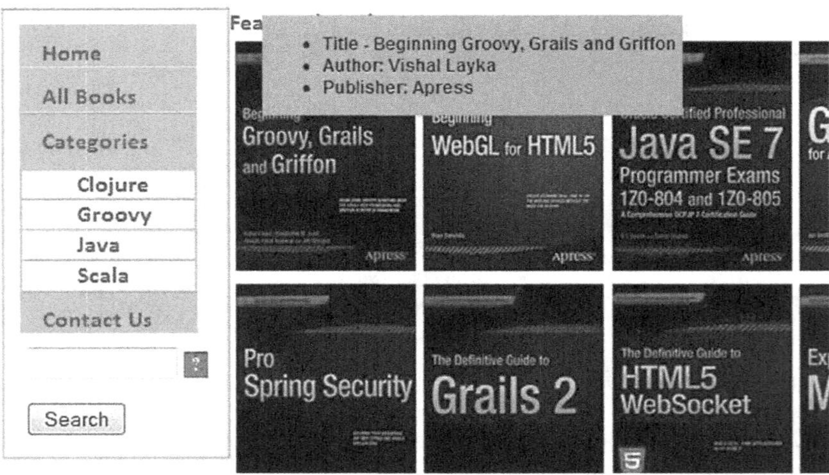

***Figure 2-41.** Tooltip for the images*

***Listing 2-40.** jQuery Function for the Image Tooltip*

```
$("span.tooltip_img1").hover(function(){$(this).append('<div class="message"><ul>
<li>Title - Beginning Groovy, Grails and Griffon</li><li>Author: Vishal Layka</li>
<li>Publisher: Apress</li></ul></div>');
}, function(){$("div.message").remove();});
```

Listing 2-41 illustrates the CSS code for the tooltip.

***Listing 2-41.** CSS for Tooltip*

```
span.tooltip_message,span.tooltip_img1 {
cursor: pointer;
display: inline-block;
background-color: #F20B26;
width: 16px;
height: 18px;
color: #ffffff;
```

```
font-size: 12px;
font-weight: bold;
text-align: center;
position: relative;
}

span.tooltip_message:hover {
background-color: #04FF97;
}

div.message {
background-color: #04FF97;
color: #000000;
position: absolute;
left: 18px;
top: -18px;
z-index: 1000000;
text-align: left;
width: 280px;
}
```

This CSS and jQuery code in Listing 2-40 and Listing 2-41 are included in `leftColumn.jsp`, as illustrated in Listing 2-42.

***Listing 2-42.** Accessing CSS and jQuery Files in leftColumn.jsp*

```
1.<link rel="stylesheet" href="css/bookstore.css" type="text/css" />
2.<script src="js/bookstore.js" type="text/javascript"></script>
3.<script type="text/javascript" src="js/jquery-1.9.1.js"></script>
```

- *Line 1*: This is the externalized CSS file for the rules illustrated in Listing 2-41
- *Line 2*: This is the externalized JavaScript file for the jQuery function in Listing 2-40
- *Line 3*: Line 3 specifies the jQuery library we are using.

Now we will begin with the search-by-keyword functionality in our web application. Listing 2-43 illustrates the search field markup.

***Listing 2-43.** Search Field Markup*

```
1.<form class="search">
2.<input type="hidden" name="action" value="search" /><input id="text"
3.type="text" name="keyWord" size="12" /><span
4.class="tooltip_message">?</span>
5.<p />
6.<input id="submit" type="submit" value="Search" />
7.</form>
```

- *Line 2*: This line specifies the action value `search`.
- *Line 6*: This line submits the request.

When the user submits the search request (again, locating the servlet from the request), step 2is executed, and this time the action has a value `search`. So, the search case in the `doPost()` method in the `BookController`, shown in Listing 2-44, is executed.

Listing 2-44. doPost() in the BookController

```
1.protected void doPost(HttpServletRequest request,
2.HttpServletResponse response) throws ServletException, IOException {
3.String base = "/jsp/";
4.String url = base + "home.jsp";
5.String action = request.getParameter("action");
6.String category = request.getParameter("category");
7.String keyWord = request.getParameter("keyWord");
8.if (action != null) {
9.switch (action) {
10.case "allBooks":
11.findAllBooks(request, response);
12.url = base + "listOfBooks.jsp";
13.break;
14.case "category":
15.findAllBooks(request, response);
16.url = base + "category.jsp?category=" + category;
17.break;
18.case "search":
19.searchBooks(request, response, keyWord);
20.url = base + "searchResult.jsp";
21.break;
22.
23.}
24.}
25.RequestDispatcher requestDispatcher = getServletContext()
26..getRequestDispatcher(url);
27.requestDispatcher.forward(request, response);
28.}
```

- *Line 18*: The case search is executed, and the value of the action is `search`
- *Line 19*: The `searchBooks()` method is called. The searchBooks() is illustrated in Listing 2-45.
- *Line 20:* Line 20 constructs the URL for the view.
- *Line 26*: The URL for the view is provided to the `RequestDispatcher`.

Listing 2-45 illustrates the `searchBooks()` helper method used by the controller to invoke the call on the DAO.

Listing 2-45. searchBooks() in the BookController

```
private void searchBooks(HttpServletRequest request,
HttpServletResponse response, String keyWord)
throws ServletException, IOException {
```

```
4.try {
5.BookDAO bookDao = new BookDAOImpl();
6.List<Book> bookList = bookDao.searchBooksByKeyword(keyWord);
7.
8.request.setAttribute("bookList", bookList);
9.
10.} catch (Exception e) {
11.System.out.println(e);
12.}
13.}
14.
```

- *Line 6*: This obtains the `bookList` based on the search keyword by invoking the `searchBooksByKeyword()` method defined in `BookDAO`. We used this method in Chapter 1 when we built the data-access layer for our web application.

Summary

This chapter introduced servlets and JSP and showed you how to make your first web application using these web components. Then the chapter implemented the real-world MVC-based Java web application, a bookstore using servlets and JSP. In the next chapter, we will augment this application to use the best practice of separating the business-logic concerns from the presentation using JSTL and Expression Language.

Chapter 3

Best Practices in Java EE Web Development

All the evolution we know of proceeds from the vague to the definite.

—Charles Sanders Peirce

Every so often good solutions are invented. At times they are discovered. Invention and discovery are not synonyms,[1] and they signify different objectives; however, both are realized through experience and expertise. Experience helps you achieve good solutions, and when you apply those good solutions to the same set of problems, patterns begin to emerge. *Patterns* are the catalog of good solutions that stem from the experience and expertise of developers.

An architect named Christopher Alexander observed that architects tend to solve the same problems in more or less the same way. This realization led him to write a book of design patterns for architects.[2] He reflected in this book, "A design pattern describes a problem which occurs over and over again, and then describes the core of the solution to that problem, in such a way that you can use this solution a million times over, without ever doing it the same way twice."

[1]*Invention* means to create a new object from preexisting objects. *Discovery* is figuring out something that preexists but not creating new objects from it.
[2]*A Pattern Language: Towns, Buildings, Construction* by Christopher Alexander, Sara Ishikawa, and Murray Silverstein (Oxford University Press, 1977). See also *The Timeless Way of Building* by Christopher Alexander (Oxford University Press, 1979).

In 1994, the book *Design Patterns: Elements of Reusable Object-Oriented Software*, by Erich Gamma, Richard Helm, Ralph Johnson, and John Vlissides (Addison-Wesley, 1994) (the "Gang of Four" or "GoF"), applied Alexander's ideas to software. This book expounded OO patterns and ushered in a wave of best-practice solutions, addressing a number of design requirements that surfaced over the years with a design strategy that is reusable across applications.

As server systems grew, enterprise infrastructure such as Java EE emerged that provided abstractions of technologies and services. However, using Java EE does not naturally lead to best-practice architecture and design. John Crupi, Dan Malks, and Deepak Alur first established Java EE design patterns based on their experience of architecting enterprise systems.

Applying these Java EE design patterns to the development of a Java EE–based application is *de rigueur* to achieving best-practice architecture and design. That said, ensuring best-practice architecture and design is not enough to ensure reusable, maintainable, extensible software. Even with the Java EE design patterns in place, a software project is often afflicted by a phenomenon called *entropy*, a measure of the degree of disorder. According to the Second Law of Thermodynamics, everything in the universe moves from low entropy (a state of order) to high entropy (disorder) and eventual chaos. Everything in nature is bound by this law of physics, and nature deals with this irrevocable law by means of evolution.

A software project too often tends to move from low entropy to high entropy, and to deal with the disordered state, it needs to keep evolving. That is not to say that evolving your project supersedes project management and methodologies; despite the most finely honed project management, sharp-edged methodologies, and a team with a keen sense of style, a software project may fall into a state of high entropy. Figure 3-1 presents the evolutionary steps in Java EE's web tier that help deal with entropy in software projects.

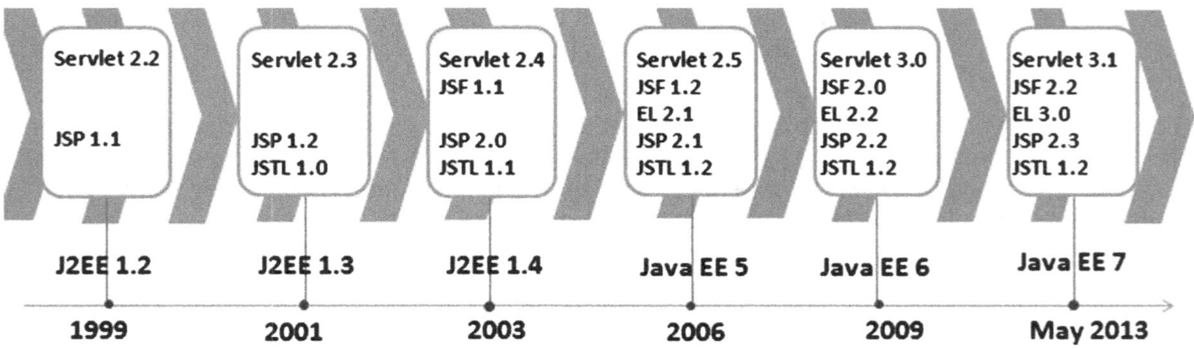

***Figure 3-1.** The evolution in the Java EE web tier*

As you can see in Figure 3-1, not only have the technologies in the Java EE web tier evolved, but new ones are added with each new release. If you are still using J2EE 1.4, for instance, you will not have the unified EL (EL 2.1) in your toolbox. It is essential to keep up with the evolution of any technology to keep from falling into the eventual state of high entropy that can afflict any software project.

This chapter elucidates the importance of gradually evolving a project with any new technologies available with each new release of Java EE and using them to deal with high entropy in the project. The chapter then discusses the importance of the Java EE patterns and explains how the web applications can be made reusable, maintainable, and extensible by using Java EE web tier patterns. Next, the chapter shows how web frameworks relinquish you from using Java EE web tier patterns by providing you out-of-the-box best-practice solutions.

Best-Practice Solutions: Using EL and JSTL

Sun released the Servlet specification in 1998. The sole purpose of servlets was to help the Java web server generate dynamic content for the client. Listing 3-1 illustrates what the first servlet looked like.

Listing 3-1. The First Servlet

```
1.import java.io.IOException;
2.import java.io.PrintWriter;
3.
4.import javax.servlet.ServletException;
5.import javax.servlet.http.HttpServlet;
6.import javax.servlet.http.HttpServletRequest;
7.import javax.servlet.http.HttpServletResponse;
8.public class Hello extends HttpServlet {
9.public void doGet(HttpServletRequest req, HttpServletResponse res)
10.throws ServletException, IOException {
11.res.setContentType ("text/html");
12.PrintWriter out = res.getWriter();
13.out.println("<HTML>");
14.out.println("<HEAD><TITLE>Hello World</TITLE></HEAD>");
15.out.println("<BODY>");
16.out.println("<BIG>Hello World</BIG>");
17.out.println("</BODY></HTML>");
18.}
19.}
```

Servlets worked fine for dynamic content generation but had one big problem. The view was hardwired into the servlet, as you can see in lines 13 to 17 in Listing 3-1. To solve this problem, JSP was born. JSP removes the need of hardwiring the view code into the business logic code. This separation of the view concern from the business-logic concern depends on the attributes shown in Listing 3-2 and Listing 3-3.

Listing 3-2. Using Attributes for Separation of Presentation(View) from Business(Servlet) Code

```
public void doPost(HttpServletRequest request, HttpServletResponse response)
throws IOException, ServletException {
String name = request.getParameter("userName");
request.setAttribute("name", name);
RequestDispatcher view = request.getRequestDispatcher("/result.jsp");
view.forward(request, response);
}
```

Listing 3-2 shows the fragment of a servlet that uses attributes.

- *Line 3*: This retrieves the `userName` from the request.
- *Line 4*: This sets the `userName` as an attribute in the request.
- *Line 5*: This retrieves the `RequestDispatcher` from the request.
- *Line 6*: This forwards to the view, passing request and response object. Note that this request object has an attribute set in it for the `userName`. The view can now make use of this attribute

Listing 3-3. The First JSP

```
1.<html><body> Hello
2.<%= request.getAttribute("name") %>
3.</body></html>
4.<html>
5.<body>
6.<% User u = (User) request.getAttribute("user"); %>
7.User  is: <%= u.getName() %>
8.</body>
9.</html>
```

The separation of the view from the business logic depends on the attributes, as illustrated in Listing 3-2 and Listing 3-3. JSP, in this manner, solved the problem of presentation cross-cutting business logic in servlets. But as you can see in Listing 3-4, with the scriptlets (Java code) intermingled in the presentation code (JSP), now the business logic cross-cuts the presentation concern.

Listing 3-4. Using a Scriptlet and an Expression in JSP

```
1.<% User u = new User(); %>
2.User  is: <%= u.getName() %>
```

- *Line 1*: The scriptlet creates an instance of a class called `User`.
- *Line 2*: This outputs the user name using Expression.

What went wrong? Scriptlets and expressions brought Java code into JSP. Prior to JSP, the presentation code cross-cut the business code. With JSP, the business code cross-cuts the presentation code. So JSP, inadvertently, didn't actually solve anything but turned the problem of cross-cutting the business and presentation logic upside down. The scriptlet and expression in Listing 3-4 could indeed be easily replaced by JSP standard actions (`<useBean>`), as shown in Listing 3-5.

Listing 3-5. Using JSP Standard Action sand Expression Language

```
1.<jsp:useBean id="user" class="com.apress.User"/>
2.User  is: ${user.name}
```

Listing 3-5 does the same thing that Listing 3-4 does but without using any Java code inside the JSP page.

- *Line 1*: This line creates the instance of the class `User` using a standard JSP action.
- *Line 2*: This line introduces the key feature of Expression Language called an *EL expression*, which replaces the scripting element called *expressions*. The syntax shown in line 2 will be discussed in greater detail in the sections that follow.

JSP standard actions are, in general, far too limited, and consequently developers had to resort to using scriptlets to create function-rich web applications. Using Java code in the form of scriptlets in JSP leads to unmaintainable JSP pages. As a result, the JSP specification has evolved to support Java-free JSP pages. This support rests primarily on the JSP Expression Language (EL) and the JSP Standard Tag Library (JSTL). In the sections that follow, we will take a closer look at EL and JSTL.

Expression Language

Beauty without expression is lifeless, JSP without Expression Language is chaos. The underlying principle of the Expression Language is to provide scriptless JSP components. The Expression Language is used in two ways.

- To retrieve objects from scoped attributes (explained in the previous chapter). These objects are JavaBeans, maps, arrays, and lists that have been stored as attributes in any of the four scopes (also explained in the previous chapter). The EL searches the attributes first in the smallest scope, which is page scope; then in request and session; and finally in the largest scope, which is application scope.
- To access request parameters, request headers, cookies, context-initialization parameters, and `pageContext` objects.

An EL expression is formed by using the construct`${expr}` or `#{expr}`. Even though both the constructs are evaluated in the same way by the EL, the `${expr}` construct is used for immediate evaluation, and the `#{expr}` construct is used for deferred evaluation.

- *Immediate evaluation*: The expression is compiled when the JSP page is compiled, and it is executed when the JSP page is executed.
- *Deferred evaluation*: The expression is not evaluated until its value is needed by the system.

> **Note** Note In JSP 2.1 and newer, `#{}` expressions are allowed only for tag attributes that accept deferred expressions. `#{expr}` will generate an error if used anywhere else.

In the sections that follow, you will look at the syntax of EL and the reserved words of the language and see how to use it on a JSP page. After you have learned the basics, you'll learn how to use EL to read values from JavaBeans, and in the final section you will learn how to use EL functions.

Literals

An EL literal can be the following types: Boolean, integer, floating-point, string, or null. Table 3-1 shows the valid values for each literal type.

Table 3-1. Literals in EL

Literal Type	Valid Literal Value
Boolean	`true` or `false`
Integer	-11 0 12345
Floating point	4.21 -8.01 1.0E12 0.12
String	Both valid: "hello" and 'hello'
Null	`null`

Reserved Words

As with any other language, EL has words that are reserved and should not be used as identifiers. Table 3-2 lists the reserved words in EL.

Table 3-2. Reserved Words in EL

and	eq	gt	true
instanceof	or	ne	le
false	empty	not	lt
ge	null	div	mod

EL Operators

The EL operations are necessary to handle data manipulations. EL supports several operators such as relational, arithmetic, logical, and others.

Arithmetic Operators

Listing 3-6 illustrates some of these operators. You can use this code on a JSP file and run it on the server. Figure 3-2 illustrates the output.

Listing 3-6. Arithmetic Operators

```
<table border="1">
<tr>
<td><b>Arithmetic Operator</b></td>
<td><b>Boolean Result</b></td>
</tr>
<tr>
<td>${'${'}2 + 2 }</td>
<td>${2 + 2}</td>
</tr>
<tr>
<td>${'${'}2 - 2 }</td>
<td>${2 - 2}</td>
</tr>
<tr>
<td>${'${'}2 * 2 }</td>
<td>${2 * 2}</td>
</tr>
<tr>
<td>${'${'}2 / 2 }</td>
<td>${2 / 2}</td>
</tr>
<tr>
<td>${'${'}2 mod 2 }</td>
<td>${2 mod 2}</td>
</tr>
</table>
```

Arithmetic Operator	**Boolean Result**
${2 + 2 }	4
${2 - 2 }	0
${2 * 2 }	4
${2 / 2 }	1.0
${2 mod 2 }	0

Figure 3-2. Arithmetic operators

Relational Operators

These operators include `==`, `!=`, `<`, `>`, `<=`, `>=`, `eq`, `ne`, `lt`, `gt`, `le`, and `ge`.

Listing 3-7 illustrates all these operators. You can use this code on a JSP file and run it on the server. The output is illustrated in Figure 3-3.

Listing 3-7. Relational Operators

```
<table border="1">
<tr>
<td><b>Relational Operator</b></td>
<td><b>Boolean Result</b></td>
</tr>
```

```
<tr>
<td>${'${'}10 &lt; 20}</td>
<td>${10 < 20}</td>
</tr>
<tr>
<td>${'${'}10 &gt; 20}</td>
<td>${10 > 20}</td>
</tr>
<tr>
<td>${'${'}10 &gt;= 10}</td>
<td>${10 >= 10}</td>
</tr>
<tr>
<td>${'${'}10 &lt;= 10}</td>
<td>${10 <= 10}</td>
</tr>
<tr>
<td>${'${'}10 == 10}</td>
<td>${10 == 10}</td>
</tr>
<tr>
<td>${'${'}10 != 20}</td>
<td>${10 != 20}</td>
</tr>
<tr>
<tr>
<td>${'${'}10 lt 20}</td>
<td>${10 lt 20}</td>
</tr>
<tr>
<td>${'${'}10 gt 20}</td>
<td>${10 gt 20}</td>
</tr>
<tr>
<td>${'${'}10 le 10}</td>
<td>${10 le 10}</td>
</tr>
<tr>
<td>${'${'}10 ge 10}</td>
<td>${10 ge 10}</td>
</tr>
<tr>
<td>${'${'}10 eq 10}</td>
<td>${10 eq 10}</td>
</tr>
<tr>
<td>${'${'}10 ne 20}</td>
<td>${10 ne 20}</td >
</tr>
</table>
```

Relational Operator	Boolean Result
${10 < 20}	true
${10 > 20}	false
${10 >= 10}	true
${10 <= 10}	true
${10 == 10}	true
${10 != 20}	true
${10 lt 20}	true
${10 gt 20}	false
${10 le 10}	true
${10 ge 10}	true
${10 eq 10}	true
${10 ne 20}	true

Figure 3-3. Relational operators

Logical Operators

Listing 3-8 illustrates the logical operators like &&, ||, and the `not` operator in action. You can use this code on a JSP file and run it on the server. The output is illustrated in Figure 3-4.

Listing 3-8. Logical Operators

```
<table border="1">
<tr>
<td><b>Logical Operator</b></td>
<td><b>Result</b></td>
</tr>
<tr>
<td>${'${'}true && false}</td>
<td>${true && false}</td>
</tr>
<tr>
<td>${'${'}true || false}</td>
<td>${true || false}</td>
</tr>
<tr>
<td>${'${'}not true}</td>
<td>${not true}</td>
</tr>
</table>
```

Logical Operator	Result
${true && false}	false
${true || false}	true
${not true}	false

Figure 3-4. Logical operators

Using EL

In this section, you will create a simple application based on the model of our bookstore application. This will not only show you how to use EL but also demonstrate its significance. Figure 3-5 illustrates the relationship between Book and Author in the application, implemented in Listings 3-9 and 3-10.

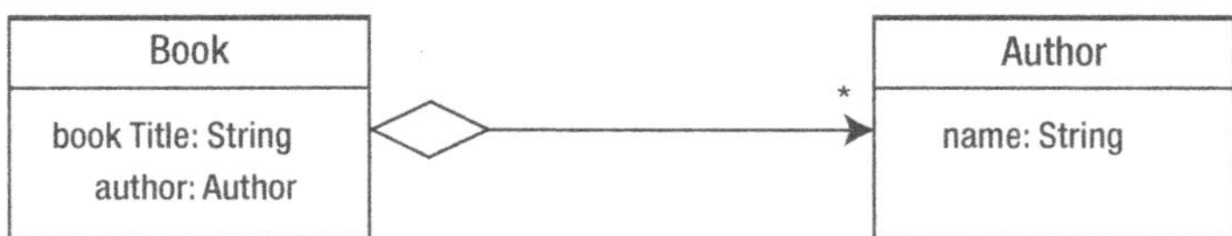

Figure 3-5. Relationship between Book and Author

Listing 3-9. Author.java

```
package com.apress.chapter03.model;

public class Author {
private String name;

public String getName() {
return name;
}

public void setName(String name) {
this.name = name;
}

}
```

Listing 3-10. Book.java

```
package com.apress.chapter03.model;

public class Book {

private String bookTitle;
private Author author;

public String getBookTitle() {
```

```
return bookTitle;
}

public void setBookTitle(String bookTitle) {
this.bookTitle = bookTitle;
}

public Author getAuthor() {
return author;
}

public void setAuthor(Author author) {
this.author = author;
}

}
```

The goal of the application is to show how to access the property of an attribute (the `bookTitle` property of `Book` in Figure 3-5) and the property of an attribute that is itself a property of the attribute (the `name` property of `Author` in Figure 3-5). In Figure 3-5,you need to output the value of the `name` property of the `Author`. It is not possible to do this using JSP standard actions, as you will see later in this section, and in such cases, scriptlets have been used. This is how scriptlets found their way into JSP. However, you should not use scriptlets because with the scriptlets (Java code) intermingled in the presentation code (JSP); the business logic cross-cuts the presentation concern, resulting in unmaintainable JSP, as explained earlier in Listing 3-4. Because JSP standard actions cannot access properties of an attribute that is itself a property of an attribute and because using scriptlets results in unmaintainable JSPs, you should use EL. In this section, you will learn how to use EL with the help of an example where `Author` class is the property of the `Book` class. Figure 3-5 shows the relationship between `Book` and `Author`. You will access the `name` property of `Author` from `Book` without using scriptlets.

Listing 3-9 illustrates the `Author` object with a single property called `name` with getters and setters. You need to output the value of the `name` property of `Author`.

Listing 3-10 illustrates the `Book` object with two properties, `bookTitle` and `author`, and their getters and setters. The `author` property in `Book` is the `Author` class, illustrated earlier in Listing 3-9. You need to access the `name` property of the `author` property.

The `Book` and `Author` objects serve as the model of the MVC application. Listing 3-11 illustratesthe controller of the application.

***Listing 3-11.** BookController.java*

```
package com.apress.chapter03.controller;

import java.io.IOException;

import javax.servlet.RequestDispatcher;
import javax.servlet.ServletException;
import javax.servlet.http.HttpServlet;
import javax.servlet.http.HttpServletRequest;
import javax.servlet.http.HttpServletResponse;
```

```
11.import com.apress.chapter03.model.Author;
12.import com.apress.chapter03.model.Book;
13.
14.public class BookController extends HttpServlet {
15.
16.protected void doGet(HttpServletRequest request,
17.HttpServletResponse response) throws ServletException, IOException {
18.Book book = new Book();
19.book.setBookTitle("Learning Java Web");
20.Author author = new Author();
21.author.setName("Vishal Layka");
22.book.setAuthor(author);
23.
24.request.setAttribute("bookAttrib", book);
25.
26.RequestDispatcher view = request.getRequestDispatcher("/book.jsp");
27.view.forward(request, response);
28.}
29.
30.}
```

Listing 3-11 is the controller part of the MVC pattern. As you learned in Listing 3-2, the separation of the view concern from the business-logic concern depends on the attributes. Hence, you have to save the model object into the attributes for the view (JSP) to be able to access the model via attributes.

- *Lines 19 to 22*: In these lines you set the `bookTitle` and `author` properties of `Book`. Note that the `name` property of `Author` is already set on line 21.
- *Line 22*: This sets the `author` property of `book`.
- *Line 24*: This sets the `Book` object as an attribute in the request.
- *Lines 26 to 27*: Line 26 should now be familiar to you. In this line, you dispatch the request to `book.jsp`.

Listing 3-12 provides the deployment descriptor for this application.

***Listing 3-12.** web.xml*

```
<?xml version="1.0" encoding="UTF-8"?>
<web-app xmlns:xsi="http://www.w3.org/2001/XMLSchema-instance"
 xmlns="http://java.sun.com/xml/ns/javaee"
 xmlns:web="http://java.sun.com/xml/ns/javaee/web-app_2_5.xsd"
 xsi:schemaLocation="http://java.sun.com/xml/ns/javaee
 http://java.sun.com/xml/ns/javaee/web-app_3_0.xsd" id="WebApp_ID" version="3.0">
<display-name>chapter03</display-name>
<servlet>
<servlet-name>BookController</servlet-name>
<servlet-class>com.apress.chapter03.controller.BookController</servlet-class>
</servlet>
<servlet-mapping>
<servlet-name>BookController</servlet-name>
```

```
<url-pattern>/book</url-pattern>
</servlet-mapping>
<welcome-file-list>
<welcome-file>index.html</welcome-file>
</welcome-file-list>
</web-app>
```

Now the only key component that is missing in this web application is the JSP page, which is where the EL code is actually written. Before we get to the JSP page, we will look at the two key operators provided by EL to access encapsulated data: the `[ ] and .` (also called *dot*) operators. After learning about the `[ ]` and `.` operators, you will be able to write `book.jsp`. Figure 3-6 illustrates the directory structure of the application.

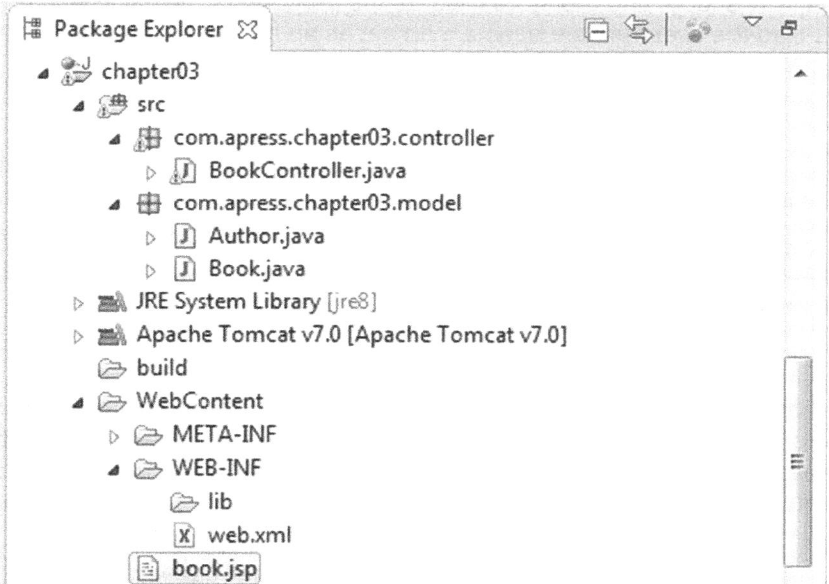

***Figure 3-6.** Directory structure*

The [ ] and . Operators

Using the `.` notation is shortcut for accessing an object's property. The dot operator was introduced in Listing 3-5. For the sake of convenience, it is shown again in Listing 3-13.

***Listing 3-13.** Using the Dot Operator*

```
<jsp:useBean id="user" class="com.apress.User"/>
User  is: ${user.name}
```

- Line 1: In Line 1, the class `User` is created using the `<jsp:useBean>` action. The `user` was set as the `request` attribute in the servlet code.
- Line 2: In Line 2, the value of name, which is a property of the User object is accessed using `${user.name}`.

The variable `user` in the expression `${user.name}` is an attribute stored in the `request` scope. The variable in the EL expression to which the dot operator is applied could be one of two kinds.

- An attribute that is stored in any of the four scopes, as it is in this case
- An EL implicit object, as explained later in this chapter

Whether this variable is an EL implicit object or an attribute stored in any of the four scopes, it can be either a JavaBean or a map. In Listing 3-13, this variable is a JavaBean that was set as an attribute in the `request` scope, and therefore `name is` the property of the JavaBean referenced by the variable `user`. Had the `user` variable been a map set as an attribute in any of the four scopes, the name would-be the key of the map.

> **Note** The variable in the EL expression to which the dot operator is applied could be either an attribute set in any of the four scopes or an EL implicit object. Furthermore, regardless of whether this variable is an attribute set in any of the four scopes or is an EL implicit object, it could be either a JavaBean or a Map. If the variable is a JavaBean, it is followed by its property right after the dot operator; if the variable is a Map, it is followed by its key right after the dot operator.

So, now it should be clear that the variable in the EL expression is either a JavaBean or a Map. But what if you want to set an array as an attribute in any of the four scopes and access its elements using an EL expression? Or what if you want to set a list as an attribute in any of the four scopes and access its elements using an EL expression? The answer lies with the [ ] operator provided by EL.

The [ ]operator is used for accessing arrays, lists, JavaBeans, and maps. That is, the variable to which the [ ] operator is applied can be an array, list, JavaBean, or map.

Inside the Brackets

There can be one of following inside the brackets of the [ ] operator:

- An index with or without quotes.
- A String literal.
- An EL implicit object or an attribute in any of the four scopes. The EL implicit object is explained later in this chapter.
- A nested expression.

If there is an index with or without quotes inside the brackets of the[ ] operator, the variable to which the [ ] operator is applied is either an array or a list. Listing 3-14 illustrates how to use the [ ] operator with a list or an array.

Listing 3-14. Using the [ ] Operator with a List or an Array

```
someArray["1"]
someArray[1]
someList["2"]
someList[2]
```

For example, the array in Listing 3-15 can be accessed as illustrated in Listing 3-16.

Listing 3-15. Setting an Array as an Attribute in the Servlet Code

```
String [ ] books = {"Clojure", "Groovy ", "Java" , "Scala"} ;
request.setAttribute("books", books);
```

Listing 3-16. Using the [ ] Operator

```
Book: ${books[0]}
```

The output displayed for Listing 3-16 is as follows:

```
Book: Clojure
```

> **Note** Lists can be accessed in the same manner as arrays.

If there is a String literal inside the brackets of the [ ] operator, the variable to which the [ ] operator is applied is either a JavaBean or a Map. Listing 3-17 illustrates the code for setting a Map as an attribute in the Servlet.

Listing 3-17. Code Fragment for Setting a Map as an Attribute in the Servlet Code

```
Map<String, String>  bookMap  = new HashMap<>();
bookMap.put("Groovy", "Beginning Groovy");
bookMap.put("Java", " Beginning Java");
bookMap.put("Scala", " Beginning Scala");
request.setAttribute("books", bookMap);
```

In Listing 3-18, EL searches for the attribute bound to the name `books` in the scope. In Listing 3-17, `books` is a Map set in the `request` attribute. Therefore, EL searches for the key `Groovy` passed in the [ ] operator of Listing 3-18 and evaluates it.

Listing 3-18. Using the [ ] Operator

```
Book : ${books["Groovy"] }
```

The output displayed for Listing 3-8 is as shown here:

```
Book: Beginning Groovy
```

Both . and [] operator can be used with JavaBeans or Maps. For example, Listing 3-18 could be written using the . operator as shown here:

```
${books.Groovy}
```

If there is neither a String literal nor an index with or without quotes inside the brackets of the [] operator and if the content inside the brackets of the [] operator is not an EL implicit object, then the content is evaluated by searching for an attribute with that name in any of the four scopes. This is illustrated using Listing 3-19 and Listing 3-20.

Listing 3-19. Code Fragment for Setting a Map as an Attribute in the Servlet Code

```
1.Map<String, String>  bookMap  = new HashMap<>();
2.bookMap.put("Groovy", "Beginning Groovy");
3.bookMap.put("Java", " Beginning Java");
4.bookMap.put("Scala", " Beginning Scala");
5.request.setAttribute("books", bookMap);
6.request.setAttribute("java", "Java");
```

Listing 3-20. Using the [] Operator

```
Book : ${books[java] }
```

Let's see how the evaluation works in Listing 3-20.

- In the code`${ books[java] }` of Listing 3-20, EL searches for an attribute bound by the name `books` in the scopes.
- EL finds this attribute in the request scope because `books` was set as a request attribute on line 5 in Listing 3-19.
- In Listing 3-20, the content of the [] operator is `java`, which is neither a String literal nor an EL implicit object; therefore, EL searches for an attribute bound by the name `java` in the scopes and finds it in the request scope because `java` was set as a request attribute on line 6 in Listing 3-19.
- Using the value `Java` of `java` on line 6 of Listing 3-19, the EL expression now becomes`${ books["Java"] }`.
- Now, because the `books` attribute is a Map set as a request attribute on line 5 in Listing 3-19, EL searches for the key `Java`, which is on line 3 in Listing 3-19. and prints its value as shown in the following output:

```
Book  : Beginning Java
```

If there is an EL expression inside the brackets of the [] operator, the content inside the brackets, which is an EL expression in this case, is evaluated by the same rules applied to any EL expression. In other words, if the EL expression is using the dot operator or [] operator and if it is a [] operator, then the same rules as explained previously are applied. This is illustrated using Listing 3-21 and Listing 3-22.

Listing 3-21. Code Fragment for Setting a Map and an Array as Attributes in the Servlet Code

```
Map<String, String>  bookMap  = new HashMap<>();
bookMap.put("Groovy", "Beginning Groovy");
bookMap.put("Java", " Beginning Java");
bookMap.put("Scala", " Beginning Scala");
request.setAttribute("books", bookMap);
String[ ] categories = {"Groovy", "Java", "Scala"};
request.setAttribute("category", categories);
```

Listing 3-22. Nested EL Expression

```
Book : ${ books[category[1]] }
```

Here's the output:

```
Book : Beginning Java
```

Now that you have learned how far you can go with the . and [ ] operators, it is time to see why EL is so important. You will now see why it is so important by completing the application you started to create, specifically, by writing the JSP page. Listing 3-23 illustrates `book.jsp`. This JSP page uses scripting elements (scriptlets and expressions) and EL. The idea is to compare the two, i.e. scripting elements and EL. This comparison is illustrated in Figure 3-7.

Listing 3-23. book.jsp

```
<%@page import="com.apress.chapter03.model.Book"%>
<%@page import="com.apress.chapter03.model.Author"%>
<%@ taglib uri="http://java.sun.com/jsp/jstl/functions" prefix="fn"%>
<%@ taglib uri="http://java.sun.com/jstl/core" prefix="c"%>
<html>
<head>
</head>
<body>
<table border="1">
<tr>
<th width= "20px">Description</th>
<th >code</th>
<th >output</th>
</tr>
<%
Book book = (Book) request.getAttribute("bookAttrib");
Author author = book.getAuthor();
%>
<tr>
<td>Author's Name using <b>Scriptlet and Expression</b>
</td>
<td>${fn:escapeXml("<%= author.getName() %>")}</td>
<td><%=author.getName()%></td>
</tr>
```

```
26.<jsp:useBean id="bookAttrib" class="com.apress.chapter03.model.Book"
27.scope="request" />
28.<tr>
29.<td>Author's Name using <b> jsp:getProperty action </b>
30.</td>
31.<td>
32.<table border="1">
33.<tr>
34.<td>${fn:escapeXml("<jsp:getProperty name = \"bookAttrib \" property= \"author \" />")}</td>
35.</tr>
36.<tr>
37.<td>${fn:escapeXml("<jsp:getProperty name = \"bookAttrib \" property= \"author.name \" />")}</td>
38.</tr>
39.</table>
40.
41.</td>
42.<td>
43.<table border="1">
44.<tr>
45.<td><jsp:getProperty name="bookAttrib" property="author" />
46.</td>
47.</tr>
48.<tr>
49.<td>
50.<%--  <jsp:getProperty name ="bookId" property="author.name" />  - this code will yield run time
exception --%>
51.Not possible
52.</td>
53.</tr>
54.</table>
55.</td>
56.</tr>
57.<tr>
58.<td>Author's Name using<b> EL </b></td>
59.<td>${fn:escapeXml("${bookAttrib.author.name}")}</td>
60.<td>${bookAttrib.author.name}</td>
61.</tr>
62.</table>
63.</body>
64.</html>
```

- *Line 23*: This outputs the name of the author using expressions.
- *Line 50*: This shows that it is not possible to output the name of the author using a JSP standard action.
- *Line 60*: This outputs the name of the author using EL.

Figure 3-7 illustrates what you will see when you run this application (`http://localhost:8080/chapter03/book`). Essentially, it is just not possible to display the value of the `name` property of `Author` using a standard JSP action; scripting elements would have been the only way to do it, had it not been for EL.

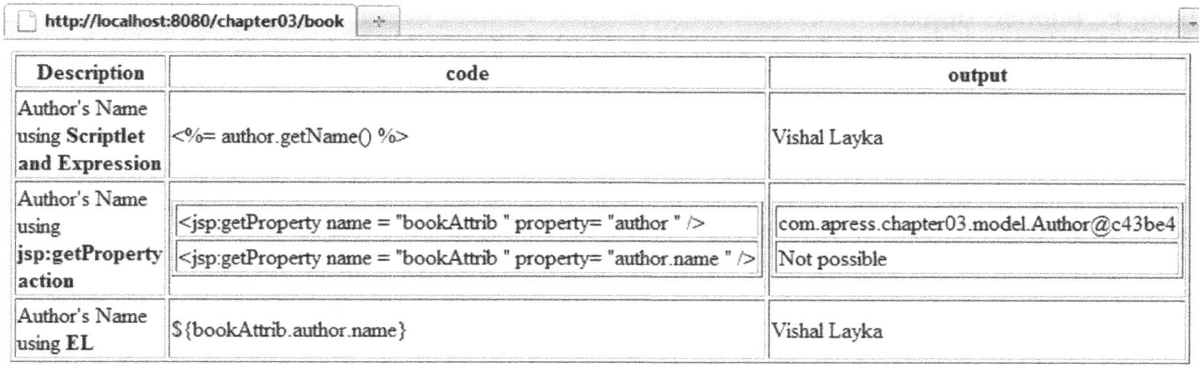

http://localhost:8080/chapter03/book

Description	code	output
Author's Name using **Scriptlet and Expression**	<%= author.getName() %>	Vishal Layka
Author's Name using **jsp:getProperty action**	<jsp:getProperty name = "bookAttrib " property= "author " /> <jsp:getProperty name = "bookAttrib " property= "author.name " />	com.apress.chapter03.model.Author@c43be4 Not possible
Author's Name using **EL**	${bookAttrib.author.name}	Vishal Layka

***Figure 3-7.** Comparing scriptlets, standard actions, and EL*

EL Implicit Objects

Scriptlets have access to several JSP implicit objects, as explained in Chapter 2. These objects allow access to any variables that are held in the particular JSP scopes. EL also provides its own implicit objects called *EL implicit objects*. EL implicit objects are not the same as JSP implicit objects (except for `pageContext`). All of these EL Implicit objects are Maps that map the respective scope attribute names to their values. For instance, using the implicit objects `param` and `paramValues`, it is possible to access HTTP request parameters. Table 3-3 describes the EL implicit objects.

***Table 3-3.** Implicit Objects in EL*

Implicit Object	Description
`cookie`	Map: maps cookie names to a single `Cookie` object.
`header`	Map: contains the values of each header name
`headerValues`	Map: maps a header name to a string array of all possible values for the header.
`initParam`	Map: maps context initialization parameter names to their string parameter values.
`param`	Map: contains the names of the parameters to a page.
`paramValues`	Map: maps a parameter nameto a string array of all the values for the parameter.
`pageContext`	The `PageContext` object.
`applicationScope`	Map: contains all application-scoped variables.
`pageScope`	Map: contains all page-scoped variables.
`requestScope`	Map: contains all request-scoped variables.
`sessionScope`	Map: contains all session-scoped variables.

Using EL Implicit Objects

Of the EL implicit objects listed in Table 3-3, `applicationScope`, `pageScope`, `requestScope`, and `sessionScope` are meant for specifying scope. These are used to access scoped attributes, that is, to access data from JavaBeans, maps, arrays, and lists that have been stored as attributes in any of the four scopes: page, request, session, and application.

The other implicit objects listed in Table 3-3 are used to access request parameters, request headers, cookies, context-initialization parameters, and `pageContext` objects. This section illustrates the usage of some of the EL implicit objects.

Accessing Request Parameters

Listing 3-24 illustrates a simple form used to submit the request parameters through `form.jsp`.

Listing 3-24. form.jsp

```
<body>
<form action="books" method="post">
<input type="hidden" name="action" value="books"/>
<p>Book Title: <input type="text" name="bookTitle"></p>
<p>Author 1 Name: <input type="text" name="authorName"></p>
<p>Author 2 Name: <input type="text" name="authorName"></p>
<input type = "submit"/>
</form>
</body>
```

In Listing 3-24, the `name` property of the `<input>` tag is the same: `authorName`.

Listing 3-25 illustrates the usage of the EL implicit objects `param` and `paramValues` to retrieve the request parameter and display the result on the `result.jsp` page.

Listing 3-25. result.jsp

```
1.<p>Book Title: ${param.bookTitle}<br>
2.Author 1: ${paramValues.authorName[0]}<br>
3.Author 2: ${paramValues. authorName[1]}
4.</p>
```

- *Line 1*: This uses the EL implicit object `param` to get the `Book` title.
- *Line 2 to Line 3*: This code uses the EL implicit object `paramValues` to get the `Author 1` and `Author 2` names.

Accessing the Header

The EL implicit objects `header` and `headerValues` give you access to the header values that can be obtained using the `request.getHeader()` and `request.getHeaders()` methods.

Listing 3-26 illustrates accessing a header named `user-agent`, using the expression `${header.user-agent}` or `${header["user-agent"]}`.

***Listing 3-26.** Using EL Implicit Object Header*

```
<span>${header["user-agent"]}</span>
```

Here's the output:

```
Mozilla/5.0 (Windows NT 6.1; rv:12.0) Gecko/20100101 Firefox/12.0
```

Accessing Cookie

The El implicit object cookie gives us access to the cookie. Listing 3-27 illustrates the cookie stored in the servlet.

***Listing 3-27.** Setting a Cookie in a Servlet*

```
String userName = "vishal";
Cookie c = new Cookie("userName", userName);
c.setPath("/");
response.addCookie(c);
```

Listing 3-28 illustrates how to use an EL implicit object to access the cookie in the JSP page.

***Listing 3-28.** Using an EL Implicit Object Cookie*

```
${cookie.userName.value}
```

Accessing a Scoped Attribute

The El implicit object `sessionScope` gives access to the attribute stored in the session scope. Listing 3-29 illustrates the attribute stored in the session in a servlet.

***Listing 3-29.** Setting a Session Attribute in a Servlet*

```
HttpSession session = request.getSession();
Book book = new Book();
book.setBookTitle("Beginning Java");
session.setAttribute("book", book);
```

Listing 3-30 illustrates using an EL implicit object called `sessionScope` to access the book title in the JSP page.

***Listing 3-30.** Using EL Implicit Object `sessionScope`*

```
<span>Book title in Session Scope ${sessionScope.book.bookTitle}</span>
```

EL Functions

EL functions let you call Java method from JSP without using scripting. An EL function is mapped to a static method of a Java class. This mapping is specified within a tag library descriptor (TLD), which is explained later in this section. Listing 3-31 illustrates a simple Java method that returns the current date and time.

Listing 3-31. Java Class with Public and Static Methods

```
package com.apress.elfunction;

import java.text.SimpleDateFormat;
import java.util.Calendar;

public class Now {

public static String now() {
Calendar currentDate = Calendar.getInstance();
SimpleDateFormat formatter = new SimpleDateFormat(
"yyyy/MMM/dd HH:mm:ss");
String now = formatter.format(currentDate.getTime());

return now;
}
}

```

The key requirement for a Java method to be used in an EL function is that the method must be `public` and `static`. The three key players in an EL function are as follows:

- A Java method defined in a class
- A JSP page that invokes the Java method using EL
- A tag library descriptor file that maps the Java method in the Java class to the JSP code that calls this Java method

Listing 3-32 illustrates the tag library descriptor file. A TLD is an XML file that declares a tag library. This TLD file contains the declarations and mappings of one or more EL functions. Each function is given a name and a specific method in a Java class that will implement the function.

Listing 3-32. Tag Library Descriptor

```
<?xml version="1.0" encoding="UTF-8"?>
<taglib version="2.1" xmlns="http://java.sun.com/xml/ns/javaee"
xmlns:xsi="http://www.w3.org/2001/XMLSchema-instance"
xsi:schemaLocation="http://java.sun.com/xml/ns/javaee
http://java.sun.com/xml/ns/javaee/webjsptaglibrary_2_1.xsd">
<tlib-version>1.2</tlib-version>
<uri>elFunction</uri>
<function>
<name>now</name>
<function-class>
```

```
11.com.apress.elfunction.Now
12.</function-class>
13.<function-signature>
14.String now()
15.</function-signature>
16.
17.</function>
18.</taglib>
```

- *Line7*: Line 7 is the URI of the function that will be used in the taglib directive in the JSP page.
- *Lines 8 to 17*: These lines specify the Java method that will be invoked with the signature and the Java class in which this method is defined.

A Java method can be called from JSP using EL in the following manner: `${prefix:function-name)`. The namespace prefix is declared by using the taglib directive in the JSP page. Listing 3-33 shows the JSP code.

Listing 3-33. Invoking an EL Function in JSP

```
1.<%@ taglib prefix="elf" uri="elFunction"%>
2.<html>
3.
4.<body>${elf:now() }
5.</body>
6.</html>
```

- *Line 1*: Line 1 is a taglib directive with the prefix `elf` and a URI. The URI is defined in the tag library descriptor.
- *Line 4*: This uses the prefix `elf` and invokes the function. This function name is defined in the tag library description.

You can create this application based on the first JSP application we created in Chapter 2. When this application is run (`http://localhost:8080/elFunctions/elTest.jsp`), it gives the output shown in Figure 3-8.

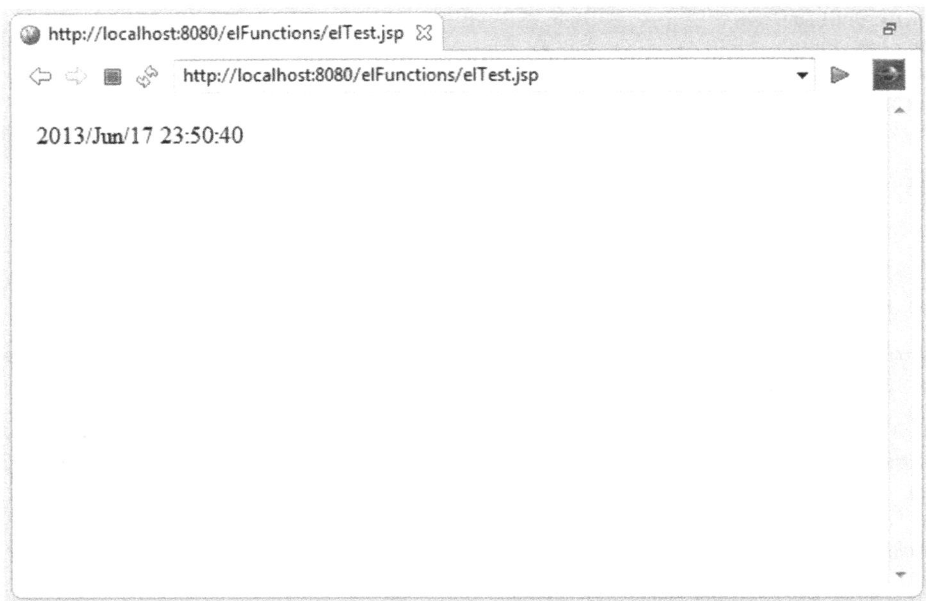

Figure 3-8. Output from invoking the EL function

JSTL

The ultimate goal of the JSP Standard Tag Library (JSTL) is to help simplify the development of Java Server Pages. As discussed in the previous section, scriptlets lead to unmaintainable JSPs and can be replaced by JSP standard actions. However, standard actions are far too limited; an even better approach is for Java developers to create their own custom actions. Still, creating a custom action is a nontrivial task. JSTL provides such custom actions that can handle common recurring tasks, and JSTL includes a wide variety of actions divided into different functional areas. Table 3-4 lists the functional areas along with the URIs used to reference the libraries and the prefixes used in the JSTL specification.

Table 3-4. JSTL Tag Libraries

Functional Area	URI	Prefix
Core	`http://java.sun.com/jsp/jstl/core`	`c`
XML processing	`http://java.sun.com/jsp/jstl/xml`	`x`
I18N-capable formatting	`http://java.sun.com/jsp/jstl/fmt`	`fmt`
Relational database access	`http://java.sun.com/jsp/jstl/sql`	`sql`
Functions	`http://java.sun.com/jsp/jstl/functions`	`fn`

Many JSTL actions export scoped variables that you can easily access through the Expression Language. As we saw in the previous chapter, scoped variables are objects stored in one of the JSP scopes: application, page, request, and session. When a JSTL action makes a scoped variable available to one or more JSP pages, it has an attribute named var that lets you specify the name of that scoped variable. Listing 3-34 illustrates the <c:set>action, available in the core tag library of JSTL, to set the value of a scoped variable.

Listing 3-34. Using<c:set>

```
<c:set var="name" value="hello" scope="session" />
```

Listing 3-34 sets a variable called name to the value hello and allows that variable to be visible in session scope. If the value for scope is not specified, the default scope is page scope. In the section that follows, you will learn all the actions in different functional areas provided in the core tag library.

The Core Tag Library

Table 3-5 describes the core actions in the core tag library.

Table 3-5. Core Actions in the Core Tag Library

Action	Description
<c:catch>	Catches exceptions thrown in the action's body
<c:choose>	Chooses one of many code fragments
<c:forEach>	Iterates over a collection of objects or iterates a fixed number of times
<c:forTokens>	Iterates over tokens in a string
<c:if>	Conditionally performs some functionality
<c:import>	Imports a URL
<c:otherwise>	Specifies default functionality in a <c:choose> action
<c:out>	Sends output to the current JspWriter
<c:param>	Specifies a URL parameter for <c:import> or <c:url>
<c:redirect>	Redirects a response to a specified URL
<c:remove>	Removes a scoped variable
<c:set>	Creates a scoped variable
<c:url>	Creates a URL, with URL rewriting as appropriate
<c:when>	Specifies one of several conditions in a <c:choose> action

The JSTL core library can be divided into four distinct functional areas, as described in Table 3-6.

Table 3-6. JSTL Core Library

Functional Areas	Description
General-purpose actions	Used to manipulate the scoped variables
Conditional actions	Used for conditional processing within a JSP page
Iterator actions	Used to iterate through collections of objects
URL-related actions	Used for dealing with URL resources in a JSP page

General-Purpose Actions

The general-purpose actions provide the means to work with scoped variables. Table 3-7 describes the general-purpose actions in the core tag library.

Table 3-7. General-Purpose Actions

Action	Description
`<c:out>`	Evaluates an expression and outputs the result to the `JspWriter` object
`<c:set>`	Sets the value of a scoped variable or a property of a target object
`<c:remove>`	Removes a scoped variable
`<c:catch>`	Catches a `java.lang.Throwable` thrown by any of its nested actions

The <c:out> Action

The `<c:out>` action evaluates an expression and displays the result. It's equivalent to the JSP syntax `<%= expression %>`.

Here's the syntax without a body:

```
<c:out value="value" [escapeXml="{true|false}"][default="defaultValue"] />
```

Here's the syntax with a body:

```
<c:out value="value" [escapeXml="{true|false}"]>
default value
</c:out>Items in brackets are optional
```

Table 3-8 describes the attributes of `<c:out>`. Since this chapter covers JSTL comprehensively, I recommend you read the JSTL specification[3] for a thorough understanding of how to use JSTL attributes.

[3]http://java.coe.psu.ac.th/J2EE/JSTL1.2/jstl-1_2-mrel2-spec.pdf

Table 3-8. <c:out> Attributes

Name	Type	Description
value	Object	This is the expression to be evaluated.
escapeXml	boolean	This determines whether the characters <,>,&,','' in the resulting string should be converted to their corresponding character entity codes. The default value is true.
default	Object	This is the default value if the resulting value is null.

The value to be written to the JspWriter is specified as a value attribute. You can use expressions in the value attribute.

- value: The expression to be evaluated is supplied via the value attribute, and the result is converted into a string before being returned as part of the response.
- default: You can optionally specify a default value that <c:out> sends to the current JspWriter if the specified value is null or is not a valid expression. You can specify the default value with the default attribute or in the body of the <c:out> action.
- escapeXml: The escapeXml attribute specifies whether to convert certain characters to the HTML character entity codes listed in Table 3-9. By default, the escapeXmlattribute is set to true. If you specify false for the escapeXml attribute, <c:out> will not convert these characters.

Table 3-9. Character Entity Codes

Character	Character Entity Code
<	<
>	>
&	&
'	'
"	"

Listing 3-35 illustrates replacing scripting elements with the <c:out> action.

Listing 3-35. Comparing <c:out> and Expression

```
<%= "hello" %>  // Ouput "hello" using Expression
<c:out  value = "hello"/> // Ouput "hello" using <c:out> action
```

The <c:set>Action

The JSTL set tag or the `<c:set>` action sets the value of a scoped variable or a property of a target object. The `<c:set>` action is a better alternative to using the `<jsp:setProperty>` JSP action. Unlike `<jsp:setProperty>`, which allows you to set only the bean property, the `<c:set>` tag can do the following:

- Set bean properties
- Set Map values
- Create scoped variables on the page, request, session, or application scope

Table 3-10 describes the attributes of the `<c:set>` action.

Table 3-10. <c:set>Attributes

Name	Type	Description
`value`	`Object`	Expression to be evaluated.
`var`	`String`	Name of the exported scoped variable to hold the value specified in the action.
`scope`	`String`	Scope for `var`.
`target`	`Object`	Target object whose property will be set. This must evaluate to a JavaBeans object with the setter property `property` or to a `java.util.Map` object.
`property`	`String`	Name of the property to be set in the target object.

The `<c:set>` tag is used to do the following:

- Set the value of a scoped variable in any JSP scope.
- Set a property of a specified target object. The target must evaluate to a JavaBean or Map object.

Setting the Value of a Scoped Variable in Any JSP Scope

One of the tasks of the `<c:set>` action is to set variables that can be used by other actions on pages.

Here's the syntax:

```
<c:set value=""value""var=""varName" " [scope=""{page|request|session|application}""]/>
```

Listing 3-36 shows an example of using `<c:set>`to set the value of the scoped variable `helloVar`.

Listing 3-36. Using <c:set>

```
<c:set var="helloVar" value="hello" />
```

Listing 3-36 creates an attribute named `helloVar` with the value `"hello"` in the default scope, which is page scope. You can also create attributes in another scope, say session scope; in that case, you need to specify the scope with `<c:set>` attribute `scope=""`. Listing 3-37 creates a variable on session scope using `<c:set>`.

Listing 3-37. Using Scope

```
<c:set var="helloVar" value="hello" scope="session" />
```

We could also have expressed this by providing the value in the body content of the action, as illustrated in Listing 3-38.

Listing 3-38. Using <c:set>with Body

```
<c:set var="hello" scope="session" >
helloworld
</c:set>
```

The value of a variable can also be an EL expression, as illustrated in Listing 3-39.

Listing 3-39. Using an EL Expression in a Value

```
<c:set var="titleVar" value="${book.title}" scope="session" />
```

In Listing 3-39, the `title` property of the `book` bean is set in the `titleVar` variable.

Listing 3-40 shows the scriptlet equivalent of `<c:set>`, as illustrated in Listing 3-36.

Listing 3-40. Scriptlet Equivalent of <c:set>

```
<%
  String helloVar = "hello";
  pageContext.setAttribute("helloVar ", helloVar);
%>
```

Setting the Property of a Specified Target Object

To be able to set bean properties or map values using `<c:set>`, we need to use `target` and `property`, instead of `var`, which will define the bean and property name to be set. If `target` is `map`, for instance, then `property` is the name of the key and `value` is the value for that key.

Here's the syntax:

```
<c:set value=""value""target=""target"" property=""propertyName""/>
```

- If using a target object, the target must evaluate to a JavaBean or a `java.util.Map` object.
- If the target is a JavaBean, it must contain the appropriate getter/setter methods.

Listing 3-41 illustrates how to set a map key using a`<c:set>` tag.

Listing 3-41. Setting a Map Key using the <c:set>Tag

```
<c:set target="bookMap" property="id" value="1">
```

This is equivalent to `bookMap.put("id", "1");`. You can also supply the value in the body of the `<c:set>` tag.

Listing 3-42 illustrates how to set bean properties using <c:set>.

Listing 3-42. Setting the bean property using the <c:set> Tag

```
<c:set target="book" property="book.title" value="Learning Java Web">
```

Listing 3-42 sets the title property of a bean named book to Learning Java Web. This is equivalent to book.setTitle("Learning Java Web");.

The <c:remove>Action

The <c:remove> action removes a variable from a specific scope. The variables set by <c:set> in any of the scopes can be removed using the <c:remove> action by specifying the variable name in the var attribute and the scope attribute.

Here's the syntax:

```
<c:remove var="varName"[scope="{page|request|session|application}"]/>
```

Table 3-11 describes the attributes of the <c:remove> action.

Table 3-11. <c:remove> Attributes

Name	Type	Description
var	String	Name of the scoped variable to be removed
scope	String	Scope for var

Listing 3-43 illustrates the simple usage of <c:remove>.

Listing 3-43. Using <c:remove>

```
<c:remove var=" helloVar " />
```

The <c:catch> Action

The <c:catch> action provides a way to catch java.lang.Throwableexceptions that are thrown by any nested actions. This action has a single var attribute that holds a reference to any java.lang.Throwable exceptions that occur during the execution of any of the nested actions.

Here is the syntax:

```
<c:catch [var="varName"]>
...nested actions in the body...
</c:catch>
```

Table 3-12 describes the attribute of the <c:catch> action.

Table 3-12. <c:catch> Attributes

Name	Type	Description
`var`	String	Name of the exported scoped variable for the exception thrown from a nested action.

The `<c:catch>` action can handle errors from any action by nesting those actions within `<c:catch>`. When an exception is thrown, it is stored in a page-scoped variable that is identified by the `var` attribute of the tag. Listing 3-44 illustrates the usage of `<c:catch>`.

Listing 3-44. Using <c:catch>

```
<body>

<c:catch var = "exception">
<% int i = 1/0;%>
</c:catch>

<c:if test = "${exception != null}">
<span> Exception : ${exception}</span>

</c:if>
</body>
```

Here's the output:

```
Exception : java.lang.ArithmeticException: / by zero
```

Conditionals

The conditional tags provided by the JSTL core tag library provide an alternative to using scriptlets for generating dynamic content based on conditions. Table 3-13 describes the actions in this functional area.

Table 3-13. Conditional Actions in the Core Tag Library

Action	Description
`<c:if>`	Evaluates its body content if the expression specified with the `test` attribute is `true`
`<c:choose>`	Provides the context for mutually exclusive conditional execution
`<c:when>`	Represents an alternative within a `<c:choose>` action
`<c:otherwise>`	Represents the last alternative within a `<c:choose>` action

The <c:if>Action

The `<c:if>` action is used for conditional processing and evaluates an expression, displaying its body content only if the expression evaluates to `true`.

Here's the syntax without body content:

```
<c:if test="testCondition"
var="varName" [scope="{page|request|session|application}"]/>
```

Here's the syntax with body content:

```
<c:if test="testCondition"
[var="varName"] [scope="{page|request|session|application}"]>
```

. . . body content . . .

```
</c:if>
```

Using the `test` attribute, a Boolean EL expression is evaluated. If the test condition evaluates to `true`, only then the body of the action is executed. The Boolean result of the expression evaluation is exported to a scoped variable using the `var` attribute. The default scope of the `var` is page, but using the `scope` attribute, the scope could be set to any of the JSP scopes.

Table 3-14 illustrates the attributes of the `<c:if>` action.

***Table 3-14.** <c:if> Attributes*

Name	Type	Description
`test`	Boolean	The test condition that determines whether the body content should be processed.
`var`	String	The name of the exported scoped variable for the resulting value of the test condition.
`scope`	String	The scope for `var`.

Listing 3-45 illustrates using <c:if> with the body content.

***Listing 3-45.** Using <c:if> with Body Content*

```
<c:set var="number" value="9"/>
<c:if test="${ number < 10}" >
<c:out value ="number is less than 10"/>
</c:if>
```

Here's the output:

```
number is less than 10
```

The <c:choose>, <c:when>, and <c:otherwise> Actions

The `<c:choose>` action enables you to handle mutually exclusive conditions. It works like a Java `switch` statement and lets you choose between a number of alternatives, using `<c:when>` instead of `case` statements and `<c:otherwise>` to provide default action just like the `switch` statement does with a default clause.

The syntax for the <c:choose> action is as follows:

```
<c:choose>
body content (<c:when> and <c:otherwise>)
</c:choose>
```

As you can see, the <c:choose> action has two possible nested actions that form its body: <c:when> and <c:otherwise>. The syntax for each is as follows:

```
<c:when test="testCondition">
body
</c:when>
<c:otherwise>
body
</c:otherwise>
```

Table 3-15 illustrates the attributes of the <c:when> action.

***Table 3-15.** <c:when> Attributes*

Name	Type	Description
test	Boolean	The test condition that determines whether the body content should be processed

Listing 3-46 illustrates a simple usage of <c:choose>.

***Listing 3-46.** Using <c:choose>*

```
<body>
<c:set var="number" value="10"/>
<c:choose>
<c:when test="${number < 10}">
       Number is less than 10.
</c:when>
<c:when test="${number > 10}">
        Number is greater than 10.
</c:when>
<c:otherwise>
        Number is equal to 10
</c:otherwise>
</c:choose>
</body>
```

Here's the output:

```
Number is equal to 10
```

Looping and Iteration

JSTL offers two useful actions for looping and iteration: <c:forEach> for general data and <c:forTokens> for string tokenizing.

Table 3-16 illustrates the actions for looping and iteration.

Table 3-16. Looping and Iteration Actions in the Core Tag Library

Action	Description
<c:forEach>	Iterates over a collection of objects
<c:forTokens>	Iterates over tokens, separated by the supplied delimiters

The <c:forEach>Action

The <c:forEach> action iterates over a collection of objects.

Here's the syntax for iterating over a collection of objects:

```
<c:forEach[var="varName"] items="collection"
[varStatus="varStatusName"]
[begin="begin"] [end="end"] [step="step"]>
```

. . . body content . . . .

```
</c:forEach>
```

Here's the syntax for iterating a fixed number of times:

```
<c:forEach [var="varName"]
[varStatus="varStatusName"]
begin="begin" end="end" [step="step"]>
```

. . . . body content . . .

```
</c:forEach>
```

Table 3-17 illustrates the attributes of the <c:forEach> action.

Table 3-17. <c:forEach> Attributes

Name	Type	Description
var	String	Name of the exported scoped variable for the current item of the iteration.
items	" Arrays, Collection, Enumeration, Iterator, Map, String	Collection of items to iterate over.
varStatus	String	Name of the exported scoped variable for the status of the iteration. The object exported is of type `javax.servlet.jsp.jstl.core.LoopTagStatus`.
begin	int	If items are specified, iteration begins at the item located at the specified index. The first item of the collection has index 0.If items are not specified, then iteration begins with index set at the value specified.
end	int	If items are specified, then iteration ends at the item located at the specified index (inclusive).If items are not specified, then iteration ends when the index reaches the value specified.
step	int	Iteration will process only every step item , starting with the first one.

To iterate over a collection of objects, use the following syntax:

```
<c:forEach[var="varName"] items="collection" [varStatus="varStatusName"]
...body  content ....
</c:forEach>
```

To iterate a fixed number of times, use the following syntax:

```
<c:forEach [var="varName"] [varStatus="varStatusName"]
begin="begin" end="end" [step="step"]>
...body content ...
</c:forEach>
```

Listing 3-47 illustrates a simple usage of `<c:forEach>`.

Listing 3-47. Using <c:forEach>

```
<body>
<c:forEach var="i" begin="1" end="3">
   Item <c:out value="${i}"/><p>
</c:forEach>
</body>
```

Here's the output:

```
Item 1
Item 2
Item 3
```

The <c:forTokens> Action

The <c:forTokens> action iterates over a string of tokens separated by a set of delimiters.

Here's the syntax:

```
<c:forTokens items="stringOfTokens" delims="delimiters"
[var="varName"] [varStatus="varStatusName"]
[begin="begin"] [end="end"] [step="step"]>
```

. . . body . . . .

```
</c:forTokens>
```

Table 3-18 describes all the attributes of <c:forTokens>.

Table 3-18. <c: for Tokens > Attributes

Name	Type	Description
var	String	Name of the exported scoped variable for the current item of the iteration.
items	String	String of tokens to iterate over.
delims	String	Set of delimiters (the characters that separate the tokens in the string).
varStatus	String	Name of the exported scoped variable for the status of the iteration. The object exported is of type javax.servlet.jsp.jstl.core.LoopTagStatus.
begin	int	Iteration begins at the token located at the specified index. The first token has index 0.
end	int	Iteration ends at the token located at the specified index (inclusive).
step	int	Iteration will process only every step tokens, starting with the first one.

The <c:forTokens> tag works with a string of characters separated by a delimiter. Listing 3-48 shows the usage of <c:forTokens>.

Listing 3-48. Using <c: for Tokens>

```
<body>
<c:forTokens items="Clojure,Groovy,Java, Scala" delims="," var="lang">
<c:out value="${lang}"/><p>
</c:forTokens>
</body>
```

Here is the output of Listing 3-48:

```
Clojure
Groovy
Java
Scala
```

URL-Related Actions

The URL-related actions are for linking, importing, and redirecting in web applications. Table 3-19 describes all the URL-related actions in the core library.

Table 3-19. URL-Related Actions

Action	Purpose
`<c:import>`	Imports the content of a URL-based resource.
`<c:param>`	Adds request parameters to a URL. This is a nested action of `<c:import>`, `<c:url>`, and `<c:redirect>`.
`<c:url>`	Builds a URL with the proper rewriting rules applied.
`<c:redirect>`	Sends an HTTP redirect to the client.

Let's take a look at these URL-related actions.

The <c:import>Action

The `<c:import>` action imports the content of a URL-based resource, providing additional functionality over the `<jsp:include>` action. The syntax of the `<c:import>` action is as follows:

```
<c:import url ="url  [context="context"] [charEncoding="charEncoding"] [scope="application|page|requ
est|session"] [var= "varName"] >
Optional body content for <c:param> sub tags
</c:import>
```

- The only required attribute is `url`, which is the URL of the resource to import.
- The `<c:param>` action, explained next, can be used as a nested tag in the body content of the `<c:import>`.

Table 3-20 describes all the attributes used with the `<c:import>` action.

Table 3-20. <c:import> Attributes

Name	Type	Description
url	String	URL of the resource to import.
context	String	Name of the context when accessing a relative URL resource that belongs to a foreign context.
var	String	Name of the exported scoped variable for the resource's content.
scope	String	Scope for var.
charEncoding	String	Character encoding of the content at the input resource.
varReader	String	Name of the exported scoped variable for the resource's content.

In the previous chapter, we saw how the `<jsp:include>` action lets us encapsulate functionality in one JSP page and include it in another; for example, you could include a header and footer as illustrated in Listing 3-49.

Listing 3-49. Using the <jsp:include> Action

```
<body>
<jsp:include page='/WEB-INF/jsp/header.jsp'/>
<%-- content -%>
<jsp:include page='/WEB-INF/jsp/footer.jsp'/>
</body>
```

The `<jsp:include>` action is limited to including the resource that belongs to the same web application as the including page and specified as a relative URL.

You can use `<c:import>` instead of `<jsp:include>` to import resources in the same web application; Listing 3-50 illustrates how to use `<c:import>` instead of `<jsp:include>`.

Listing 3-50. Using <c:import>

```
<body>
<c:import url='/WEB-INF/jsp/header.jsp'/>
<%-- content --%>
<c:import url='/WEB-INF/jsp/footer.jsp'/>
</body>
```

With the `<c:import>` action, other than accessing resources in the same web application, you can also access external resources or resources in a foreign context. To access an external resource, you specify an absolute URL for the `url` attribute, and to access a resource in a foreign context, you specify a value for the `context` attribute that represents a context path for the foreign context along with the `url` attribute, which represents a context-relative path to the resource. Listing 3-51 illustrates how to use the `<c:import>` action to import a resource from a foreign context.

Listing 3-51. Importing a Resource from a Foreign Context

```
<c:import url='/jsp/book.jsp' context='/foreigncontext'/>
```

Note The charEncoding attribute is required when accessing absolute URL resources where the protocol is not HTTP and where the encoding is not ISO-8859-1.

The <c:param>Action

The <c:import>, <c:url>, and <c:redirect> actions explained later in this section all deal with URLs. The <c:param> action is used to pass request parameters and is used as a nested tag in the body of either the <c:import>, <c:url>, or <c:redirect> action. The <c:param> action also does the URL encoding.

Here's the syntax with a parameter value specified in the attribute value.

```
<c:param name="name" value="value"/>
```

Here's the syntax with a parameter value specified in the body content.

```
<c:param name="name">
parameter value
</c:param>
```

Table 3-21 describes the attributes of <c:param>.

Table 3-21. <c:param> Attributes

Name	Type	Description
name	String	Name of the query string parameter
value	String	Value of the parameter

Listing 3-52 illustrated how you can use <c:import> instead of <jsp:include>. You can also specify request parameters for included files with the <jsp:param> action, as shown in Listing 3-52.

Listing 3-52. Using <jsp:param>

```
<body>
<jsp:include page='/WEB-INF/jsp/company/companyHeader.jsp'>
<jsp:param name='user'
value='<%=session.getAttribute("userName")%>'/>
</jsp:include>
<%-- Page content goes here--%>
<jsp:include page='/WEB-INF/jsp/company/companyFooter.jsp'/>
</body>
```

Listing 3-53 illustrates how you can use <c:param> instead of <jsp:param>.

Listing 3-53. Using <c:param>

```
<body>
<c:import url='/WEB-INF/jsp/header.jsp'>
<c:param name='user'
value='${sessionScope.userName}'/>
</c:import>
<%-- body content --%>
<c:import url='/WEB-INF/jsp/footer.jsp'/>
</body>
```

The <c:url>Action

The `<c:url>` action builds a URL with the proper rewriting rules applied. It can format a URL and store it in a variable specified by the `var` attribute.

Here's the syntax without body content:

```
<c:url value [context] [var] [scope]/>
```

Here's the syntax with body content to specify query string parameters:

```
<c:url value [context] [var] [scope]>
<c:param> actions
</c:url>
```

- The only required attribute is `value`, which is the URL to be processed.
- `<c:param>` subtags can also be specified within the body of `<c:url>` for adding to the URL query string parameters, which will be properly encoded if necessary.

The attributed of <c:url> are listed in the Table 3-22.

***Table 3-22.** <c:url> Attributes*

Name	Type	Description
`value`	String	URL to be processed.
`context`	String	Name of the context when specifying a relative URL resource that belongs to a foreign context.
`var`	String	Name of the exported scoped variable for the processed URL.
`scope`	String	Scope for `var`.

Listing 3-54 shows the simple usage of `<c:url>`.

Listing 3-54. Using <c:url>

```
<c:url var="homePage" scope="session"value="http://www.yourbookstore.com" />
```

If you specify a context-relative or page-relative URL for the value attribute, <c:url> prepends the context path of the web application to the URL; for example, if the context path of the web application is /bookWeb/books, the <c:url> action <c:url value='/book.jsp'/> will result inurl:/bookWeb/books/book.jsp.

The <c:redirect>Action

The <c:redirect> action sends an HTTP redirect to the client, redirecting the browser to an alternate URL. The <c:redirect> action provides the URL rewriting with a redirect.

Here's the syntax without body content:

```
<c:redirect url="value" [context="context"]/>
```

Here's the syntax with body content to specify query string parameters:

```
<c:redirect url="value" [context="context"]>
<c:param> subtags
</c:redirect>
```

The <c:redirect>action has two attributes: the URL that will be used to redirect to and an optional context.

The attributes of <c:redirect> are listed in the Table 3-23.

Table 3-23. <c:redirect> Attributes

Name	Type	Description
url	String	The URL of the resource to redirect to
context	String	The name of the context when redirecting to a relative URL resource that belongs to a foreign context

The URL, relative or absolute, follows the same URL rewriting rules as <c:url>. Listing 3-55 illustrates redirecting to an external resource, which is an absolute URL.

Listing 3-55. Using <c:redirect>

```
<c:redirect url="http://www.yourbookstore.com" />
```

You can redirect to a resource in a foreign context using the context attribute. The URL specified must start with a / as a context-relative URL, and as defined, the context name must also start with a /. Listing 3-56 illustrates redirecting to a foreign resource in a foreign context.

Listing 3-56. redirecting to a foreign resource in a foreign context.

```
<c:redirect url="/foreignresource.html" context="/foreigncontext" />
```

In this chapter, we have looked at the nuts and bolts of the Java EE machine in the web tier: the web components (servlets and JSP), the feature-rich Expression Language, and the ready-to-use custom actions (JSTL). Now we'll talk about best-practice solutions using patterns.

Best-Practice Solutions: Using Patterns

While Java EE does a great job of standardizing the enterprise infrastructure, of providing an application model, and of providing components adequate to develop web applications, interacting directly with the Java EE components often results in massive amounts of boilerplate code and even code redundancy. Using Java EE does not naturally lead to best-practice architecture and design. To that end, Deepak Alur, John Crupi, and Dan Malks first established the Java EE design patterns based on their experience of architecting enterprise systems. In this section, you will be introduced to the Java EE patterns in the web tier established by Alur, Crupi, and Malks.

> **Note** The book *Core J2EE Patterns: Best Practices and Design Strategies* by Alur, Crupi, and Malks (Prentice Hall, 2003) is highly recommended for learning about best-practice architecture and design. However, there have been substantial changes in the business and persistence JavaEE patterns with the Java EE 6 and Java EE 7. For instance, some patterns such as Service Locator have been dropped in favor of the Dependency Injection pattern. But the web tier patterns remain the same. You can find substantial literature on the new business and persistence Java EE patterns in *Real World Java EE Patterns: Rethinking Best Practices* (second edition) by Adam Bien.

The web tier encapsulates the presentation logic that is required to provide the service to the clients. The presentation tier does the following:

- Intercepts the client requests
- Provides functionality such as authentication, authorization, encryption, and session management, to name a few
- Accesses business services
- Constructs the response
- Renders the response to the client

In general, web application development requires you to address a common set of problems.

- When a request enters a web application, it often has to be preprocessed to provide certain functionality such as authentication, authorization, and encryption.
- The presentation tier and the business logic are often intermingled. This makes the presentation tier difficult to maintain.
- Views are often encoded with the view navigation logic. This results in intermingled view content and view navigation.
- There is no centralized component for view management, which results in code redundancy and code scattering across the views.

This is not a complete list of problems, but these are the most common of them in a web application. Fortunately, these problems in a web application can be addressed using web tier Java EE patterns. How to use these Java EE patterns differs with each problem. Table 3-24 describes these patterns.

Table 3-24. Presentation Tier Java EE Patterns

Presentation Tier Pattern	Description
Intercepting Filter	Preprocessing and postprocessing of a client web request and response
Front Controller	Centralized access point for presentation tier request handling to support the integration of system services, content retrieval, view management, and navigation
View Helper	Encapsulating business logic so that it is not intertwined with the presentation logic
Composite View	Managing the layout of the view independent of the content
Service to Worker	Assembling a microframework of front controller and view helper with a dispatcher component
Dispatcher View	Assembling a microframework of front controller and view helper with a dispatcher component

Note A good enterprise application consists of multiple tiers, and each tier concentrates on its own responsibilities/concerns, as explained in Chapters 1 and 2.

In the sections that follow we will look at each of these Java EE web tier patterns.

Intercepting Filter

A web application receives different types of requests that require some kind of processing, for example, to check whether the client has to be authenticated before proceeding with navigation. The best technique to provide a processing mechanism for requests is to use a processing component called a *filter*. Filters are used when you need to provide request preprocessing or postprocessing functionalities. The Intercepting Filter pattern comes along with the introduction of filters to the Servlet specification. This pattern uses one or more filters plugged into the current application to provide services such as authorization, compression, encryption, and logging. Figure 3-9 illustrates the Intercepting Filter pattern.

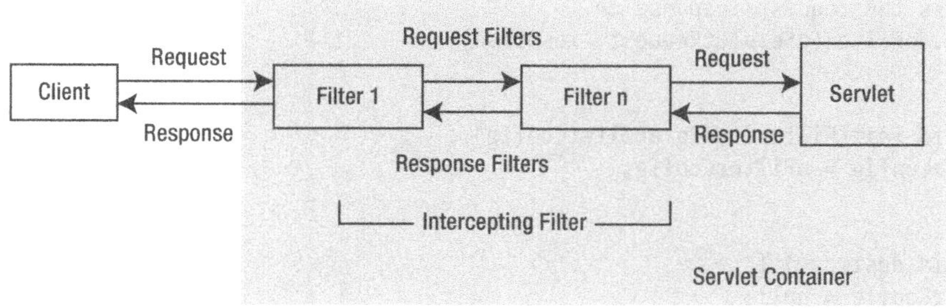

Figure 3-9. Intercepting Filter pattern

The Intercepting Filter pattern is used for preprocessing and postprocessing of client requests and also the responses by intercepting requests and responses. The filters are pluggable in the sense that you can add or remove them without changing the code.

One of the use cases for which the Intercepting Filter pattern is deemed best fit is when you want to enable theIE9 document mode of the browser by default. IE has two modes: browser mode and document mode. The browser always sends browser mode data to the server, and the server always responds with document mode data. The browser mode data consists of a user agent string with a version and trident token information, while the document mode data consists of metatags that dictate the mode in which the response will be rendered on the browser.

Listing 3-57 shows a simple response filter that enables the IE9 document mode of the browser by default.

Listing 3-57. Simple Response Filter

```
package com.apress.filters
import javax.servlet.*;
import javax.servlet.http.HttpServletResponse;
import java.io.IOException;
import java.util.Enumeration;

/**
 * filter for enabling IE9 document mode by default
 *
 */
public class ResponseHeaderFilter implements Filter {
    private FilterConfig filterConfig = null;

    public void doFilter(ServletRequest aServletRequest, ServletResponse aServletResponse,
FilterChain chain)
            throws IOException, ServletException {

        HttpServletResponse response = (HttpServletResponse) aServletResponse;

        // set the provided HTTP response parameters
        for (Enumeration e = filterConfig.getInitParameterNames(); e.hasMoreElements();) {
            String headerName = (String) e.nextElement();
            response.addHeader(headerName, filterConfig.getInitParameter(headerName));
        }

        // pass the request/response on
        chain.doFilter(aServletRequest, response);
    }

    public void init(FilterConfig aFilterConfig) {
        filterConfig = aFilterConfig;
    }

    public void destroy() {
        filterConfig = null;
    }
}
```

- *Line 20*: This line fetches all the initialization parameters from the deployment descriptor.
- *Line 22*: This line adds these parameters to the response.

Listing 3-58 illustrates the configuration of the response filter in the deployment descriptor.

***Listing 3-58.** Configuring Simple Response Filter*

```
 1.<filter>
 2.<filter-name>HTML5</filter-name>
 3.<filter-class>com.apress.filters.ResponseHeaderFilter</filter-class>
 4.<init-param>
 5.<param-name>X-UA-Compatible</param-name>
 6.<param-value>IE=edge,chrome=1</param-value>
 7.</init-param>
 8.</filter>
 9.<filter-mapping>
10.<filter-name>HTML5</filter-name>
11.<url-pattern>/*</url-pattern>
12.</filter-mapping>
```

- *Line 5 to 6*: These lines define the init parameters.

Front Controller

For web applications to be maintainable, all requests must pass through a common central component. The lack of a centralized mechanism leads to the following problems:

- There is no centralized component for view management, which results in code redundancy and code scattering across the views.
- Views are often encoded with view navigation logic. This results in intermingled view content and view navigation.

The Front Controller pattern provides a centralized access for the request handling to provide content retrieval, view management, navigation, validation, error handling, centralized security control, and so on. The Front Controller pattern is best implemented with a servlet. Using a centralized servlet to handle all requests and responses provides the following advantages:

- It provides a single location from which to control decisions related to authentication and authorization.
- All URLs that the front controller is required to handle can be mapped to this servlet.
- It provides a centralized access point to support the view management and navigation.
- You can apply common logic to several views.
- It provides the separation of the presentation logic from the navigation and business logic. This leads to loose coupling between the two.

Figure 3-10 shows the structure of the Front Controller pattern.

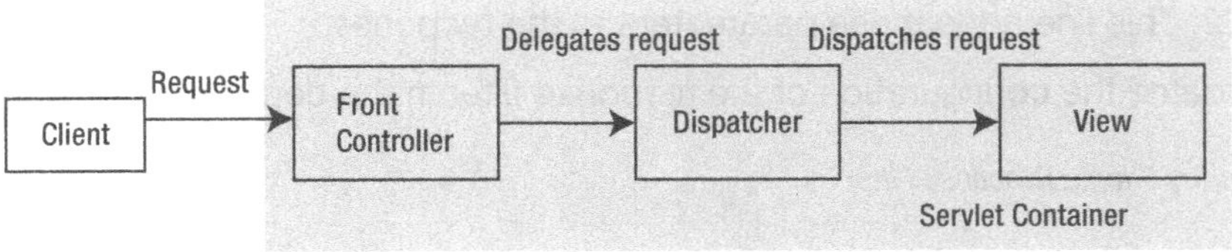

***Figure 3-10.** Front Controller class diagram*

The components of the Front Controller pattern are as follows:

- Controller
- Dispatcher
- View

Controller

The controller is the initial point for handling a request and coordinates with a dispatcher component. The controller manages the following:

- Handling the request, including invoking security services such as authentication and authorization
- Delegating to the business service
- Handling errors

Dispatcher

The dispatcher is responsible for view management and navigation.

View

The view represents and displays information to the client.

Figure 3-11 illustrates the sequence diagram of the front controller.

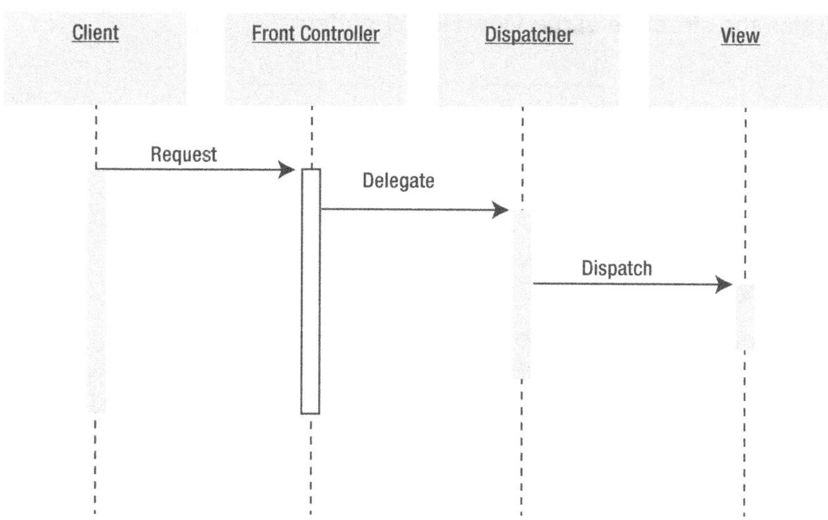

Figure 3-11. Front controller sequence diagram

View Helper

In a web application, the presentation content (that is, the content of the JSP page) requires the processing of dynamic content. Presentation tier changes occur often and are difficult to develop and maintain when the business logic and presentation logic are intermingled. In fact, intermingling the business logic and presentation logic makes the presentation unmaintainable. The View Helper design pattern decouples the presentation tier from with the business tier and generates views based on a template. The components in the View Helper pattern are as follows:

- View
- View helper

View

A view contains the presentation formatting logic and delegates the business processing logic in the presentation to the helper.

View Helper

The view helper does the following:

- A view helper can be implemented as a JavaBean implementation or a custom tag implementation. We used this pattern in Chapter 2.
- Helpers serve as the view's intermediate data model.
- Helpers are responsible for getting data from a business service.
- Presentation business logic is encapsulated in the helper.

Figure 3-12 illustrates the structure of the View Helper pattern.

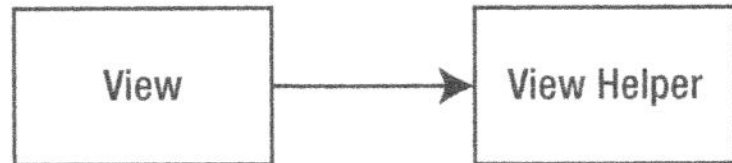

***Figure 3-12.** View Helper class diagram*

Composite View

In web applications, views are often built by embedding formatting code directly within each view. This makes modifying the layout of multiple views difficult. The Composite View pattern allows a parent view to be composed of subviews. Hence, the overall view becomes a composition of smaller subviews that are included dynamically in the overall view.

The components of the Composite View pattern are as follows:

- *Basic view*: This is the basic abstraction of the view.
- *Composite view*: This is a view that is composed of a number of subviews.
- *The view*: This is a simple view that has no subviews.

Figure 3-13 shows the basic structure for the Composite View pattern.

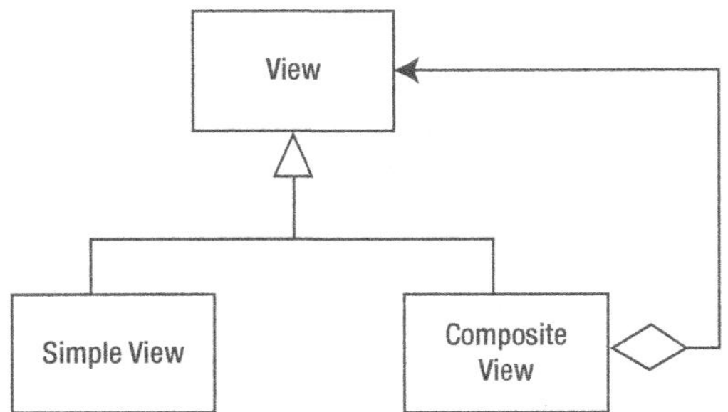

***Figure 3-13.** Composite View class diagram*

Figure 3-14 illustrates the usage of the Composite View pattern.

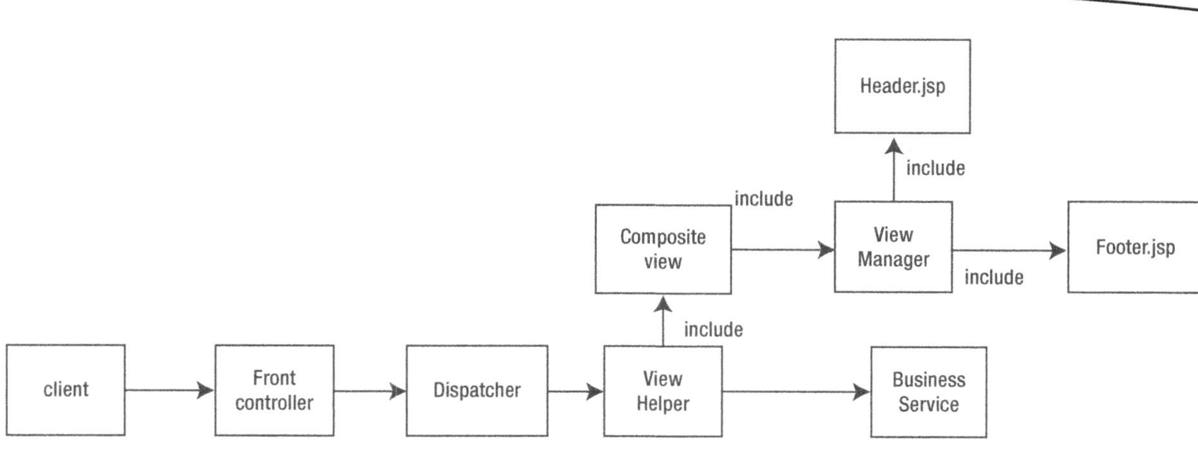

Figure 3-14. Composite View usage

Dispatcher View

The Dispatcher View design pattern assembles two patterns, Front Controller and View Helper, into a microframework with a dispatcher component to utilize the benefits associated with each pattern.

In the Dispatcher View pattern, the dispatcher is responsible for choosing and providing the mechanism to statically or dynamically present the subsequent view to the user.

The members of the Dispatcher View pattern, as illustrated in Figure 3-15, are as follows:

- Front controller
- Dispatcher
- Helper
- View
- View helper

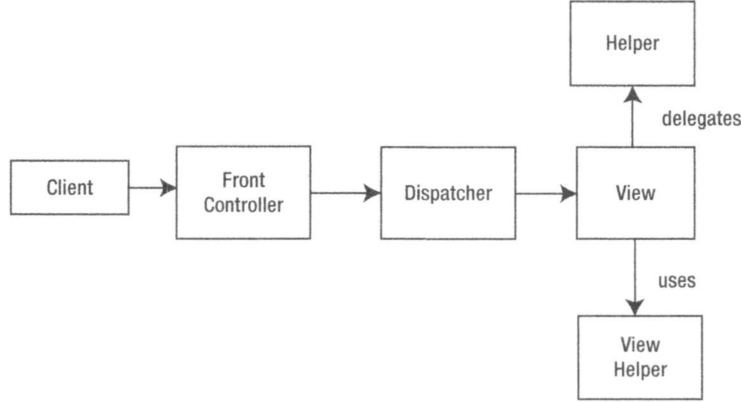

Figure 3-15. Dispatcher class diagram

Front Controller

The front controller does the following:

- Centralizes request processing
- Delegates to the view using the dispatcher
- Uses the view helper to separate the business logic concerns from the presentation logic concerns

Dispatcher

The dispatcher does the following:

- Is responsible for view management and navigation
- Delegates to the view
- Uses a helper to push data into the view

Helper

The helper does the following:

- Helps the view or the controller to complete its processing

View

The view does the following:

- Represents and displays information to the client
- Pulls the data from the data source using a view helper

Figure 3-16 illustrates the sequence diagram of the Dispatcher View pattern.

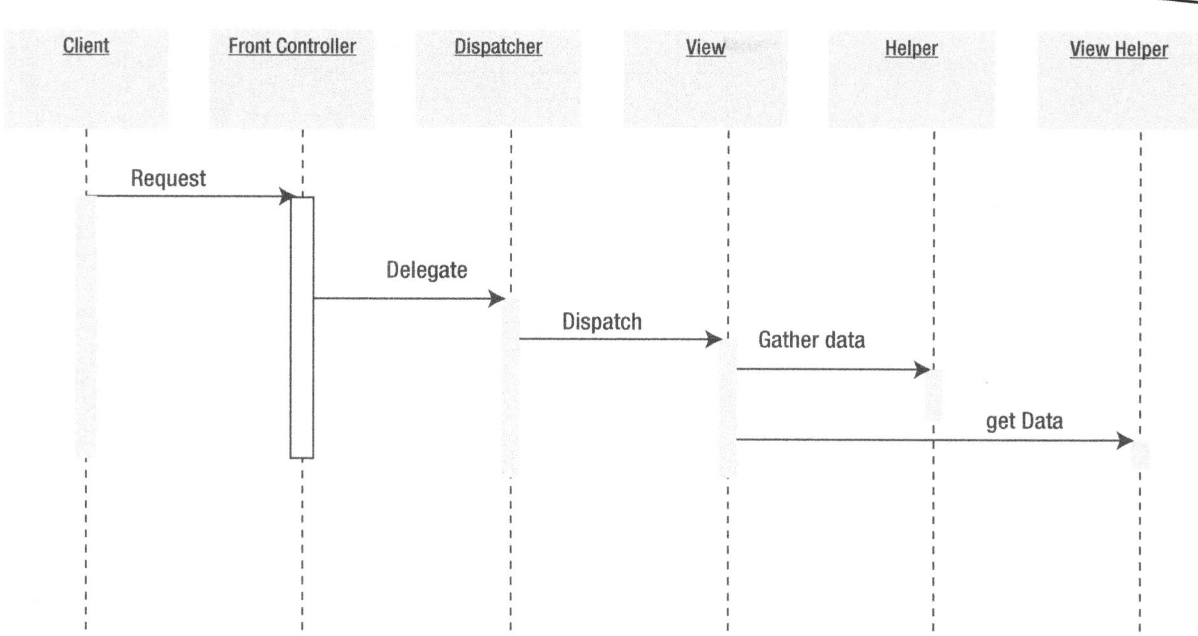

***Figure 3-16.** Dispatcher View sequence diagram*

Service to Worker

The Service to Worker design pattern assembles two patterns, Front Controller and View Helper, into a microframework with a dispatcher component to utilize the benefits associated with each pattern.

The Service to Worker pattern is a combination of a dispatcher with views and helpers to handle client requests and to generate dynamic content as the response. The Service to Worker pattern can be used in an application when the application requires dynamic content generation.

The members of the Service to Worker pattern, as illustrated in Figure 3-17, are as follows:

- Front controller
- Dispatcher
- Helper
- View
- View helper

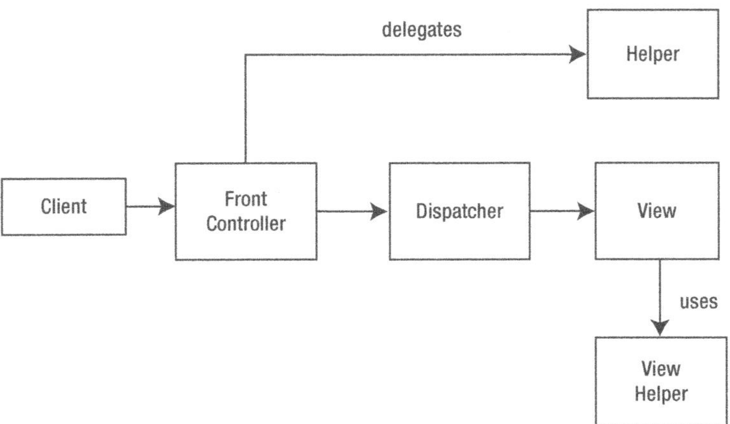

Figure 3-17. Service to Worker class diagram

Front Controller

The front controller does the following:

- Centralizes request processing
- Delegates to the view using the dispatcher
- Uses a view helper to separate the business logic concerns with the presentation logic concerns

Dispatcher

The dispatcher does the following:

- Is responsible for view management and navigation
- Delegates to the view
- Uses a helper to push data into the view

Helper

The helper does the following:

- Helps the view or the controller to complete its processing
- Pushes data into the view

Figure 3-18 illustrates the sequence diagram of the Service to Worker pattern.

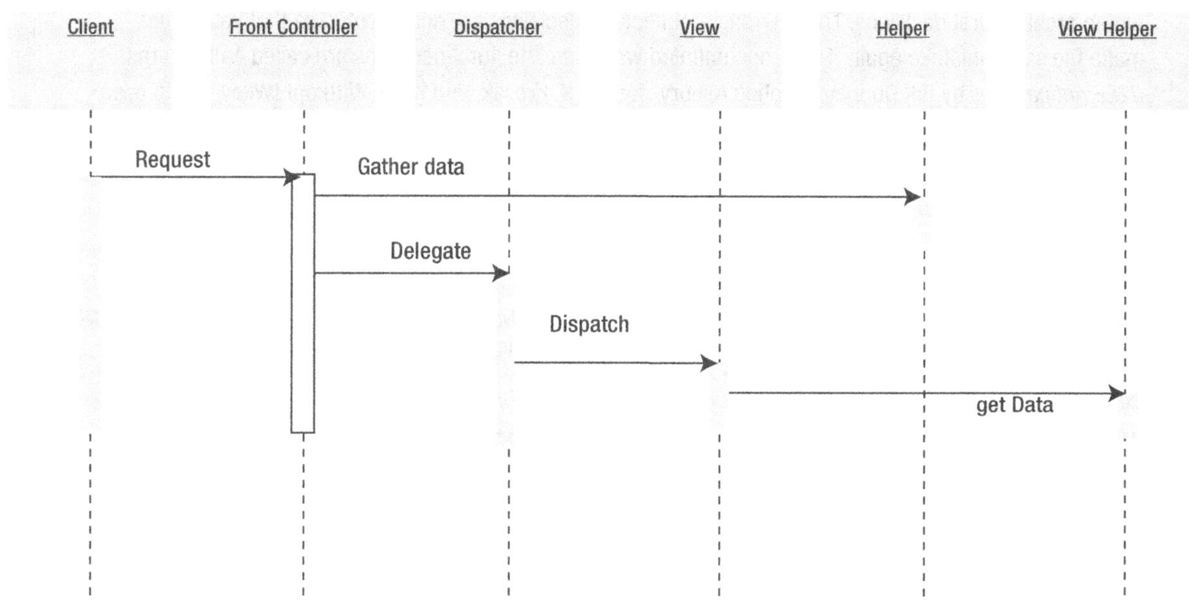

***Figure 3-18.** Service to Worker sequence diagram*

The Service to Worker pattern, like the Dispatcher View pattern, consists of a combination of other patterns from the catalog. Both of these microframework patterns describe the combination of a controller and dispatcher with views and helpers, but the difference is that the Dispatcher View pattern delays content retrieval until dynamic view generation, while the Service to Worker pattern does content retrieval in the front controller.

We just covered all the Java EE web tier patterns. Using these patterns, you can address the architectural domain problem and business problem areas. However, you must also use *OO patterns* to address the architectural problem domain. Many design patterns can be applied to attain reusability, maintainability and extensibility. For instance, you can attain this trinity in the web application using OO patterns such as the following:

- Abstract Factory
- Builder
- Decorator
- Façade
- Template Method

Note In spite of applying the Java EE patterns and incremental evolution, some applications fail due to wrong architectural decisions. These wrong architectural decisions are documented so that you do not make the same mistake again. These documented wrong architectural decisions are called Antipatterns. *J2EE Antipatterns* by Bill Dudney, Stephen Asbury, Joseph K. Krozak, and Kevin Wittkopf (Wiley, 2003) is an excellent resource for Antipatterns.

Java Web Frameworks

You learned that MVC and the Java EE web tier patterns together facilitate the architectural foundation for building reusable, maintainable, and extensible web applications. As developers gather more experience, they start discovering generic objects that can be used over and over, and patterns begin to emerge. Once you have a collection of such generic objects, a framework begins to emerge. A *framework* is a collection of generic objects and other supporting classes that provide the infrastructure for application development. Frameworks are, essentially, a collection of design patterns guarded by the basic framework principles discussed next. A Java framework uses two types of patterns.

- OO patterns
- Java EE patterns

A framework uses OO patterns for its own construction to address the *architectural problem domain*, such as extensibility, maintainability, reusability, performance, and scalability. Both OO patterns and Java EE patterns address the *business problem domain areas*, such as processing requests, authentication, validation, session management, and view management to name a few. .Frameworks address these two major architectural and business problem areas by providing patterns based generic objects and supporting classes, closely guarded by the following key principles:

- *Configurability*: Configurability is the ability of the framework to be able to use the metadata to alter the behavior of the framework.
- *Inversion of control*: In traditional programming style, the problem domain code controls the flow of the application execution. Inversion of control refers to the technique where reusable code controls the execution of the problem domain code, thus controlling the flow of the application execution.
- *Loose coupling*: This principle refers to the independence of the collaborating classes in the framework with which each collaborating class can be altered without influencing the other collaborating class.
- *Separation of concerns*: This principle refers to the need to classify the problem domain areas and deal with them in an isolated manner so that the concerns of one problem area do not influence the concerns of another problem area. The multitiered Java EE architecture we saw in Chapter 1 is driven by the principle of the separation of concerns.
- *Automating common functionalities*: A framework provides mechanisms for automated solutions to the mundane functionalities of the domain.

Why Use a Framework?

While Java EE does a great job of standardizing the enterprise infrastructure and providing an application model, there are few major problems associated with it.

- Interacting directly with the Java EE components often results in massive boilerplate code and even code redundancy.
- You have to write code for dealing with common business domain problems.
- You have to write code for solving architectural domain problems.

You could roll your own framework to address the problems associated with building Java EE based web applications using OO patterns and Java EE patterns. But writing an in-house framework entails efforts that are orthogonal to the business goals of the application; in addition, the in-house framework is unlikely to be upgraded, and the new versions of the in-house framework will never see the sun, unlike mainstream frameworks that continuously evolve instead of falling into architectural entropy. With that in mind, it's time to look at some of the available JVM-based web frameworks (see Table 3-25). This table is far from exhaustive; a myriad of frameworks are available, but this book will cover the most successful JVM-based web frameworks listed in the table.

Table 3-25. JVM-Based Web Frameworks

Web Frameworks	Category	Language	Download From
Struts 2	Request-based framework	Java	`http://struts.apache.org/download.cgi#struts2314`
Spring Web MVC	Request-based framework	Java	`www.springsource.org/spring-community-download`
JSF 2	Component-based framework	Java	`www.oracle.com/technetwork/java/javaee/downloads/index.html`
Grails 2	Rapid web development framework	Groovy	`www.grails.org/download`
Play 2	Rapid web development framework	Java and Scala	`www.playframework.com/download`

All the web frameworks listed in Table 3-25 follow the MVC Model-2 architecture, the basic architectural pattern you learned about in Chapter 2. In a typical web application, there are several tasks that you want to do for every incoming request, such as encryption. A single controller for the web application lets you centralize all the tasks that the controller has to perform in a web application, such as the following:

- Centralizing the logic for dispatching requests to views
- Checking whether the user requesting an operation has valid authorization

As the MVC-based web application grows larger with more and more views to display, the controller in the MVC-application model becomes a procedural object that takes too many decisions to render those views. This problem can be alleviated by using the front controller and configuration metadata, instead of using pure MVC architecture. This solution is illustrated in Figure 3-19.

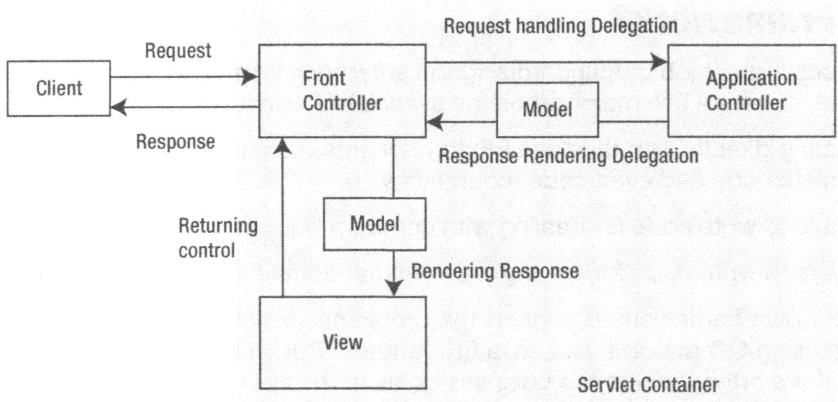

***Figure 3-19.** MVC with front controller*

When the HTTP request arrives from the client, the front controller looks up in the configuration metadata file to decide on the right application controller that should handle theHTTP request. The application controller consists ofthe business logic invocations and presentation logic controls for the HTTP request.The difference between using pure MVC and the Front Controller pattern with MVC is that the front controller servlet looks up the configuration metadata to figure out the application controller that handles the HTTP request processing instead of itself deciding to call specific HTTP request handler objects.

In essence, this is the pattern that is common to many leading web frameworks. For instance, Struts 2 and Spring Web MVC are front controller–based MVC frameworks that delegate the control to the application controller using configuration metadata stored in, for example , an XML file. In Struts 2, the `ServletFilter` is a manifestation of the front controller in Figure 3-19. In JSF 2, it's `FacesServlet`; in Spring Web MVC, it's `DispatcherServlet`; and in Grails 2, it's the subclass of `DispatcherServlet`.

This concludes the chapter. From the next chapter onwards, this book will navigate through the labyrinth of Web frameworks that capitalize on the strengths of Java EE and JVM.

Summary

This chapter focused on evolving the technologies and tools used in a Java EE project. The chapter introduced you to the common problems associated with developing a web application and showed how these problems can be solved and how web applications can be made reusable, maintainable, and extensible by using tools (such as unified EL) available with Java EE.

EL and JSTL are two picture-perfect implementations of the theory of the separation of business and view concerns, and they can be used to build reusable, easy-to-maintain, function-rich web applications. This chapter also introduced you to the Java EE web tier patterns and how these JavaEE patterns provide solutions to the recurring problems in a particular context. Then the chapter showed how frameworks address architectural and business problem areas by providing patterns-based generic objects and supporting classes. Finally, the chapter showed how web frameworks relinquish you from using Java EE design patterns by providing you out-of-the-box best-practice solutions.

Chapter 4

Building a Web Application Using Struts 2

A wounded deer leaps the highest.

—Emily Dickinson

The Struts framework is an old living tree whose ring patterns tell the story of the legacy Java web forests. Struts, released in June 2001, pioneered an essential evolution of the Model-2 development model to address the vicissitudes of web development. You can see Struts' DNA assimilated in many other architecturally diverse action-based frameworks that evolved to address Model-2 development. Struts gave birth to the Tiles framework, which can now be used with a myriad of web frameworks.

The growth in Struts' popularity began to lose momentum because of the ever-increasing complexities of web applications and because of the competition from other evolving web frameworks. The WebWork framework that was built on classic Struts later unified with it to create the Struts 2 framework. Struts 2 is a complete rewrite of the architecture of classic Struts, aimed at addressing the aforementioned needs. Struts 2 provides the architectural foundations for web applications, provides architectural mechanisms to automate recurring tasks and to separate cross-cutting concerns, and saves developers from maintaining a plethora of configuration code by means of convention over configuration.

One chapter is not enough to demonstrate the full capabilities of any framework, so my intention here is to demonstrate the fundamentals of Struts 2 web framework. Beginning with this chapter and through the subsequent chapters, you will progressively learn how modern web frameworks provide architectural foundations centered on Java EE web tier patterns.

Struts 2 Framework Overview

Table 4-1 describes the key features of the Struts 2 framework.

Table 4-1. Key Features of the Struts 2 Framework

Features	Description
Ajax support	Struts 2 integrates Ajax support. Besides out-of-the-box Ajax, Struts 2 also supports a myriad of Ajax-centric plug-ins.
Convention over configuration	Struts 2 adheres to the principle of convention over configuration and eliminates unnecessary configuration.
Declarative architecture using annotations	Struts 2's declarative architecture using annotations reduces XML configuration and keeps the configuration closer to the action class.
Data conversion	Struts 2 provides automatic type conversion of string-based form field values to objects or primitivetypes, removing the need to provide conversion code in the action class.
Dependency injection	Struts 2 uses dependency injection for the action to collaborate with the components it needs.
Extensibility	Struts 2 is extensible, in that the classes in the framework are interface based.
Plug-in architecture	The core Struts 2behavior can be enhanced with plug-ins. You can find a number of plug-ins available for Struts 2 here: `https://cwiki.apache.org/S2PLUGINS/home.html`
POJO forms and actions	Unlike classic Struts that used ActionForms, in Struts 2 you can use any POJO to receive the form input. And any POJO can work as an action.
View technologies	Struts 2supports multiple views such as JSP, FreeMarker, Velocity, XSLT, and so on.

Before diving into Struts 2, it is worthwhile to understand the architecture of classic Struts (hereafter referred to as Struts). Struts is an MVC-based framework. The central component of a Struts framework is the `ActionServlet`, which implements the Front Controller web-tier Java EE pattern. Figure 4-1 illustrates the architecture of Struts.

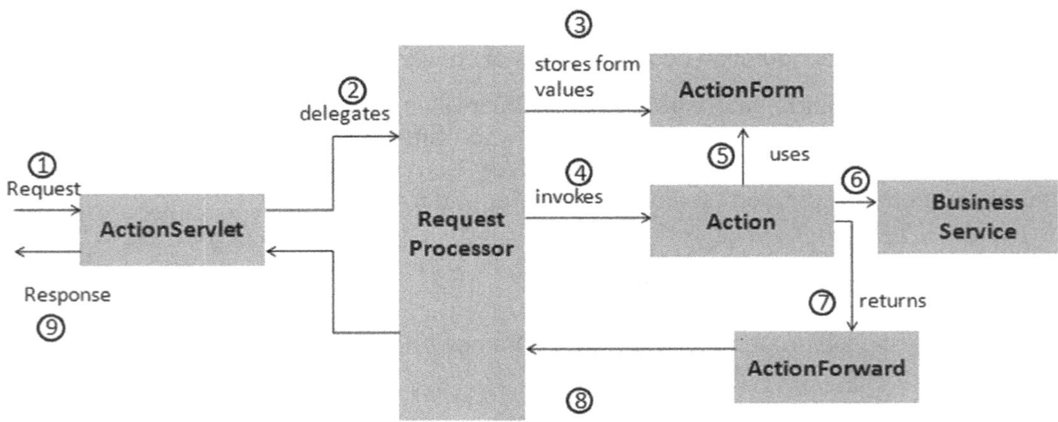

Figure 4-1. Architecture of the Struts framework

The sequence of events in Struts is as follows:

1. The `ActionServlet` delegates request processing to a `RequestProcessor`.
2. The `RequestProcessor` processes the request and stores the form values in the `ActionForm`.
3. The `RequestProcessor` then invokes the `Action` class.
4. The `Action` class accesses the `ActionForm` to retrieve the form values.
5. The `Action` class invokes the call to the service layer.
6. The `Action` class returns the `ActionForward`, which is used to encapsulate the response view.

Struts 2, however, is different from Struts. Unlike Struts, which follows a push-MVC architecture where data is expected to be present in the page or scope, Struts 2is a pull-MVC architecture; that is, the data can be pulled from the `Action`. Table 4-2 shows a one-to-one mapping of the Struts and Struts 2 framework elements.

***Table 4-2.** One-to-One Mapping of Struts and Struts 2Framework Elements*

Struts Framework Elements	Struts 2 Framework Elements
`ActionServlet`	Servlet filter
`RequestProcessor`	Interceptor
`Action`	`Action`
`ActionForm`	Action or POJOs
`ActionForward`	`Result`

> **Note** You can find a comprehensive list of similarities and differences between Struts and Struts 2 at `http://struts.apache.org/release/2.3.x/docs/comparing-struts-1-and-2.html`.

Figure 4-2 illustrates the key elements of Struts 2 that provide a cleaner implementation of MVC.

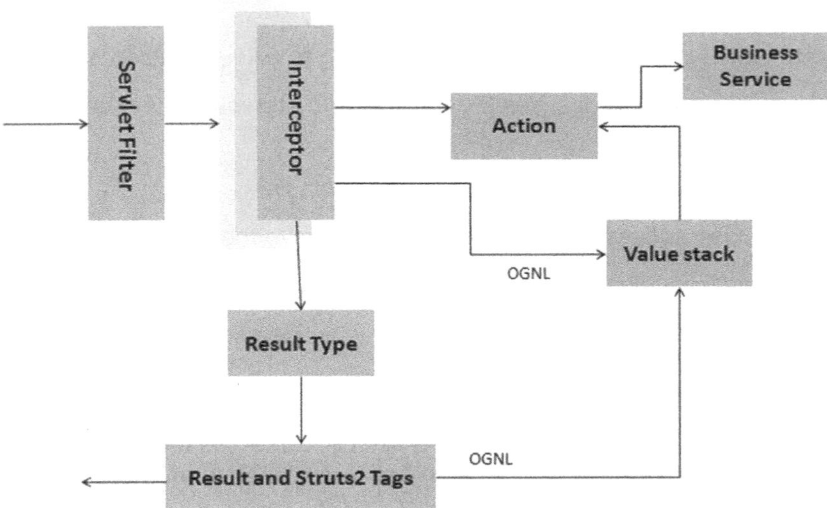

Figure 4-2. Architecture of Struts 2

As you can see from Figure 4-2, Struts 2 is also an MVC-based framework that implements the Front Controller pattern. The sequence of events in Struts 2 framework is as follows:

1. The request is mapped to the configuration metadata.
2. The request passes through a stack of interceptors that provide preprocessing and postprocessing for the request and cross-cutting features.
3. The `Action` and the method in the `Action` that provides the logic to process this request is invoked.
4. The `Result` is invoked to render the response.
5. The response is returned to the user.

The key elements of Struts 2 illustrated in Figure 4-2 are discussed next.

Action

Actions are the core of the action-oriented Struts 2 framework because they provide the necessary logic for request processing. Actions are not required to implement any interface or extend any class, and actions can be POJOs. Listing 4-1 illustrates the action called `HelloWorldAction`.

Listing 4-1. An Action as a POJO

```
public class HelloWorldAction{
//...
public String execute() {
return "success";
}
}
```

This action class is configured in the struts.xml file, as illustrated in Listing 4-2.

Listing 4-2. Configuring the Action Class in struts.xml

```
<package name="helloWorld" " extends="struts-default" namespace="/ >

<action name="hello" class=" HelloWorldAction">
<result name="success"> /hello.jsp</result>
</action>

<package>
```

The action mapping in Listing 4-2 uses the name attribute to define the name of the action you can use to access this action class and uses the result tag to define which result page should be returned to the user. Now you can access the action via an .action extension.

```
http://localhost:8080/helloWorldExample//hello.action
```

Even though you can use POJO actions, Struts 2 provides two action helpers that can be used: the Action interface and the ActionSupport class.

Action Interface

Struts 2 comes with an optional Action interface, as illustrated in Listing 4-3.

Listing 4-3. Action Interface

```
package com.opensymphony.xwork2;

public interface Action {
public static final String ERROR = "error";
public static final String INPUT = "input";
public static final String LOGIN = "login";
public static final String NONE = "none";
public static final String SUCCESS = "success";

public String execute();
}
```

This interface provides the common string-based return values as constants and the default execute() method that should be implemented by the implementing classes.

The action class that implements this interface can use the constant value directly, as illustrated in Listing 4-4.

Listing 4-4. Using the Action Interface

```
import com.opensymphony.xwork2.Action;
public class HelloWorldAction implements Action{
//..
public String execute() {
return SUCCESS;
}
}
```

ActionSupport Class

The ActionSupport class implements the Action interface and provides an implementation of the execute() method that returns the SUCCESS value. The ActionSupport class also implements some interfaces that provide support for validation, localization, and internationalization, as illustrated in the code fragment of the ActionSupport class in Listing 4-5.

Listing 4-5. ActionSupportClass

```
public class ActionSupport implements Action, Validateable, ValidationAware,TextProvider,
LocaleProvider, Serializable {
...
public String execute(){
return SUCCESS;
}
}
```

Listing 4-6 shows the code fragment through which the ActionSupport class can be used to provide validation.

Listing 4-6. Using ActionSupport

```
import com.opensymphony.xwork2.ActionSupport;

public class LoginAction extends ActionSupport{
private String username;
private String password;
public String getPassword() {
return password;
}
public void setPassword(String password) {
this.password = password;
}

public String getUsername() {
return username;
}

public void setUsername(String username) {
this.username = username;
}
```

```
//getters and setters
// ...
public String execute() {
return "SUCCESS";
}

public void validate(){
if("".equals(getUsername())){
addFieldError("username", getText("username.required"));
}
if("".equals(getPassword())){
addFieldError("password", getText("password.required"));
}
}
}
```

Interceptors

Interceptors promote the separation of concerns by separating the implementation of the cross-cutting concerns from the action. Struts 2 comes with a set of prebuilt interceptors and interceptor stacks that you can use out of the box. Listing 4-7 illustrates the declaration of an action that belongs to a package that extends the `struts-default` package, which contains the default set of interceptors.

***Listing 4-7.** Declaring an Action*

```
<package name="default" namespace="/" extends="struts-default">
<action name="helloAction"
class="HelloWorldAction" >
<result name="success">/hello.jsp</result>
</action>
</package>
```

When you extend your package from the `struts-default` package, by default the `defaultStack` will be used for all the actions in your package. The `defaultStack` is configured in the `struts-default.xml` file, and it provides all the core Struts 2 functionality. The `struts-default.xml` file is located in the `struts 2-core.jar` file. To map other interceptors to an action, you can use the `interceptor-ref` element, as illustrated in Listing 4-8.

***Listing 4-8.** Mapping Interceptors to the Action*

```
<package name="default" namespace="/" extends="struts-default">
<action name="helloAction"
class="HelloWorldAction" >
<interceptor-ref name="logger"/>
<result name="success">/hellot.jsp</result>
</action>
</package>
```

In Listing 4-8, the action mapping maps the logger interceptors to the HelloWorldAction action class via the interceptor-ref element. Since the HelloWorldAction is declared its own interceptors, it loses the default set of interceptors, and you have to explicitly declare the defaultStack in order to use it, as illustrated in Listing 4-9.

Listing 4-9. Declaring a Default Stack

```
<package name="default" namespace="/" extends="struts-default">
<action name="helloAction"
class="HelloWorldAction" >
<interceptor-ref name="logger"/>
<interceptor-ref name="defaultStack"/>
<result name="success">/hello.jsp</result>
</action>
</package>
```

ValueStack and OGNL

The Object-Graph Navigation Language (OGNL[1]) is a powerful expression language that is used to set and get properties from JavaBeans and to invoke methods from Java classes. It also helps in data transfer and type conversion. OGNL is similar to EL and JSTL, which evaluate expressions and navigate object graphs using dot notation. As you saw in Figure 4-2, OGNL and the ValueStack, though not part of MVC, are at the core of the Struts 2 framework. All the MVC components interact with ValueStack to provide contextual data. These components access ValueStack using OGNL syntax, and OGNL and ValueStack work together in Struts 2 to handle a request. Specifically, when a request is sent to the Struts 2 application, a ValueStack object is created for that request, and the references to all the objects that are created to serve that request as well as scope attributes are maintained in the ValueStack. All these objects are available to the view through OGNL. You will not find OGNL difficult to use because it is similar to EL and JSTL (which are covered in Chapter 3). Listing 4-10 illustrates how OGNL looks. Notice that OGNL uses #, unlike JSP EL, which uses $.

Listing 4-10. Using OGNL

```
<s:property value="#book.bookTitle" />
```

ResultType and Result

In Struts 2, the rendering of the response consists of the result type and the result. The result type provides the implementation details for the type of view that is returned to the user. Each method on an action returns a result, which includes specifying the result type. If no result type is specified, then the default result type is used, which forwards to a JSP page, as illustrated in Listing 4-11.

Listing 4-11. Default Result Type

```
<result name="success">
   /hello.jsp
</result>
```

---

[1]http://commons.apache.org/proper/commons-ognl/

Struts 2 comes with a number of predefined result types. Struts allows you to use other view technologies to present the results including Velocity, FreeMarker, and Tiles, as illustrated in Listing 4-12.

Listing 4-12. Declaring Tiles as the Result Type

```
<action name="login" class="com.apress.bookstore.action.LoginAction">
<result name="success" type="tiles">home</result>
<result name="error" type="tiles">login</result>
</action>
```

Struts 2 Tags

The Struts 2 framework provides a high-level and portable tag API that you can use with JSP. You will learn how the tags work and how to use OGNL to reference values on the ValueStack in the sections that follow. Table 4-3 describes the different categories of Struts 2 tag libraries.

Table 4-3. Struts 2Tags

Struts 2 Tags	Description
Ajax tags	Struts 2provides Ajax support by means of Ajax tags.
Control tags	These are tags that provide ways to manipulate collections of elements.
Data tags	These are tags that render data from the action, internationalized text, and URLs.
Form tags	These are tags that provide wrappers for HTML form tags, as well as additional widgets such as a date picker.
Non form UI tags	The tags in this group are used in forms but are not directly form entry elements. They include error message displays, tabbed panels, and tree views.

Note You can find the full list of Struts 2 tags in the online documentation at `http://struts.apache.org/release/2.3.x/docs/tag-reference.html`.

Getting Started with Struts 2

In this section, you will develop a HelloWorld Struts 2 application. You will use the build and dependency management tool called Maven.[2] Maven is a command-line tool that is used to build and package projects and to manage dependencies. It makes life easier for developers working across multiple projects by providing the same directory structure across multiple projects.

[2]`http://maven.apache.org/`

The dependencies, explicitly configured and transitive, described in the Maven configuration file (pom.xml) will be accessed from a local repository or downloaded to the local repository during the build process. This feature allows developers to create new projects without creating the common directory structure, creating the configuration files, and coding default classes and tests from scratch. The benefit of using Maven for runtime dependencies is that you don't need to remember and search for required dependencies manually. You will use Maven 4 to import Struts 2 runtime dependencies. Maven 4 is integrated with Eclipse-kepler, as mentioned in Chapter 1. So, you do not have to install the Maven plug-in for Eclipse. To create the Maven project, click New ➤ Other, as illustrated in Figure 4-3.

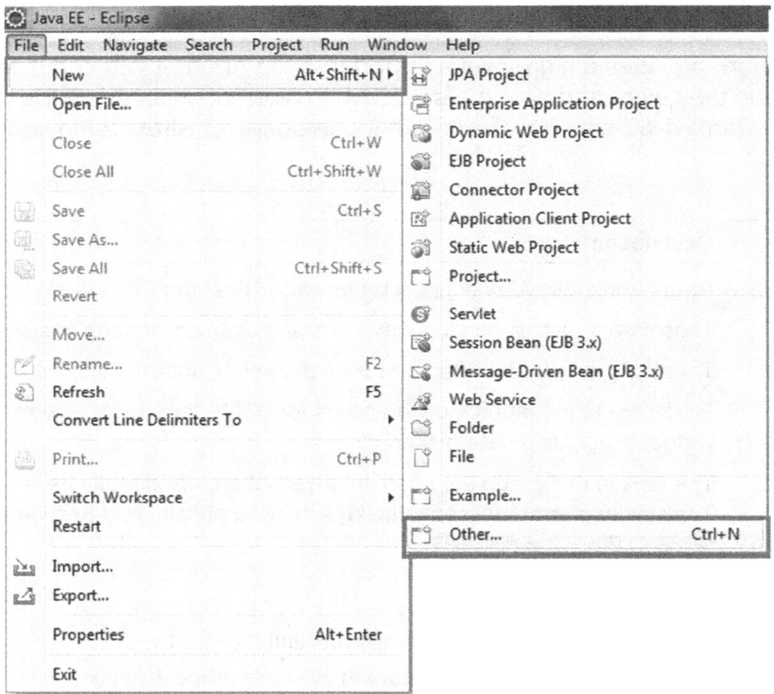

Figure 4-3. Selecting a Maven project

Select Maven Project in the wizard, as illustrated in Figure 4-4.

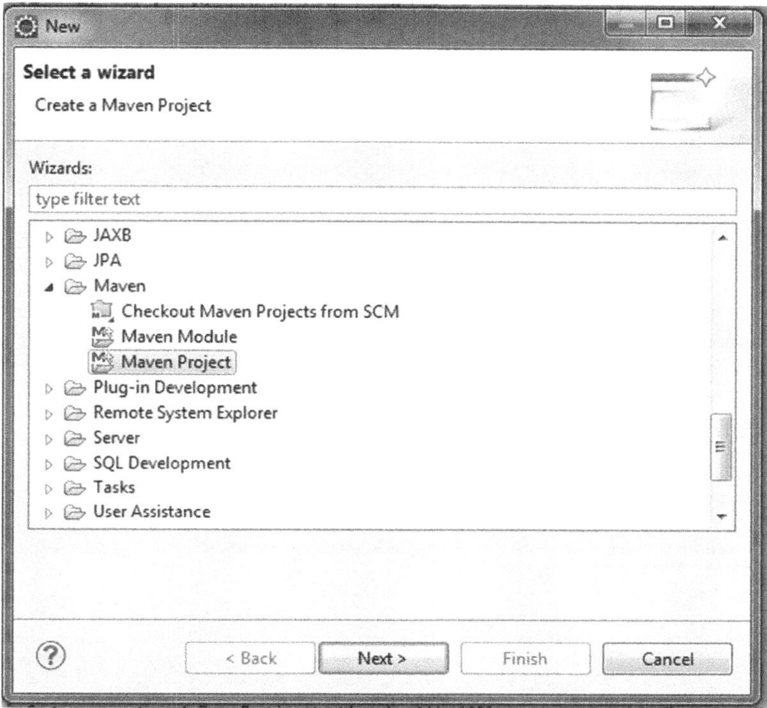

Figure 4-4. Selecting the option Maven Project

Click Next and configure the options as illustrated in Figure 4-5.

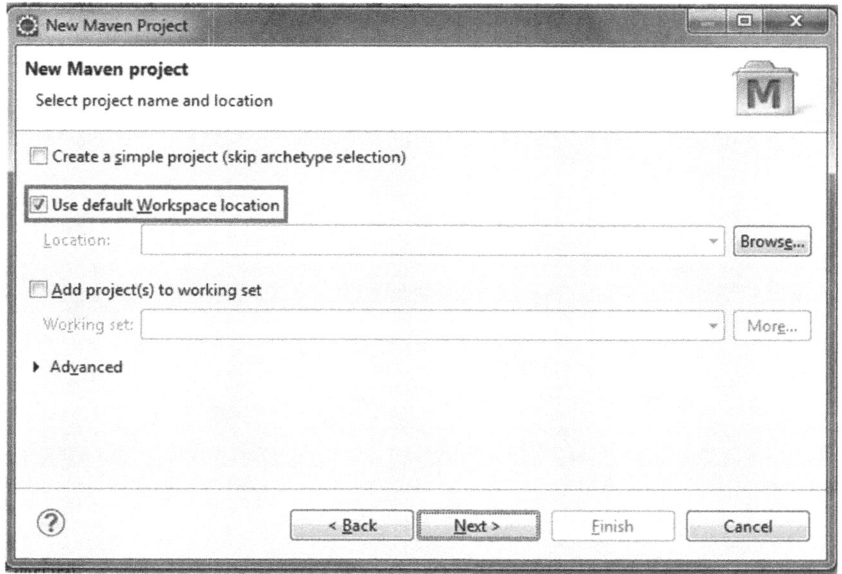

Figure 4-5. Configuring a Maven project

Click Next and as illustrated in Figure 4-6 select Catalog, GroupId, and ArtifactId.

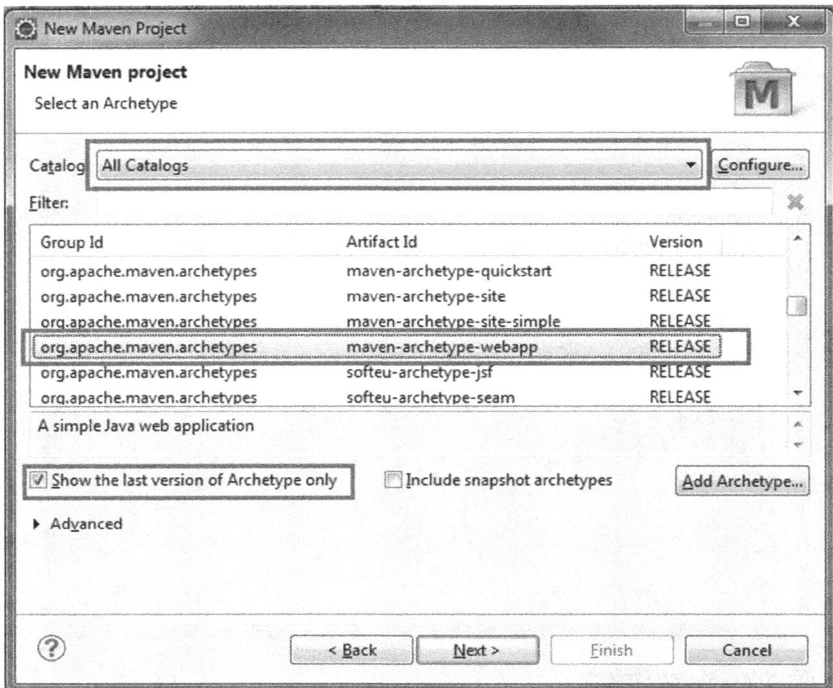

Figure 4-6. Selecting archetypes

Click Next and enter the group ID, artifact ID, and package details, as illustrated in Figure 4-7.

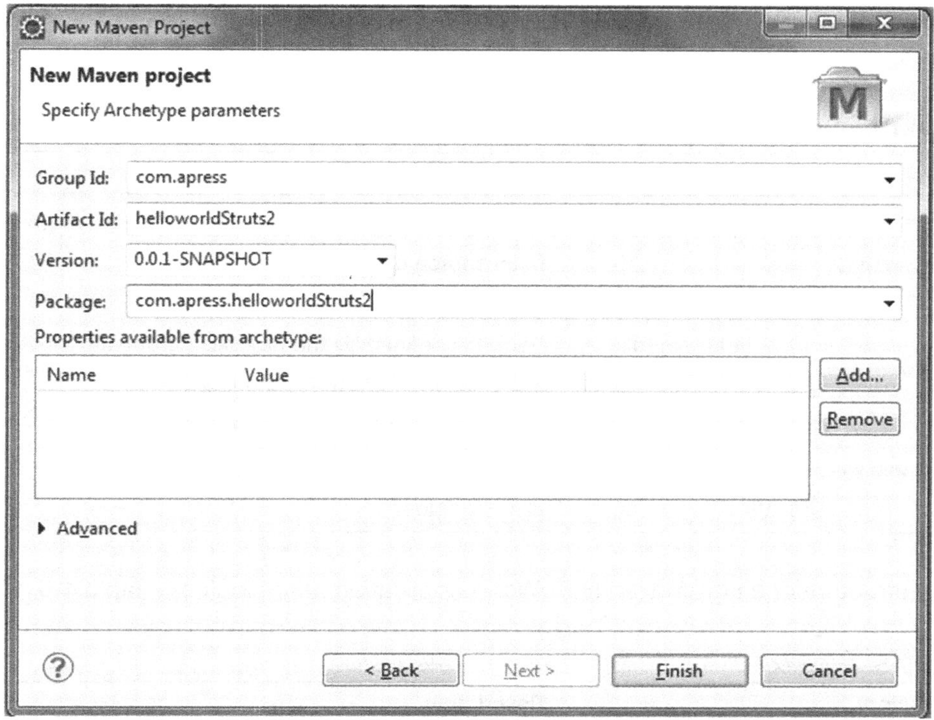

Figure 4-7. Specifying archetype parameters

Click Finish. The project with the name described in the Artifact Id field in Figure 4-7 is created. Figure 4-8 shows the directory structure of the project created.

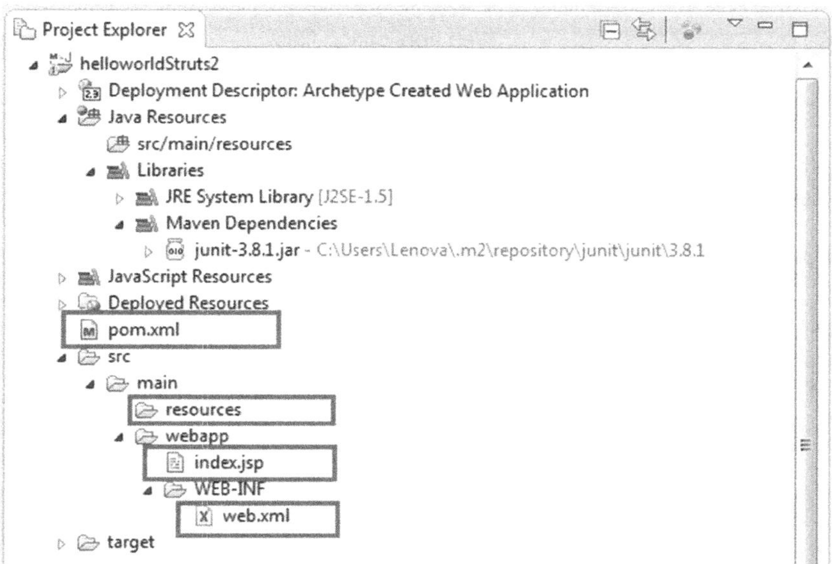

Figure 4-8. Directory structure of the created project

The directory structure illustrated in Figure 4-8 follows the normal Maven directory structure. Table 4-4 describes the directory structure of the HelloWorld application.

Table 4-4. Directory Structure of a Maven-Based Application

Directory	Description
Src	All source
: - main	Main source directory
: : - java	Java source
: : - helloworld	Package defined by the groupID parameter
: : - action	The package from the archetype
: :- resources	Resources(configuration, properties, and so on)
: - webapp	Web application files
: : - WEB-INF	WEB-INF folder

The directory structure of a non-Maven HelloWorld application might look like Table 4-5.

Table 4-5. Directory Structure of a Non-Maven-Based Application

Directory	Description
Src	All source
: - helloworld	Helloworld package
: - action	Action package
- struts.xml	Resources(configuration, properties, and so on)
Web	Web application files
: - WEB-INF	WEB-INF folder

You need to add the `struts 2-core` dependency to the generated `pom.xml` file of the HelloWorld application. Listing 4-13 shows the code fragment to add to `pom.xml`.

Listing 4-13. struts 2-core Dependency

```
<dependency>
<groupId>org.apache.struts</groupId>
<artifactId>struts 2-core</artifactId>
<version>2.3.15.1</version>
<type>jar</type>
<scope>compile</scope>
</dependency>
```

Your pom.xml file will look like Listing 4-14.

Listing 4-14. pom.xml

```
<project xmlns="http://maven.apache.org/POM/4.0.0"
xmlns:xsi="http://www.w3.org/2001/XMLSchema-instance"
 xsi:schemaLocation="http://maven.apache.org/POM/4.0.0 http://maven.apache.org/maven-v4_0_0.xsd">
<modelVersion>4.0.0</modelVersion>
<groupId>com.apress</groupId>
<artifactId>helloworldStruts2</artifactId>
<packaging>war</packaging>
<version>0.0.1-SNAPSHOT</version>
<name>helloworldStruts2Maven Webapp</name>
<url>http://maven.apache.org</url>
<dependencies>
<dependency>
<groupId>junit</groupId>
<artifactId>junit</artifactId>
<version>3.8.1</version>
<scope>test</scope>
</dependency>
<dependency>
<groupId>org.apache.struts</groupId>
<artifactId>struts2-core</artifactId>
<version>2.3.15.1</version>
<type>jar</type>
<scope>compile</scope>
</dependency>
</dependencies>
<build>
<finalName>helloworldStruts2</finalName>
</build>
              </project>
```

> **Note** You can find the list of dependencies of Struts 2 at
> http://struts.apache.org/development/2.x/struts2-core/dependencies.html.

Listing 4-15 shows the empty deployment descriptor created in the project.

Listing 4-15. web.xml

```
<!DOCTYPE web-app PUBLIC
"-//Sun Microsystems, Inc.//DTD Web Application 2.3//EN"
 "http://java.sun.com/dtd/web-app_2_3.dtd" >
<web-app>
<display-name>Archetype Created Web Application</display-name>
</web-app>
```

You need to configure the servlet filter in the deployment descriptor, as illustrated in Listing 4-16.

Listing 4-16. web.xml

```
1.<!DOCTYPE web-app PUBLIC
2. "-//Sun Microsystems, Inc.//DTD Web Application 2.3//EN"
3. "http://java.sun.com/dtd/web-app_2_3.dtd" >
4.
5.<web-app>
6.<display-name>Hello World Struts2 Web App</display-name>
7.<filter>
8.<filter-name>struts2</filter-name>
9.<filter-class>org.apache.struts2.dispatcher.ng.filter.StrutsPrepareAndExecuteFilter</filter-class>
10.</filter>
11.
12.<filter-mapping>
13.<filter-name>struts2</filter-name>
14.<url-pattern>/*</url-pattern>
15.</filter-mapping>
16.</web-app>
```

- *Lines 7 to 10*: These lines define the `StrutsPrepareAndExecuteFilter` that is used as the servlet filter in Struts 2 to which all URLs are mapped.

> **Note** The `FilterDispatcher` (`org.apache.struts2.dispatcher.FilterDispatcher`) was used in early Struts 2 development, and it has been deprecated since Struts 2.1.3.

Listing 4-17 illustrates the `struts.xml` file.

Listing 4-17. struts.xml

```
1.<?xml version="1.0" encoding="UTF-8"?>
2.<!DOCTYPE struts PUBLIC
3.    "-//Apache Software Foundation//DTD Struts Configuration 2.0//EN"
4.    "http://struts.apache.org/dtds/struts-2.0.dtd">
5.
6.<struts>
7.<constant name="struts.devMode" value="true" />
8.<package name="basicstruts2" extends="struts-default">
9.<action name="index">
10.<result>/index.jsp</result>
11.</action>
12.</package>
13.</struts>
```

- *Lines 9 to 11*: These lines define the `index` action, which renders the result `index.jsp`.

Listing 4-18 illustrates index.jsp.

Listing 4-18. index.jsp

```
<html>
<body>
<h2>Hello World!</h2>
</body>
</html>
```

Deploy the web application to the servlet container Tomcat 7, open a web browser, and access `http://localhost:8080/helloworldStruts2/`, as illustrated in Figure 4-9.

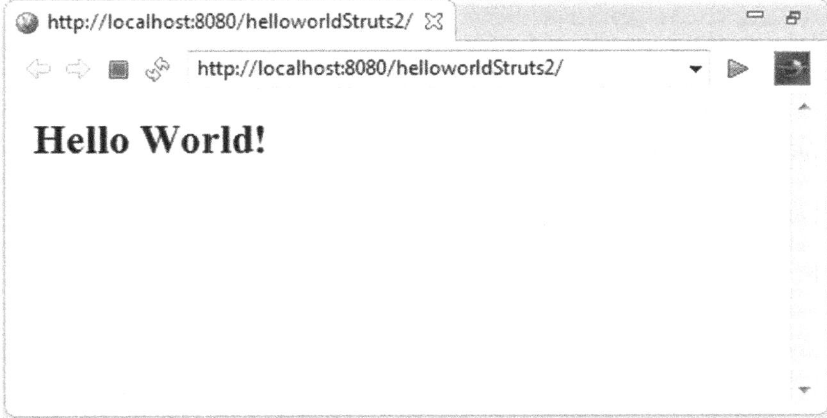

***Figure 4-9.** Running the HelloWorld application*

The HelloWorld application you developed didn't comprise any actions but a single JSP file that was generated when you created the project. The purpose of the HelloWorld application you created was to test the configuration of Struts 2. You will create actions in the following section.

You will create a HelloWorld project that displays a welcome message to the user, as illustrated in Figure 4-10.

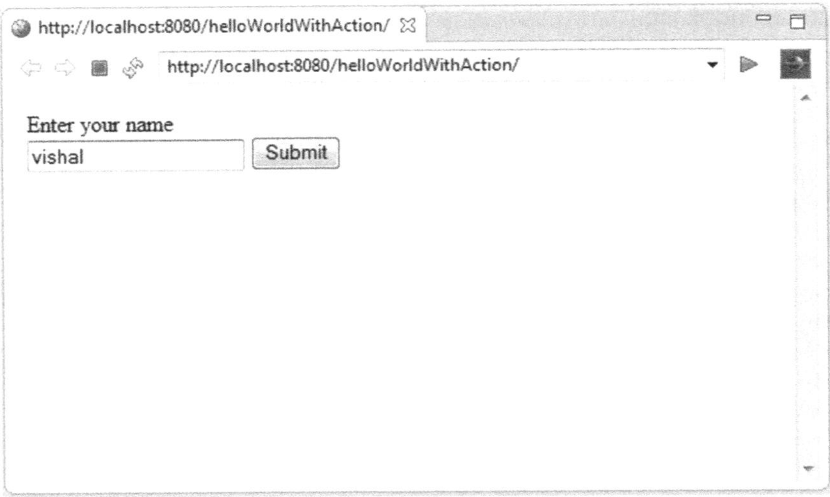

Figure 4-10. *Form of the HelloWorld project*

When you submit an HTML form in a Struts 2 web application, the input is sent to the Java class called `Action`. After the action executes, a result selects a resource to render the response, as illustrated in Figure 4-11.

Figure 4-11. *Greeting the user*

Let's modify the HelloWorld project you created earlier to add an action, the form that accepts a user's input, and the view that greets the user, as illustrated in the directory structure shown in Figure 4-12.

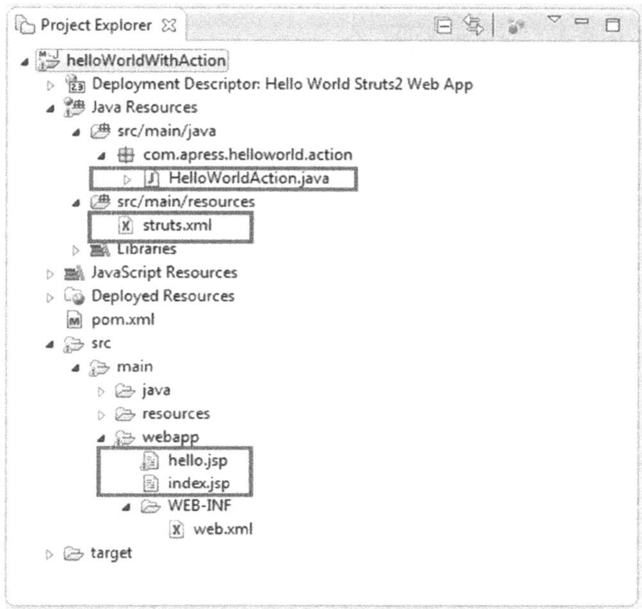

***Figure 4-12.** The directory structure of the project*

Listing 4-19 illustrates the form that allows the user to enter a name and submit it.

***Listing 4-19.** index.jsp*

```
1.<html>
2.<body>
3.
4.<form action="hello">
5.<label for="name">Enter your name</label><br /><input type="text"
6.name="name" /><input type="submit" value="Submit" />
7.</form>
8.</body>
9.</html>
```

- *Line 4*: When the user submits the form, the action name `hello` is sent to the container.

You need a mapping to map the URL to the `HelloWorldAction` controller. The mapping tells the Struts 2 framework which class will respond to the user's action, which method of that class will be executed, and which view will be rendered as the response. Listing 4-20 illustrates this mapping file.

***Listing 4-20.** struts.xml*

```
<?xml version="1.0" encoding="UTF-8"?>
<!DOCTYPE struts PUBLIC
    "-//Apache Software Foundation//DTD Struts Configuration 2.0//EN"
    "http://struts.apache.org/dtds/struts-2.0.dtd">
```

```
6.<struts>
7.<constant name="struts.devMode" value="true" />
8.<package name="basicstruts2" extends="struts-default"
9.namespace="/">
10.
11.<action name="index">
12.<result>/index.jsp</result>
13.</action>
14.
15.<action name="hello" class="com.apress.helloworld.action.HelloWorldAction"
16.method="execute">
17.<result name="success">/hello.jsp</result>
18.</action>
19.</package>
20.</struts>
```

- *Line 15*: This line declares the action mapping for `HelloWorldAction`. `HelloWorldAction` is mapped to the action name `hello`.
- *Line 16*: This line declares that the `execute()` method of the action is to be executed.
- *Line 17*: This line declares that `hello.jsp` is designated as a `success` page and will be rendered as the response.

We need an `Action` class to act as the controller. The `Action` class responds to a user action of submitting the form and sending the `hello` action to the container. Listing 4-21 illustrates `HelloWorldAction`.

***Listing 4-21.** HelloWorldAction.java*

```
1.package com.apress.helloworld.action;
2.
3.public class HelloWorldAction {
4.private String name;
5.
6.public String execute() throws Exception {
7.return "success";
8.}
9.
10.public String getName() {
11.return name;
12.}
13.
14.public void setName(String name) {
15.this.name = name;
16.}
17.}
18.
```

- *Lines 6 to 7*: The Struts 2 framework will create an object of the `HelloWorldAction` class and call the execute method in response to a user's action. And the execute method returns the success string, which is mapped to `hello.jsp` in `struts.xml`.

Listing 4-22 illustrates hello.jsp.

Listing 4-22. hello.jsp

```
1.<%@ page language="java" contentType="text/html; charset=ISO-8859-1"
2.pageEncoding="ISO-8859-1"%>
3.<%@ taglib prefix="s" uri="/struts-tags"%>
4.<html>
5.<head>
6.<title>Hello World</title>
7.</head>
8.<body>
9.Hello
10.<s:property value="name" />
11.</body>
12.</html>
```

- *Line 3*: The taglib directive tells the servlet container that this page will be using the Struts 2 tags.
- *Line 10*: The s:property tag displays the value returned by calling the method getName of the HelloWorldAction class. The getName method returns a String. It is this String returned by getName that will be displayed by the s:property tag.

Now you will learn a different technique of declarative configuration provided by Struts 2: annotations. You can create the new project or modify the project created earlier. Figure 4-13 illustrates the directory structure.

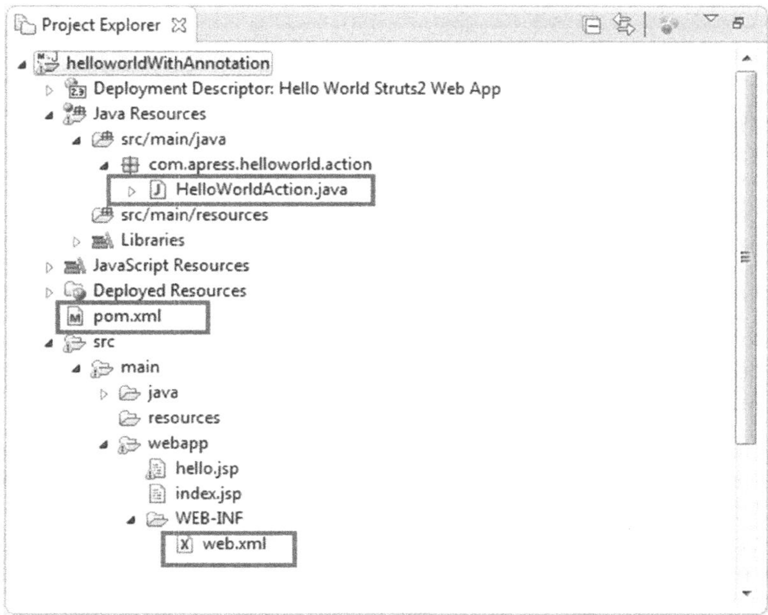

***Figure 4-13.** HelloWorld project using Struts 2 annotations*

To use Struts 2 annotations, you need the plug-in called `struts 2-convention-plugin`. Add the dependency to the `pom.xml` file using the fragment illustrated in Listing 4-23.

Listing 4-23. struts 2-convention-plugin

```
<dependency>
<groupId>org.apache.struts</groupId>
<artifactId>struts2-convention-plugin</artifactId>
<version>2.3.15.1</version>
</dependency>
```

Listing 4-24 illustrates `HelloWorldAction` configured with Struts 2 annotations.

Listing 4-24. HelloWorldAction

```
1.package com.apress.helloworld.action;
2.
3.import org.apache.struts2.convention.annotation.Action;
4.import org.apache.struts2.convention.annotation.Result;
5.
6.@Action(value = "/hello", results = { @Result(name = "success", location = "/hello.jsp") })
7.public class HelloWorldAction {
8.private String name;
9.
10.public String execute() throws Exception {
11.return "success";
12.}
13.
14.public String getName() {
15.return name;
16.}
17.
18.public void setName(String name) {
19.this.name = name;
20.}
21.}
```

- *Line 6*: `@Action` defines the URL of an action. Since the value of the action annotation is `"/hello"`, the action will be invoked for the request URL `"/hello"`.
- *Line 6*: `@Result` defines a result for an action. The result annotation maps the result code to the result page. Here the result code `"success"` is mapped to the result `"/hello.jsp"`.

Listing 4-24 uses action and result annotations just to show you how to use them. You can also use the intelligent defaults provided by the Convention plug-in. If you set the `actionPackages` filter init parameter to a comma-separated list of packages containing action classes in `web.xml`, as illustrated in Listing 4-25, the packages and their subpackages will be scanned. All classes in the designated packages that implement `Action` or the POJO actions that don't implement the `Action` interface and end with `Action` are examined.

Listing 4-25. actionPackages Init Parameter

```
<init-param>
<param-name>actionPackages</param-name>
<param-value>com.apress.helloworld.action</param-value>
</init-param>
```

The Convention plug-in uses the `Action` class name to map the action URL. The Convention plug-in first removes the word `Action` at the end of the class name and then converts the camel-case name to dashes. So, by default `HelloWorldAction` will be invoked for the request URL `hello-world`. But if you want the action to be invoked for a different URL, then you can do this by using the action annotation.

> **Tip** You can find the list of all Struts 2 annotations at `http://struts.apache.org/release/2.3.x/docs/annotations.html`.

In the section that follows, you will develop the bookstore web application using Struts 2.

Bookstore Web Application

In this section, you will progressively develop the bookstore application including the following functionality:

- The login functionality
- Templates
- Integration with the data access layer
- Login via a database
- Selection of categories from a database
- Listing books by category

The complete code for the application is available in the downloadable archive on the Apress website.

The Login Functionality

Figure 4-14 shows the initial login screen.

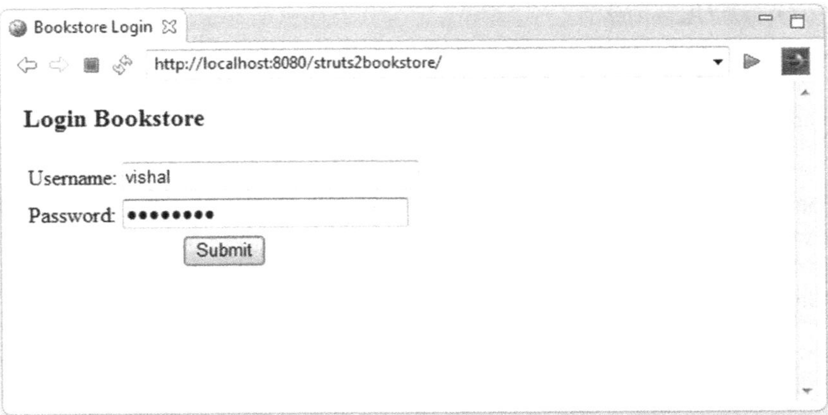

Figure 4-14. Login page of the bookstore application

When the user submits a valid name and password combination, the user will be logged in, and the user's name is displayed as illustrated in Figure 4-15.

Figure 4-15. Login successful

If the user enters an incorrect username or password, an error message will be displayed to the user, as illustrated in Figure 4-16.

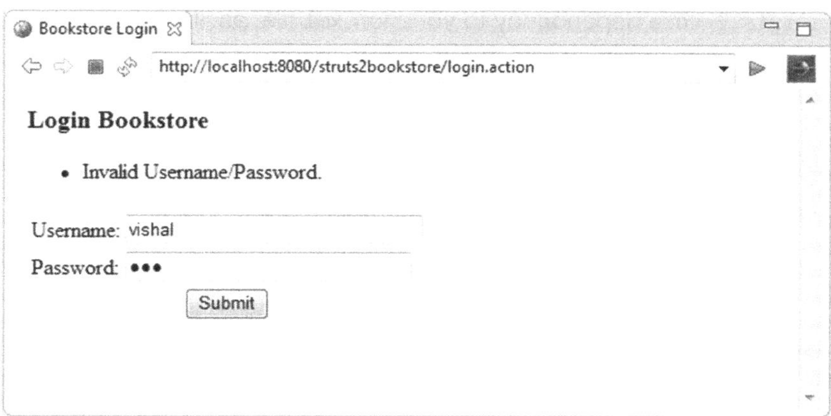

Figure 4-16. Login failed

Figure 4-17 illustrates the directory structure of the application. You can download the source code for the application from the Apress website, and then as you move along with each section, you can refer to the source for imports and other artifacts.

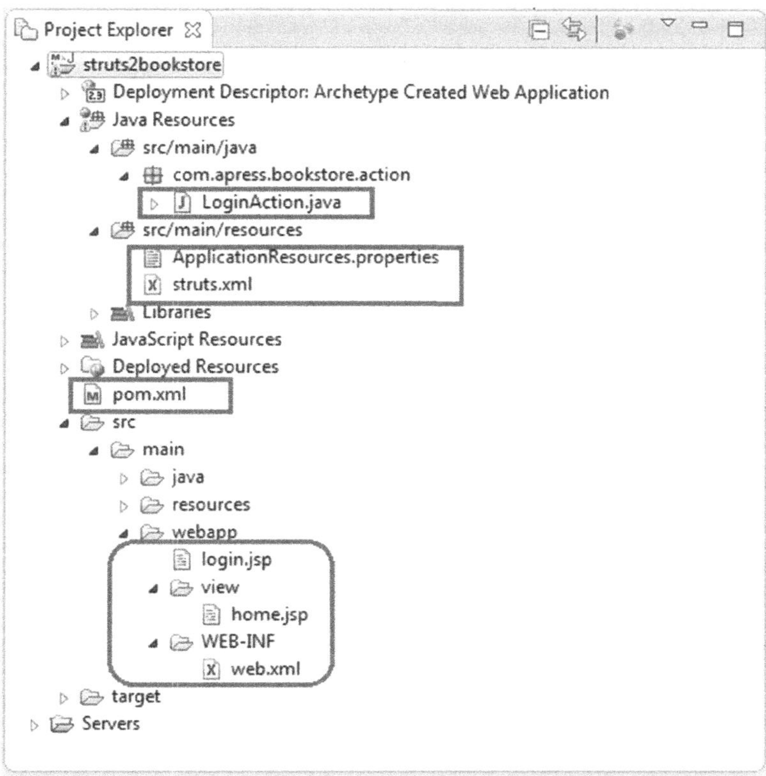

Figure 4-17. Directory structure of the bookstore application

You can add the struts 2-core dependency to your pom.xml file, as illustrated in Listing 4-26.

Listing 4-26. struts 2-core Dependency

```
<dependency>
<groupId>org.apache.struts</groupId>
<artifactId>struts 2-core</artifactId>
<version>2.3.15.1</version>
<type>jar</type>
<scope>compile</scope>
</dependency>
```

You can use the same web.xml file used earlier in the HelloWorld project. Modify the welcome-file-list file, as illustrated in Listing 4-27.

Listing 4-27. Welcome File

```
<welcome-file-list>
<welcome-file>login.jsp</welcome-file>
</welcome-file-list>
```

Listing 4-28 illustrates the login.jsp file.

Listing 4-28. login.jsp

```
1.<%@ page contentType="text/html; charset=UTF-8"%>
2.<%@ taglib prefix="s" uri="/struts-tags"%>
3.<html>
4.<head>
5.<title>Bookstore Login</title>
6.</head>
7.<body>
8.<h3>Login Bookstore</h3>
9.<s:actionerror />
10.<s:form action="login.action" method="post">
11.<s:textfield name="username" key="label.username" size="30" />
12.<s:password name="password" key="label.password" size="30" />
13.<s:submit method="execute" align="center" />
14.</s:form>
15.</body>
16.</html>
```

Listing 4-28 illustrates the usage of several Struts 2 tags. This is a login form that allows the user to input a username and password. In line 10, the name of the action login is sent to the container when the user submits the form. This action name is mapped to LoginAction via struts.xml, as illustrated in Listing 4-29.

Listing 4-29. struts.xml

```
1.<?xml version="1.0" encoding="UTF-8" ?>
2.<!DOCTYPE struts PUBLIC
3."-//Apache Software Foundation//DTD Struts Configuration 2.3//EN"
4."http://struts.apache.org/dtds/struts-2.3.dtd">
5.
6.
7.<struts>
8.<constant name="struts.enable.DynamicMethodInvocation" value="false" />
9.<constant name="struts.devMode" value="true" />
10.<constant name="struts.custom.i18n.resources" value="ApplicationResources" />
11.
12.<package name="default" extends="struts-default" namespace="/">
13.<action name="login" class="com.apress.bookstore.action.LoginAction">
14.<result name="success">view/home.jsp</result>
15.<result name="error">login.jsp</result>
16.</action>
17.</package>
18.</struts>
```

In Listing 4-29, line 13 maps the `LoginAction` class of the `login` name to the URL, and line 14 renders `home.jsp` when the String `success` is returned by the `LoginAction` class. If the `LoginAction` class returns the String `error`, then `login.jsp` is rendered again with the error message.

Listing 4-30 illustrates `LoginAction`.

Listing 4-30. LoginAction.java

```
package com.apress.bookstore.action;
import com.opensymphony.xwork2.ActionSupport;
public class LoginAction extends ActionSupport {
private String username;
private String password;
public String execute() {
if (this.username.equals("vishal") && this.password.equals("password")) {
return "success";
} else {
addActionError(getText("error.login"));
return "error";
}
}
public String getUsername() {
return username;
}
public void setUsername(String username) {
this.username = username;
}

public String getPassword() {
return password;
}

```

```
25.public void setPassword(String password) {
26.this.password = password;
27.}
28.}
```

In lines 7 to 9 of Listing 4-30, the username and password are hard-coded. Later you will see how to authenticate against a database. If the username or password is invalid, the `addActonError` method in line 10 gets the `error.login` message mapped to the `ApplicationResources.properties`, illustrated in Listing 4-31, and returns the String `error`.

Listing 4-31. ApplicationResources.properties

```
label.username= Username
label.password= Password
error.login= Invalid Username/Password
```

Listing 4-32 illustrates `home.jsp`, which is rendered when the `LoginAction` class returns the String `success`.

Listing 4-32. home.jsp

```
<%@ page contentType="text/html; charset=UTF-8"%>
<%@ taglib prefix="s" uri="/struts-tags"%>
<html>
<head>
<title>Home</title>
</head>
<body>
<s:property value="username" />
</body>
</html>
```

Listing 4-32 displays the username using the `s:property` tag when `LoginAction` returns the String `success`.

Developing Templates

In this section, you will see how to integrate the Tiles framework with Struts 2. We will add Tiles support to the HelloWorld Struts application created in the previous section. Tiles is a templating system that reduces code duplication and maintains a consistent look and feel across all the pages of a web application. With Tiles, you define a common layout in a configuration file, and this layout is extended across all the webpages of the web application. This means you can change the look and feel of all the pages of a web application by changing just the template file, instead of changing all the pages. For the bookstore application, you will add a header and menu, as illustrated in Figure 4-18.

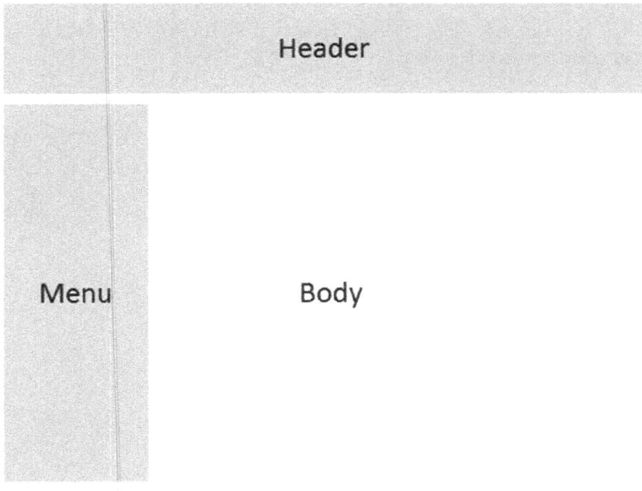

Figure 4-18. Template for the bookstore application

Figure 4-19 illustrates the login screen with the header. When the authentication is successful, the user is logged in, and the home page with the menu bar is rendered, as illustrated in Figure 4-20. If the username or password is invalid, the user remains on the login screen, and an error message is displayed, as illustrated in Figure 4-21.

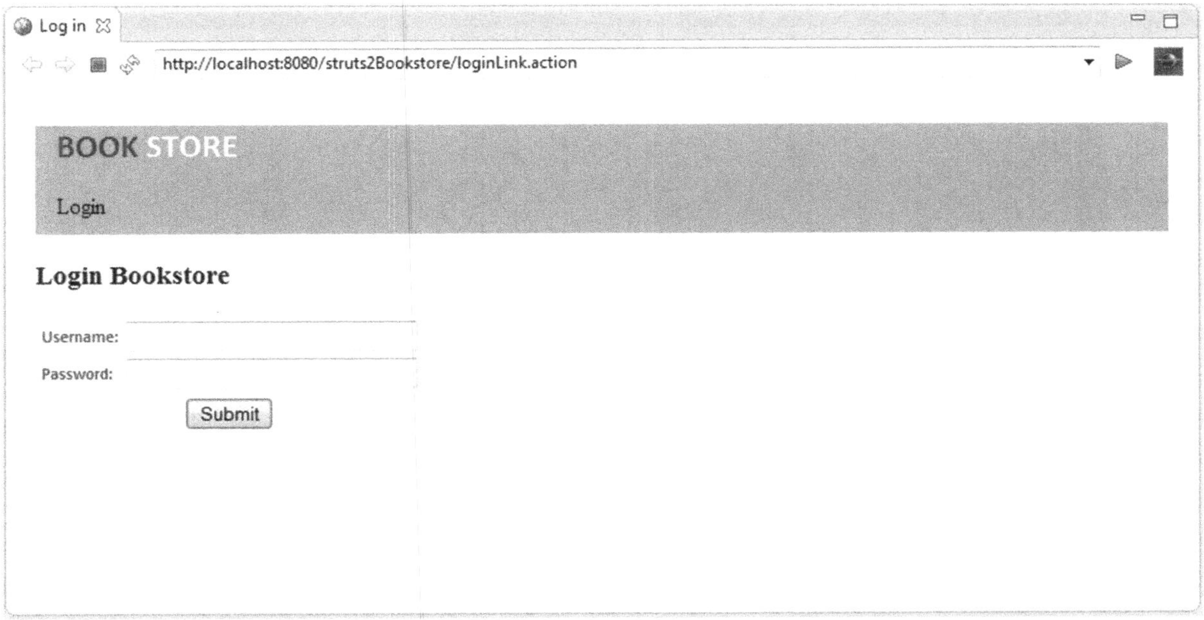

Figure 4-19. Login screen with header

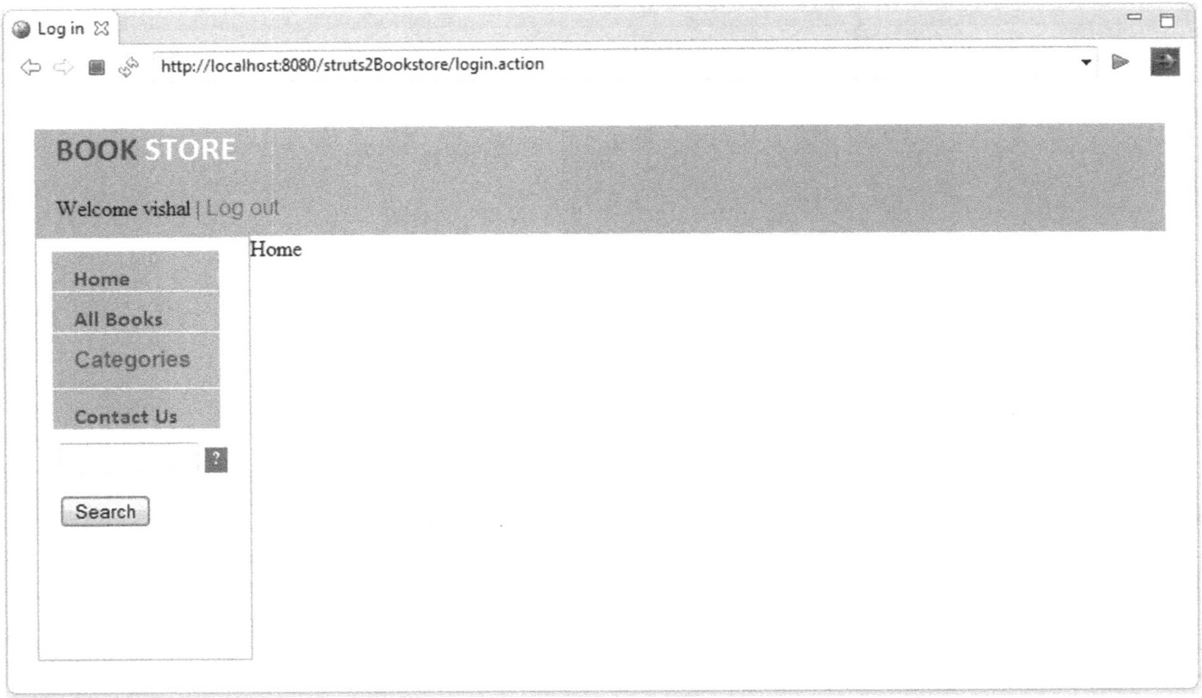

Figure 4-20. Menu displayed on successful login

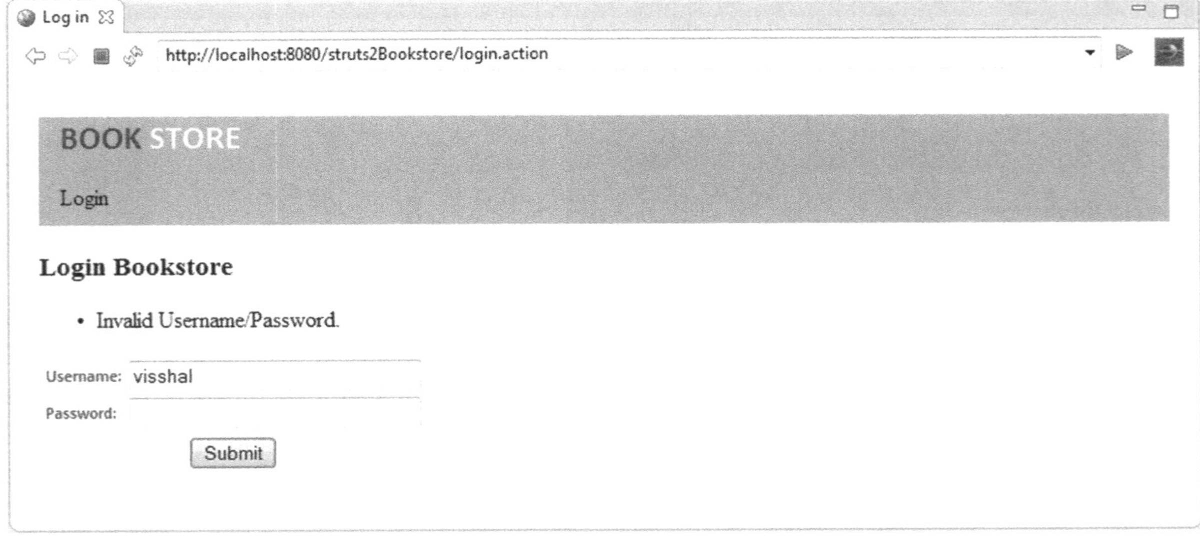

Figure 4-21. Login failed with header

When the user is logged in, the user's name is displayed on the header, and the menu appears, as illustrated in Figure 4-20.

Figure 4-22 illustrates the directory structure with the template files.

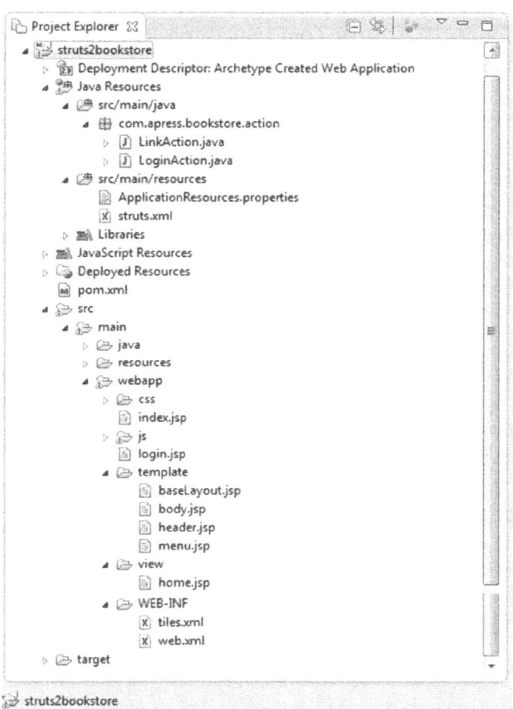

***Figure 4-22.** The directory structure with the template files*

You need to modify the `pom.xml` file with struts 2-tiles3-plugin and slf4j-log4j12, as illustrated in Listing 4-33. These plug-ins are required to integrate Tiles with Struts 2.

***Listing 4-33.** struts-tiles and slf4j-log4j12 Plug-Ins*

```
<dependency>
<groupId>org.apache.struts</groupId>
<artifactId>struts2-tiles3-plugin</artifactId>
<version>2.3.15.1</version>
</dependency>
<dependency>
<groupId>org.slf4j</groupId>
<artifactId>slf4j-log4j12</artifactId>
<version>1.5.6</version>
</dependency>
```

Listing 4-34 illustrates the `struts.xml` file.

Listing 4-34. struts.xml

```
1.<?xml version="1.0" encoding="UTF-8" ?>
2.<!DOCTYPE struts PUBLIC
3."-//Apache Software Foundation//DTD Struts Configuration 2.3//EN"
4."http://struts.apache.org/dtds/struts-2.3.dtd">
5.
6.
7.<struts>
8.<constant name="struts.enable.DynamicMethodInvocation" value="false" />
9.<constant name="struts.devMode" value="true" />
10.<constant name="struts.custom.i18n.resources" value="ApplicationResources" />
11.
12.<package name="default" extends="struts-default" namespace="/">
13.<result-types>
14.<result-type name="tiles"
15.class="org.apache.struts2.views.tiles.TilesResult" />
16.</result-types>
17.<action name="*Link" method="{1}"
18.class="com.apress.bookstore.action.LinkAction">
19.<result name="login" type="tiles">login</result>
20.<result name="allBooks" type="tiles">allBooks</result>
21.</action>
22.<action name="login" class="com.apress.bookstore.action.LoginAction">
23.<result name="success" type="tiles">home</result>
24.<result name="error" type="tiles">login</result>
25.</action>
26.<action name="logout">
27.<result name="success" type="tiles">logout</result>
28.</action>
29.</package>
30.</struts>
```

- *Lines 19, 20, 23, 24, and 27*: These lines define the result type as Tiles and the tile name, such as `home` and `login`, which is defined in `tiles.xml`. Depending on the result string returned by the action, in other words, `success` or `error`, the corresponding JSP file defined in `tiles.xml` is mapped with the definition name in `tiles.xml` to the tile name in `struts.xml`.

Listing 4-35 illustrates the tiles.xml file.

Listing 4-35. tiles.xml

```
<?xml version="1.0" encoding="UTF-8" ?>

<!DOCTYPE tiles-definitions PUBLIC "-//Apache Software Foundation//DTD Tiles Configuration 3.0//EN"
"http://tiles.apache.org/dtds/tiles-config_3_0.dtd">

<tiles-definitions>
```

```
<definition name="baseLayout" template="/template/baseLayout.jsp">
<put-attribute name="title" value="Template" />
<put-attribute name="header" value="/template/header.jsp" />
<put-attribute name="menu" value="/template/menu.jsp" />
<put-attribute name="body" value="/template/body.jsp" />
</definition>

<definition name="login" extends="baseLayout">
<put-attribute name="title" value="Log in" />
<put-attribute name="menu" value="" />
<put-attribute name="body" value="/login.jsp" />
</definition>
<definition name="error" extends="baseLayout">
<put-attribute name="title" value="Log in" />
<put-attribute name="menu" value="" />
<put-attribute name="body" value="/login.jsp" />
</definition>
<definition name="home" extends="baseLayout">
<put-attribute name="title" value="Log in" />
<put-attribute name="menu" value="/template/menu.jsp" />
<put-attribute name="body" value="/view/home.jsp" />
</definition>
<definition name="logout" extends="baseLayout">
<put-attribute name="title" value="Log in" />
<put-attribute name="menu" value="" />
<put-attribute name="body" value="/login.jsp" />
</definition>

<definition name="allBooks" extends="baseLayout">
<put-attribute name="title" value="All Books" />
<put-attribute name="body" value="/allBooks.jsp" />
</definition>


</tiles-definitions>
```

Listing 4-36 illustrates the baselayout.jsp file, which defines where the header, footer, and body content should be inserted.

Listing 4-36. ***Base layout***

```
<%@ taglib uri="http://tiles.apache.org/tags-tiles" prefix="tiles"%>
<!DOCTYPE HTML PUBLIC "-//W3C//DTD HTML 4.01 Transitional//EN"
   "http://www.w3.org/TR/html4/loose.dtd">

<html>
<head>
<meta http-equiv="Content-Type" content="text/html; charset=UTF-8">
<link rel="stylesheet" href="css/bookstore.css" type="text/css" />
<script type="text/javascript" src="js/jquery-1.9.1.js"></script>
<script src="js/bookstore.js"></script>
<title><tiles:insertAttribute name="title" ignore="true" /></title>
</head>
```

```
<body>
<div id="centered">
<tiles:insertAttribute name="header" />
<tiles:insertAttribute name="menu" />
<tiles:insertAttribute name="body" />
</div>
</body>
</html>
```

Listing 4-37 illustrates the header.jsp file.

Listing 4-37. header.jsp

```
1.<%@ page language="java" contentType="text/html; charset=ISO-8859-1"
2.pageEncoding="ISO-8859-1"%>
3.<%@ taglib prefix="s" uri="/struts-tags"%>
4.
5.<div class="header">
6.<h2>
7.<span style="margin-left: 15px; margin-top: 15px;" class="label">BOOK
8.<span style="color: white;">STORE</span>
9.</span>
10.</h2>
11.<span style="color: black; margin-left: 15px;">
12.
13.
14.<s:if test="%{username!=null && !hasActionErrors() }">Welcome <s:property value="username" /> |
<a href='<s:url action="logout.action"/>'>Log out</a></s:if>
15.<s:else>
16.Login
17.</s:else>
18.
19.
20.
21.
22.</span>
23.
24.</div>
25.
```

Lines 14 to 17 use Struts 2 s:if, s:else, and s:property tags to welcome the user when logged in and allow the user to log out. Since this code is in the header, this functionality will be available to all the pages in the application.

Listing 4-38 illustrates the web.xml file.

Listing 4-38. web.xml

```
1.<!DOCTYPE web-app PUBLIC
2. "-//Sun Microsystems, Inc.//DTD Web Application 2.3//EN"
3. "http://java.sun.com/dtd/web-app_2_3.dtd" >
4.
5.<web-app>
6.<display-name>Archetype Created Web Application</display-name>
7.<context-param>
8.<param-name>org.apache.tiles.impl.BasicTilesContainer.DEFINITIONS_CONFIG</param-name>
9.<param-value>/WEB-INF/tiles.xml</param-value>
10.</context-param>
11.
12.<filter>
13.<filter-name>struts2</filter-name>
14.<filter-class>org.apache.struts2.dispatcher.ng.filter.StrutsPrepareAndExecuteFilter</filter-class>
15.</filter>
16.<filter-mapping>
17.<filter-name>struts2</filter-name>
18.<url-pattern>/*</url-pattern>
19.</filter-mapping>
20.<listener>
21.<listener-class>org.apache.tiles.extras.complete.CompleteAutoloadTilesListener</listener-class>
22.</listener>
23.<welcome-file-list>
24.<welcome-file>index.jsp</welcome-file>
25.</welcome-file-list>
26.
27.</web-app>
```

Lines 7 to 10 and lines 21 to 22 are required to configure Tiles with Struts 2.

Integrating the Data Access Layer

In this section, you will integrate the web application you created with the data access layer. You can use the data access layer you created in Chapter 1. You will then authenticate the user against the database. Next, you will show the categories in the bookstore database on the menu bar. Then you will retrieve the list of books from the database by category. Figure 4-23 illustrates the directory structure of the application.

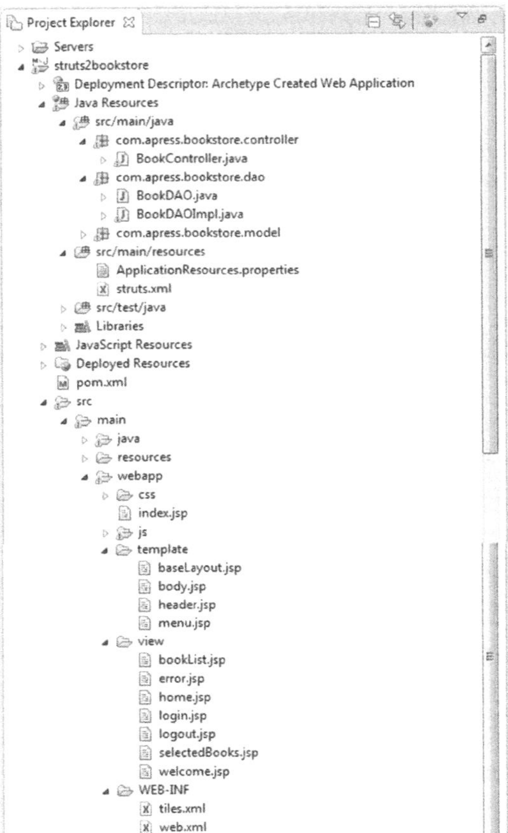

***Figure 4-23.** Directory structure with the data access layer*

As you can see in the directory structure there is a single `BookController` in the application. The methods in this controller are illustrated in the Listing 4-39.

***Listing 4-39.** BookController*

```
public class BookController extends ActionSupport  {

        //properties

        public String login() {}

        public String executelogin() {}

        public String error() {}

        public String allBooks() {}

        public String booksByCategory() {}

```

```
15.            public String searchByKeyword() {}
16.
17.            public String home() {}
18.
19.            public String selectedBooks(){}
20.
21.            public String logout() {}
22.
23.           // getters and setters
24.
25.     }
```

- *Line 5*: responsible for displaying the login form.
- *Line 7*: authenticates the user against the database.
- *Line 9*: displays the error message, for example if the user is invalid.
- *Line 11*: lists all the books in the bookstore.
- *Line 13*: lists the books by category.
- *Line 15*: allows user to search the books by keyword: book title or author's name.
- *Line 17*: displays the home page when clicked on home link.
- *Line 19*: displays the list of selected books.
- *Line 21*: allows the user to log out.

Login Using Database

Listing 4-40 illustrates the `executelogin()` method responsible for authenticating user against the database. For this you need to add the USER table to the data model you developed in chapter 1 using the following DDL:

```
CREATE TABLE USER(
ID INT NOT NULL AUTO_INCREMENT,
FIRST_NAME VARCHAR(60) NOT NULL,
LAST_NAME VARCHAR(60) NOT NULL,
USERNAME VARCHAR(60) NOT NULL,
PASSWORD VARCHAR(60) NOT NULL,
PRIMARY KEY (ID)
);
```

***Listing 4-40.** executelogin()method in the BookController*

```
public String executelogin() {
            String executelogin = "failed";
            session = ActionContext.getContext().getSession();
            dao = new BookDAOImpl();
            user = new User();
            user.setUserName(getUsername());
```

```
7.                  user.setPassword(getPassword());
8.                  setUser(user);
9.                  if (dao.isUserAllowed(user)) {
10.
11.                         setCategoryList(dao.findAllCategories());
12.                         session.put("username", username);
13.                         session.put("categoryList", getCategoryList());
14.                         executelogin = "success";
15.                 }
16.                 else {
17.                         addActionError(getText("error.login"));
18.                         return "error";
19.                 }
20.                 // return result;
21.                 return "executelogin";
22.         }
```

Figure 4-24 illustrates the USER table.

Field	Type	Null	Key	Default	Extra
ID	int(11)	NO	PRI	NULL	auto_increment
FIRST_NAME	varchar(60)	NO		NULL	
LAST_NAME	varchar(60)	NO		NULL	
USERNAME	varchar(60)	NO		NULL	
PASSWORD	varchar(60)	NO		NULL	

***Figure 4-24.** USER table*

- *Line 9*: The user is authenticated against the database. As you can see in the Line 9 replaces the hard-coded username and password in the Listing 4-31 by invoking `isUserAllowed()` on the DAO The `isUserAllowed()` method selects the username and password from the USER table (as shown in Figure 4-24) in the resultset based on the username and password entered in the login form.
- *Line 11-14*: If the user is valid, categories are retrieved from the database, and the list of categories is stored in the session.
- *Lines 16-19*: Line 16 sets the valid boolean variable to true if the resultset contains the username and password If the user is not valid, the String `error` is returned.

Displaying Categories Retrieved from the Database

Listing 4-41 illustrates the menu that shows the categories returned from the database. In Listing 4-40, you retrieved the categories and stored them in the session for a valid user. These categories will be displayed in `menu.jsp`.

Listing 4-41. menu.jsp

```
1.<li><div>
2.
3.<span class="label" style="margin-left: 15px;">
4.<a href="<s:url action=""/>">Categories</a></span>
5.</div>
6.<ul>
7.<li><s:form action=" booksByCategoryLink">
8.
9.<s:select name="category" list="#session['categoryList']"
10.listValue="categoryDescription" listKey="id" />
11.<s:submit value="Select" />
12.</s:form><a class="label" href=""><span class="label"
13.style="margin-left: 30px;"></span></a></li>
14.
15.</ul></li>
```

- *Lines 9 to 10*: These lines display the categories in the list that was stored in the session in `LoginAction` using the expression language of Struts 2.
- *Line 11*: When the user clicks the select button, the selected category and the action name in line 7, `booksByCategoryLink`, are sent to the container, and then mapped via `struts.xml` to the action, which retrieves the list of books.

Listing Books by Category

In this section, you will retrieve the list of books by category from the database. The selected category and the action name `booksByCategoryLink` are sent to the container, and then mapped via `struts.xml` to `BookController`. Listing 4-42 illustrates the code fragment of `struts.xml`.

Listing 4-42. Declaring BookController in struts.xml

```
1.      <action name="*Link" method="{1}"
2.                              class="com.apress.bookstore.controller.BookController">
3.                              <result name="login" type="tiles">login</result>
4.                              <result name="allBooks" type="tiles">booklist</result>
5.                              <result name="booksByCategory" type="tiles">booklist</result>
6.                              <result name="searchByKeyword" type="tiles">booklist</result>
7.                              <result name="home" type="tiles">home</result>
8.                              <result name="executelogin" type="tiles">executelogin</result>
9.                              <result name="selectedBooks" type="tiles">selectedBooks</result>
10.                             <result name="logout" type="tiles">logout</result>
11.                             <result name="error" type="tiles">error</result>
12.                     </action>
```

The * in the Line 1 of the Listing 4-42 is the wildcard character. Any action name values that end in `Link` will be handled by this action mapping. Whatever value is before `Link` will be the value used for the method attribute (the {1} place holder will be replaced with that value). So instead of writing nine separate action mapping nodes in the configuration file for this simple application you can simply use the wildcard character, *, in your name value and an attribute value place holder ({1}) for the method value. This enables the Struts 2 framework to dynamically select the correct method to call at runtime. Listing 4-43 illustrates `booksByCategory()`.

Listing 4-43. booksByCategory()

```
public String booksByCategory() {
                dao = new BookDAOImpl();
                setBookList(dao.findBooksByCategory(category));
                return "booksByCategory";
        }
```

When `booksByCategory()` in the Listing 4-43 returns it is mapped to the tile name `booklist` as it was illustrated in Line 5 of Listing 4-42. This maps to `booklist` defined in the tiles.xml as illustrated in Listing 4-44 which renders the `booklist.jsp` file. Listing 4-44 illustrates the code fragment in `tiles.xml`.

Listing 4-44. tiles.xml

```
<definition name="booklist" extends="baseLayout">
<put-attribute name="title"  value="Log in"/>
<put-attribute name="menu"   value="/menu.jsp"/>
<put-attribute name="body"   value="/view/bookList.jsp"/>
</definition>
```

Listing 4-45 illustrates the `bookList.jsp`.

Listing 4-45. booklist.jsp

```
<%@  taglib uri="/struts-tags" prefix="s"%>
<body>
<div id="centered">
<s:form action=" selectedbooksLink" theme="simple">
<center>
<table id="grid">
<thead>
<tr>
<th id="th-title">Book Title</th>
<th id="th-author">Author</th>
<th id="th-price">Price</th>
</tr>
</thead>
<tbody>
<s:iterator value="bookList" id="book">
<tr>
<td>
<s:checkboxname="selectedBooks" fieldValue="%{bookId}" />
 <s:propertyvalue="#book.bookTitle" />
</td>
```

```
30.<td>
31.<s:iterator value="#book.authors" id="author">
32.<s:if test="%{#book.id == #author.bookId}">
33.<s:property value="#author.firstName" />
34.<s:property value="#author.lastName" />
35.</s:if>
36.</s:iterator>
37.</td>
39.<td><s:property value="price" /></td>
40.</tr>
42.</s:iterator>
43.</tbody>
45</table>
47.</center><br>
49.<s:submit value="Add to the shopping cart" />
51.</s:form>
52.
53.</div>
54.</body>
```

Listing 4-45 illustrates the usage of Struts 2 tags and how Struts 2 OGNL is used to navigate the property `bookTitle` on line 27 and the properties `firstName` and `lastName` (of the author) on lines 33 and 34. Line 31 illustrates the usage of a simple and nested `s:iterator`. Line 26 allows the user to select books to add to the shopping cart. The user can check the books to select and submit them by clicking the button on line 49. When the user clicks the Add to Cart button, the action name `selectedbooksLink` on line 8 and the bookId on line 26 are sent to the container, which is then mapped to the`AddToCart`action via `struts.xml`. The `AddToCart` action then stores the book to the cart in the database, and the `AddToCart` action returns the String `success`, which is mapped via action mapping in `struts.xml` and the tile in the `tiles.xml` file to the view `selectedBooks.jsp`. The user can click the Purchase button on the `selectedBooks.jsp` page to call `PurchaseAction` in the same manner. This chapter sketched a brief overview of Struts 2. For more detailed coverage of Struts 2, I recommend *Practical Apache Struts 2 Web 2.0 Projects* by Ian Roughley.

Summary

In this chapter, you saw the Struts 2 framework's core components, which follow the MVC design pattern, and you saw how Struts 2separates the cross-cutting concerns by means of interceptors. You saw how the Struts 2 framework provides a declarative architecture in two forms: XML and annotations. In the next chapter, you will learn another action-oriented framework, called Spring Web MVC.

Chapter 5

Building Java Web Applications with Spring Web MVC

Anything you can do, I can do Meta.

—Daniel Dennett

Mark Twain once said, "In the spring, I have counted 136 different kinds of weather." Almost certainly, he wasn't referring to the Spring Framework. Or was he clairvoyant? The Spring Framework has grown to become an ecosystem of projects; it includes many distinct modules, integrates numerous frameworks and libraries, and provides a varied range of capabilities in diverse areas such as Flash, enterprise applications, web services, data stores, OSGi,[1] and even .NET. Spring applications are supported on all popular cloud platforms such as Cloud Foundry,[2] Google App Engine, and Amazon EC2[3] and can leverage traditional RDBMSs as well as new NoSQL[4] solutions and data stores like PostgreSQL,[5] MySQL, MongoDB,[6] and Redis.[7] Unlike many other frameworks such as Struts, which is confined to developing web applications, the Spring Framework can be used to build stand-alone, web, and JEE applications. Spring provides support for building modern web applications including REST, HTML5, and Ajax, as well as mobile client platforms including Android and iPhone. The Spring Framework has remarkably changed the enterprise Java landscape forever by connecting components with systems so that you do not have to write the plumbing code, thus allowing you to focus on the business of the application.

---

[1]`www.osgi.org/Main/HomePage`
[2]`www.cloudfoundry.com/`
[3]`http://aws.amazon.com/ec2/`
[4]`http://nosql-database.org/`
[5]`www.postgresql.org/`
[6]`www.mongodb.org/`
[7]`http://redis.io/`

Spring Framework Overview

The Spring Framework consists of features in these categories:

- AOP and instrumentation
- Core container
- Data access/integration
- Web
- Test

The modules in each of these categories are described in the following sections.

AOP and Instrumentation

The AOP and instrumentation category consists of the AOP, Aspects, and Instrumentation modules, as described in Table 5-1.

Table 5-1. AOP Modules

Module	Description
AOP	Spring's AOP module provides an AOP Alliance-compliant aspect-oriented programming implementation.
Aspects	The Aspects module provides integration with AspectJ.
Instrumentation	The Instrumentation module provides class instrumentation support and classloader implementations.

Core Container

The core container category consists of the Beans, Core, Context, and Expression Language modules, as described in Table 5-2.

Table 5-2. Core Modules

Module	Description
Beans	The Beans module provides IoC and dependency injection features.
Core	The Core module provides IoC and dependency injection features.
Context	The Context module builds on the Core and Beans modules and adds support for internationalization, event propagation, resource loading, EJB, and JMX.
Expression Language	The Expression Language module provides the Spring expression language.

Data Access/Integration

The data access/integration layer consists of the JDBC, ORM, OXM, JMS, and Transaction modules, as described in Table 5-3.

Table 5-3. Data Access/Integration Modules

Modules	Description
JDBC	The JDBC module provides a JDBC abstraction layer that removes the need to use pure JDBC.
ORM	The ORM module provides integration for ORM frameworks, such as JPA, JDO, Hibernate, and iBatis.
OXM	The OXM module supports object/XML mapping implementations for JAXB, Castor, XMLBeans, JiBX, and XStream.
JMS	The JMS module provides features for producing and consuming messages.
Transaction	The Transaction module supports programmatic and declarative transaction management.

Test

The test category consists of the Test module, as described in Table 5-4.

Table 5-4. Test Module

Modules	Description
Test	The Test module supports the testing of Spring components with JUnit or TestNG.

Web

The web layer consists of the Web, Web-Servlet, Web-Struts, and Web-Portlet modules, as described in Table 5-5.

Table 5-5. Web Modules

Modules	Description
Web	Spring's Web module provides basic web-oriented integration features and a web-oriented application context. It also provides several remoting options such as Remote Method Invocation (RMI), Hessian, Burlap, JAX-WS, and Spring's own HTTP invoker.
Web-Servlet	The Web-Servlet module contains Spring's Model-View-Controller (MVC) implementation for web applications.
Web-Struts	The Web-Struts module provides support for integrating a classic Struts web tier within a Spring application. Note that this support is now deprecated as of Spring 3.0.
Web-Portlet	The Web-Portlet module provides the MVC implementation to be used in a portlet environment.

> **Note** The core of the Spring Framework is based on the principle of Inversion of Control (IoC) that provides injection of dependencies. However, Spring is not the only framework offering dependency injection features; there are several other frameworks such as Seam[8], Google Guice[9], and JEE6 and newer that offer dependency injection.

At the time of writing, Spring 3.2.2 is expected to be released; Spring 3.1 was released in December 2011. Spring Framework 4.0 is expected by the end of 2013, with plans to support Java SE 8, Groovy 2, and some aspects of Java EE 7.

Spring Framework Fundamentals

An application is composed of components such as web components and business logic components. These components need to collaborate with each other to fulfill the common business goals of the application, so these components depend on one another. This dependency, if uncontrolled, often leads to tight coupling between them, resulting in an unmaintainable application. Controlling this coupling so that it does not result in a tightly coupled application is a nontrivial task. By contrast, if a component of the application does not depend on another component, it will not have to look for it, all the components will be fully isolated, and the resulting application will be loosely coupled. But such an application will not do anything. Essentially, components should depend on other components but should not look for these components on which they depend. Instead, such dependencies should be provided to the dependent components. This is the essence of Inversion of Control. The Spring Framework is one such IoC framework, which provides the dependencies to the dependent components by means of dependency injection.

> **Note** IoC is based on the Hollywood principle[10]: "Don't call us; we'll call you."

Figure 5-1 is a high-level view of how Spring works.

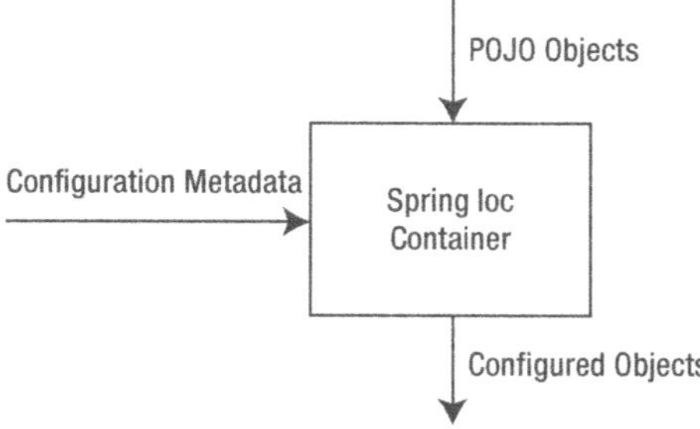

Figure 5-1. *Spring IoC container*

---

[8]www.seamframework.org/
[9]http://code.google.com/p/google-guice/
[10]http://martinfowler.com/bliki/InversionOfControl.html

As illustrated in Figure 5-1, the Spring IoC container produces fully configured application objects by using application POJO objects and configuration metadata.

- *Application POJO objects*: In Spring, the application objects that are managed by the Spring IoC container are called *beans*. A Spring bean is an object that is instantiated, assembled, and managed by a Spring IoC container.

> **Note** In Spring, components are also called *beans*. The Spring beans are different from the JavaBeans convention. The Spring beans can be any plain old Java objects (POJOs). A POJO is an ordinary Java object without any specific requirements, such as extending a specific class or implementing a specific interface.

- *Configuration metadata*: The configuration metadata specifies the objects that comprise your application and the interdependencies between such objects. The container reads the configuration metadata and figures out from it which objects to instantiate, configure, and assemble. The container then injects those dependencies when it creates the bean. The configuration metadata can be represented by either XML, annotations, or Java code.

In terms of implementation, the Spring container can inject objects in arguments of instance and static methods and can inject constructors via dependency injection. Say you have an application that has a component called `ClassA` that depends on `ClassB`. In other words, `ClassB` is the dependency. Your standard code would look like Listing 5-1.

Listing 5-1. Tightly Coupled Dependency

```
1.    public class ClassA {
2.       private ClassB classB;
3.       public ClassA() {
4.          classB = new ClassB();
5.       }
6.    }
```

We create a dependency between `ClassA` and `ClassB` in line 3-4 of Listing 5-1. This tightly couples `ClassA` with `ClassB`. This tight coupling can be circumvented using IoC, and in order to that, first we need to change the code in Listing 5-1 to Listing 5-2.

Listing 5-2. Removing the Tight Coupling Between ClassA and ClassB

```
public class ClassA {
   private ClassB classB;
   public ClassA(ClassB classB) {
      this.classB = classB;
   }
}
```

As you can see in Listing 5-2, `ClassB` is implemented independently, and the Spring container provides this implementation of `ClassB` to `ClassA` at the time of instantiation of `ClassA`, and the dependency (in other words, class `ClassB`) is injected into class `ClassA` through a constructor. Thus, the control has been removed from ClassA and kept elsewhere (that is, in an XML configuration file, illustrated in Listing 5-3) and thus “inverted” by dependency injection (DI) because the dependency is delegated to an external system, in other words, the configuration metadata. Listing 5-3 illustrates a typical Spring configuration metadata file.

Listing 5-3. Configuration Metadata

```
1.    <?xml version="1.0" encoding="UTF-8"?>
2.    <beans xmlns="http://www.springframework.org/schema/beans"
3.        xmlns:xsi="http://www.w3.org/2001/XMLSchema-instance"
4.        xsi:schemaLocation="http://www.springframework.org/schema/beans
5.            http://www.springframework.org/schema/beans/spring-beans-3.2.xsd">
6.
7.
8.    <bean id=" .." class=".."/>
9.
10.   <!-- more bean definitions -- >
11.
12.   </beans>
```

- *Line 2*: To use tags such as `<beans>`, `<bean>`, and so on, certain namespaces need to be declared. The core Spring Framework comes with ten configuration namespaces. For now let’s concentrate on the `beans` namespace; as the chapter progresses, other namespaces will be used. However, in this book we require only the `aop`, `beans`, and `context` schemas, so if you are interested in using others, you can find them at `http://static.springsource.org/spring/docs/3.2.2.RELEASE/spring-framework-reference/html/xsd-config.html`.
- *Line 2*: When describing beans in an XML-based configuration, the root element of the XML file is `<beans>` from Spring’s bean schema. The entire Spring configuration, including `<bean>` declarations, is placed in the top-level `<beans>`.
- *Line 8*: `<bean>` is the most basic configuration unit in Spring. It tells Spring to create an object for the application. These `<bean>` definitions correspond to the actual objects that make up the application.
- *Line 8*: The `id` attribute is a string that helps identify the individual bean definition. The `class` attribute defines the type of the bean and uses the fully qualified class name. The value of the `id` attribute refers to the collaborating objects.

> **Note** While XML is a classic way for defining configuration metadata, you can use annotations (from Spring 2.5 and newer) or Java code (from Spring 3.0 and newer).

Listing 5-4 illustrates the bean definition that should be included in the configuration metadata file illustrated in Listing 5-3 to inject the `classB` dependency in Listing 5-2.

Listing 5-4. Configuring Dependency

```
1.    <!-- Definition for classA bean -->
2.       <bean id="classA" class="ClassA">
3.          <constructor-arg ref="classB"/>
4.       </bean>
5.
6.       <!-- Definition for classB bean -->
7.       <bean id="classB" class="ClassB">
8.       </bean>
```

- *Line 2*: This specifies the `classA` bean to be created and managed by the Spring container.
- *Line 3*: `<constructor-arg>` configures bean properties via constructor injection by declaring them in the elements.
- *Line 7*: This specifies that `classB` bean should be created and managed by the Spring container.

The dependency injection depicted in Listing 5-4 is called *constructor*-based dependency injection. Constructor-based DI is accomplished when the container invokes a class constructor with a number of arguments, each representing a dependency on another class. There is another variant of DI called *setter*-based dependency injection. In setter-based DI, the container, after invoking a no-argument constructor or no-argument static factory method to instantiate your bean, calls the setter methods on your beans. To use setter-based DI, you need to modify Listing 5-2 to look like Listing 5-5.

Listing 5-5. Setter Method to Inject Dependency

```
public class ClassA{
   private ClassB classB;

   // a setter method to inject the dependency.
   public void setClassB(ClassB classB) {
      this.classB = classB;
   }
   // a getter method to return classB
   public ClassB getClassB() {
      return classB;
   }

}
```

In Listing 5-5, the DI takes place through setter methods of the `ClassA` class in which the `ClassB` instance is created, and this instance is used to call setter methods to initialize `ClassA`'s properties. Listing 5-6 illustrates the bean definition that should be included in the configuration metadata file illustrated in Listing 5-3 to achieve the setter-based dependency injection required in Listing 5-5.

Listing 5-6. Configuring Dependency Through Setter-Based DI

```
<bean id="classA" class="ClassA">
<property name="classB" ref="classB" />
</bean>
<bean id="classB" class="ClassB" />
```

The `<property>` tag defines a property for dependency injection. Listing 5-6 can be translated into the Java code illustrated in Listing 5-7.

Listing 5-7. Java Code Equivalent of Listing 5-6

```
ClassA classA = new ClassA();
ClassB classB = new ClassB();
classA.setClassB(classB);
```

> **Tip** Constructor-based and setter-based DI can be used simultaneously, but it is recommended to use constructor arguments for mandatory dependencies and setters for optional dependencies.

The Spring container is essentially a factory that creates objects encapsulating the creation of objects and configures these objects using the configuration metadata that contains information about the collaborating objects in the application that must be created. Spring provides two types of IoC container implementation.

- Bean factories (defined by the `org.springframework.beans.factory.BeanFactory` interface)
- Application contexts (defined by the `org.springframework.context.ApplicationContext` interface)

Bean factories are the simplest of containers and provide basic support for DI. `ApplicationContext` is a subinterface of `BeanFactory` that provides application framework services, such as the following:

- The ability to resolve textual messages from a properties file
- The ability to publish application events to interested event listeners
- The application-layer specific contexts such as the `WebApplicationContext` to be used in the web tier

> **Note** Web applications have their own `WebApplicationContext`. The `WebApplicationContext` will be explained when we discuss web-based Spring applications later in this chapter.

Application Context

Spring comes with several implementations of the `ApplicationContext` interface out of the box. The three most commonly used are the following:

- `ClassPathXmlApplicationContext`: Loads a context definition from an XML file located in the class path
- `FileSystemXmlApplicationContext`: Loads a context definition from an XML file in the file system
- `XmlWebApplicationContext`: Loads context definitions from an XML file contained within a web application

In stand-alone applications, it is common to create an instance of `ClassPathXmlApplicationContext` or `FileSystemXmlApplicationContext`.

Following Figure 5-1, you have to instantiate the Spring IoC container (`ApplicationContext`) for it to create bean instances by reading their configurations (configuration metadata). Then, you can get the bean instances from the IoC container to use.

Listing 5-8 illustrates the instantiation of the `ClassPathXmlApplicationContext`, an implementation of `ApplicationContext`. The `ClassPathXmlApplicationContext` implementation builds an application context by loading an XML configuration file from the class path.

Listing 5-8. ***Instantiation of ClassPathXmlApplicationContext***

```
ApplicationContext context = new ClassPathXmlApplicationContext("beans.xml");
```

Listing 5-9 illustrates the instantiation of the `FileSystemXmlApplicationContext`.

Listing 5-9. ***Instantiation of the FileSystemXmlApplicationContext***

```
ApplicationContextcontext=new FileSystemXmlApplicationContext("c:/beans.xml");
```

> **Note** The `FileSystemXmlApplicationContext` looks for *beans.xml* in a specific location within the file system, whereas `ClassPathXmlApplicationContext` looks for *beans.xml* anywhere in the class path (including JAR files).

In the section that follows, you will learn how to use the application context when you create your first Spring-based stand-alone application.

Key Objectives of the Spring Framework

Dependency injection is not the only key benefit of using the Spring Framework. The goal of the Spring Framework is to simplify the complexity of developing an enterprise application. This complexity manifests itself in an enterprise application in several ways, and most enterprise applications prior to the Spring Framework were inadvertently afflicted with few or even all of the following tribulations:

- Tight coupling
- Cross-cutting concerns
- Boilerplate code

Fundamentally, Spring enables you to build applications from POJOs and apply enterprise services nonintrusively to POJOs so that the domain model has no dependencies on the framework itself. Thus, the driving force behind the Spring Framework was to promote best practices in Java EE development by enabling a POJO-based programming model.

Dealing with Tight Coupling Using Dependency Injection

Now let's see how Spring enables loose coupling through dependency injection with the help of a simple stand-alone application. The code for this application is available in a downloadable archive on the Apress web site. In addition, this application will be a preamble into the Spring forest. Listing 5-10, 5-11, and 5-12 illustrate the hierarchy of service provider objects and the dependencies of the `VehicleService` illustrated in Listing 5-13.

Listing 5-10. Vehicle Interface

```
public interface Vehicle {
public String drive();
}
```

Listing 5-11. Vehicle Implementation: Bike

```
public class Bike implements Vehicle{
    public String drive() {
        return " driving a bike";
    }
}
```

Listing 5-12. Vehicle Implementation: Car

```
public class Car implements Vehicle {

    public String drive() {
        return " driving a car";
    }
}
```

These service provider objects are used by the class `VehicleService`, as illustrated in Listing 5-13, which is then used by the client object, as illustrated in Listing 5-14.

Listing 5-13. Vehicle Service

```
1.    public class VehicleService {
2.
3.        private Vehicle vehicle = new Bike();
4.
5.        public void driver() {
6.            System.out.println(vehicle.drive());
7.
8.        }
9.
10.   }
```

- *Line 3*: In Listing 5-13, class `Bike` is the dependency of class `VehicleService` and is instantiated on line 3. This is a case of tight coupling because the class `VehicleService` is implementation-aware of the `Vehicle` object, which is `Bike` in this case.

Listing 5-14 illustrates the stand-alone `VehicleApp`.

Listing 5-14. Stand-Alone VehicleApp

```
public class VehicleApp {
    public static void main(String[] args) {
        VehicleService service = new VehicleService();
        service.driver();
    }
}
```

As illustrated in Listing 5-14, `VehicleService` is implementation-aware of the `Vehicle` object and hence tightly coupled to it. Now let's decouple this application through the Spring Framework's DI. The first step is to create a Java project using the Eclipse IDE. Select File ➤ New ➤ Project and then select Java Project Wizard from the wizard list. Name your project **looselyCoupledApplication** using the wizard, as illustrated in Figure 5-2.

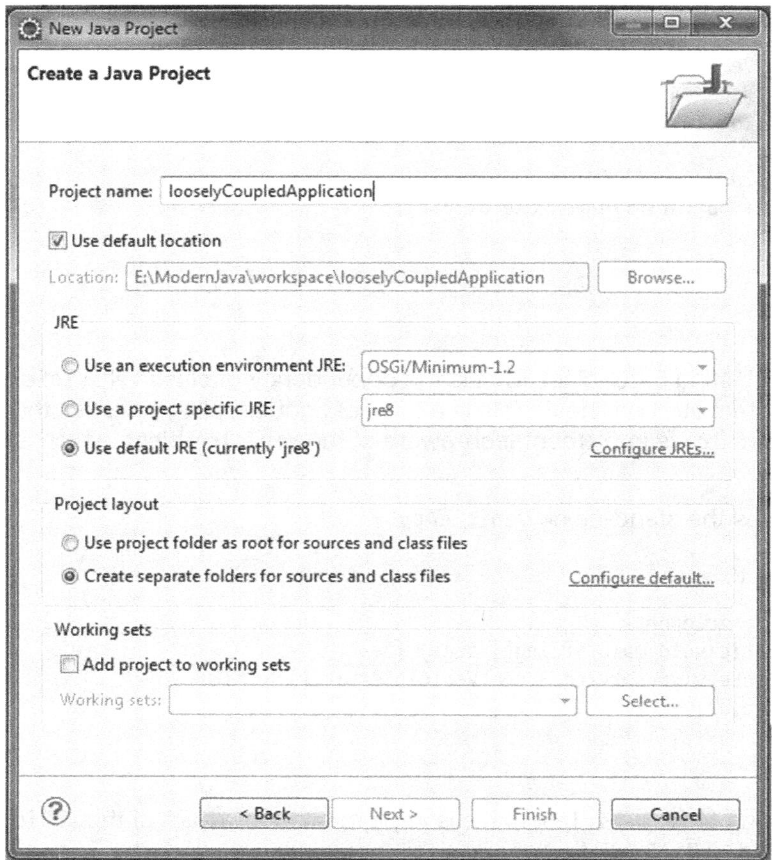

Figure 5-2. Creating the Java project

Now you need to add the Spring Framework and common logging API libraries in your project. You can download the Spring Framework libraries from `http://projects.spring.io/spring-framework/`. You can use Maven as explained in the previous chapter to configure the Spring Framework in your project. When using Maven, you need to add following to your `pom.xml` file:

```
<dependencies>
    <dependency>
        <groupId>org.springframework</groupId>
        <artifactId>spring-context</artifactId>
        <version>3.2.5.RELEASE</version>
    </dependency>
</dependencies>
```

Using Maven is much easier, but to know which key libraries are used for the three applications you will make in this section, you can manually configure the libraries in Eclipse. These libraries are available in the downloadable archive available from the Source Code/Download tab on the book's Apress webpage (`www.apress.com/9781430259831`).

To add the Spring Framework to your project, right-click your project and select Build Path ➤ Configure Build Path to display the Java Build Path window as illustrated in Figure 5-3. Now add the external JARs that you downloaded in your file system from the Apress website.

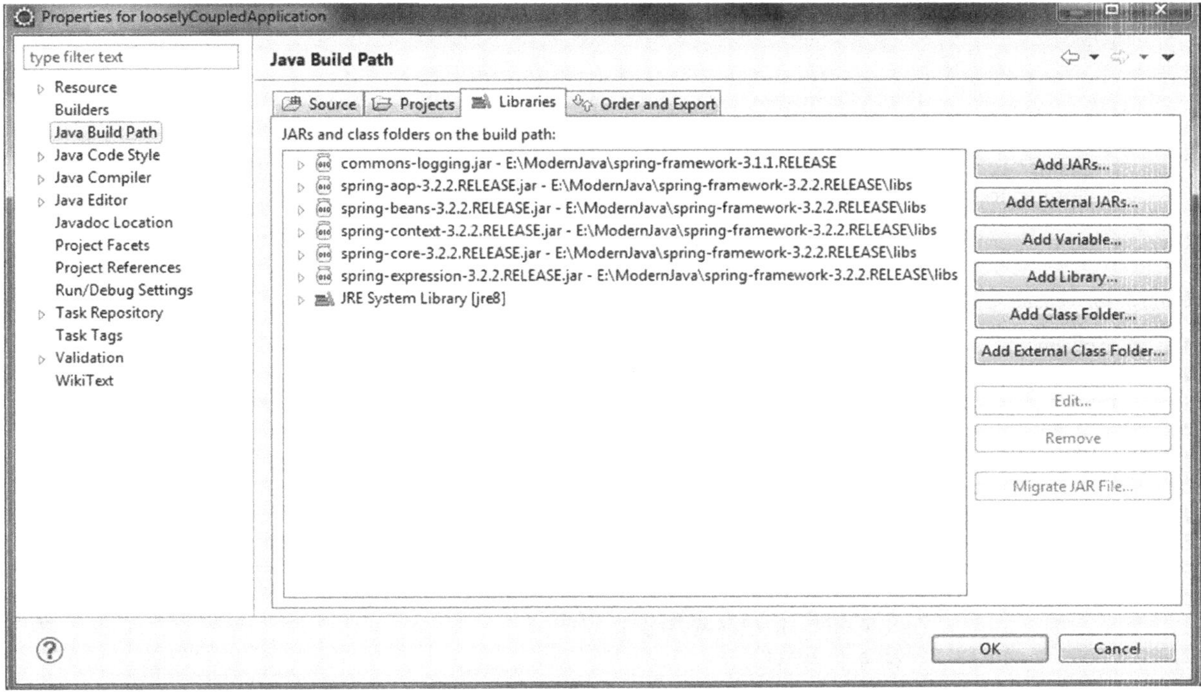

Figure 5-3. Adding external JARs

Now let's create actual source files under the looselyCoupledApplication project. First we need to create a package called `com.apress.decoupled`. To do this, right-click src in the Package Explorer section, select New ➤ Package, and create the package `com.apress.decoupled`. Then create `Vehicle.java`, `Car.java`, and `Bike.java`, which is the code illustrated in Listings 5-10, 5-11, and 5-12, under the `com.apress.decoupled` package.

Then create the class `VehicleService` as illustrated in Listing 5-15.

Listing 5-15. Loosely Coupled VehicleService

```
package com.apress.decoupled;

public class VehicleService {

    private Vehicle vehicle;

    public void setVehicle(Vehicle vehicle) {
        this.vehicle = vehicle;
    }
```

```
10.
11.     public void driver() {
12.         System.out.println(vehicle.drive());
13.
14.     }
15.
16. }
17.
```

- *Line 7*: In Listing 5-15, we have removed total control from the class VehicleService and kept it in the XML configuration file, and the dependency is being injected into the class VehicleService through a setter method on line 7.

Now create a client class VehicleApp, as illustrated in Listing 5-16.

***Listing 5-16.** Vehicle Application*

```
1.  package com.apress.decoupled;
2.  import org.springframework.context.ApplicationContext;
3.  import org.springframework.context.support.ClassPathXmlApplicationContext;
4.
5.  public class VehicleApp {
6.
7.      public static void main(String[] args) {
8.          ApplicationContext  context = new ClassPathXmlApplicationContext(
9.                  "beans.xml");
10.         VehicleService contestService = (VehicleService) context
11.                 .getBean("vehicleService");
12.         contestService.driver();
13.     }
14.
15. }
```

- *Lines 8 to 9*: These lines instantiate the application context and pass the configuration file.
- *Lines 10 to 11*: These lines get the bean from the configuration file. To get a declared bean from a bean factory or an application context, you make a call to the getBean() method, pass in the unique bean name, and cast the return type to its actual type before using it.

Now, you need to create a bean configuration file, which is an XML file (as illustrated in Listing 5-17), that connects the beans.

***Listing 5-17.** Configuration File*

```
<?xml version="1.0" encoding="UTF-8"?>
<beans xmlns="http://www.springframework.org/schema/beans"
       xmlns:xsi="http://www.w3.org/2001/XMLSchema-instance"
       xsi:schemaLocation="http://www.springframework.org/schema/beans
       http://www.springframework.org/schema/beans/spring-beans-3.0.xsd">
<bean id="car" class="com.apress.decoupled.Car" />
```

```
<bean id="bike" class="com.apress.decoupled.Bike" />
<bean id="vehicleService" class="com.apress.decoupled.VehicleService">
<property name="vehicle">
<ref local="car" />
</property>
</bean>
</beans>
```

You can choose any name you like for `beans.xml`. You have to make sure that this file is available in `CLASSPATH` and use the same name in the main application while creating the application context, as shown in the `VehicleApp.java` file. Figure 5-4 shows the directory structure of the application.

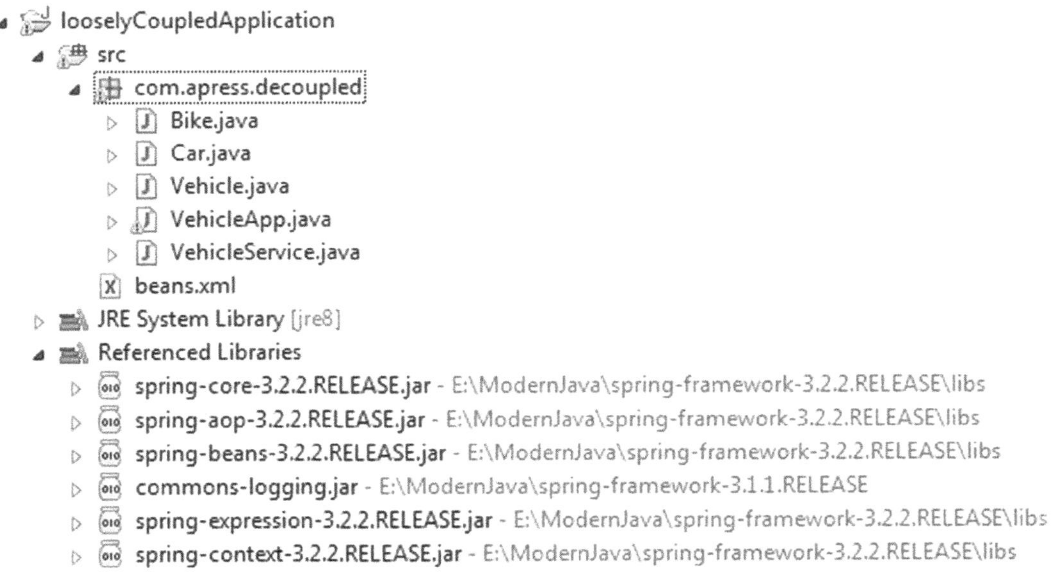

***Figure 5-4.** Directory structure*

Addressing Cross-Cutting Concerns Using AOP

A separation of concerns is achieved in Spring by means of aspect-oriented programming (AOP). AOP encapsulates the cross-cutting concerns in separate, reusable components called aspects and adds them to the application. This process is called *weaving*. This results in the cohesive components that concentrate on the business functions and are totally unaware of system services such as logging, security, transaction, and so on. To understand how aspects can be applied in Spring, you will now create a simple `BookService` that retrieves a list of all books, adding a basic logging aspect to the `BookService`. The code for this application is available in a downloadable archive on the Apress web site. Listing 5-18 illustrates the `BookService`.

Listing 5-18. BookService Interface

```
package com.apress.aop;

import java.util.List;

public interface BookService {
    public List<Book> getAllBooks();

}
```

Listing 5-19 illustrates the implementation of this `BookService`.

Listing 5-19. BookService Implementation

```
package com.apress.aop;

import java.util.ArrayList;
import java.util.List;

public class BookServiceImpl implements BookService{
    private static List<Book> bookList;
    static {

        Book book1 = new Book();
        book1.setId((long)1);
        book1.setBookTitle("Modern Java");

        Book book2 = new Book();
        book2.setId((long)2);
        book2.setBookTitle("Beginning Groovy");

        Book book3 = new Book();
        book3.setId((long)2);
        book3.setBookTitle("Beginning Scala");

        bookList = new ArrayList<Book>();
        bookList.add(book1);
        bookList.add(book2);
        bookList.add(book3);
    }


    public List<Book> getAllBooks() {
        for(Book b: bookList){
            System.out.println("Books:"+b.getBookTitle());
        }
        return bookList;
    }
}
```

Logging is not the concern of BookServiceImpl. For logging, create an aspect as illustrated in Listing 5-20 that will be woven into the BookService object, providing the logging wherever needed.

Listing 5-20. Aspect for Logging

```
1.    package com.apress.aop;
2.
3.    public class LoggingAspect {
4.        public void logBefore() {
5.
6.            System.out.println("Before calling getAllBooks");
7.        }
8.
9.        public void logAfter() {
10.           System.out.println("After calling getAllBooks");
11.       }
12.   }
13.
```

- *Line 3*: LoggingAspect is a simple class with two methods.
- *Line 4*: The logBefore() method that should be invoked before getAllBooks() is called.
- *Line 9*: the logAfter() method that should be invoked after the getAllBooks() is called.

The LoggingAspect does its job without the BookServiceImpl asking it to do so. Furthermore, because the BookServiceImpl does not need to know about the LoggingAspect, you are not required to inject the LoggingAspect into the BookServiceImpl. This removes the unneeded complexity from the BookServiceImpl code of having to inject LoggingAspect and having to check whether LoggingAspect is null. As you may have noticed, LoggingAspect is a POJO. It becomes an aspect when it is declared as an aspect in the Spring context. LoggingAspect can be applied to the BookServiceImpl without the BookServiceImpl needing to explicitly call on it. In fact, BookServiceImpl remains totally unaware of LoggingAspect's existence. To make LoggingAspect work as an aspect, all you need to do is declare it as one in the Spring configuration file. Listing 5-21 illustrates the application context XML file that declares LoggingAspect as an aspect.

Listing 5-21. Configuration File

```
<?xml version="1.0" encoding="UTF-8"?>
<beans xmlns="http://www.springframework.org/schema/beans"
    xmlns:xsi="http://www.w3.org/2001/XMLSchema-instance" xmlns:context=
    "http://www.springframework.org/schema/context"
    xmlns:aop="http://www.springframework.org/schema/aop"
    xsi:schemaLocation="http://www.springframework.org/schema/beans
        http://www.springframework.org/schema/beans/spring-beans-3.2.xsd
        http://www.springframework.org/schema/context
        http://www.springframework.org/schema/context/spring-context-3.2.xsd
        http://www.springframework.org/schema/aop
        http://www.springframework.org/schema/aop/spring-aop-3.2.xsd">

```

```
12.
13.     <bean id="bookService" class="com.apress.aop.BookServiceImpl"/>
14.
15.     <bean id="logAspect" class="com.apress.aop.LoggingAspect"/>
16.
17.     <aop:config>
18.         <aop:aspect  ref = "logAspect">
19.             <aop:pointcut id = "log"
20.                 expression="execution(* *.getAllBooks())" />
21.             <aop:before  pointcut-ref = "log"
22.                 method="logBefore" />
23.             <aop:after  pointcut-ref = "log"
24.                 method="logAfter" />
25.         </aop:aspect>
26.     </aop:config>
27. </beans>
```

- *Lines 9 to 10*: You use Spring's aop configuration namespace to declare that the LoggingAspect bean is an aspect.
- *Line 15*: You declare the LoggingAspect as a bean. Even if the Spring Framework transforms a POJO to an aspect by declaring it as an aspect in the context, it still has to be declared as a Spring <bean>.
- *Line 18*: Then you refer to that bean in the <aop:aspect> element.
- *Lines 19 to 20*: The pointcut is defined in the preceding <pointcut> element with an expression attribute set to select where the advice should be applied. The expression syntax is AspectJ's pointcut expression language.
- *Lines 21 to 22*: You declare (using <aop:before>) that before the getAllBooks() method is executed, the LoggingAspect's logBefore method should be called. This is called *before advice*. The pointcut-ref attribute refers to a pointcut named log.
- *Lines 23 to 24*: You (using <aop:after>) declare that the logAfter method should be called after getAllBooks() has executed. This is known as *after advice*. The pointcut-ref attribute refers to a pointcut named log.

Listing 5-22 illustrates the stand-alone Java application.

***Listing 5-22.** Stand-Alone Java Application*

```
package com.apress.aop;
import org.springframework.context.ApplicationContext;
import org.springframework.context.support.ClassPathXmlApplicationContext;

public class Driver {

        public static void main(String...args){
    ApplicationContext context = new ClassPathXmlApplicationContext("beans.xml");

```

```
        BookService bookService = (BookService)context.getBean("bookService");
                bookService.getAllBooks();

            }
    }
```

Figure 5-5 illustrates the directory structure of this application.

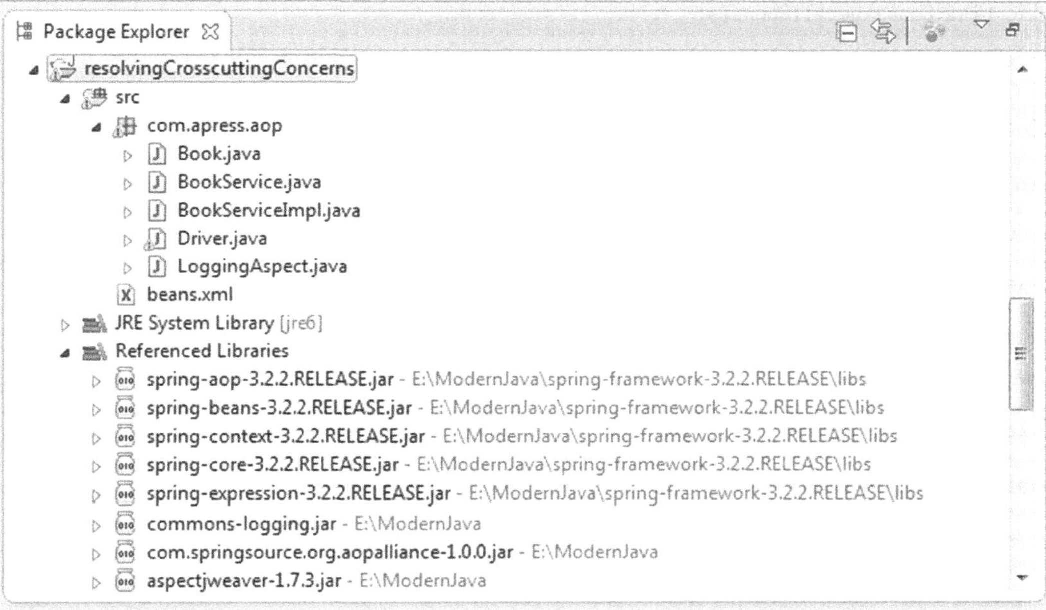

***Figure 5-5.** Directory structure*

Thus, Spring AOP can be employed to provide services such as transactions and security declaratively without tangling up your code that, in first place, should remain concerned only with its business functions.

Removing Boilerplate Code Using Templates

In Chapter 1 we built the data access layer of the bookstore application and used pure JDBC in the `BookDAOImpl` to connect to the database. In this section, you will see how the Spring Framework, by means of Spring's `JDBCTemplate`, transforms the `BookDAOImpl`, eliminating the boilerplate code that results from using pure JDBC to obtain a connection to a data store, and cleans up resources. The code for this application is available in the downloadable archive on the Apress web site. Listing 5-23 illustrates the `BookService`.

Listing 5-23. BookService

```
package com.apress.books.service;

import java.util.List;

import com.apress.books.model.Book;

public interface BookService {
    public List<Book> getAllBooks();

}
```

Listing 5-24 illustrates the BookService implementation.

Listing 5-24. BookService Implementation

```
package com.apress.books.service;

import java.util.List;

import com.apress.books.dao.BookDAO;
import com.apress.books.model.Book;

public class BookServiceImpl implements BookService{

    private  BookDAO bookDao ;

    public void setBookDao(BookDAO bookDao) {
        this.bookDao = bookDao;
    }

    public List<Book> getAllBooks() {
        List<Book> bookList = bookDao.findAllBooks();

        return bookList;
    }
}
```

Listing 5-25 illustrates the BookDAO.

Listing 5-25. BookDAO

```
package com.apress.books.dao;

import java.util.List;

import com.apress.books.model.Book;
import com.apress.books.model.Category;
```

```
public interface BookDAO {
    public List<Book> findAllBooks();

}
```

Listing 5-26 illustrates the BookDAO implementation.

Listing 5-26. BookDAO Implementation

```
package com.apress.books.dao;

import java.sql.Connection;
import java.sql.DriverManager;
import java.sql.PreparedStatement;
import java.sql.ResultSet;
import java.sql.SQLException;
import java.sql.Statement;
import java.util.ArrayList;
import java.util.List;

import javax.sql.DataSource;

import org.springframework.beans.factory.annotation.Autowired;
import org.springframework.jdbc.core.JdbcTemplate;

import com.apress.books.model.Author;
import com.apress.books.model.Book;
import com.apress.books.model.Category;

public class BookDAOImpl implements BookDAO {


    DataSource dataSource;


    public void setDataSource(DataSource dataSource) {
        this.dataSource = dataSource;
    }

    public List<Book> findAllBooks() {
      List<Book> bookList = new ArrayList<>();

    String sql = "select * from book inner join author on book.id = author.book_id";

    JdbcTemplate jdbcTemplate = new JdbcTemplate(dataSource);
    bookList = jdbcTemplate.query(sql, new BookRowMapper());
      return bookList;
     }

}
```

Compare this `findAllBooks()` method of `BookDAOImpl` with the `findAllBooks()` method of Chapter 1, and you will see that `JDBCTemplate` eliminates the boilerplate code that results from using pure JDBC to obtain a connection to our data store and cleans up resources.

- *Line 36*: This creates a `JDBCTemplate` using the data source passed to it. Note the `JDBCTemplate` is instantiated this way for the sake of explanation. In a production ready application you should inject `JDBCTemplate` as a dependency like any other dependency as explained in Listing 5-15.
- *Line 37*: A row mapper implementation is used. The `BookRowMapper` is explained next.

Listing 5-27 illustrates the `BookRowMapper` object to query one or more rows and then transform each row into the corresponding domain object instead of retrieving a single value.

Listing 5-27. ***The BookMapper Object***

```
1.    package com.apress.books.dao;
2.
3.    import java.sql.ResultSet;
4.    import java.sql.SQLException;
5.
6.    import org.springframework.jdbc.core.RowMapper;
7.
8.    import com.apress.books.model.Book;
9.
10.   public class BookRowMapper implements RowMapper<Book> {
11.
12.        @Override
13.        public Book mapRow(ResultSet resultSet, int line) throws SQLException {
14.         BookExtractor bookExtractor = new BookExtractor();
15.         return bookExtractor.extractData(resultSet);
16.        }
17.
18.      }
```

- *Line 10*: Spring's `RowMapper<T>` interface (under the package `org.springframework.jdbc.core`) provides a simple way for you to perform mapping from a JDBC resultset to POJOs.
- *Line 14*: This uses `BookExtractor` to extract the data.

Listing 5-28 illustrates the `BookExtractor` object.

Listing 5-28. ***BookExtractor Object***

```
package com.apress.books.dao;

import java.sql.ResultSet;
import java.sql.SQLException;
import java.util.ArrayList;
import java.util.List;

```

```
8.     import org.springframework.dao.DataAccessException;
9.     import org.springframework.jdbc.core.ResultSetExtractor;
10.
11.    import com.apress.books.model.Author;
12.    import com.apress.books.model.Book;
13.
14.    public class BookExtractor implements ResultSetExtractor<Book> {
15.
16.        public Book extractData(ResultSet resultSet) throws SQLException,
17.          DataAccessException {
18.
19.         Book book = new Book();
20.         Author author = new Author();
21.       List<Author> authorList = new ArrayList<>();
22.
23.         book.setId(resultSet.getLong(1));
24.         book.setCategoryId(resultSet.getLong(2));
25.         book.setBookTitle(resultSet.getString(3));
26.         book.setPublisherName(resultSet.getString(4));
27.         book.setAuthorId(resultSet.getLong(5));
28.         author.setBookId(resultSet.getLong(6));
29.         author.setFirstName(resultSet.getString(7));
30.         author.setLastName(resultSet.getString(8));
31.         authorList.add(author);
32.         book.setAuthors(authorList);
33.
34.         return book;
35.        }
36.
37.       }
```

- *Line 14*: BookExtractor implements ResultSetExtractor provided by Spring (under the package org.springframework.jdbc.core). The RowMapper is suitable only for mapping to a single domain object. But since we are joining two tables in Listing 5-26 on line 34, we need to use the ResultSetExtractor interface to transform the data to a nested domain object.

Listing 5-29 illustrates the configuration file for this stand-alone application.

***Listing 5-29.** Configuration File*

```
<?xml version="1.0" encoding="UTF-8"?>
<beans xmlns="http://www.springframework.org/schema/beans"
    xmlns:xsi="http://www.w3.org/2001/XMLSchema-instance" xmlns:context=
    "http://www.springframework.org/schema/context"
    xmlns:aop="http://www.springframework.org/schema/aop"
    xsi:schemaLocation="http://www.springframework.org/schema/beans
        http://www.springframework.org/schema/beans/spring-beans-3.2.xsd
        http://www.springframework.org/schema/context
        http://www.springframework.org/schema/context/spring-context-3.2.xsd
        http://www.springframework.org/schema/aop
        http://www.springframework.org/schema/aop/spring-aop-3.2.xsd">

```

```
12.         <!-- telling container to take care of annotations stuff -->
13.     <context:annotation-config />
14.
15.     <!-- declaring base package -->
16.     <context:component-scan base-package="com.apress.books" />
17.
18.
19.         <bean id="dao" class="com.apress.books.dao.BookDAOImpl" >
20.         <property name="dataSource" ref="dataSource">
21.             </property>
22.         </bean>
23.
24.         <bean id="service" class="com.apress.books.service.BookServiceImpl">
25.             <property name="bookDao" ref="dao">
26.             </property>
27.         </bean>
28.
29.         <bean id="dataSource"
30.       class="org.springframework.jdbc.datasource.DriverManagerDataSource">
31.     <property name="driverClassName" value="com.mysql.jdbc.Driver" />
32.     <property name="url" value="jdbc:mysql://localhost:3306/books" />
33.     <property name="username" value="root" />
34.     <property name="password" value="password" />
35.     </bean>
36.     </beans>
```

- *Line 20*: Configures dao with the data source

In this way, the Spring Framework eliminates the boilerplate code. Now with a stand-alone Java application you can query the new data access layer that we built using the Spring Framework. Listing 5-30 illustrates the stand-alone Java application that queries the data access through the service-layer component BookService.

Listing 5-30. Stand-Alone Application

```
package com.apress.books.client;
import java.util.List;
import org.springframework.context.ApplicationContext;
import org.springframework.context.support.ClassPathXmlApplicationContext;
import com.apress.books.model.Book;
import com.apress.books.service.BookService;

public class BookApp {

    public static void main(String[] args) {
        ApplicationContext context = new ClassPathXmlApplicationContext("beans.xml");
        BookService bookService = (BookService)context.getBean("service");
        // List all books
        System.err.println("Listing all Books:");
        List<Book> bookList= bookService.getAllBooks();
```

```
        for(Book b: bookList){
            System.out.println(b.getId()+"--"+b.getBookTitle());
        }
    }
}
```

In this section, you learned the key objectives of the Spring Framework, which aims to simplify the complexity that trickles into any enterprise application via tight coupling, cross-cutting concerns, and boilerplate code. In the next section, we will implement the web layer using the Web MVC module of the Spring Framework.

Building Web Application with Spring Web MVC

In Chapter 1, Spring Web MVC provided the Model-View-Controller architecture and myriad of components that together help you develop loosely coupled web applications built on the Spring IoC container.

Spring Web MVC Architecture

Spring's Web MVC framework, like many other web MVC frameworks, is request-driven, designed around a central servlet called `DispatcherServlet` that dispatches requests to controllers and offers other functionality that facilitates the development of web applications. `DispatcherServlet` implements one of the Java EE web-tier patterns, called Front Controller. As such, `DispatcherServlet` acts as the front controller of the Spring MVC framework, and every web request has to go through it so that it can control and administer the entire request-handling process. The request-processing workflow of the Spring Web MVC `DispatcherServlet` is illustrated in Figure 5-6.

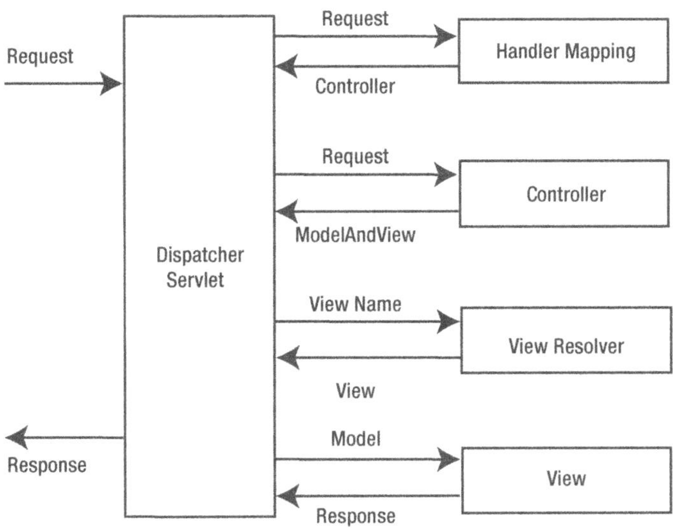

Figure 5-6. Request-processing workflow of the Spring Web MVC DispatcherServlet

Following from Figure 5-6, the high-level overview of the workflow is as follows:

1. The client sends a request to the web container in the form of an HTTP request.
2. `DispatcherServlet` intercepts the request to figure out the appropriate handler mappings.
3. With the help of handler mappings thus figured out, the `DispatcherServlet` dispatches the request to the appropriate controller.
4. The controller processes the request and returns the model and view objects to `DispatcherServlet` in the form of a `ModelAndView` instance.
5. `DispatcherServlet` then resolves the `View` (which can be JSP, FreeMarker, Velocity, and so on) by consulting the `ViewResolver` object.
6. The selected view is then rendered back to the client.

`DispatcherServlet` is the heart of Spring Web MVC framework, but before you dive into `DispatcherServlet`, first you must look at `ApplicationContext` in a web application. As mentioned earlier, a web application has its own specialized `WebApplicationContext` that must be loaded before `DispatcherServlet` is initialized. When the Spring Web MVC application starts and before the web application is ready to serve the requests, the `WebApplicationContext` and `DispatcherServlet` come into action, as explained here:

1. The servlet container initializes the web application and then triggers the `contextInitialized` event, which is listened to by the `ContextLoaderListener`.
2. `ContextLoaderListener` creates the root `WebApplicationContext`.
3. The `DispatcherServlet` is initialized, creating its own `WebApplicationContext` and nesting it inside the root `WebApplicationContext`.
4. `DispatcherServlet` searches for components such as ViewResolvers and HandlerMappings. If a component is found, it will be initialized; otherwise, the default for the component is initialized.

You will look at these steps in greater detail in the sections that follow.

WebApplicationContext

In web applications, the `ApplicationContext` used is called `WebApplicationContext`, and it is a specialized `ApplicationContext` that is aware of the servlet environment. It is the root `ApplicationContext` in a web application and must be loaded before `DispatcherServlet` initializes to ensure that all of the services such as the data source are available that are required by the web application. `WebApplicationContext` is configured in the `web.xml` file using `ContextLoaderListener`, as illustrated in Listing 5-31.

Listing 5-31. Configuring ContextLoaderListener in web.xml

```
<listener>
<listener-class>
org.springframework.web.context.ContextLoaderListener
</listener-class>
</listener>
```

By default, `ContextLoaderListener` loads the application context file stored in your `WEB-INF` directory. This location can be overridden by defining the `contextConfigLocation` context parameter in `web.xml`, as shown in Listing 5-32.

Listing 5-32. File Locations Using the contextConfigLocation Parameter

```
<context-param>
<param-name>contextConfigLocation</param-name>
<param-value>
classpath:service-context.xml
classpath:data-access-context.xml
</param-value>
</context-param>
```

At this point, the configuration of `WebApplicationContext` in `web.xml` looks like Listing 5-33.

Listing 5-33. Web.xml with ContextLoaderListener and contextConfigLocation

```
<context-param>
<param-name>contextConfigLocation</param-name>
<param-value>
classpath:service-context.xml
classpath:data-access-context.xml
</param-value>
</context-param>
<listener>
<listener-class>
org.springframework.web.context.ContextLoaderListener
</listener-class>
</listener>
```

> **Note** `ContextLoaderListener` by default looks for a `/WEB-INF/applicationContext.xml` file if you do not specify a `<context-param>` named `contextConfigLocation`.

Now that you know how to configure `WebApplicationContext` in a web application, we can move on to the second object, `DispatcherServlet`, that is configured in the `web.xml` file.

The DispatcherServlet

Like any servlet, DispatcherServlet needs to be configured in web.xml to be able to handle requests. Configuring and using the DispatcherServlet requires the following:

1. You have to indicate to the container to load DispatcherServlet and map it to URL patterns.
2. After the DispatcherServlet is loaded, it creates its own org.springframework.web.context.WebApplicationContext.
3. The DispatcherServlet then detects the SpringMVC components from this application context, and if not found, it will use the default. These SpringMVC components and their defaults will be explained later.
4. DispatcherServlet then delegates tasks to each of the SpringMVC components (or their defaults) depending on the request.

> **Note** DispatcherServlet creates its own WebApplicationContext, which contains the web-specific components such as Controllers and ViewResolver. This WebApplicationContext is then nested inside the root WebApplicationContext, which is loaded before the DispatcherServlet is initialized to ensure that the web components in WebApplicationContext of DispatcherServlet can find their dependencies.

DispatcherServlet, like any other servlet, is declared in the web.xml file of your web application. You need to map requests that you want DispatcherServlet to handle, by using a URL mapping in the same web.xml file. Listing 5-34 illustrates a DispatcherServlet declaration and mapping.

Listing 5-34. Declaring and Mapping DispatcherServlet

```
<web-app>
<servlet>
<servlet-name>bookstore</servlet-name>
<servlet-class>org.springframework.web.servlet.DispatcherServlet</servlet-class>
<load-on-startup>1</load-on-startup>
</servlet>
<servlet-mapping>
<servlet-name>bookstore</servlet-name>
<url-pattern>/bookstore/*</url-pattern>
</servlet-mapping>
</web-app>
```

In a Servlet 3.0 and newer environment, you can also use WebApplicationInitializer, an interface provided by the Spring MVC framework, to configure the servlet container programmatically. Listing 5-35 illustrates the programmatic equivalent of the previous web.xml example.

Listing 5-35. Programmatic Equivalent of Listing 5-43

```
public class ExampleWebApplicationInitializer implements WebApplicationInitializer {
    @Override
    public void onStartup(ServletContext container) {
        ServletRegistration.Dynamic registration = container.addServlet("dispatcher",
        new DispatcherServlet());
        registration.setLoadOnStartup(1);
        registration.addMapping("/bookstore/*");
    }
}
```

By default, `DispatcherServlet` looks for a file named `WEB-INF/<servlet-name>-servlet.xml`, where `<servlet-name>` is replaced with the value declared in `web.xml` in the `<servlet-name>` tag. `DispatcherServlet` uses this `<servlet-name>-servlet.xml` file to create `WebApplicationContext`.

Spring MVC Components

As mentioned earlier, `DispatcherServlet` searches the SpringMVC components from the `WebApplicationContext` it created, and if not found, it uses the default. These Spring MVC components are expressed as interfaces. Table 5-6 gives an overview of all the main component types involved in the request-processing workflow.

Table 5-6. Spring MVC Components

Bean type	Explanation
`HandlerMapping`	Maps incoming requests to handlers and interceptors
`HandlerAdapter`	For extending `DispatcherServlet` to customize the web workflow
`HandlerExceptionResolver`	Maps exceptions to views
`ViewResolver`	Resolves logical view names to actual views
`LocaleResolver`	Resolves the locale a client is using for internationalized views
`ThemeResolver`	Resolves themes for personalizing layouts
`MultipartResolver`	Parses multipart for file uploads
`FlashMapManager`	Supports FlashMap to pass attributes from one request to another

The Spring `DispatcherServlet` uses Spring MVC components that need to be configured in `WebApplicationContext` to process requests. However, if you don't configure these components, Spring Web MVC uses the default. Table 5-7 lists the default implementation of the components.

Table 5-7. The DispatcherServlet's Default Components

Component	Default Implementation
MultipartResolver	No default; explicit configuration required
LocaleResolver	AcceptHeaderLocaleResolver
ThemeResolver	FixedThemeResolver
HandlerMapping	BeanNameUrlHandlerMapping DefaultAnnotationHandlerMapping
HandlerAdapter	HttpRequestHandlerAdapter SimpleControllerHandlerAdapter AnnotationMethodHandlerAdapter
HandlerExceptionResolver	AnnotationMethodHandlerExceptionResolver ResponseStatusExceptionResolver DefaultHandlerExceptionResolver
RequestToViewNameTranslator	DefaultRequestToViewNameTranslator
ViewResolver	InternalResourceViewResolver
FlashMapManager	SessionFlashMapManager

Getting Started with a Spring Web MVC Application

In this section, I will walk you through the steps of creating a Hello World Spring MVC application using Spring Tool Suite (an Eclipse-based IDE). You will learn the fundamental concepts of Spring MVC while building the sample application. The tools used in this application include the following:

- Spring Framework 3.2.1
- Spring Tool Suite IDE 3.2.0 (based on Eclipse Juno 4.2.2)
- vFabric tc Server Developer Edition v2.8 (based on Apache Tomcat and optimized for Spring applications)

Spring Tool Suite (STS) is an Eclipse-based IDE that is actively developed and maintained by the SpringSource community. STS provides project templates such as Spring Batch, Spring Integration, Spring Persistence (Hibernate + JPA), Spring MVC, and so on. In addition, STS always gets the latest update of Spring artifacts from the Maven repository.

You can choose to download and install STS in one of three ways:

- Download and install STS from the installer program.
- Install STS through an Eclipse update.
- Download and extract the zip archive.

Start STS in your own workspace. From the main menu, select File ➤ New ➤ Spring Template Project (see Figure 5-7).

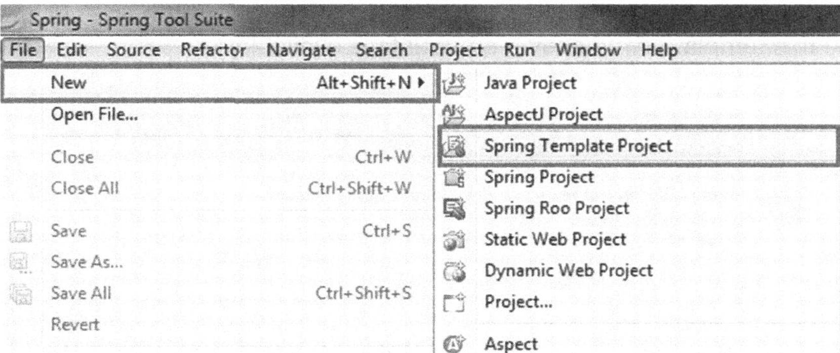

***Figure 5-7.** Selecting a SpringTemplate project*

In the New Template Project dialog, select Spring MVC Project (see Figure 5-8).

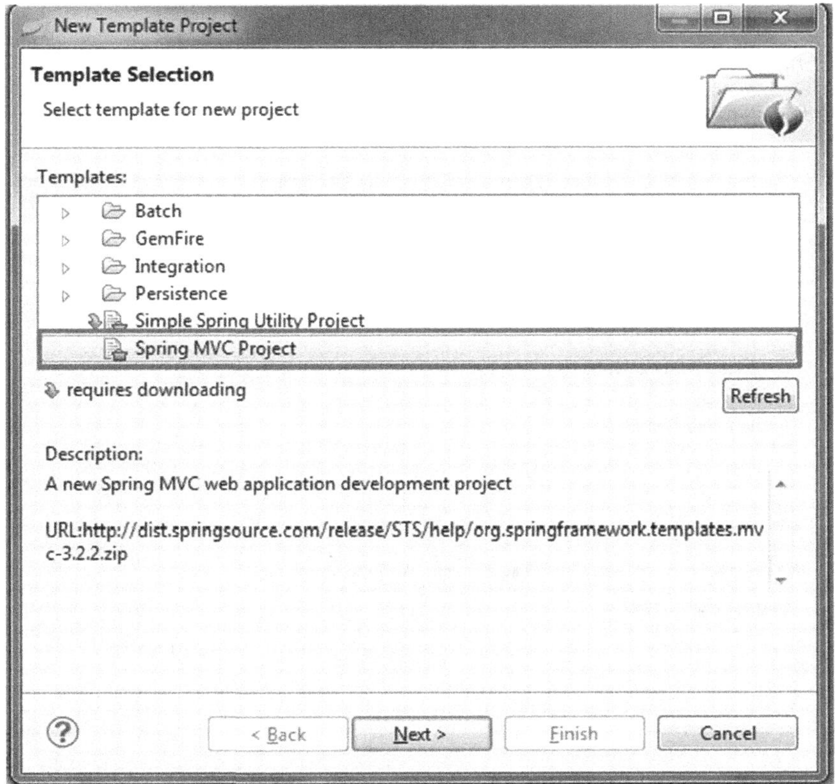

***Figure 5-8.** Selecting a SpringMVC project*

Click Next, which requires downloading an update of the template, as shown in Figure 5-9 (for the first time you use this template or whenever an update is available).

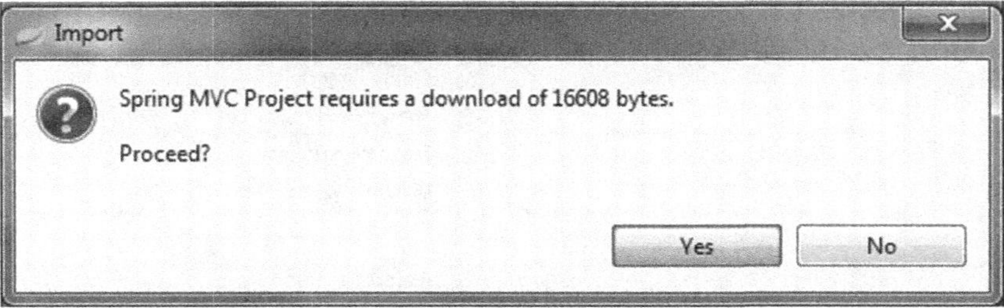

***Figure 5-9.** Downloading the update*

Click Yes to download the update, which should bring up the New Spring MVC Project dialog.

Enter the following information in the window illustrated in Figure 5-10:

- *Project name*: **helloworld**
- *Top-level package*: **com.apress.helloworld**

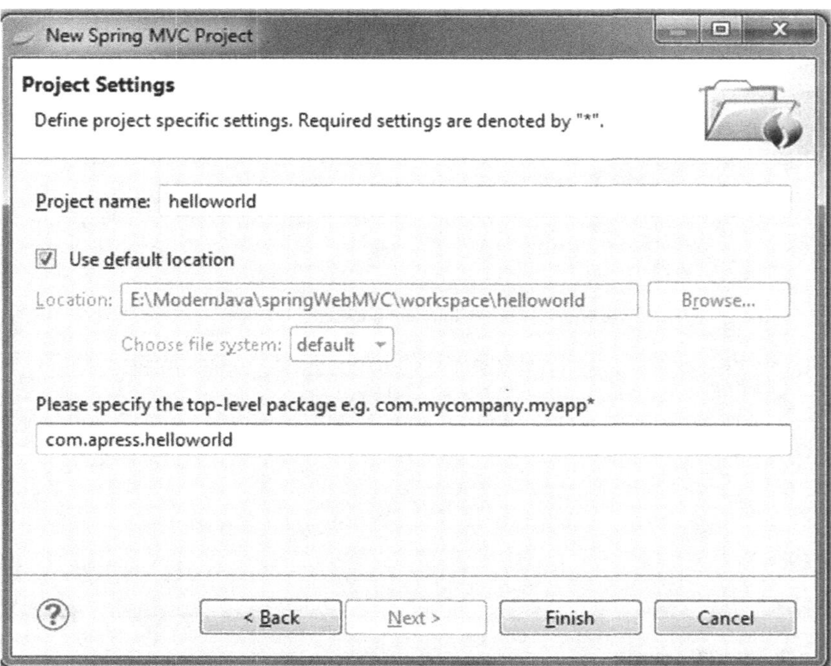

***Figure 5-10.** New Spring MVC Project dialog*

Click Finish, and STS will create a Spring MVC-based project with some defaults for the controller, views, and configuration. We didn't write any lines of code yet, but the application is ready to be deployed and run.

Right-click in the Servers view and select New ➤ Server.

In the New Server dialog, select VMware ➤ VMware vFabric tc Server..., as shown in Figure 5-11.

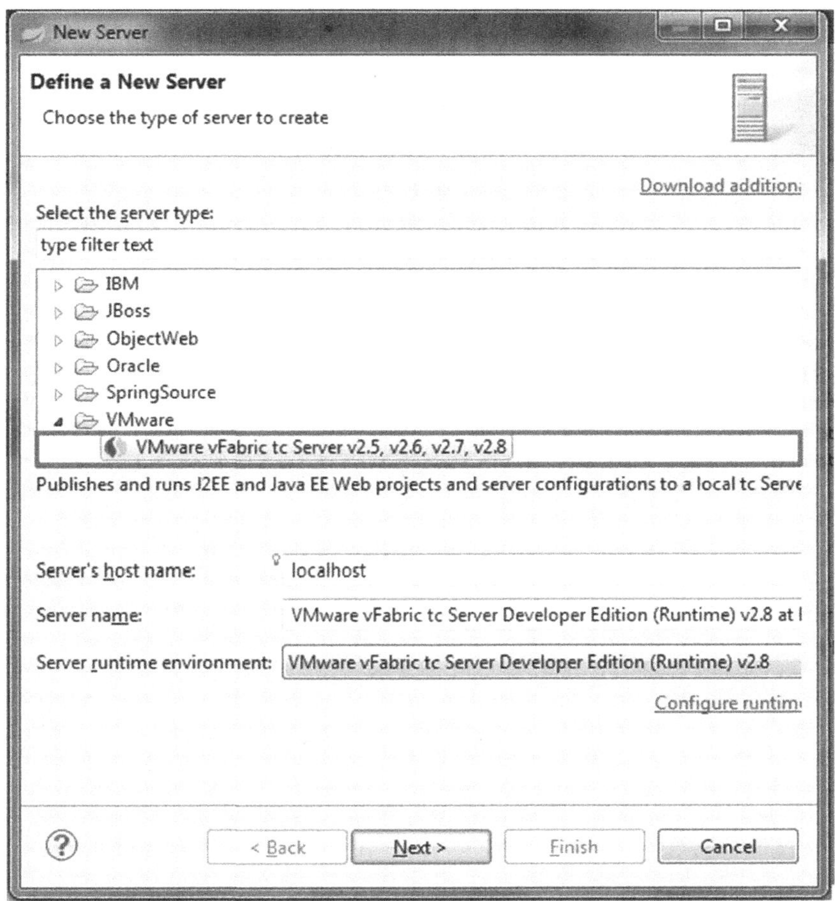

***Figure 5-11.** Defining a new server*

Click Next. On the next screen, keep the option "Create new instance" selected (see Figure 5-12).

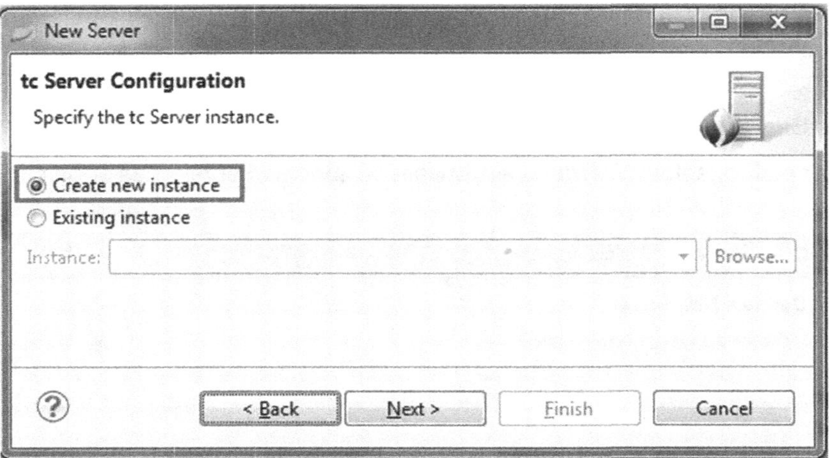

***Figure 5-12.** Creating a new instance*

Click Next. On the next screen, type **tcServer** as name for the new instance and select base as the template (see Figure 5-13).

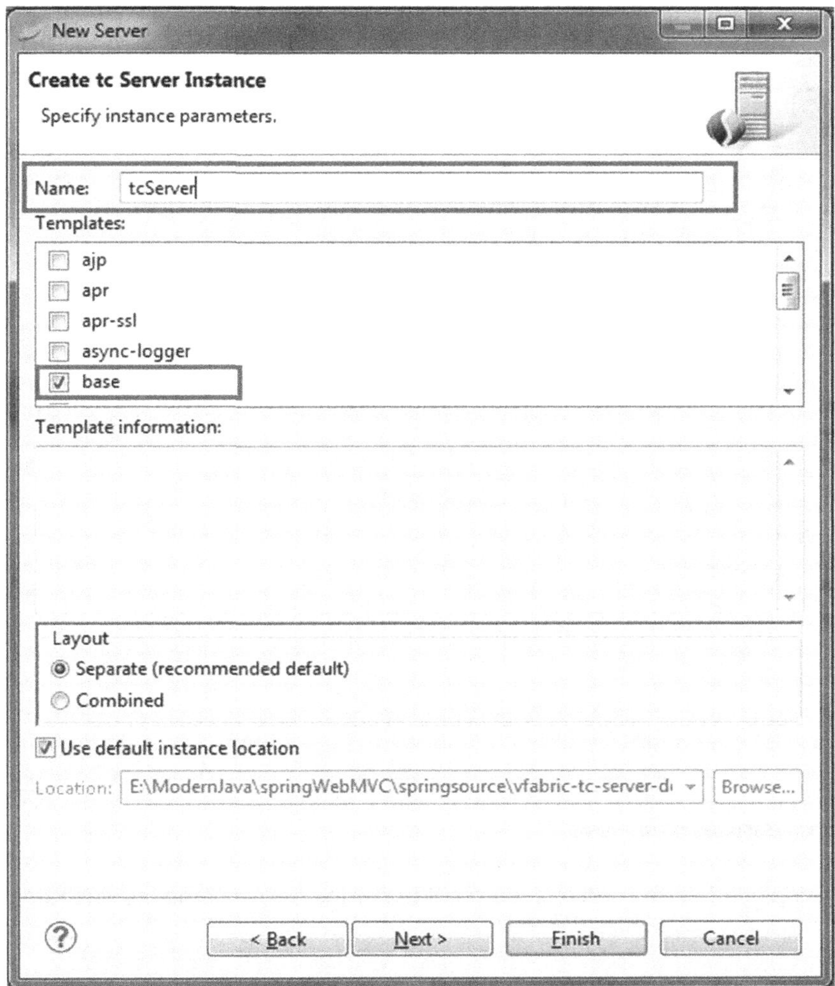

Figure 5-13. Specifying instance parameters

Add helloworld and click Finish to complete the server setup (see Figure 5-14). Now deploy the helloworld application.

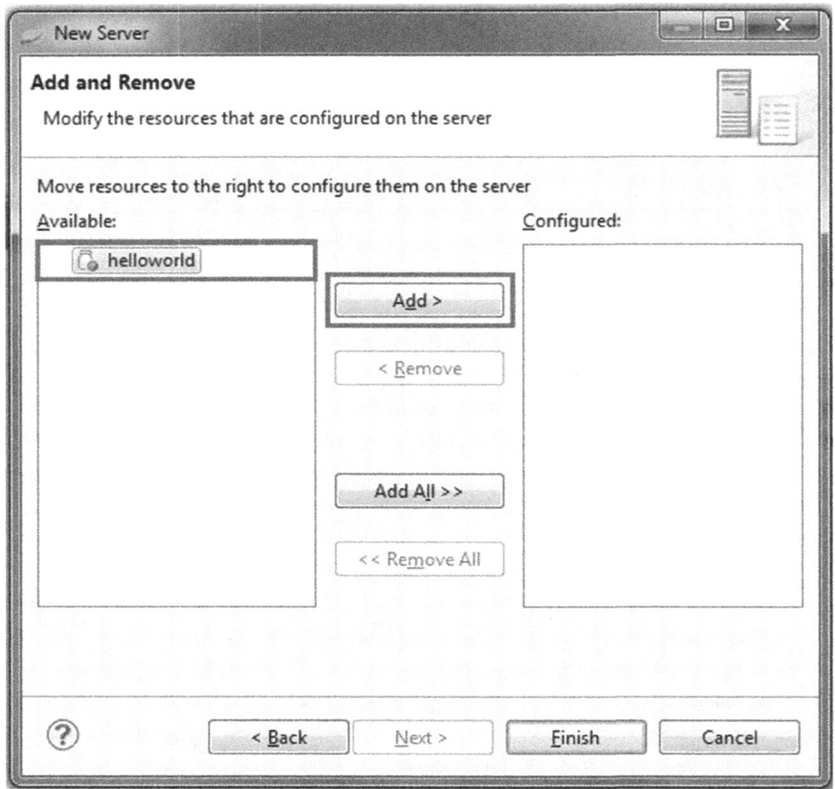

Figure 5-14. Configuring resources on the server

The application is deployed on the server if we see it under the server name, as illustrated in Figure 5-15.

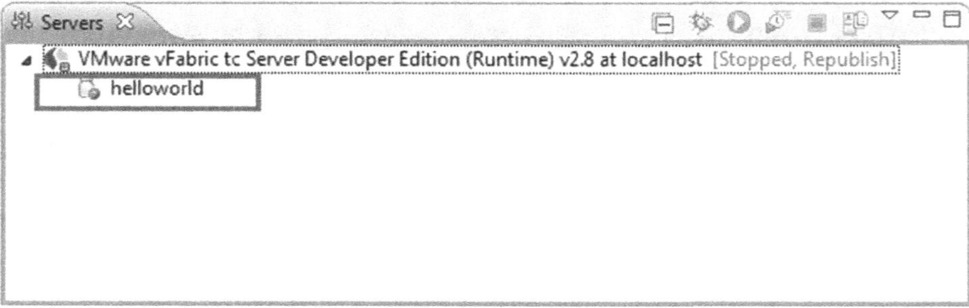

Figure 5-15. Deployed application

Start the server and run the application using the URL `http://localhost:8080/helloworld` (see Figure 5-16).

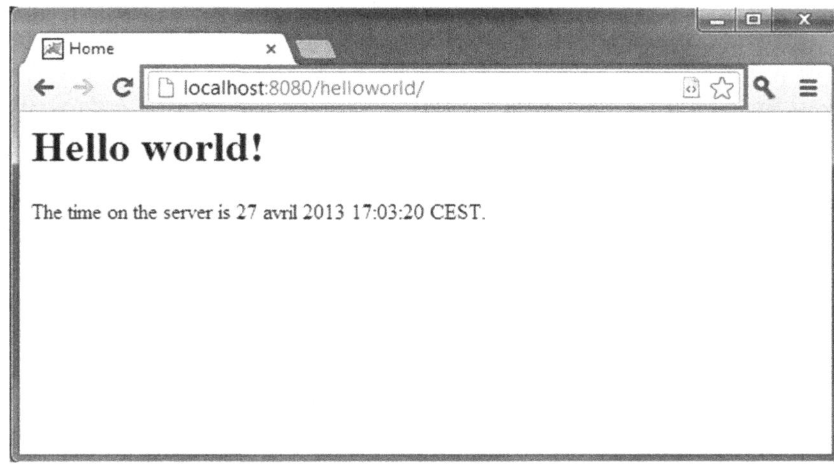

Figure 5-16. Running the application

Now let's explore what has been created by the Spring MVC Project template. Expand the branches in the Project Explorer view to see how the project is structured, as illustrated in Figure 5-17.

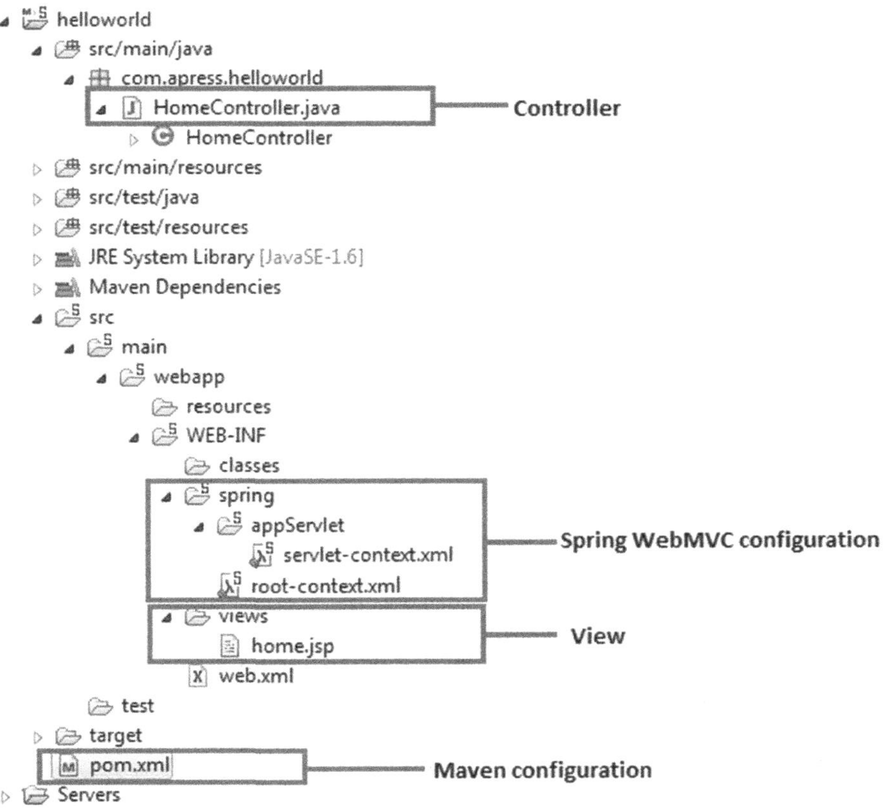

Figure 5-17. Directory structure of the Hello World application

We will go through each of the components illustrated in Figure 5-17. Figure 5-18 illustrates the content of the generated web.xml file.

```
<?xml version="1.0" encoding="UTF-8"?>
<web-app version="2.5" xmlns="http://java.sun.com/xml/ns/javaee"
    xmlns:xsi="http://www.w3.org/2001/XMLSchema-instance"
    xsi:schemaLocation="http://java.sun.com/xml/ns/javaee
    http://java.sun.com/xml/ns/javaee/web-app_2_5.xsd">

    <!-- The definition of the Root Spring Container shared by all Servlets and Filters -->
    <context-param>
        <param-name>contextConfigLocation</param-name>
        <param-value>/WEB-INF/spring/root-context.xml</param-value>
    </context-param>

    <!-- Creates the Spring Container shared by all Servlets and Filters -->
    <listener>
        <listener-class>org.springframework.web.context.ContextLoaderListener</listener-class>
    </listener>

    <!-- Processes application requests -->
    <servlet>
        <servlet-name>appServlet</servlet-name>
        <servlet-class>org.springframework.web.servlet.DispatcherServlet</servlet-class>
        <init-param>
            <param-name>contextConfigLocation</param-name>
            <param-value>/WEB-INF/spring/appServlet/servlet-context.xml</param-value>
        </init-param>
        <load-on-startup>1</load-on-startup>
    </servlet>

    <servlet-mapping>
        <servlet-name>appServlet</servlet-name>
        <url-pattern>/</url-pattern>
    </servlet-mapping>

</web-app>
```

***Figure 5-18.** Generated web.xml*

This is the typical configuration for a Spring MVC-based application with a declaration for the following:

- Spring's ContextLoaderListener
- Spring's DispatcherServlet
- Spring configuration file root-context.xml
- Spring configuration file servlet-context.xml
- The URL mapping for Spring's DispatcherServlet

We will look at the use of each one of these, but before that, we will modify web.xml. In the Spring MVC template project, the web.xml file it generates supports Servlet 2.5. In this chapter, we will use Servlet 3.0 (the tcServer that comes with STS is built on top of Apache Tomcat 7, which already supports Servlet 3.0), so we need to change the XML header from 2.5 to 3.0 too. Listing 5-36 shows the revised <web-app> tag.

Listing 5-36. The Web Deployment Description for Spring MVC

```
1.     <?xml version="1.0" encoding="UTF-8"?>
2.     <web-app xmlns="http://java.sun.com/xml/ns/javaee" xmlns:xsi=
       "http://www.w3.org/2001/XMLSchema-instance"
3.         xsi:schemaLocation="http://java.sun.com/xml/ns/javaee
           http://java.sun.com/xml/ns/javaee/web-app_3_0.xsd"
4.         version="3.0">
5.
6.         <!-- The definition of the Root Spring Container shared by all Servlets and Filters -->
7.         <context-param>
8.             <param-name>contextConfigLocation</param-name>
9.             <param-value>/WEB-INF/spring/root-context.xml</param-value>
10.        </context-param>
11.
12.        <!-- Creates the Spring Container shared by all Servlets and Filters -->
13.        <listener>
14.            <listener-class>org.springframework.web.context.ContextLoaderListener</listener-class>
15.        </listener>
16.
17.        <!-- Processes application requests -->
18.        <servlet>
19.            <servlet-name>appServlet</servlet-name>
20.            <servlet-class>org.springframework.web.servlet.DispatcherServlet</servlet-class>
21.            <init-param>
22.                <param-name>contextConfigLocation</param-name>
23.                <param-value>/WEB-INF/spring/appServlet/servlet-context.xml</param-value>
24.            </init-param>
25.            <load-on-startup>1</load-on-startup>
26.        </servlet>
27.
28.        <servlet-mapping>
29.            <servlet-name>appServlet</servlet-name>
30.            <url-pattern>/</url-pattern>
31.        </servlet-mapping>
32.
33.    </web-app>
```

- *Lines 2 to 4*: In the `<web-app>` tag, the version attribute and the corresponding URL are changed to version 3.0 to indicate to the web container that the web application will use Servlet 3.0.
- *Lines 7 to 10*: In the `<context-param>` tag, the `contextConfigLocation` param is provided, which defines the location of Spring's root `WebApplicationContext` configuration file.
- *Lines 13 to 15*: A listener of class `org.springframework.web.context.ContextLoaderListener` is defined. This is for Spring to load the root `WebApplicationContext`.
- *Lines 18 to 26*: One dispatcher servlet (called `appServlet`) is defined. We use the one generated by the template project for the application's presentation layer. The `WebApplicationContext` for the dispatcher servlet is located at `/src/main/webapp/WEB-INF/spring/appServlet/servlet-context.xml`.

The servlet-context.xml file is loaded by the Spring's DispatcherServlet, which receives all requests coming into the application. Listing 5-37 illustrates servlet-context.xml.

Listing 5-37. The servlet-context.xml of the Hello World Application

```
1.  <?xml version="1.0" encoding="UTF-8"?>
2.  <beans:beans xmlns="http://www.springframework.org/schema/mvc"
3.      xmlns:xsi="http://www.w3.org/2001/XMLSchema-instance"
4.      xmlns:beans="http://www.springframework.org/schema/beans"
5.      xmlns:context="http://www.springframework.org/schema/context"
6.      xsi:schemaLocation="http://www.springframework.org/schema/mvc
7.      http://www.springframework.org/schema/mvc/spring-mvc.xsd
8.          http://www.springframework.org/schema/beans
9.          http://www.springframework.org/schema/beans/spring-beans.xsd
10.         http://www.springframework.org/schema/context
11.         http://www.springframework.org/schema/context/spring-context.xsd">
12.
13.     <!-- DispatcherServlet Context: defines this servlet's request-processing
14.     infrastructure -->
15.
16.     <!-- Enables the Spring MVC @Controller programming model -->
17.     <annotation-driven />
18.
19.     <!-- Handles HTTP GET requests for /resources/** by efficiently serving up
20.     static resources in the ${webappRoot}/resources directory -->
21.     <resources mapping="/resources/**" location="/resources/" />
22.
23.     <!-- Resolves views selected for rendering by @Controllers to .jsp resources
24.     in the /WEB-INF/views directory -->
25.     <beans:bean class="org.springframework.web.servlet.view.InternalResourceViewResolver">
26.         <beans:property name="prefix" value="/WEB-INF/views/" />
27.         <beans:property name="suffix" value=".jsp" />
28.     </beans:bean>
29.
30.     <context:component-scan   base-package="com.apress.helloworld" />
31.
32.
33.
34. </beans:beans>
```

- *Line 17*: <annotation-driven /> tells the framework to use an annotations-based approach to scan files in the packages. Thus, we can use the @Controller annotation for the controller class instead of declaring XML elements.
- *Line 21*: <resources mapping=.../> maps static resources directly with HTTP GET requests. For example, images, JavaScript, and CSS resources do not have to go through controllers.

- *Lines 25 to 28*: This bean declaration tells the framework how to find physical JSP files according to logical view names returned by the controllers, by attaching the prefix and the suffix to a view name. For example, if a controller's method returns `home` as logical view name, then the framework will find a physical file `home.jsp` under the `/WEB-INF/views` directory.
- *Line 30*: `<context:component-scan .../>` tells the framework which packages to be scanned when using an annotations-based strategy. Here the framework will scan all classes under the package `com.apress.helloworld`. When the application grows, you can add more configurations for business beans, DAOs, transactions, and so on.

Now that we have the infrastructure in place to detect the controller that will handle the request, it's time to look at the controller.

> **Note** Prior to Spring 2.5, one of the interface-based controllers was used. As of Spring 3.0, the interface-based controllers have been deprecated in favor of annotated classes.

Listing 5-38 illustrates the code of the controller class `HomeController` generated by STS.

***Listing 5-38.** HomeController of the Hello World Application*

```
package com.apress.helloworld;

import java.text.DateFormat;
import java.util.Date;
import java.util.Locale;

import org.slf4j.Logger;
import org.slf4j.LoggerFactory;
import org.springframework.stereotype.Controller;
import org.springframework.ui.Model;
import org.springframework.web.bind.annotation.RequestMapping;
import org.springframework.web.bind.annotation.RequestMethod;

/**
 * Handles requests for the application home page.
 */
@Controller
public class HomeController {

    private static final Logger logger = LoggerFactory.getLogger(HomeController.class);

    /**
     * Simply selects the home view to render by returning its name.
     */
    @RequestMapping(value = "/", method = RequestMethod.GET)
    public  String  home(Locale locale, Model model) {
```

```
27.             logger.info("Welcome home! The client locale is {}.", locale);
28.
29.             Date date = new Date();
30.             DateFormat dateFormat = DateFormat.getDateTimeInstance(DateFormat.LONG,
                DateFormat.LONG, locale);
31.
32.             String formattedDate = dateFormat.format(date);
33.
34.             model.addAttribute("serverTime", formattedDate );
35.
36.             return "home";
37.         }
38.
39.     }
```

- *Line 17*: The `@Controller` annotation is used to specify that this class is a Spring controller. `DispatcherServlet` scans such annotated classes for mapped handler methods by means of `@RequestMapping` annotations.
- *Line 25*: The `@RequestMapping` annotation specifies that the `home()` method will handle a GET request with the URL / (the default page of the application).
- *Line 26 to 37*: The `home()` method creates a `String` object to hold the current date based on the current locale and adds this object to the model with the name `serverTme`. And finally the method returns a view named `home`, which will be resolved by the view resolver specified in the `servlet-context.xml` file, to find the actual view file. In one controller class, we can write many methods to handle different URLs.

`@Controller` and `@RequestMapping` and a number of other annotations form the basis for the Spring MVC implementation. To define a controller class in Spring 3.0 and newer, you have to mark the class with the `@Controller` annotation. When an `@Controller`-annotated class receives a request, it looks for an appropriate handler method to handle the request. Each method to which the request is to be mapped is decorated with the `@RequestMapping` annotation, making the method a handler method to which the request is mapped by means of handler mappings.

As you saw in Listing 5-38, the `home()` method in `HomeController` returns a view named `home`, which is resolved by the view resolver specified in `servlet-context.xml`. Now it is time to look at the view, which is the `home.jsp` file generated in the `/WEB-INF/views` directory. Listing 5-39 illustrates `home.jsp`.

Listing 5-39. home.jsp of the Hello World Application

```
<%@ taglib uri="http://java.sun.com/jsp/jstl/core" prefix="c" %>
<%@ page session="false" %>
<html>
<head>
    <title>Home</title>
</head>
<body>
<h1>
    Hello world!
</h1>
```

```
11.
12.     <P>  The time on the server is ${serverTime}. </P>
13.     </body>
14.     </html>
```

Listing 5-39 looks familiar. This is a simple JSP file that uses an EL expression on line 12 to print the value of the variable `serverTime` that is passed by the controller.

As you may have noticed, STS created two Spring configuration files: `root-context.xml` and `servlet-context.xml`. We have not looked at `root-context.xml` yet because our Hello World application does not require this file to display the content of `home.jsp`. This file is empty by default, as illustrated in Figure 5-19.

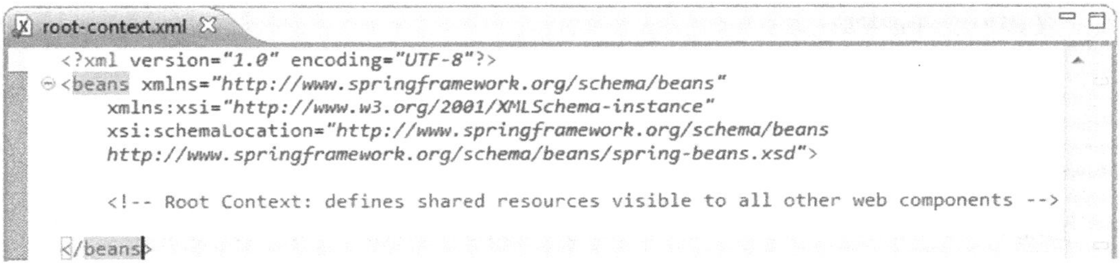

```
root-context.xml
<?xml version="1.0" encoding="UTF-8"?>
<beans xmlns="http://www.springframework.org/schema/beans"
    xmlns:xsi="http://www.w3.org/2001/XMLSchema-instance"
    xsi:schemaLocation="http://www.springframework.org/schema/beans
    http://www.springframework.org/schema/beans/spring-beans.xsd">

    <!-- Root Context: defines shared resources visible to all other web components -->

</beans>
```

Figure 5-19. Generated root-context.xml

This file, as the name suggests, specifies the root configuration for the Spring container. The `root-context.xml` file is loaded by the Spring's `ContextLoaderListener` upon the application's start-up, as you learned in the previous section.

So far, we have gone through all the files generated by the Spring MVC Project template, so you should be equipped enough to dive deeper, building the bookstore application along the way.

Implementing Spring Web MVC in the Bookstore Application

In this section, you will learn how to develop the bookstore web application using the Spring Web MVC framework. The code for the application is available as a downloadable archive from the Apress web site. As mentioned earlier, all incoming requests flow through `DispatcherServlet`. Hence, like any other servlet in a Java EE application, the Java EE container needs to be informed to load this servlet on start-up via `web.xml`. You have to create a new Spring MVC project first. Listing 5-40 illustrates `web.xml` of the bookstore application.

Listing 5-40. web.xml

```
<?xml version="1.0" encoding="UTF-8"?>
<web-app xmlns="http://java.sun.com/xml/ns/javaee" xmlns:xsi=
"http://www.w3.org/2001/XMLSchema-instance"
    xsi:schemaLocation="http://java.sun.com/xml/ns/javaee
    http://java.sun.com/xml/ns/javaee/web-app_3_0.xsd"
    version="3.0">
```

```
5.        <!-- Processes application requests -->
6.        <servlet>
7.            <servlet-name>bookstore</servlet-name>
8.            <servlet-class>org.springframework.web.servlet.DispatcherServlet</servlet-class>
9.            <init-param>
10.               <param-name>contextConfigLocation</param-name>
11.               <param-value>/WEB-INF/spring/bookstore/bookstore-servlet.xml</param-value>
12.           </init-param>
13.           <load-on-startup>1</load-on-startup>
14.       </servlet>
15.
16.       <servlet-mapping>
17.           <servlet-name>bookstore</servlet-name>
18.           <url-pattern>*.html</url-pattern>
19.       </servlet-mapping>
20.
21.       <welcome-file-list>
22.           <welcome-file>/list_book.html</welcome-file>
23.       </welcome-file-list>
24.   </web-app>
```

- *Lines 7 to 8*: DispatcherServlet is registered as a servlet called bookstore.
- *Line 10*: The Spring configuration file can be explicitly specified in the contextConfigLocation servlet parameter to ask Spring to load the configurations besides the default <servletname>-servlet.xml.

Listing 5-41 illustrates bookstore-servlet.xml.

Listing 5-41.* *bookstore-servlet.xml

```
<?xml version="1.0" encoding="UTF-8"?>
<beans:beans xmlns="http://www.springframework.org/schema/mvc"
    xmlns:xsi="http://www.w3.org/2001/XMLSchema-instance" xmlns:beans=
    "http://www.springframework.org/schema/beans"
    xmlns:context="http://www.springframework.org/schema/context"
    xsi:schemaLocation="http://www.springframework.org/schema/mvc
    http://www.springframework.org/schema/mvc/spring-mvc.xsd
        http://www.springframework.org/schema/beans http://www.springframework.org/schema/
        beans/spring-beans.xsd
        http://www.springframework.org/schema/context http://www.springframework.org/schema/
        context/spring-context.xsd">

    <!-- DispatcherServlet Context: defines this servlet's request-processing
        infrastructure -->

    <beans:bean name="/list_book.html"
        class="com.apress.bookstore.controller.BookController" />

    <!-- Resolves views selected for rendering by @Controllers to .jsp resources
        in the /WEB-INF/views directory -->
    <beans:bean
```

```
            class="org.springframework.web.servlet.view.InternalResourceViewResolver">
            <beans:property name="prefix" value="/WEB-INF/views/" />
            <beans:property name="suffix" value=".jsp" />
        </beans:bean>
    </beans:beans>

```

As soon as the user requests a list of books using `http://localhost:8080/bookstore`, the request hits the servlet engine, which routes the call to the bookstore web app, which is deployed in the servlet container. The `web.xml` file shown in Listing 5-40 provides the welcome file that should serve the request.

```
        <welcome-file-list>
            <welcome-file>/list_book.html</welcome-file>
        </welcome-file-list>
```

The URL in the welcome file matches the URL pattern that has been registered for `DispatcherServlet`, and the request is routed to it. Based on the configuration available in `bookstore-servlet.xml`, the request is routed to a specific controller, illustrated in line 12 of Listing 5-41. Here the `list_book.html` file is declared as a bean and mapped to the `BookController` class. This means if a URL with `/list_book.html` is requested, it will ask the `BookController` to handle the request. Listing 5-42 illustrates the interface-based `BookController`. Later you will see how to replace this interface-based controller with an annotated controller.

***Listing 5-42.** Interface-Based Controller for the Bookstore Application*

```
package com.apress.bookstore.controller;

import javax.servlet.http.HttpServletRequest;
import javax.servlet.http.HttpServletResponse;

import org.springframework.web.servlet.ModelAndView;
import org.springframework.web.servlet.mvc.Controller;

import com.apress.bookstore.service.BookService;

public class BookController implements Controller{

    @Override
    public ModelAndView handleRequest(HttpServletRequest arg0,
            HttpServletResponse arg1) throws Exception {
        BookService bookservice = new BookService();
        ModelAndView modelAndView = new ModelAndView("bookList");
        modelAndView.addObject("bookList", bookservice.getBookList());
        return modelAndView;
    }
}
```

The controller instantiates the `BookService` that is responsible for returning the required book data. `ModelAndView("booklist")` calls the view named `bookList` by passing `bookList` to Spring's view resolver to identify which view should be returned to the user. In this case, the BookController returns a ModelAndView object named bookList. The fragment of the view resolver in bookstore-servlet.xml (from Listing 5-41) is shown here:

```
    <beans:bean
        class="org.springframework.web.servlet.view.InternalResourceViewResolver">
        <beans:property name="prefix" value="/WEB-INF/views/" />
        <beans:property name="suffix" value=".jsp" />
    </beans:bean>
```

Based on the definition, the view resolver finds the file using the following mechanism:

```
Prefix + ModelAndView name + suffix, which translates to : /WEB-INF/jsp/bookList.jsp
```

ModelAndView.addObject("bookList", bookService.getBookList()) adds the book data returned by getBookList() to the model named bookList, which is formatted and rendered by the view.

Finally, the servlet engine renders the response via the specified JSP illustrated in Listing 5-43.

Listing 5-43. View

```
<%@page contentType="text/html" pageEncoding="UTF-8"%>
<%@ taglib prefix="c" uri="http://java.sun.com/jsp/jstl/core"%>
<!DOCTYPE html>
<html>
<head>
<meta http-equiv="Content-Type" content="text/html; charset=UTF-8">
<title>Your Book store</title>
</head>
<body>
    <h1>Books List</h1>
    <table border="1">
        <tr>
            <th align="left">Author</th>
            <th align="left">Book Title</th>
        </tr>
        <c:forEach items="${bookList}" var="book">
            <tr>
                <td>${book.author.authorName}</td>

                <td>${book.bookTitle}</td>
            </tr>
        </c:forEach>
    </table>
</body>
</html>
```

Figure 5-20 illustrates the directory structure of the bookstore application.

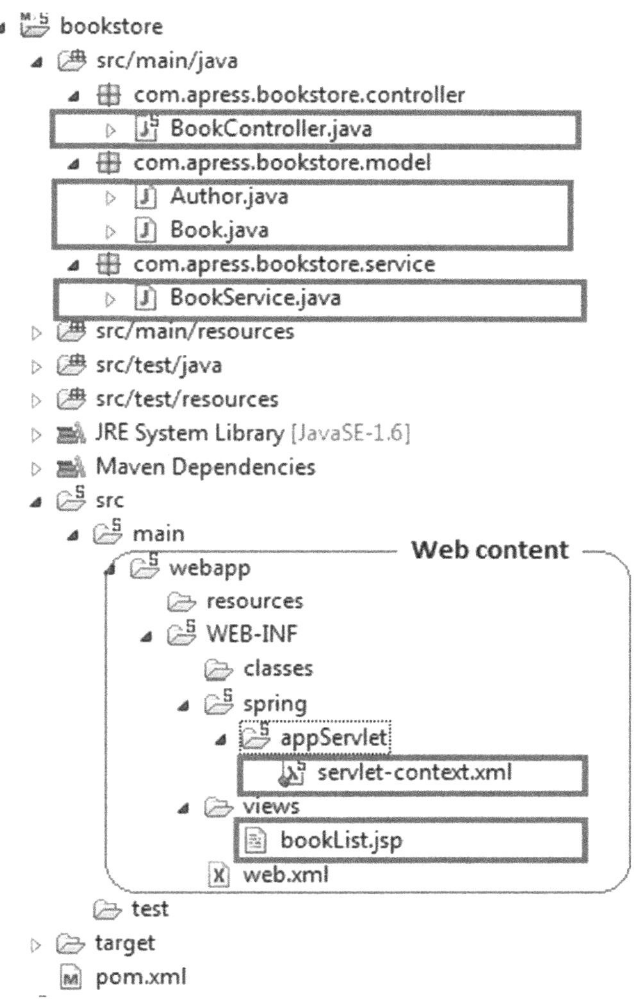

Figure 5-20. Directory structure of the bookstore application

Let's replace the interface-based controller in Listing 5-42 with an annotations-based controller. Listing 5-44 illustrates the annotations-based BookController.

Listing 5-44. Annotations-Based BookController

```
package com.apress.bookstore.controller;
import com.apress.bookstore.service.BookService;
import org.springframework.stereotype.Controller;
import org.springframework.web.bind.annotation.RequestMapping;
import org.springframework.web.bind.annotation.RequestMethod;
import org.springframework.web.servlet.ModelAndView;

@Controller
@RequestMapping("/list_book.html")
```

```
10.     public class BookController {
11.         @RequestMapping(method = RequestMethod.GET)
12.         public ModelAndView bookListController() {
13.             BookService bookManager = new BookService();
14.             ModelAndView modelAndView = new ModelAndView("bookList");
15.             modelAndView.addObject("bookList", bookManager.getBookList());
16.             return modelAndView;
17.         }
18.     }
```

- *Line 8*: In an annotations-based application, a form controller is created using `@Controller`. `@Controller` indicates that a particular class serves the role of a controller. `@Controller` also allows for autodetection, aligned with Spring's general support for detecting the component classes in the class path and autoregistering bean definitions for them. In this example, the `@Controller` annotation indicates that the `BookListControler` class is a controller class.
- *Line 9*: `@RequestMapping` is used to map URLs such as `/list_book.html` onto an entire class or a particular handler method. `@RequestMapping` on the class level indicates that all handling methods on this controller are relative to the `/list_book.html` path.
- *Line 13*: `@RequestMapping` on the method level indicates that the method accepts only GET requests; in other words, an HTTP GET for `/list_book.html` involves `bookListController()`.

Listing 5-45 illustrates the modified `bookstore-servlet.xml` to have the annotations-based `BookController` discovered.

***Listing 5-45.** bookstore-servlet.xml to Support Annotations-Based Controller*

```
<?xml version="1.0" encoding="UTF-8"?>
<beans:beans xmlns="http://www.springframework.org/schema/mvc"
    xmlns:xsi="http://www.w3.org/2001/XMLSchema-instance" xmlns:beans=
    "http://www.springframework.org/schema/beans"
    xmlns:context="http://www.springframework.org/schema/context"
    xsi:schemaLocation="http://www.springframework.org/schema/mvc
    http://www.springframework.org/schema/mvc/spring-mvc.xsd
        http://www.springframework.org/schema/beans
        http://www.springframework.org/schema/beans/spring-beans.xsd
        http://www.springframework.org/schema/context
        http://www.springframework.org/schema/context/spring-context.xsd">

    <!-- DispatcherServlet Context: defines this servlet's request-processing
        infrastructure -->

    <context:component-scan base-package="com.apress.bookStore.controller" />
    <beans:bean name="/list_book.html"
        class="com.apress.bookstore.controller.BookController" />


    <!-- Resolves views selected for rendering by @Controllers to .jsp resources
        in the /WEB-INF/views directory -->
```

```
19.        <beans:bean
20.            class="org.springframework.web.servlet.view.InternalResourceViewResolver">
21.            <beans:property name="prefix" value="/WEB-INF/views/" />
22.            <beans:property name="suffix" value=".jsp" />
23.        </beans:bean>
24.    </beans:beans>
```

- *Line 12*: `<context:component-scan>` of the dispatcher servlet registers `@Controller`-annotated classes as beans. The `BookListController` class is automatically discovered and registered as a bean.

Working with Forms Using Annotations

Form processing is greatly simplified with annotations-driven configuration in Spring Web MVC. Spring removes the need for traditional form handling via the data binding mechanism that automatically populates Java objects from the submitted form and by supporting validation and error reports. Listing 5-46 demonstrates using a form and then processing the user-entered data. Figure 5-21 illustrates the new files added to the bookstore directory structure.

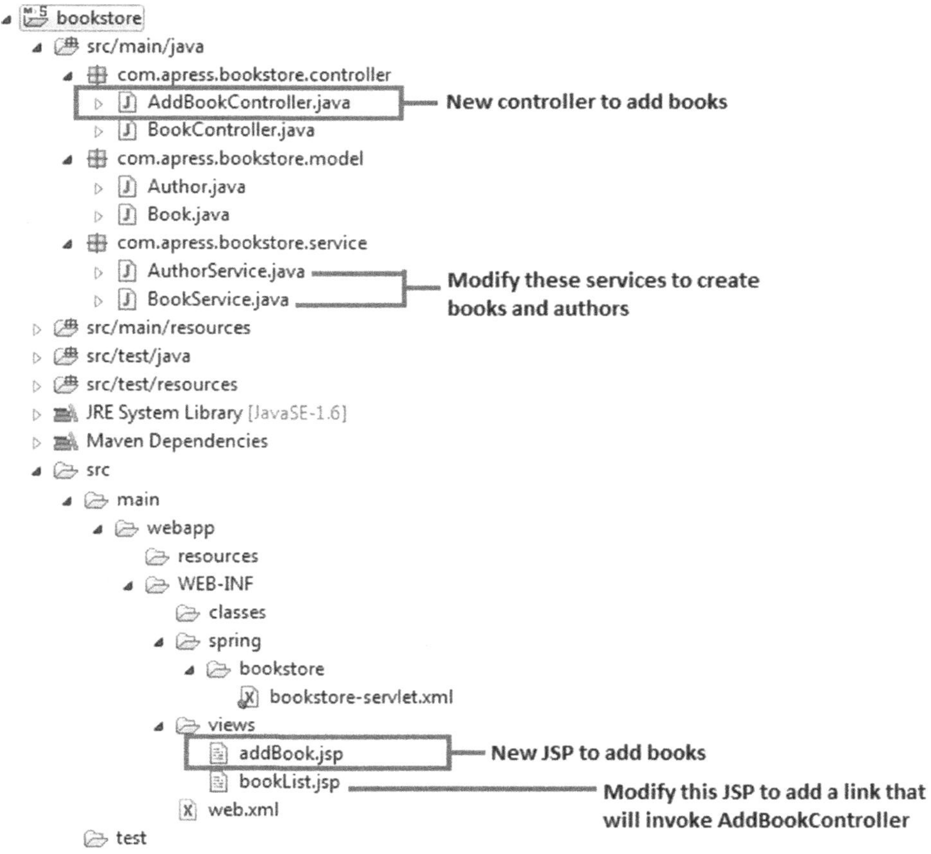

Figure 5-21. New files in the application for form processing

A new controller, AddBookController, is added that takes care of all the form processing using annotations. Listing 5-46 illustrates the AddBookController.

Listing 5-46. AddBookController for Form Processing

```
package com.apress.bookstore.controller;

import java.util.List;

import org.springframework.stereotype.Controller;
import org.springframework.ui.ModelMap;
import org.springframework.validation.BindingResult;
import org.springframework.web.bind.WebDataBinder;
import org.springframework.web.bind.annotation.InitBinder;
import org.springframework.web.bind.annotation.ModelAttribute;
import org.springframework.web.bind.annotation.RequestMapping;
import org.springframework.web.bind.annotation.RequestMethod;
import org.springframework.web.bind.support.SessionStatus;
import org.springframework.web.context.request.WebRequest;

import com.apress.bookstore.model.Author;
import com.apress.bookstore.model.Book;
import com.apress.bookstore.service.AuthorService;
import com.apress.bookstore.service.BookService;

@Controller
@RequestMapping("/addBook.html")
public class AddBookController {
    @RequestMapping(value="/addBook.html", method = RequestMethod.GET)
    public String initForm(ModelMap model) {
    Book book = new Book();
    book.setBookTitle("Add  Book :");
        model.addAttribute("book", book);
    return "addBook";
    }

    @InitBinder
    public void initBinder(WebDataBinder binder, WebRequest request) {
    binder.setDisallowedFields(new String[] {"author"});
        Book book = (Book)binder.getTarget();
    AuthorService authorService = new AuthorService();
    Long authorId = null;
    try {
            authorId = Long.parseLong(request.getParameter("author"));
        } catch (Exception e) {}
        if (authorId != null) {
            Author author = authorService.getAuthorById(authorId);
            book.setAuthor(author);
        }
    }

```

```
47.         @ModelAttribute("authorList")
48.         public List<Author> populateAuthorList() {
49.         AuthorService authorService = new AuthorService();
50.         return authorService.getAuthorList();
51.         }
52.
53.         @RequestMapping(method = RequestMethod.POST)
54.         public String processSubmit(@ModelAttribute("book") Book book, BindingResult result,
            SessionStatus status) {
55.             BookService bookService = new BookService();
56.             bookService.createBook(book);
57.         return "redirect:/list_book.html";
58.         }
59.     }
```

- *Line 22*: The `AddBookController` class is annotated with `@RequestMapping("/addBook.html")`, which means that all the methods in this class will handle the request for the URL"`/ addBook.html`".
- *Line 24*: The initialization for binding is done by annotating the method name with `@RequestMapping(method=RequestMethod.GET)`.
- *Line 25*: `initForm()` handles the `GET` request type and shows the add new book form.
- *Line 28*: `initForm()` also adds a new instance to the model map so that the new instance can be associated with the form.
- *Line 32*: Binding is defined by annotating the method name with `@InitBinder`.
- Annotating controller methods with `@InitBinder` allows configuring the web data binding directly within the controller class. `@InitBinder` identifies methods that initialize the `WebDataBinder` that is used to populate the command and form object arguments of annotated handler methods. Such init-binder methods support all arguments that `@RequestMapping` supports, except for command/form objects and the corresponding validation result objects. Init-binder methods that are declared must not have a return value. Thus, they are usually declared as void.
- *Line 33*: Typical arguments include `WebDataBinder` in combination with `WebRequest` or `java.util.Locale`, allowing code to register context-specific editors.
- Data binding is configured using the `WebDataBinder` class. `WebDataBinder` is a special `DataBinder` for data binding from web request parameters to JavaBean objects.
- Spring injects an instance of this class into any controller method that has been annotated with `@InitBinder`. This object is then used to define the data binding rules for the controller.
- `WebRequest` allows for generic request parameter access as well as request/session attribute access without ties to the native Servlet API.
- *Line 34*: `setDisallowedFields()` registers the fields that are not allowed for binding.

- *Line 47*: The reference data is put into the model so that the form view can access it, by annotating the method name with `@ModelAttribute`.
  - When `@ModelAttribute` is placed on a method parameter, it maps a model attribute to the specific annotated method parameter. This is how the controller gets a reference to the object holding the data entered in the form.
  - `@ModelAttribute` annotation informs the Spring MVC framework that the `authorList` instance should be assigned as an instance of the `Author` class and should be passed to populate the `AuthorList()`.
- *Line 53*: The form submission is handled by annotating the method name with `@RequestMapping(method= RequestMethod.POST)`.
- *Line 54*: `processSubmit()` accepts POST requests; that is, an HTTP POST for `/new_book.html` invokes `processSubmit()`. `processSubmit()` processes the form data. `processSubmit()` takes three parameters:
  - `@ModelAttribute(value="book") Book book`: The model attribute annotation informs the Spring MVC framework that the `Book` model instance should be assigned as an instance of the `Book` class and should be passed to the method `processSubmit()`.
  - `BindingResult result`: Spring determines errors, if any, during the creation of the `Book` class. If it finds errors, its description is passed to the method as a `BindingResult` instance.
  - `SessionStatus status`: `SessionStatus` is a status handle for marking form processing as complete.
- *Line 57*: The `redirect`: prefix in the return statement triggers an HTTP redirect back to the browser. This is necessary when delegating the response to another controller, rather than just rendering the view.

Listing 5-47 illustrates the modified service layer of the bookstore application for form processing.

***Listing 5-47.** BookService*

```
package com.apress.bookstore.service;

import java.util.LinkedList;
import java.util.List;

import com.apress.bookstore.model.Author;
import com.apress.bookstore.model.Book;

public class BookService {

    private static List<Book> bookList;

    static {

        Author author1 = new Author();
        author1.setAuthorId((long) 1);
```

```
        author1.setAuthorName("Vishal Layka");
        Book book1 = new Book();
        book1.setBookId((long) 1);
        book1.setBookTitle("Beginning Groovy, Grails and Griffon");
        book1.setAuthor(author1);

        Book book2 = new Book();
        book2.setBookId((long) 2);
        book2.setBookTitle("Modern Java Web Development");
        book2.setAuthor(author1);

        bookList = new LinkedList<Book>();
        bookList.add(book1);
        bookList.add(book2);
    }

    public List<Book> getBookList() {
        return bookList;
    }

     public Book createBook(Book b) {
            Book book = new Book();
            book.setBookId((long)bookList.size() + 1);
            book.setAuthor(b.getAuthor());
            book.setBookTitle(b.getBookTitle());
            bookList.add(book);
            return book;
            }

}
```

Listing 5-48 illustrates the modified `bookList.jsp` of the bookstore application for form processing.

Listing 5-48. bookList.jsp

```
<%@page contentType="text/html" pageEncoding="UTF-8"%>
<%@ taglib prefix="c" uri="http://java.sun.com/jsp/jstl/core"%>
<!DOCTYPE html>
<html>
<head>
<meta http-equiv="Content-Type" content="text/html; charset=UTF-8">
<title>Your Book store</title>
</head>
<body>
    <h1>Books List</h1>
    <table border="1">
        <tr>
            <th align="left">Author</th>
            <th align="left">Book Title</th>
        </tr>
        <c:forEach items="${bookList}" var="book">
```

```
17.             <tr>
18.                 <td>${book.author.authorName}</td>
19. 
20.                 <td>${book.bookTitle}</td>
21.             </tr>
22.         </c:forEach>
23.     </table>
24.     <br/>
25.     <a href="addBook.html">Add books.</a>
26. </body>
27. </html>
```

- *Line 25*: The form controller is called using `addBook.html`, which is mapped on lines 22 and 24 of the `AddBookController` in Listing 5-46.

Listing 5-49 illustrates the new JSP page of the bookstore application for form processing that will be displayed when the `AddBookController` is invoked using `<a href="addBook.html">Add books.</a>` on line 25 of Listing 5-48.

Listing 5-49. addBook.jsp

```
<%@page contentType="text/html" pageEncoding="UTF-8"%>
<%@ taglib prefix="c" uri="http://java.sun.com/jsp/jstl/core" %>
<%@ taglib prefix="form" uri="http://www.springframework.org/tags/form" %>

<!DOCTYPE html>
<html>
<head>
<meta http-equiv="Content-Type" content="text/html; charset=UTF-8">
<title>Your Book store</title>
</head>
<body>
<h1>Add  Book</h1>
    <form:form method="post" commandName="book">
            Author<br />
<form:select path="author">
<form:options items="${authorList}" itemValue="authorId" itemLabel="authorName" />
</form:select>
<br /><br />
            Book Name<br />
<form:input path="bookTitle"/><br /><br />
<br />
<input type="submit" value="Submit">
    </form:form>
</body>
</html>
```

Listing 5-49 illustrates the form displayed. It also shows the usage of Spring form tags.

Annotations-Based Validation

The following section demonstrates how you can validate the user-entered data using annotations. Figure 5-22 illustrates the modified files and newly added files in the application.

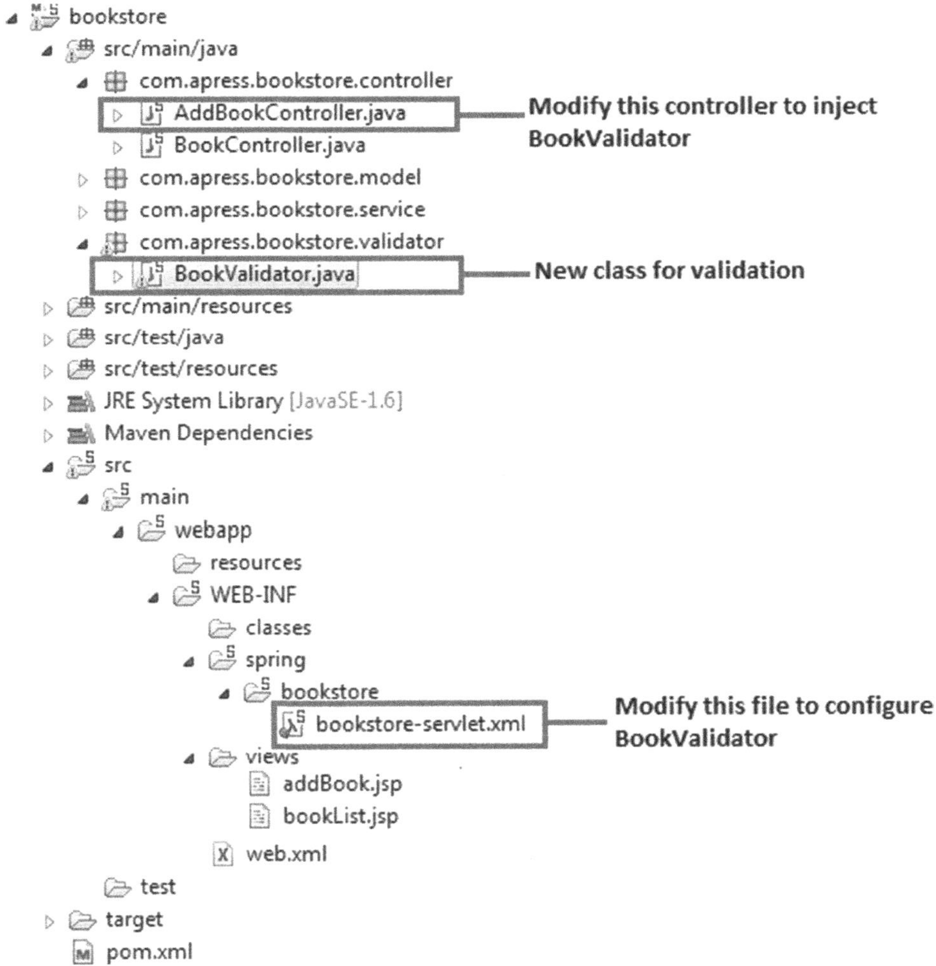

Figure 5-22. Modified files and new files in the directory structure for annotations-based validation

Listing 5-50 illustrates the BookValidator.

Listing 5-50. Validations in the BookValidator

```
package com.apress.bookstore.validator;

import org.springframework.validation.Errors;
import org.springframework.validation.ValidationUtils;
import org.springframework.validation.Validator;

```

```
7.  import com.apress.bookstore.model.Book;
8.
9.  public class BookValidator implements Validator {
10.     @Override
11.     public boolean supports(Class clazz) {
12.         return Book.class.equals(clazz);
13.     }
14.
15.     @Override
16.     public void validate(Object obj, Errors errors) {
17.         Book book = (Book) obj;
18.         ValidationUtils.rejectIfEmptyOrWhitespace(errors, "bookTitle", "field.required",
            "Required Field");
19.         if ( ! errors.hasFieldErrors("bookTitle")) {
20.             if (book.getBookTitle().isEmpty())
21.                 errors.rejectValue("Title", "", "Cannot be left empty!");
22.         }
23.     }
24.
25.
26. }
```

- *Lines 19 to 23*: Typical validations in the application

The controller named AddBookController is updated for the validation, as shown in Listing 5-51.

***Listing 5-51.** Updating the AddBookController*

```
package com.apress.bookstore.controller;

import java.util.List;

import org.springframework.beans.factory.annotation.Autowired;
import org.springframework.stereotype.Controller;
import org.springframework.ui.ModelMap;
import org.springframework.validation.BindingResult;
import org.springframework.web.bind.WebDataBinder;
import org.springframework.web.bind.annotation.InitBinder;
import org.springframework.web.bind.annotation.ModelAttribute;
import org.springframework.web.bind.annotation.RequestMapping;
import org.springframework.web.bind.annotation.RequestMethod;
import org.springframework.web.bind.support.SessionStatus;
import org.springframework.web.context.request.WebRequest;

import com.apress.bookstore.model.Author;
import com.apress.bookstore.model.Book;
import com.apress.bookstore.service.AuthorService;
import com.apress.bookstore.service.BookService;
import com.apress.bookstore.validator.BookValidator;

```

```
@Controller
@RequestMapping("/addBook.html")
public class AddBookController {
    BookValidator bookValidator;

    @Autowired
    public AddBookController(BookValidator bookValidator) {
        this.bookValidator = bookValidator;
    }

    @RequestMapping(value="/addBook.html", method = RequestMethod.GET)
    public String initForm(ModelMap model) {
    Book book = new Book();
    book.setBookTitle("Add  Book :");
        model.addAttribute("book", book);
    return "addBook";
    }

    @InitBinder
    public void initBinder(WebDataBinder binder, WebRequest request) {
    binder.setDisallowedFields(new String[] {"author"});
        Book book = (Book)binder.getTarget();
    AuthorService authorService = new AuthorService();
    Long authorId = null;
    try {
            authorId = Long.parseLong(request.getParameter("author"));
        } catch (Exception e) {}
        if (authorId != null) {
            Author author = authorService.getAuthorById(authorId);
            book.setAuthor(author);
        }
    }

    @ModelAttribute("authorList")
    public List<Author> populateAuthorList() {
    AuthorService authorService = new AuthorService();
    return authorService.getAuthorList();
    }

    @RequestMapping(method = RequestMethod.POST)
    public String processSubmit(@ModelAttribute("book") Book book, BindingResult result,
    SessionStatus status) {
        BookService bookService = new BookService();
        bookService.createBook(book);
        if(result.hasErrors()) {
            return "addBook";
        } else {
    bookService.createBook(book);
            return "redirect:/list_book.html";
        }

    }
}
```

- *Line 29*: The `BookValidator` class is injected using the setter method.
- *Line 63*: In `processSubmit()`, `validate()` of the `BookValidator` is called to check whether the book details are entered by the user. `validate()` is passed the value of the `Book` model and the `BindingResult` object to hold errors, if any.
- *Line 66*: A check is made whether the result variable holds any errors. If there are errors, then the application displays the same page with the error messages. If there are no errors, that is, the user has entered all the correct data, then the application displays the list of the book details along with the newly entered book details.

Configuring the Validator

Now you have to declare the validator for the URL `addBook.html` in `bookstore-servlet.xml`, as illustrated in Listing 5-52.

***Listing 5-52.** Declaring the BookValidator*

```
1.    <?xml version="1.0" encoding="UTF-8"?>
2.    <beans:beans xmlns="http://www.springframework.org/schema/mvc"
3.        xmlns:xsi="http://www.w3.org/2001/XMLSchema-instance" xmlns:beans=
          "http://www.springframework.org/schema/beans"
4.        xmlns:context="http://www.springframework.org/schema/context"
5.        xsi:schemaLocation="http://www.springframework.org/schema/mvc http://www.springframework.org/
          schema/mvc/spring-mvc.xsd
6.            http://www.springframework.org/schema/beans http://www.springframework.org/schema/
              beans/spring-beans.xsd
7.            http://www.springframework.org/schema/context
              http://www.springframework.org/schema/context/spring-context.xsd">
8.
9.        <!-- DispatcherServlet Context: defines this servlet's request-processing
10.           infrastructure -->
11.
12.       <context:component-scan base-package="com.apress.bookstore.controller" />
13.       <beans:bean class="com.apress.bookstore.validator.BookValidator" />
14.
15.       <!-- Resolves views selected for rendering by @Controllers to .jsp resources
16.           in the /WEB-INF/views directory -->
17.       <beans:bean
18.           class="org.springframework.web.servlet.view.InternalResourceViewResolver">
19.           <beans:property name="prefix" value="/WEB-INF/views/" />
20.           <beans:property name="suffix" value=".jsp" />
21.       </beans:bean>
22.   </beans:beans>
```

- *Line 13*: The `BookValidator` class is defined. The container creates the `BookValidator` class by calling its constructor.

Summary

This chapter first briefly introduced the Spring Framework and went on to show how you can deal with tight coupling, cross-cutting concerns, and boilerplate code. This chapter transformed the data access layer built in Chapter 1 to eliminate the boilerplate code resulting from using pure JDBC. Then it discussed Spring MVC's architecture, including its request-handling life cycle. Next it showed you how to develop a Hello World application using Spring Web MVC. Then it began implementing the bookstore application using Spring Web MVC, and as the application progressed, it introduced the annotations programming model of Spring Web MVC and processing forms in the web application.

Chapter 6

Component-Based Web Development Using JSF 2

It's so beautifully arranged on the plate—you just know someone's fingers have been all over it.

—Julia Child

JavaServer Faces (JSF) is a component-based framework for developing web applications. The distinctive feature that sets component-based frameworks apart is the ability to create and distribute *reusable UI components*. In general, a component represents an abstraction, a well-defined contract with the implementation details hidden from the user of the component. That is, the user of the component does not need to know the internal mechanisms of the component in order to be able to use it. Struts and Spring Web MVC alleviate the increasing complexities of building sophisticated user interfaces for the Web, but these web frameworks are not component-centric and therefore unqualified for engineering truly reusable UI components. To that end, different web frameworks, such as Tapestry and Wicket, emerged to offer a component-centric approach to web application development. However, because of a lack of existing standards for component-centric development, the ways in which these web frameworks implemented reusable UI components appeared to an experienced web developer to be tedious or limited.

JSF standardizes component-based web development and provides numerous and broad-ranging UI components to reduce the complexities in web application development. JSF provides out-of-the-box reusable UI components so that the application developers can concentrate on the application's business logic rather than striving to develop and maintain dynamic and rich user interfaces. JSF is the evolution of a few frameworks such as Struts and was inspired by Swing's component model. JSF represents, and requires, a paradigm shift to let you think in terms of components instead of requests and responses. Its goal is to make web development rapid by promoting and standardizing an ecosystem to engineer reusable UI components.

The Architecture of JSF

A JSF web framework uses the Model-View-Controller (MVC) design pattern like request-based web frameworks such as Struts and SpringMVC do. Figure 6-1 shows a high-level architecture of the JSF framework.

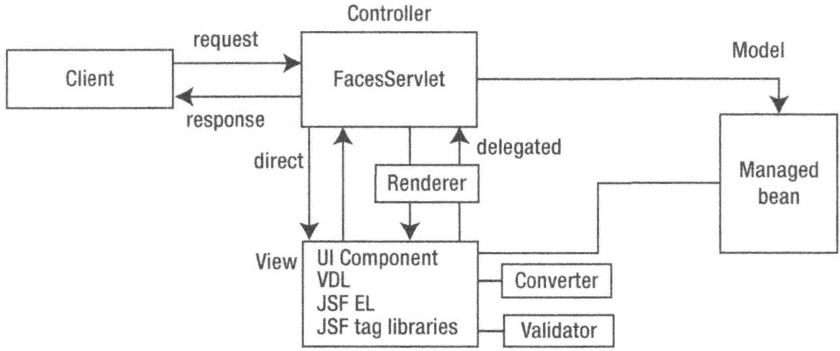

Figure 6-1. A high-level architecture of the JSF framework

Figure 6-1 presents several important parts of JSF that make its architecture rich and flexible. This architecture allows you to do the following:

- Plug in any view declaration language (VDL) such as JSP and Facelets
- Render the display in different devices, such as desktops, tablets, and so on
- Create pages using components

FacesServlet

FacesServlet is the controller in the MVC, as shown in Figure 6-1, and implements the Front Controller pattern that intercepts every interaction between Facelets (the view) and the model. FacesServlet is configured through annotations on managed beans, converters, components, renderers, and validators or optionally through the `faces-config.xml` descriptor file.

Managed Bean

Managed beans serve as the model for the UI component. They are responsible for the following:

- Synchronizing data with components
- Processing business logic
- Handling navigation between pages

VDL

JSF uses a view declaration language (VDL) to display a page to the client on various devices such as the desktop, portables, and so on. The default VDL for JavaServer Faces (JSF) is Facelets, but JSF allows multiple VDLs, such as JSP.

JSF EL

In the Hello World application in Chapter 5, you saw how to access managed bean properties and invoke managed bean actions using EL expressions with the delimiters `#{` and `}`. The EL used in JSF 1.0 and 1.1 (and later in JSP versions 1.2 and 2.0) was an extension of the EL that was part of the JSP Standard Tag Library (JSTL), as explained in Chapter 3. The difference in JSF EL and the JSP EL is that of evaluation. In JSP, as you have seen in Chapter 3, any `${}` expression that appears in the page is evaluated immediately during page rendering. Such expressions are called *immediate expressions*.

JSF allows expressions to be available both during the rendering of the page and when that is posted back again. This type of expression in JSF is called a *deferred expression* and is expressed with the delimiters `#{}`.

JSF Tag Library

The standard JSF library consists of four parts that the page needs to access in order to use the JSF components.

- *HTML components library*: This defines elements that represent common HTML user interface components. The standard HTML library is accessible in Facelets and JSP as a tag library with a URI of `http://java.sun.com/jsf/html` and a default prefix of `h`.
- *JSF core library*: The standard core library is associated with the `f:` namespace and provides common application development utilities for validation and conversion.
- *Facelets library*: The standard Facelets templating library is accessible in Facelets as a tag library with a URI of `http://java.sun.com/jsf/facelets` and a default prefix of `ui`.
- *Composite library*: The standard composite component library is accessible in Facelets as a tag library with a URI of `http://java.sun.com/jsf/composite` and a default prefix of `composite`.

The standard JSF component libraries are part of the specification and also come with any standard JSF implementation such as the reference implementation or the MyFaces implementation. The section that follows shows how to download and install the JSF implementation, known as Mojarra, and integrate it into a web application.

UI Component

JSF has a rich component model provided in a standard UI component framework, as illustrated in Figure 6-2. The JSF component model includes the following:

- A rendering model that defines a myriad of forms in which the component can be rendered such as for desktop application devices and mobile app devices
- An event and event listener model that define how to handle component events
- A conversion model that defines the ways to register data converters to a component for data conversion
- A validation model that defines the ways to register validators to a component for the server-side validation

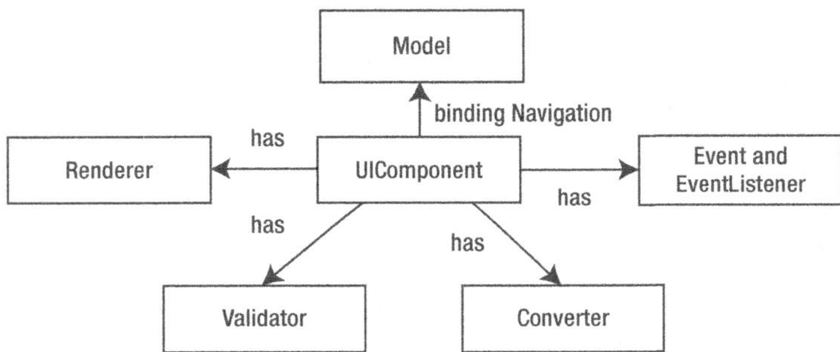

***Figure 6-2.** The JSF component model*

The UI component model is the core of JSF; it allows you to develop the view of a web application from collections of standard, out-of-the-box UI components. These UI components are responsible for the behavior and are utilized in the JSF pages by including four tag libraries provided by JSF, depending on the type of UI component you want to use.

Renderer

The renderer is responsible for displaying a component, in other words, rendering the markup to the client and translating a user's input into the component's value. JSF supports two programming models for displaying components.

- *Direct renderer model*: When the direct model is used, components decode from, and encode to, the view. The decoding and encoding processes are explained in the next section.
- *Delegated renderer model*: When the delegated model is used, the decoding and encoding are delegated to a renderer.

Converter and Validator

JSF provides out-of-the-box converters to convert its UI component's data to objects used in a managed bean, and vice versa. For example, they convert a component's Date value to and from String values that come from the HTML markup.

JSF also provides out-of-the-box validators to validate its UI components to ensure that the value entered by the user is valid. These tags can, for example, validate a range of Long or the length of a string.

Events and Event Listeners

When the user clicks a button or link on the JSF page, a JSF UI component triggers an event. To handle such an event, an event listener is registered on the managed bean. The UI component calls the event notification on the event listener for the specific event.

As you have seen, JSF pages consist of a tree of components. This tree of components is managed by the JSF request-processing life cycle behind the scenes. To understand the JSF request-processing life cycle, first you will create a Hello World web application, and then through this application you will learn how the JSF life cycle works behind the scenes.

Getting Started with JSF

In this section, you will create a simple Hello World JSF web application using Eclipse 3.8 or newer, which supports JSF2.*x*. Create a dynamic web project as illustrated in Figure 6-3 by selecting File ➤ New ➤ Project ➤ Web ➤ Dynamic Web Project. Specify Apache Tomcat v7.0 in Target Runtime, select JavaServer Faces Project in the configuration, and click Next.

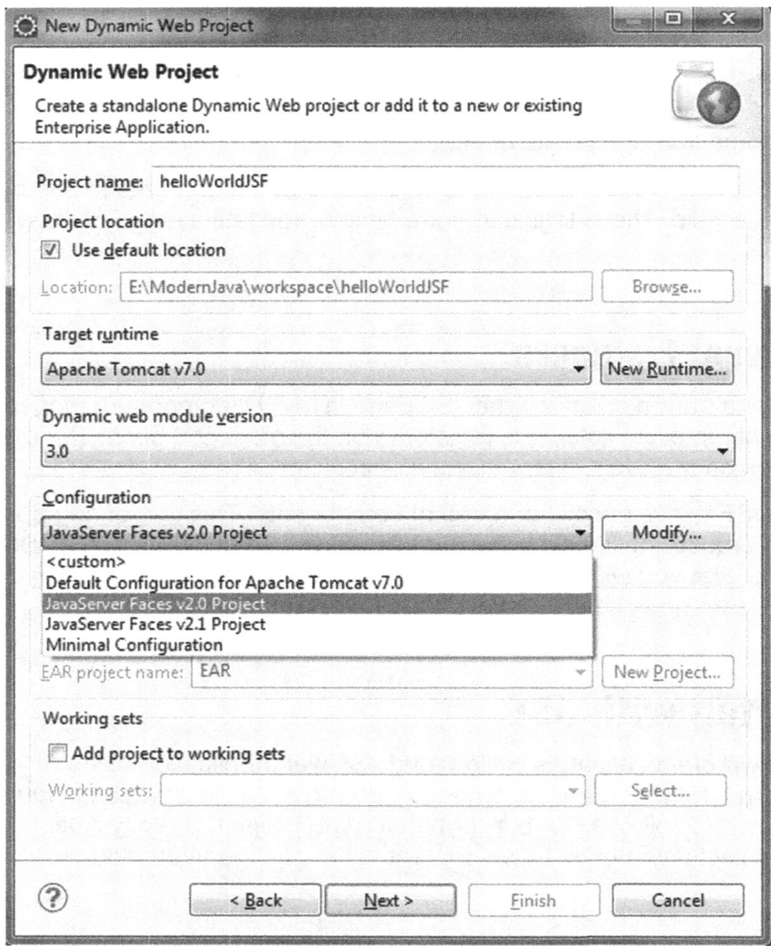

***Figure 6-3.** Creating a JSF project*

Configure the project for building a Java application, as illustrated in Figure 6-4, and click Next.

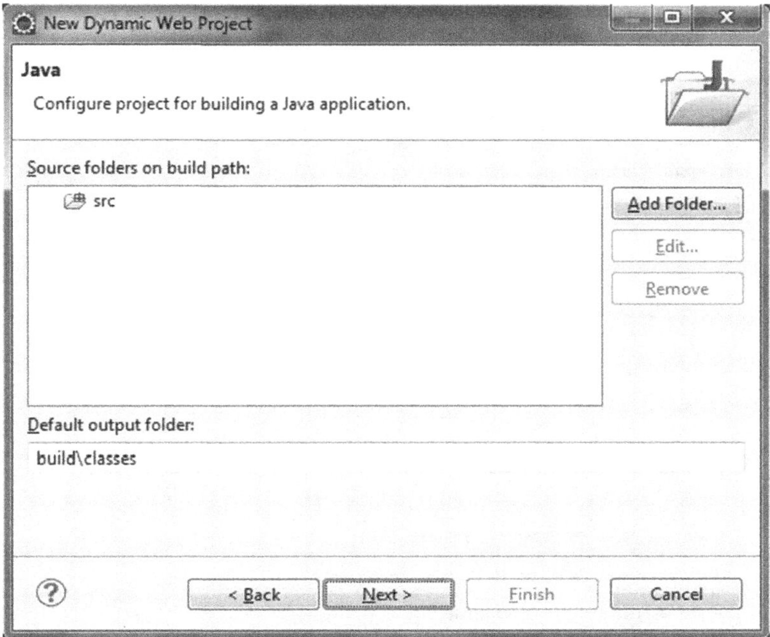

Figure 6-4. Configuring a dynamic web project

Configure the web module settings, as illustrated in Figure 6-5, and click Next.

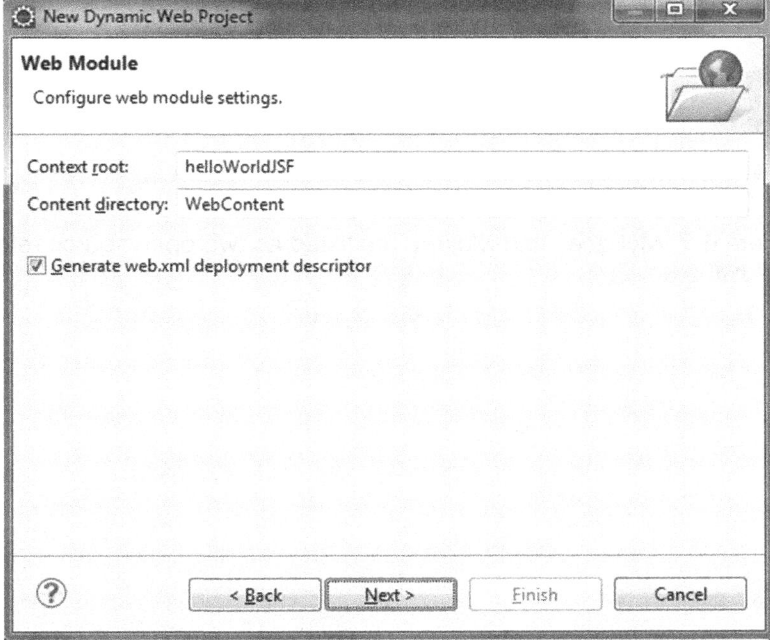

Figure 6-5. Configuring the web module settings

You need to select the JSF implementation library, as illustrated in Figure 6-6. You can do so by downloading the library by clicking Download.

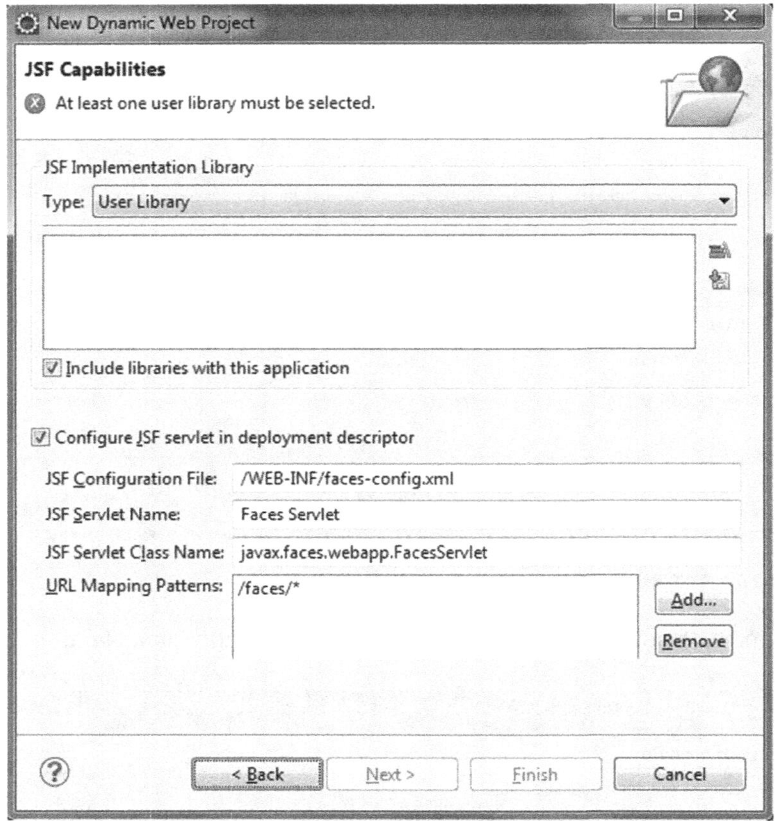

Figure 6-6. Downloading JSF implementation libraries

As illustrated in Figure 6-7, MyFaces and Mojarra are listed as two open source reference implementations of JSF 2.0.

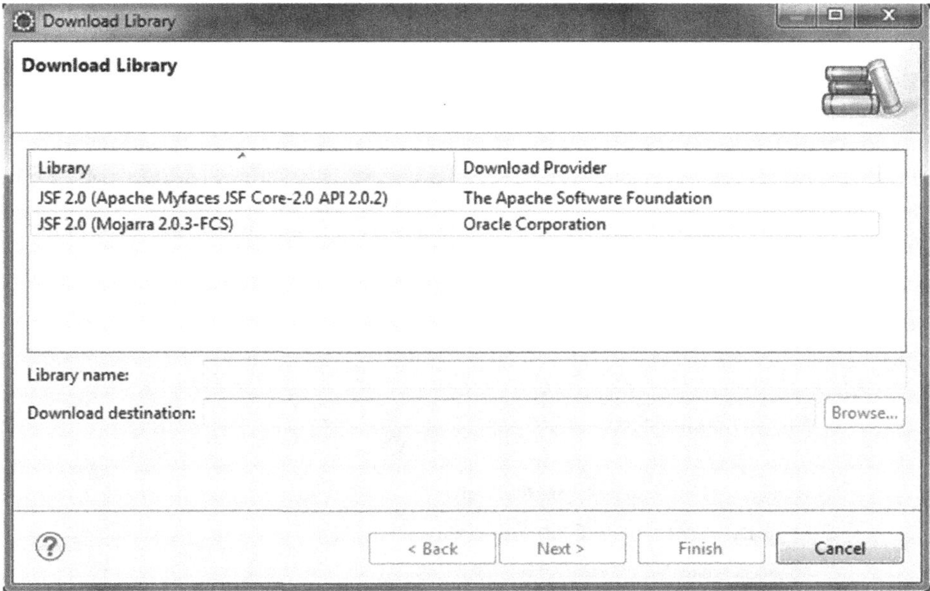

Figure 6-7. JSF implementation libraries

Select Mojarra, click Next, and accept the license terms, as illustrated in Figure 6-8.

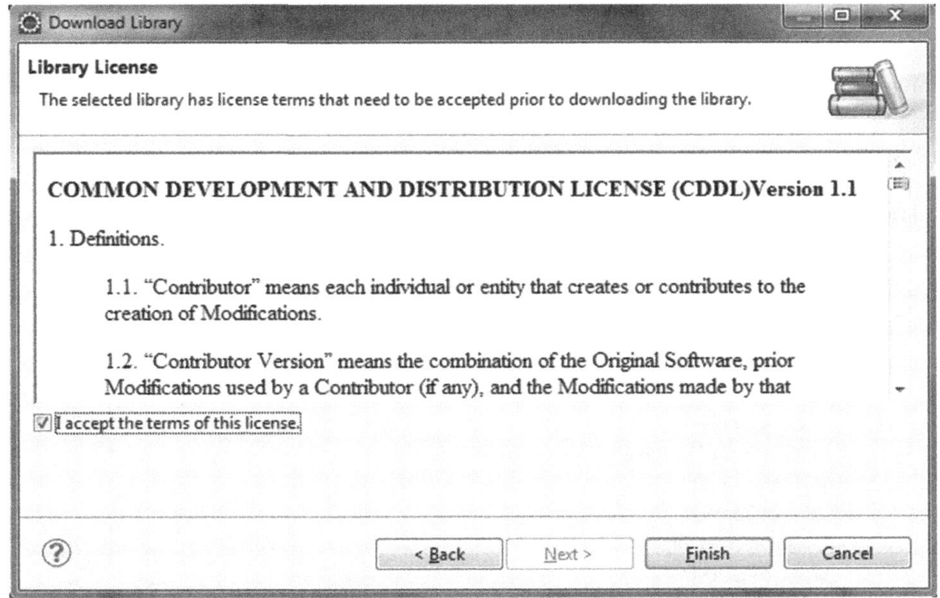

Figure 6-8. Accept the terms of license

Click Finish. Mojarra will be listed as the selected implementation library, as illustrated in Figure 6-9.

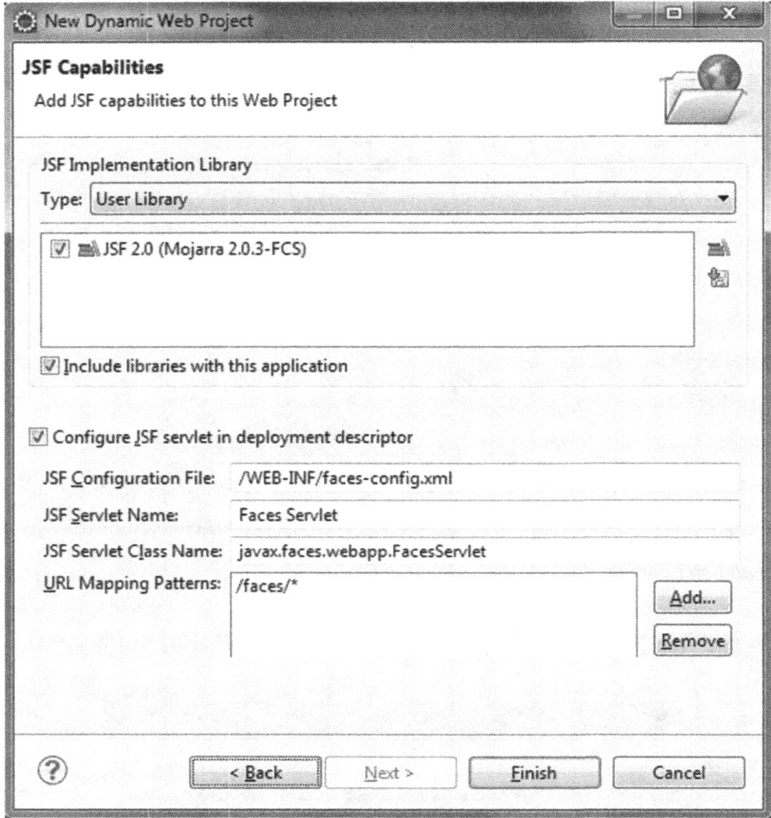

Figure 6-9. Adding JSF capabilities

Click Finish. The project is created, as illustrated in Figure 6-10.

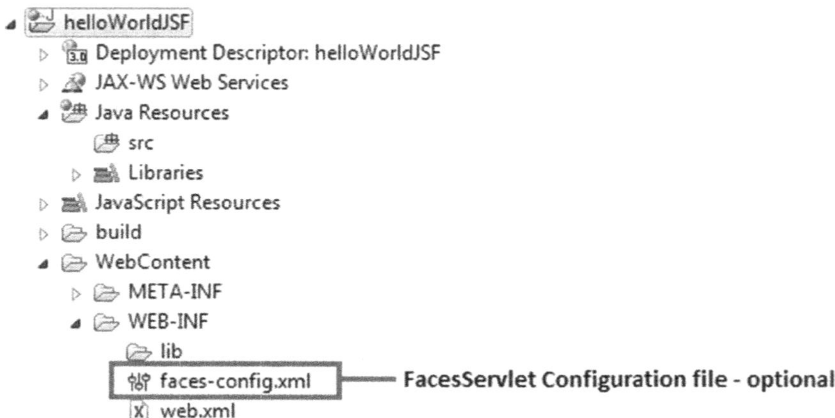

Figure 6-10. Directory structure of the created JSF project

You will create the following files in the project:

- *Managed bean*: `HelloBean.java`.
- *form.xhtml*: This is a view file that comprises JSF core tags and deferred EL. When the application is run, the `form.xhtml` file looks like Figure 6-11. This screen provides an input field and a Submit button.

***Figure 6-11.** The form to enter the name*

- *hello.xhtml*: When users enter a name and click the Submit button in `form.xhtml`, they are greeted by name. `hello.xhtml` displays the name of the user entered in `form.xhtml` along with the greeting, as illustrated in Figure 6-12.

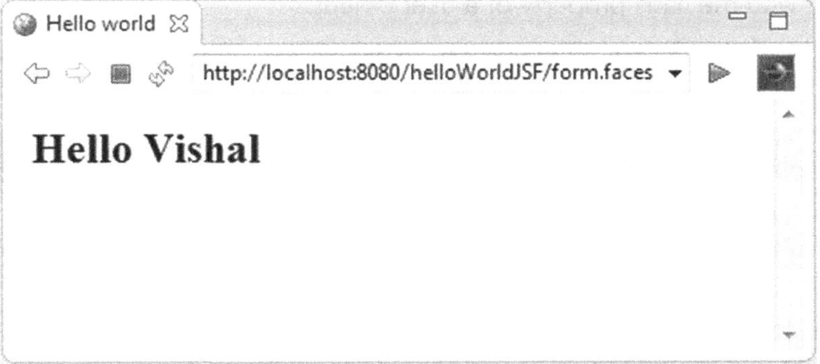

***Figure 6-12.** Hello screen*

Listing 6-1 illustrates the code of the form.xhtml file.

Listing 6-1. form.xhtml

```
1.  <?xml version="1.0" encoding="UTF-8"?>
2.  <!DOCTYPE html >
3.  <html xmlns="http://www.w3.org/1999/xhtml"
4.  xmlns:h="http://java.sun.com/jsf/html">
5.
6.  <h:head>
7.      <title>First JSF app</title>
8.  </h:head>
9.  <h:body>
10.     <h3>Enter your name:</h3>
11.
12.     <h:form>
13.         <h:inputText value="#{helloBean.name}"></h:inputText>
14.         <h:commandButton value="Submit" action="hello"></h:commandButton>
15.     </h:form>
16.  </h:body>
17.  </html>
```

- *Line 4*: The xmlns attribute declares the JSF namespace.
- *Lines 6, 9, 12, 13, and 14*: Some tags have prefixes, such as h:head and h:inputText. These are JSF tags. The h:inputText and h:commandButton tags correspond to the text field and Submit button in Figure 6-11.
- *Line 13*: The input fields are linked to object properties. For example, attributevalue="#{helloBean.name}" tells the JSF implementation to link the text field with the name property of a user object.
- *Line 14*: The #{...} delimiters enclose expressions in the JSF expression language.
- *Line 14*: When you enter the name and click the Submit button, the hello.xhtml file is displayed, as specified in the action attribute of the h:commandButton tag.

Listing 6-2 illustrates the code of the hello.xhtml file.

Listing 6-2. hello.xhtml

```
<?xml version="1.0" encoding="UTF-8"?>
<!DOCTYPE html>
<html xmlns="http://www.w3.org/1999/xhtml"
    xmlns:h="http://java.sun.com/jsf/html">

<h:head>
    <title>Hello world</title>
</h:head>
<h:body>
    <h2>Hello  #{helloBean.name}</h2>
 </h:body>
 </html>
```

- *Line 10*: When the page is submitted, JSF will find the `helloBean` and set the submitted name value via the `setName()` method. When `hello.xhtml` is displayed, JSF will find the `helloBean` and display the `name` property value via its `getName()` method.

Listing 6-3 illustrates the `helloBean`.

Listing 6-3. Managed Bean

```
1.    package com.apress.jsf.helloworld;
2.    import javax.faces.bean.ManagedBean;
3.    import javax.faces.bean.SessionScoped;
4.    import java.io.Serializable;
5.
6.    @ManagedBean
7.    @SessionScoped
8.    public class HelloBean implements Serializable {
9.
10.        private static final long serialVersionUID = 1L;
11.
12.        private String name;
13.
14.        public String getName() {
15.            return name;
16.        }
17.        public void setName(String name) {
18.            this.name = name;
19.        }
20.     }
```

- *Line 6*: A managed bean is a Java bean that is accessed from a JSF page. The `@ManagedBean` annotation specifies the name by which an object of this class is referenced in the JSF pages.
- *Line 7*: A managed bean must have a name and a scope. Session scope signifies that the bean object is available for one user across multiple pages.

> **Note** There are two annotations for naming a bean. `@Named` is the best choice with a Java EE 6 and newer application server.

Like Struts and Spring MVC web applications, when you deploy a JSF web application inside an application server, you need to provide a deployment descriptor file named `web.xml`. Listing 6-4 shows this file. For the sake of brevity, the `web-app` declaration and the list of files in the `welcome-file-list` are not completely shown.

Listing 6-4. web.xml

```
1.	<web-app ..... >
2.	<display-name>helloWorldJSF</display-name>
3.	<welcome-file-list>
4.	    ...
5.	</welcome-file-list>
6.	<servlet>
7.	<servlet-name>Faces Servlet</servlet-name>
8.	<servlet-class>javax.faces.webapp.FacesServlet</servlet-class>
9.	<load-on-startup>1</load-on-startup>
10.	 </servlet>
11.	 <servlet-mapping>
12.	 <servlet-name>Faces Servlet</servlet-name>
13.	 <url-pattern>/faces/*</url-pattern>
14.	 </servlet-mapping>
15.	 <servlet-mapping>
16.	 <servlet-name>Faces Servlet</servlet-name>
17.	 <url-pattern>*.faces</url-pattern>
18.	 </servlet-mapping>
19.	 <context-param>
20.	 <description>State saving method: 'client' or 'server' (=default). See JSF Specification
2.5.2</description>
21.	 <param-name>javax.faces.STATE_SAVING_METHOD</param-name>
22.	 <param-value>client</param-value>
23.	 </context-param>
24.	 <context-param>
25.	 <param-name>javax.servlet.jsp.jstl.fmt.localizationContext</param-name>
26.	 <param-value>resources.application</param-value>
27.	 </context-param>
28.	 <listener>
29.	 <listener-class>com.sun.faces.config.ConfigureListener</listener-class>
30.	 </listener>
31.	 </web-app>
```

- *Lines 11 to 14*: The `servlet-mapping` element makes certain that all URLs with the prefix `/faces` are processed by `FacesServlet`.
- *Lines 15 to 18*: The `servlet-mapping` element makes certain that all URLs ending with the `faces` extension are processed by `FacesServlet`.

Figure 6-13 shows the directory structure of the Hello World web application.

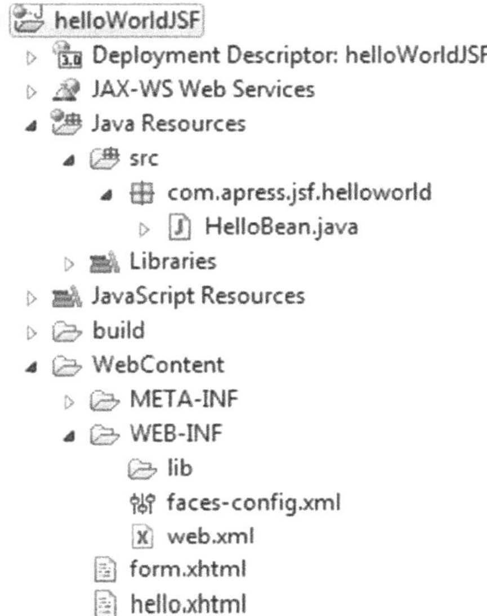

***Figure 6-13.** Directory structure of the Hello World web application*

Life Cycle of a JSF Application

Unlike Struts and Spring Web MVC, the JSF life cycle performs the following request-processing tasks in well-defined phases during which specific tasks are performed:

- Checking whether the incoming data is valid
- Triggering application logic to fulfill the request
- Binding the field properties directly to properties of the model and having their values updated upon form submissions
- Rendering the response to the client

The following are the six phases of the JSF application life cycle, as illustrated in Figure 6-14:

- Restore View phase
- Apply Request Values phase
- Process Validation phase
- Update Model phase
- Invoke Application phase
- Render Response phase

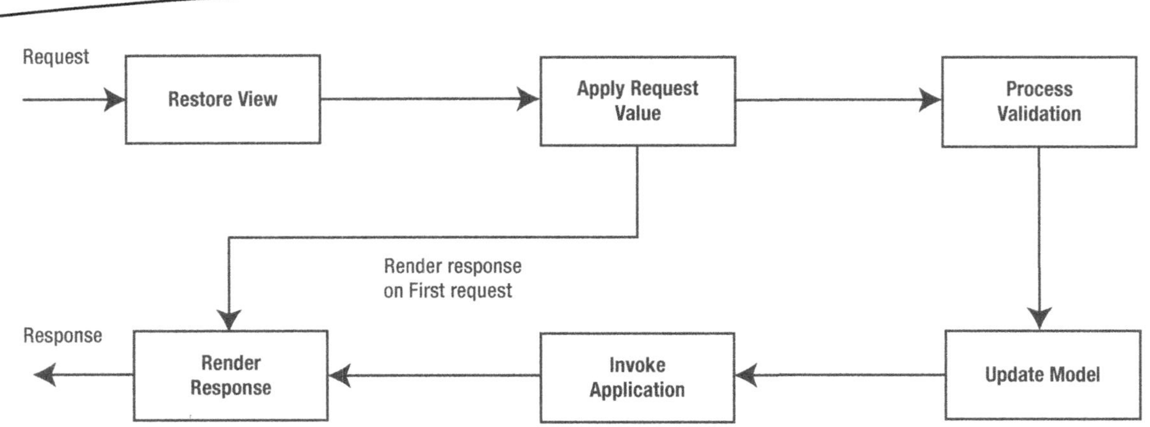

Figure 6-14. The phases of the JSF life cycle

Phase 1: Restore View

JSF begins the Restore View phase as soon as a link or button is clicked and JSF receives a request. During this phase, JSF does the following:

- Builds a component tree from the page. This component tree contains the information associated with all components of the page. If the page is requested for the first time, JSF creates an empty view.
- Wires event handlers and validators to UI components.
- Saves the view in the `FacesContext` instance.

Phase 2: Apply Request Values

After the component tree is created/restored, the JSF runtime runs the `decode` method of each component in the component tree that extracts the values from the request parameters. The values that are extracted by the `decode` method are stored in the component, after performing data conversion if necessary. If the conversion fails, an error message is generated and queued on `FacesContext`.

Phase 3: Process Validation

During this phase, the JSF runtime processes validators registered on the component tree during the Restore View phase. If there are validation errors, JSF adds an error message to the `FacesContext` instance, skips the fourth and fifth phases, enters the Render Response phase, and displays the error messages.

Phase 4: Update Model

If there are no validation errors in the Process Validation phase, the JSF runtime updates the managed bean's properties that are bound to the UI components with the new values of the UI components. The conversion is also performed in this phase if necessary.

Phase 5: Invoke Application

During this phase, the JSF runtime processes the application events by executing the corresponding event listeners. When the user submits a form, the JSF FacesServlet generates an application event that returns an outcome string that is passed to the navigation handler. The navigation handler looks up the next page to be rendered.

Phase 6: Render Response

In this phase, each component in the component tree renders itself, and the state of the response is saved so that the FacesServlet can access it during the Restore View phase, which will occur if subsequent requests are made to the same page.

Let's look behind the scenes of the Hello World application from the viewpoint of the request-processing life cycle.

1. The browser first connects to `http://localhost:8080/helloWorldJSF/form.faces`.
2. The JSF implementation initializes the JSF code and reads the `form.xhtml` page. That page contains tags, such as `h:form`, `h:inputText`, and `h: commandButton`. Each tag has an associated tag handler class. When the page is read, the tag handler class associated with each tag is executed, and a component tree is constructed. This is the first phase: Restore View. Since this is the first request and the component tree does not already exist, a new but empty component tree is created instead of restoring the component tree. Figure 6-15 shows the component tree for the code fragment of the `form.xhtml` file in Listing 6-1.

```
<h:form>
<h:inputText value="#{helloBean.name}"></h:inputText>
<h:commandButton value="Submit" action="hello"></h:commandButton>
</h:form>
```

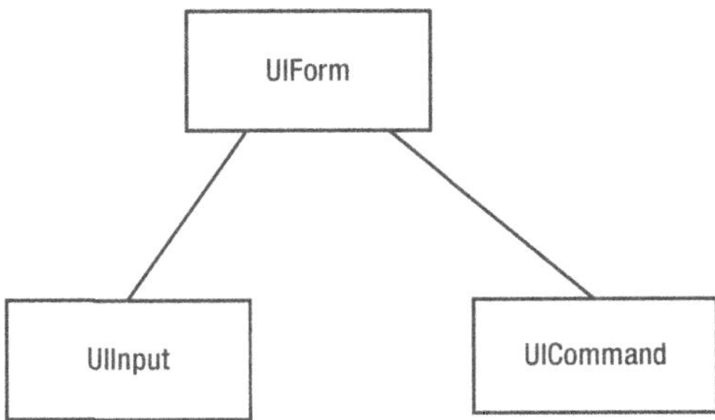

Figure 6-15. The component tree of form.xhtml

3. Now the JSF runtime enters the second phase: Apply Request Values. The `UIForm` object corresponds to the `h:form`, the `UIInput` object corresponds to the `h:inputText`, and the `UICommand` object corresponds to `h:commandButton` in the JSF file. Since this is the first request to this page and there are no request parameters available or events to process, nothing to update the model with, nothing to convert and validate, and no application-level events, the JSF runtime skips the second, third, fourth, and fifth phases and enters the sixth phase: Render Response. Each component object in the created component tree has a renderer that generates HTML. This process of generating HTML by the renderer of the component is called *encoding*. This encoded page is then displayed in the browser.

4. The user now fills in the name field in the form and clicks the Submit button.

5. The browser sends the form data to the web server, formatted as a POST request. The JSF runtime enters the first phase again, Restore View, and the component tree is restored to reflect the values the user entered in the form. And then the JSF runtime enters the second phase, Apply Request Values.

6. In the Apply Request Values phase, the JSF runtime performs the process called *decoding* in which each component in the component tree decodes the form data and the component stores this value. If the conversion fails while storing, an error message is generated and queued on `FacesContext`.

7. The JSF runtime enters the third phase: Process Validation. At this point, the JSF runtime processes the validators registered with the component tree during the first phase. If there are any validation errors, such as if the name field in the Hello World application is empty, JSF adds an error message to the `FacesContext` instance, skips the other phases, and enters the sixth phase: Render Response. It also displays the error messages, such as "name field cannot be empty." Since there is no validation in the Hello World application, the JSF runtime enters the fourth phase: Update Model.

8. In the Update Model phase, the JSF runtime updates the managed bean, namely, `helloBean`'s property name, with the value entered on the form. The `UIInput` component updates the `helloBean` property `name` referenced in the `value` attribute and invokes the setter methods with the value that the user entered. In this phase, conversion is also performed if necessary via the converters registered with the component. Since the conversion is not necessary in this case, the JSF runtime enters the fifth phase, Invoke Application, or triggers an action event.

9. In the Invoke Application phase, the `UICommand` component checks whether the button was clicked. If so, it triggers an action event, namely, the `hello` action referenced in the `action` attribute, which tells the navigation handler to look for the `hello.xhtml` page, and the JSF runtime enters the sixth phase: Render Response.
10. FacesServlet creates a response component tree, and each component renders itself as the JSF runtime goes through the corresponding JSF tags. At the end of this phase, the state of the response is saved so that `FacesServlet` can access it during the Restore View phase of subsequent requests to the same page.

Managed Beans

A *managed bean* is a regular JavaBean class registered with JSF and managed by the JSF framework and serves as the model for the UI component. The managed bean contains the getter and setter methods, business logic, or a backing bean that is a bean that contains all the values of the form. The managed beans are responsible for the following:

- Synchronizing server-side data with components in the component tree
- Processing business logic
- Handling navigation between pages

The component is associated with a specific managed bean property or action by means of the EL. As you saw in the Hello World application, you do not need to write any code to construct and manipulate the `HelloBean`. The JSF runtime constructs the beans and accesses them. Managed beans can be easily registered in a JSF configuration file (that is, `faces-config.xml`) or using annotations.

Listing 6-5 illustrates registering a managed bean using XML configuration.

Listing 6-5. Registering a Managed Bean Using XML

```
<managed-bean>
<managed-bean-name>helloWorld</managed-bean-name>
<managed-bean-class>com..apress.jsf.helloWorld.HelloBean</managed-bean-class>
<managed-bean-scope>session</managed-bean-scope>
</managed-bean>
```

Listing 6-6 illustrates registering a managed bean using an annotation.

Listing 6-6. Registering Managed Bean Using an Annotation

```
@ManagedBean
@SessionScoped
public class HelloWorld {

}
```

Note Contexts and dependency injection (CDI) beans are much more powerful than managed beans. You should use CDI beans if you deploy your application in a Java EE application server such as Glassfish. A Java EE 6 and newer application server automatically supports CDI. The CDI beans are used in the same way as managed beans but instead of `@ManagedBean`, they are declared with the `@Named` annotation, as shown here:

```
@Named("helloBean")
@SessionScoped
public class HelloBean implements Serializable {
...
}
```

Facelets

Facelets was created to replace the use of JSP as a view declaration language for JSF; it was designed exclusively for JSF and provides templating and extensible tag libraries to refrain from using scriptlets (Java code) in the HTML pages. The significant differences between Facelets and JSP are that Facelets provides the ability to write pages in pure HTML markup and provides server-side templating.

Templating with Facelets

You learned templating in Chapter 4 using the Tiles framework where you saw how templates encapsulate common layout to be used across all the pages, and you now understand how templates work. Facelets is similar to the Tiles framework for templating and composing pages. Consequently, templating is very much the same, other than six tags provided by Facelets for templating in the `ui:` tag library.

- `ui:composition`
- `ui:decorate`
- `ui:define`
- `ui:include`
- `ui:insert`
- `ui:param`

ui:composition

The `ui:composition` tag is used in template client files acting as template clients and indicates that enclosing content should be included in the `UIComponent` hierarchy at the specific point in the page. Listing 6-7 illustrates the syntax of `ui:composition`.

Listing 6-7. ui:composition Tag

```
<ui:composition template="optional">
```

The optional attribute declares a template to which the enclosed content should be applied using the template attribute.

ui:decorate

The difference between the ui:decorate tag and the ui:composition tag is that, unlike ui:composition, ui:decorate causes surrounding content to be included in the page as well. Listing 6-8 illustrates the syntax of ui:decorate.

Listing 6-8. ui:decorate Tag

```
<ui:decorate template="required">
```

ui:define

The ui:define tag is used inside a ui:composition tag in template client files to define a region that will be inserted into the composition at the point provided by the ui:insert tag. Listing 6-9 illustrates the syntax of ui:define.

Listing 6-9. ui:define Tag

```
<ui:define name="required">
```

ui:insert

The ui:insert tag is used in the template files to indicate where the ui:define in the template client should be inserted. Listing 6-10 illustrates the syntax of ui:insert.

Listing 6-10. ui:insert Tag

```
<ui:insert name="optional">
```

If no name is specified, the content in the body of the ui:insert tag is added to the view.

ui:include

The ui:include can be used in the template files or template client files. Listing 6-11 illustrates the syntax of ui:include.

Listing 6-11. ui:include Tag

```
<ui:include src="required">
```

ui:param

The `ui:param` tag is used inside `ui:include` tags to define name-value pairs for parameterized inclusion of the pages. Listing 6-12 illustrates the syntax of `ui:param`.

Listing 6-12. ui:param Tag

```
<ui:param name="required" value="required">
```

Next you will implement templating with Facelets. Create a JSF project similar to the Hello World project in the earlier section. In this application, you will create the header and sidebar template that will be used in the bookstore application. Figure 6-16 illustrates the directory structure of the application.

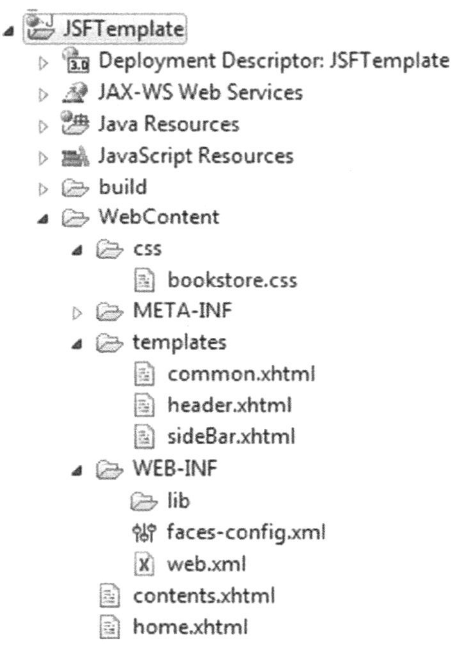

***Figure 6-16.** Directory structure of the JSFTemplate application*

Listing 6-13 illustrates the template file `common.xhtml`.

Listing 6-13. common.xhtml

```
<?xml version="1.0" encoding="UTF-8"?>
<html xmlns="http://www.w3.org/1999/xhtml"
    xmlns:h="http://java.sun.com/jsf/html"
    xmlns:ui="http://java.sun.com/jsf/facelets">
<h:head>
    <link rel="stylesheet" href="css/bookstore.css" type="text/css" />
</h:head>
```

```
8.     <h:body>
9.         <div id="centered">
10.            <div>
11.                <ui:insert name="header">
12.                    <ui:include src="/templates/header.xhtml" />
13.                </ui:insert>
14.            </div>
15.            <div>
16.                <ui:insert name="sideBar">
17.                    <ui:include src="/templates/sideBar.xhtml" />
18.                </ui:insert>
19.            </div>
20.            <div>
21.                <ui:insert name="content">
22.                    <ui:include src="/templates/contents.xhtml" />
23.                </ui:insert>
24.            </div>
25.        </div>
26.    </h:body>
27.    </html>
```

- *Line 3*: Declares the namespace for the HTML library
- *Line 4*: Declares the namespace for the Facelet library
- *Line 5 to 7*: Show the usage of the `h:head` tag instead of using the markup `<head/>`
- *Line 8*: Shows the usage of the `h:body` tag instead of using the markup `<body/>`
- *Lines 11 to 13*: Show the usage of the `u:insert` tag for templating the body content of the `<ui:insert>` tag that is added to the view
- *Line 12*: Shows the usage of the `ui:include` tag for the inclusion of `header.xhtml`
- *Line 17*: Shows the usage of the `ui:include` tag for the inclusion of `sideBar.xhtml`
- *Line 22*: Shows the usage of the `ui:include` tag for the inclusion of `contents.xhtml`

Listing 6-14 illustrates the template client `header.xhtml`.

Listing 6-14. header.xhtml

```
<?xml version="1.0" encoding="UTF-8"?>
<html xmlns="http://www.w3.org/1999/xhtml"
    xmlns:h="http://java.sun.com/jsf/html"
    xmlns:ui="http://java.sun.com/jsf/facelets">
```

```
5.    <h:body>
6.        <ui:composition>
7.            <div class="header">
8.                <h2>
9.                <span style="margin-left: 15px; margin-top: 15px;" class="label">BOOK
10.                        <span style="color: white;">STORE</span>
11.                    </span>
12.                 </h2>
13.             </div>
14.         </ui:composition>
15.     </h:body>
16.     </html>
```

- *Line 6*: The ui:composition tag indicates to the Facelets system that the enclosing children will be grafted into the UIComponent hierarchy where header.xhtml is inserted in common.xhtml.

Listing 6-15 illustrates sideBar.xhtml.

***Listing 6-15.** sideBar.xhtml*

```
<div class="leftbar">
    <ul id="menu">
        <li><div>
                <a class="link1" href=""><span class="label"
                    style="margin-left: 15px;">Home</span>
                </a>
            </div></li>
        <li><div>
        <a class="link1" href="listOfBooks.xhtml"><span
             style="margin-left: 15px;" class="label">All Books</span></a>
             </div></li>
         <li><div>
         <span class="label" style="margin-left: 15px;">Categories</span>
             </div>
             <ul>
                 <li><a class="label" href=""><span class="label"
                         style="margin-left: 30px;"></span></a></li>
             </ul></li>
         <li><div>
                 <span class="label" style="margin-left: 15px;">Contact Us</span>
             </div></li>
     </ul>
 </div>
```

Listing 6-15 is the same sidebar file used in Chapter 2.

Listing 6-16 illustrates the template client contents.xhtml.

Listing 6-16. contents.xhtml

```
1.    <?xml version="1.0" encoding="UTF-8"?>
2.    <html xmlns="http://www.w3.org/1999/xhtml"
3.        xmlns:ui="http://java.sun.com/jsf/facelets">
4.    <body>
5.        <ui:composition>
6.            <h1>Book Store Home</h1>
7.        </ui:composition>
8.    </body>
9.    </html>
```

- *Line 5*: The ui:composition tag indicates to the Facelets system that the enclosing children should be grafted into the UIComponent hierarchy at the point where contents.xhtml is inserted.

Listing 6-17 illustrates the home.xhtml file that defines content.xhtm.

Listing 6-17. home.xhtml

```
1.    <?xml version="1.0" encoding="UTF-8"?>
2.    <!DOCTYPE html>
3.    <html xmlns="http://www.w3.org/1999/xhtml"
4.        xmlns:h="http://java.sun.com/jsf/html"
5.        xmlns:ui="http://java.sun.com/jsf/facelets">
6.    <h:body>
7.        <ui:composition template="templates/common.xhtml">
8.            <ui:define name="content">
9.                  <ui:include src="/contents.xhtml" />
10.            </ui:define>
11.        </ui:composition>
12.     </h:body>
13.     </html>
```

- *Line 7*: The ui:composition tag declares the template common.xhtml to which the enclosed content contents.xhtml should be applied using the template attribute.

You can now run this application using the URL http://localhost:8080/JSFTemplate/home.faces, as shown in Figure 6-17.

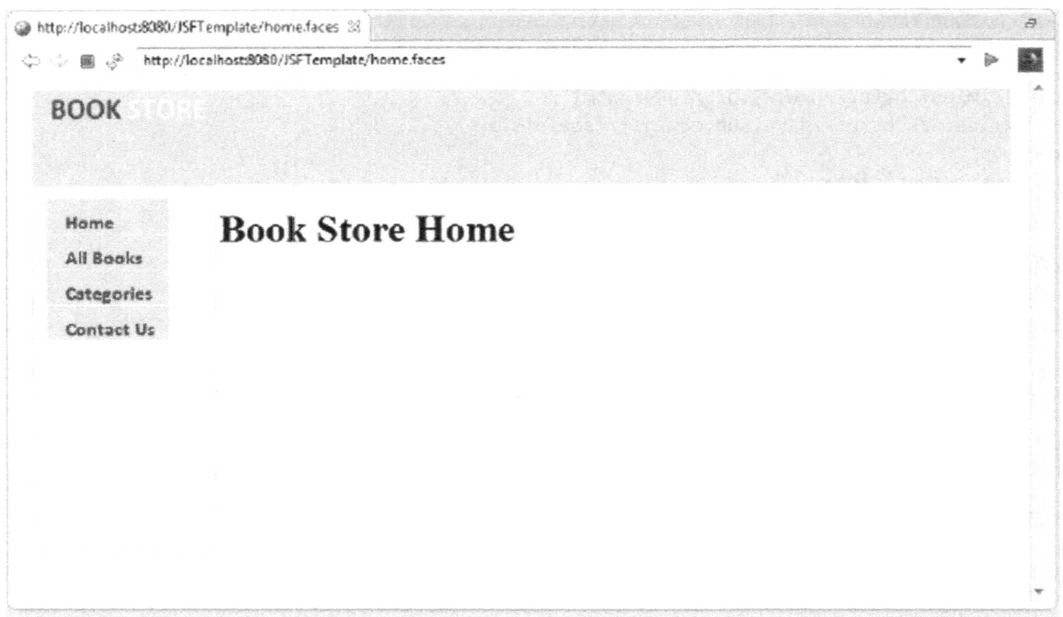

Figure 6-17. Header and sidebar using templates

Building the Bookstore Application Using JSF 2

In this section, you will develop the bookstore application using JSF. In Chapter 1 you developed the data access layer for the bookstore application and queried it via a stand-alone application developed using Java. In Chapter 5 you refactored the stand-alone application to integrate it with the Spring Framework in order to use the robust features offered by Spring's `JDBCTemplate`. Then you used the Spring `JDBCTemplate` with a Spring Web MVC web application. In this chapter, you will use the same Spring `JDBCTemplate` with a JSF-based web application to leverage the benefits of the Spring template discussed in Chapter 5. To do so, you need to integrate JSF with the Spring Framework. In the section that follows, you will learn to integrate JSF with Spring. Then you will develop the web layer of the application using JSF. You will develop this application in the following four steps:

1. Integrate JSF with the Spring Framework.
2. Access the database from the web layer via Spring `JDBCTemplate`.
3. Develop templates reusing the templates developed earlier.
4. Develop the user interface using UI components and JSF EL.

Figure 6-18 illustrates the directory structure of the application you are going to develop.

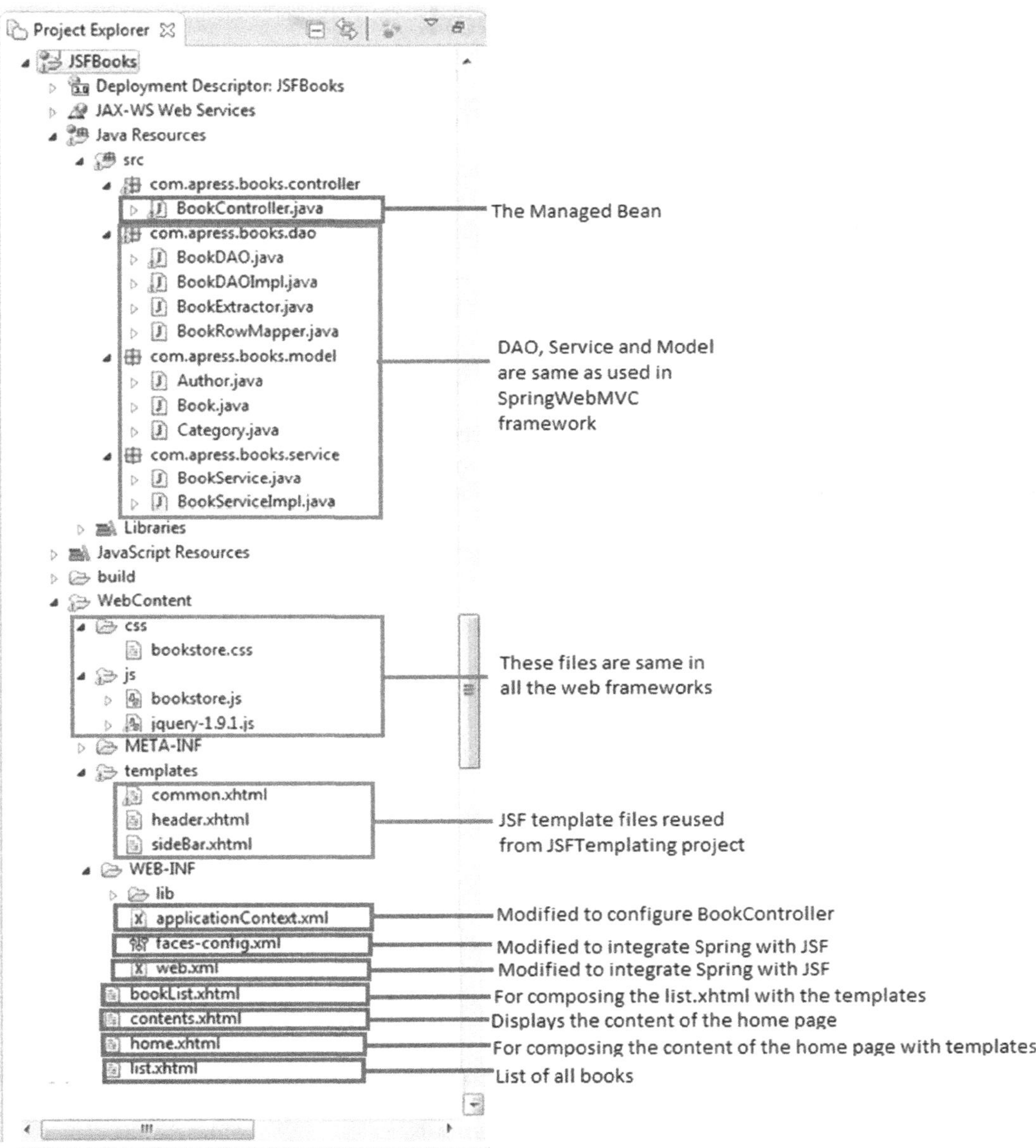

Figure 6-18. Directory structure of the bookstore web application

Integrating JSF with Spring Framework

To integrate JSF with the Spring dependency injection framework, you have to do the following:

- Add the `ContextLoaderListener` and `RequestContextListener` listeners provided by the Spring Framework in `web.xml`
- Add an `el-resolver` entry in `faces-config.xml` to point to the Spring class `SpringBeansFacesELResolver`

Listing 6-18 illustrates adding `ContextLoaderListener` and `RequestContextListener` in the `web.xml` file.

Listing 6-18. web.xml

```
<?xml version="1.0" encoding="UTF-8"?>
<web-app xmlns:xsi="http://www.w3.org/2001/XMLSchema-instance" xmlns="http://java.sun.com/xml/ns/javaee" xmlns:web="http://java.sun.com/xml/ns/javaee/web-app_2_5.xsd" xsi:schemaLocation="http://java.sun.com/xml/ns/javaee http://java.sun.com/xml/ns/javaee/web-app_3_0.xsd" metadata-complete="true" version="3.0">
<display-name>JSFBooks</display-name>
<servlet>
<servlet-name>Faces Servlet</servlet-name>
<servlet-class>javax.faces.webapp.FacesServlet</servlet-class>
<load-on-startup>1</load-on-startup>
</servlet>
<servlet-mapping>
 <servlet-name>Faces Servlet</servlet-name>
 <url-pattern>/faces/*</url-pattern>
 </servlet-mapping>
 <servlet-mapping>
 <servlet-name>Faces Servlet</servlet-name>
 <url-pattern>*.jsf</url-pattern>
 </servlet-mapping>
 <servlet-mapping>
 <servlet-name>Faces Servlet</servlet-name>
 <url-pattern>*.faces</url-pattern>
 </servlet-mapping>
 <context-param>
 <description>State saving method: 'client' or 'server' (=default). See JSF Specification 2.5.2</description>
 <param-name>javax.faces.STATE_SAVING_METHOD</param-name>
 <param-value>client</param-value>
 </context-param>
 <context-param>
 <param-name>javax.servlet.jsp.jstl.fmt.localizationContext</param-name>
 <param-value>resources.application</param-value>
 </context-param>
 <listener>
 <listener-class>com.sun.faces.config.ConfigureListener</listener-class>
 </listener>
```

```
33.    <listener>
34.    <listener-class>
35.            org.springframework.web.context.ContextLoaderListener
36.    </listener-class>
37.    </listener>
38.    <listener>
39.    <listener-class>
40.            org.springframework.web.context.request.RequestContextListener
41.    </listener-class>
42.    </listener>
43.    </web-app>
```

- *Line 33 to 37*: Configures `ContextLoaderListener`
- *Line 38 to 42*: Configures `RequestContextListener`

`SpringBeanFacesELResolver` is an `ELResolver` implementation that delegates to Spring's `WebApplicationContext` and the default resolver of the underlying JSF implementation. Listing 6-19 illustrates adding the `el-resolver`.

Listing 6-19. ***faces-config.xml***

```
1.    <?xml version="1.0" encoding="UTF-8"?>
2.    <faces-config
3.        xmlns="http://java.sun.com/xml/ns/javaee"
4.        xmlns:xsi="http://www.w3.org/2001/XMLSchema-instance"
5.        xsi:schemaLocation="http://java.sun.com/xml/ns/javaee
http://java.sun.com/xml/ns/javaee/web-facesconfig_2_0.xsd"
6.        version="2.0">
7.    <application>
8.        <el-resolver>
9.            org.springframework.web.jsf.el.SpringBeanFacesELResolver
10.        </el-resolver>
11.        </application>
12.    </faces-config>
```

- *Lines 7 to 11*: Configures Spring EL resolver

JSF is now integrated with the Spring Framework, and you should be able to access the database via Spring `JDBCTemplate`.

Accessing a Database from the Web Layer via Spring JDBCTemplate

Next you will create the managed bean to access the database from the web layer. You already created the Spring `JDBCTemplate` in Chapter 5. The managed bean you are going to create now will use the `JDBCTemplate` created earlier via the `BookService`, which was also created in Chapter 5. In other words, we will create the managed bean to access the database via the service layer and data access layer created in Chapter 5. Listing 6-20 illustrates the `BookController` managed bean.

Listing 6-20. BookController.java

```
1.  package com.apress.books.controller;
2.
3.  import javax.faces.bean.ManagedBean;
4.  import javax.faces.bean.RequestScoped;
5.  import com.apress.books.model.Book;
6.  import com.apress.books.service.BookService;
7.  import java.util.List;
8.
9.  @ManagedBean
10.  @RequestScoped
11.  public class BookController {
12.
13.        private BookService bookService ;
14.        private List<Book> bookList;
15.
16.      public String listAllBooks() {
17.          bookList = bookService.getAllBooks();
18.              return "bookList.xhtml";
19.          }
20.
21.      public BookService getBookService() {
22.          return bookService;
23.      }
24.
25.      public void setBookService(BookService bookService) {
26.          this.bookService = bookService;
27.      }
28.
29.      public List<Book> getBookList() {
30.            return bookList;
31.      }
32.      public void setBookList(List<Book> bookList) {
33.          this.bookList = bookList;
34.      }
35.  }
```

- *Line 17*: Invokes the `getAllBooks()` method on `bookService`
- *Line 18*: Returns the `booklist.xhtml` file that is composed with the template and `list.xhtml`, which displays the list of books see later in Figure 6-20

Listing 6-21 illustrates the configuration metadata that is provided to the Spring IoC container. This file is the same as created in Chapter 5 with a slight modification to configure the managed bean `BookController` with the `BookService`.

Listing 6-21. applicationContext.xml

```
1.    <?xml version="1.0" encoding="UTF-8"?>
2.    <beans xmlns="http://www.springframework.org/schema/beans"
3.        xmlns:xsi="http://www.w3.org/2001/XMLSchema-instance"
xmlns:context="http://www.springframework.org/schema/context"
4.        xmlns:aop="http://www.springframework.org/schema/aop"
5.        xsi:schemaLocation="http://www.springframework.org/schema/beans
6.            http://www.springframework.org/schema/beans/spring-beans-3.2.xsd
7.            http://www.springframework.org/schema/context
8.            http://www.springframework.org/schema/context/spring-context-3.2.xsd
9.            http://www.springframework.org/schema/aop
10.            http://www.springframework.org/schema/aop/spring-aop-3.2.xsd">
11.
12.        <!-- telling container to take care of annotations stuff -->
13.        <context:annotation-config />
14.
15.        <!-- declaring base package -->
16.        <context:component-scan base-package="com.apress.books" />
17.
18.        <bean id="bookController" class="com.apress.books.controller.BookController">
19.            <property name="bookService" ref="service"></property>
20.        </bean>
21.
22.        <bean id="dao" class="com.apress.books.dao.BookDAOImpl" >
23.        <property name="dataSource" ref="dataSourceBean">
24.            </property>
25.        </bean>
26.
27.        <bean id="service" class="com.apress.books.service.BookServiceImpl">
28.            <property name="bookDao" ref="dao">
29.            </property>
30.        </bean>
31.
32.        <bean id="dataSourceBean"
33.            class="org.springframework.jdbc.datasource.DriverManagerDataSource">
34.            <property name="driverClassName" value="com.mysql.jdbc.Driver" />
35.            <property name="url" value="jdbc:mysql://localhost:3306/books" />
36.            <property name="username" value="root" />
37.            <property name="password" value="password" />
38.        </bean>
39.    </beans>
```

- *Lines 18 to 20*: Configures bookController with bookService

Developing Templates

You will reuse the template and the template client file developed earlier for the header and sidebar of the bookstore application. However, you need to modify sideBar.xhtml to invoke the listOfAllBooks action in the bookController bean, as illustrated in Listing 6-22.

Listing 6-22. sideBar.xhtml

```
1.   <?xml version="1.0" encoding="UTF-8"?>
2.   <!DOCTYPE html >
3.   <html xmlns="http://www.w3.org/1999/xhtml"
4.       xmlns:h="http://java.sun.com/jsf/html"
5.       xmlns:ui="http://java.sun.com/jsf/facelets">
6.   <h:form>
7.       <div class="leftbar">
8.           <ul id="menu">
9.               <li><div>
10.                       <a class="link1" href=""><span class="label"
11.                           style="margin-left: 15px;">Home</span>
12.                       </a>
13.                   </div></li>
14.               <li><div>
15.               <h:commandLink class="link1" action="#{bookController.listAllBooks}">
16.                   <span style="margin-left: 15px;" class="label">All Books</span>
17.               </h:commandLink>
18.                   </div></li>
19.               <li><div>
20.                   <span class="label" style="margin-left: 15px;">Categories</span>
21.                   </div>
22.                   <ul>
23.                       <li><a class="label" href=""><span class="label"
24.                       style="margin-left: 30px;"></span></a></li>
25.                   </ul></li>
26.               <li><div>
27.                   <span class="label" style="margin-left: 15px;">Contact Us</span>
28.                   </div></li>
29.            </ul>
30.        </div>
31.  </h:form>
32.
33.  </html>
```

- *Line 6*: Shows the usage of the `h:form` tag instead of using the markup `<form>`
- *Line 15*: Shows the usage of the `h:commandlink` tag that triggers the `listAllBooks` action on the `bookController` managed bean using the deferred EL

Developing the User Interface Using UI Components and JSF EL

Now you will develop the UI of the application. Figure 6-19 illustrates the home page of the application. When the user clicks All Books in the sidebar, the list of all books is displayed, as illustrated in Figure 6-20.

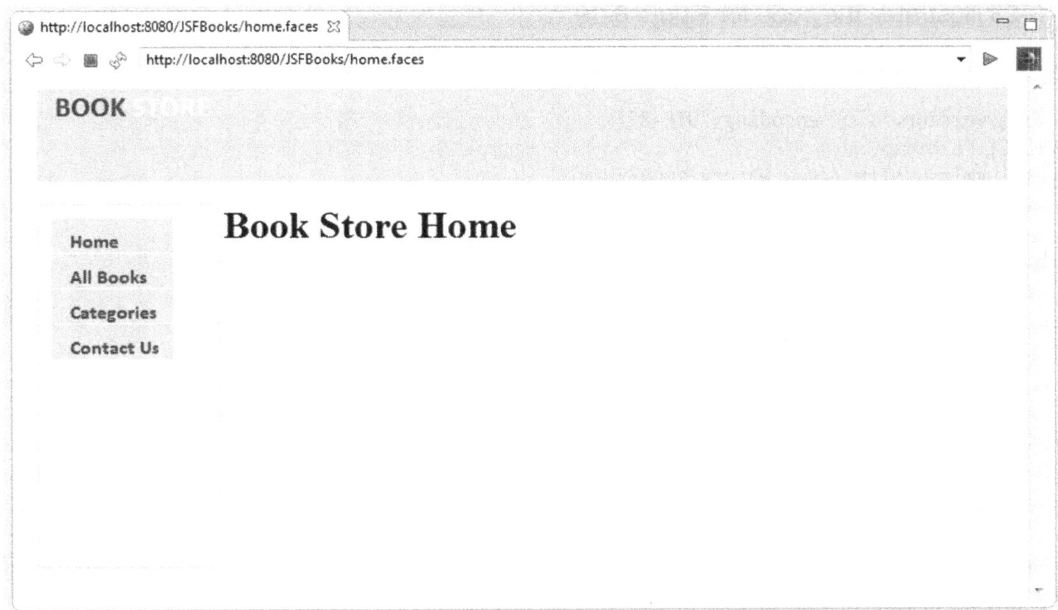

Figure 6-19. Home page of the bookstore web application

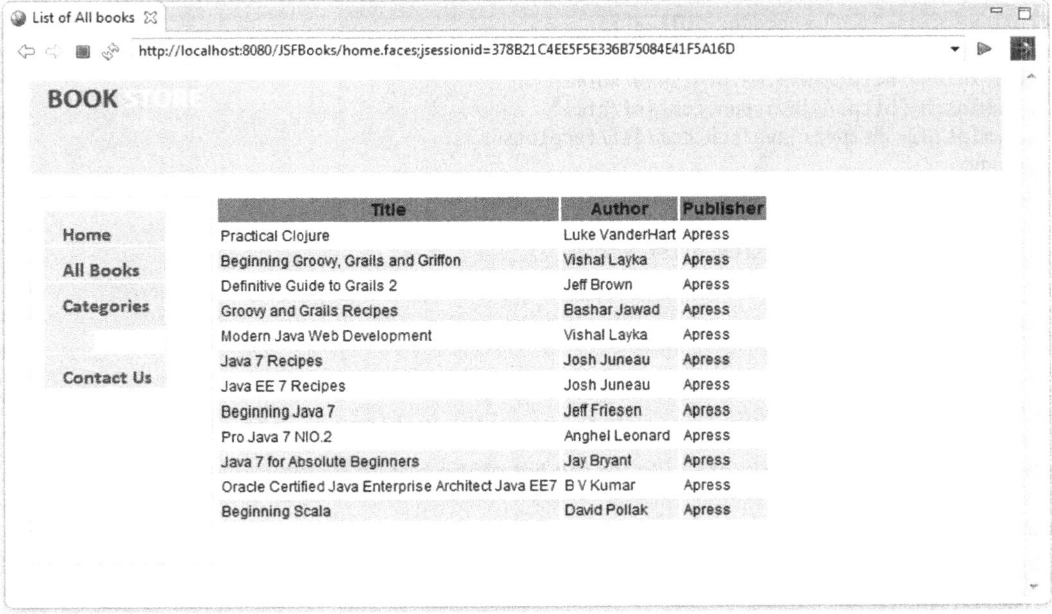

Figure 6-20. List of books

Listing 6-23 illustrates the code for Figure 6-19.

Listing 6-23. home.xhtml

```
1.    <?xml version="1.0" encoding="UTF-8"?>
2.    <!DOCTYPE html>
3.    <html xmlns="http://www.w3.org/1999/xhtml"
4.        xmlns:h="http://java.sun.com/jsf/html"
5.        xmlns:ui="http://java.sun.com/jsf/facelets">
6.    <h:body>
7.        <ui:composition template="templates/common.xhtml">
8.            <ui:define name="content">
9.                <ui:include src="/contents.xhtml" />
10.            </ui:define>
11.        </ui:composition>
12.    </h:body>
13.    </html>
```

- *Line 9*: The usage of the `ui:include` tag for the inclusion of `contents.xhtml`

When the user clicks All Books in the sidebar of the home page, the list of all books is displayed, as illustrated in Figure 6-20.

Listing 6-24 and Listing 6-25 illustrate the code for Figure 6-20.

Listing 6-24. bookList.html

```
1.    <?xml version="1.0" encoding="UTF-8"?>
2.    <!DOCTYPE html>
3.    <html xmlns="http://www.w3.org/1999/xhtml"
4.        xmlns:h="http://java.sun.com/jsf/html"
5.        xmlns:ui="http://java.sun.com/jsf/facelets">
6.    <h:body>
7.        <ui:composition template="templates/common.xhtml">
8.            <ui:define name="content">
9.                <ui:include src="/list.xhtml" />
10.            </ui:define>
11.        </ui:composition>
12.    </h:body>
13.    </html>
```

- *Line 9*: The usage of the `ui:include` tag for the inclusion of `list.xhtml`

Listing 6-25 illustrates the `list.xhtml` file for the list of the books displayed in Figure 6-20.

Listing 6-25. list.xhtml

```
1.    <?xml version="1.0" encoding="UTF-8"?>
2.    <!DOCTYPE html>
3.    <html xmlns="http://www.w3.org/1999/xhtml"
4.        xmlns:h="http://java.sun.com/jsf/html"
5.        xmlns:ui="http://java.sun.com/jsf/facelets"
6.        xmlns:f="http://java.sun.com/jsf/core">
```

```
7.  <h:head>
8.      <title>List of All books</title>
9.      <link rel="stylesheet" href="css/bookstore.css" type="text/css" />
10.      <script type="text/javascript" src="js/jquery-1.9.1.js"></script>
11.      <script src="js/bookstore.js"></script>
12.  </h:head>
13.  <h:body>
14.      <h:dataTable id="grid" value="#{bookController.bookList}" var="book">
15.          <h:column>
16.              <f:facet name="header" id="th-title">
17.                  <h:outputText value="Title" />
18.              </f:facet>
19.              <h:outputText value="#{book.bookTitle}" />
20.          </h:column>
21.          <h:column>
22.              <f:facet name="header" id="th-author">
23.                  <h:outputText value="Author" />
24.              </f:facet>
25.              <ui:repeat value="#{book.authors}" var="content">
26.                  <h:outputText value="#{content.firstName} #{content.lastName}" />
27.              </ui:repeat>
28.          </h:column>
29.          <h:column>
30.              <f:facet name="header" id="th-price">
31.                  <h:outputText value="Publisher" />
32.              </f:facet>
33.              <h:outputText value="#{book.publisherName}" />
34.          </h:column>
35.      </h:dataTable>
36.  </h:body>
37.  </html>
```

- *Line 6*: Declares the namespace for the JSF core library
- *Line 14*: Shows the usage of the h:dataTable tag instead of using the markup <table/>
- *Line 14*: Shows the deferred EL expression that uses the bookList property of the managed bean bookController
- *Line 15*: Shows the usage of h:column instead of using the markup <td/>
- *Line 16*: Shows the usage of the f:facet tag to add the facet
- *Line 17*: Shows the usage of h:outputText that displays the book title

Summary

JSF is a component-based MVC framework, at the heart of which is the UI component model; this model allows the development of a web application's view from collections of standard, out-of-the-box, reusable UI components. Unlike Struts and Spring Web MVC, the JSF lifelife cycle performs mundane and recurring request-processing tasks in well-defined phases, allowing the developer to concentrate on the business logic of the web application.

Chapter 7

Rapid Web Development with Grails

Live in fragments no longer, only connect.

—Edgar Morgan Foster

Grails takes web development to the next level of abstraction. The fact that Java EE was not written with an application level of abstraction led to the development and subsequent popularity of Java frameworks such as Spring, Hibernate, and so on. But most of the Java frameworks take a fragmented approach toward web development. You have to maintain the configuration for each layer. Grails embraces convention over configuration and wraps these powerful frameworks with a layer of abstraction via the Groovy language, thus providing a complete development platform that allows you to take full advantage of Java and the JVM.

This chapter will reach under the covers of the Grails machine and look at its parts: its wheels and gears all moving in a coordinated motion, its workability, its leading-edge engine, and its underlying form. It will take a closer look at the interactions in the Grails ecosystem. It will show how controllers handle, manage, direct, and orchestrate the logical flow of the application and how they handle requests, redirect requests, execute and delegate actions, or render views as the need arises. It will explore views and unravel how Grails uses SiteMesh, the page decoration framework, to give a consistent look to pages, as well as how views draw on Grails' built-in tags and dynamic tags in its tag library to create well-formed markup and promote a clean separation of concerns. It's quite a machine.

Grails Features

Grails is a request-based, MVC, open-source web development framework. More than just that, though, it is a complete development platform in which everything runs on top of the robust Java and Java EE platforms as illustrated in Figure 7-1. It leverages the existing popular Java frameworks, and it includes a web container, database, build system, and test harness that exploit the dynamism of the Groovy language.

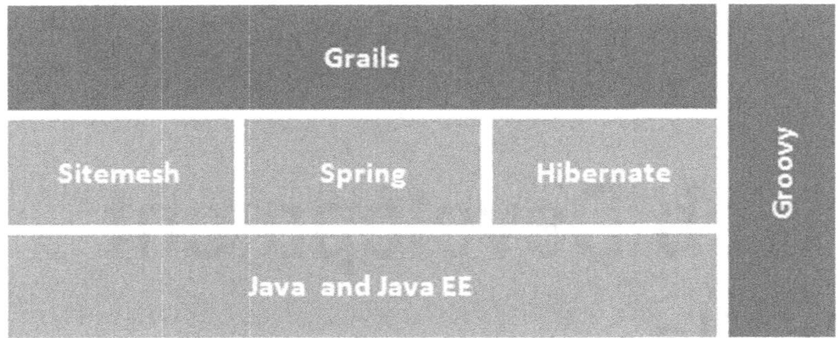

Figure 7-1. *Grails platform*

Grails provides best practices, such as convention over configuration, and unit testing using frameworks such as Spring, Hibernate, and SiteMesh, to name a few. This section will highlight some of the important best practices.

Convention over Configuration

Rather than configuration, Grails gives precedence to convention. *Convention over configuration*, in simple terms, means writing configuration code only when you deviate from the convention. These ingenious conventions correspond to the directory structure; Grails brings into play the name and location of the files instead of relying on explicit configuration via the wiring of XML configuration files. This means if you create a class following the Grails conventions, Grails will wire it into Spring or treat it as a Hibernate entity. If you create a new domain class called `Book`, Grails will automatically create a table called `book` in the database. By using the convention-over-configuration paradigm, Grails can envisage a component from its name and its location in the directory structure. One immediate consequence of this, other than speeding up application development, is that you have to configure a particular aspect of a component only when that configuration deviates from the standard.

Scaffolding

The Grails scaffolding generates an application's CRUD functionality from the domain classes, at either runtime or development time. The generated application consists of the controller and GSP views associated with the domain class. The scaffolding also generates the database schema, including tables for each of the domain classes.

Object-Relational Mapping

Grails includes a powerful object-relational mapping (ORM) framework called Grails Object Relational Mapping (GORM). Like most ORM frameworks, GORM maps objects to relational databases; but unlike other ORM frameworks, GORM is based on a dynamic language. Therefore GORM can inject the CRUD methods right into the class without having to implement them or inherit them from persistent superclasses.

Note ORM is a way to map objects from the OO world onto tables in a relational database and provides an abstraction above SQL.

Plug-Ins

Instead of providing out-of-the-box solutions for every possible requirement, Grails offers a plug-in architecture, and you can find plug-ins for a plethora of functionalities.

Unit Testing

For improving the quality of the deliverables, Grails provides unit tests, integration tests, and functional tests for automating the web interface.

Integrated Open Source

Grails integrates industry-standard and proven open source frameworks, several of which are briefly described in this section.

Table 7-1 illustrates the frameworks that Grails leverages.

***Table 7-1.** Frameworks That Grails Leverages*

Integrated Open Source Technology	Description
Ajax frameworks	Grails ships with the jQuery library but also provides support for other frameworks such as Prototype, Dojo, Yahoo UI, and the Google Web Toolkit through the plug-in system.
Hibernate	Hibernate is an ORM framework that provides the foundation for GORM.
H2	Grails uses the in-memory H2[1] database and enables the H2 database console in development mode (at the URI `/dbconsole`) so that the in-memory database can be easily queried from the browser.
Spring	Spring Framework provides an application level of abstraction on top of the Java EE API. Grails developers can build an application that internally uses Spring and Hibernate without knowing these frameworks. Grails abstracts most of the details of these frameworks from Grails developers.
SiteMesh	SiteMesh[2] is a layout-rendering framework that implements the Decorator design pattern for rendering HTML with headers, footers, and navigation elements. Grails abstracts most of the SiteMesh details from the Grails developer.
Tomcat	By default, Grails uses an embedded Tomcat container.

[1]`www.h2database.com/html/main.html`

[2]`http://wiki.sitemesh.org/display/sitemesh/Home`

Installing Grails

Before installing Grails, you will need as a minimum a Java Development Kit (JDK) version 1.6 or newer. Download the appropriate JDK for your operating system, run the installer, and then set up an environment variable called `JAVA_HOME` pointing to the location of this installation.

> **Note** A JDK is required in your Grails development environment. A JRE is not sufficient.

The first step to getting up and running with Grails is to install the distribution. To do so, follow these steps:

1. Download a binary distribution of Grails from `http://grails.org/` and extract the resulting ZIP file to a location of your choice.
2. Set the `GRAILS_HOME` environment variable to the location where you extracted the ZIP file.
   - On Unix/Linux-based systems, this is typically a matter of adding something like the following to your profile: `export GRAILS_HOME=/path/to/grails`.
   - On Windows, this is typically a matter of setting an environment variable under `My Computer/Advanced/Environment Variables`.
3. Then add the `bin` directory to your `PATH` variable.
   - On Unix/Linux-based systems, this can be done by adding `export PATH="$PATH:$GRAILS_HOME/bin"` to your profile.
     - On Windows, this is done by modifying the `PATH` environment variable under `My Computer/Advanced/Environment Variables`.

If Grails is working correctly, you should now be able to type `grails -version` in the terminal window and see output similar to this:

```
E:\>grails -version
Grails version: 2.2.4
```

Hello World Application

In this section, you will create your first Grails web application. To create a Grails application, you need to familiarize yourself with the usage of the `grails` command:

```
grails [command name]
```

Run `create-app` to create an application.

```
grails create-app helloworld
```

This will create a new directory called helloworld inside the current one that contains the project, in other words, your workspace. Navigate to this directory in your console:

```
cd helloworld
```

Change into the helloworld directory you just created and start the Grails interactive console by typing the grails command.

```
\grails2-workspace\helloworld>grails
```

This will download several resources, and then you should see a prompt, as illustrated in Figure 7-2.

```
E:\ModernJava\grails2-workspace\helloworld>grails
| Enter a script name to run. Use TAB for completion:
grails>
```

Figure 7-2. *Grails interactive console*

What we want is a simple page that just prints the message "Hello World" to the browser. In Grails, whenever you want a new page, you create a new controller action for it. Since we don't yet have a controller, let's create one now with the create-controller command.

```
grails> create-controller hello
```

The previous command will create a new controller called HelloController.groovy as illustrated in Listing 7-1, in the grails-app/controllers/helloworld directory.

Listing 7-1. *HelloController.groovy*

```
package helloworld

class HelloController {

    def index() { }
}
```

We now have a controller, so let's add an action to generate the "Hello World" page. The code looks like Listing 7-2.

Listing 7-2. *Modifying the Index Action*

```
def index() { render "Hello World" } }
```

The action is simply a method. In this particular case, it calls a special method provided by Grails to render the page.

To see your application in action, you need to start up a server with another command called run-app.

```
grails> run-app
```

This will start an embedded server on port 8080 that hosts your application. You should now be able to access your application at the URL `http://localhost:8080/helloworld/`. The result will look like Figure 7-3.

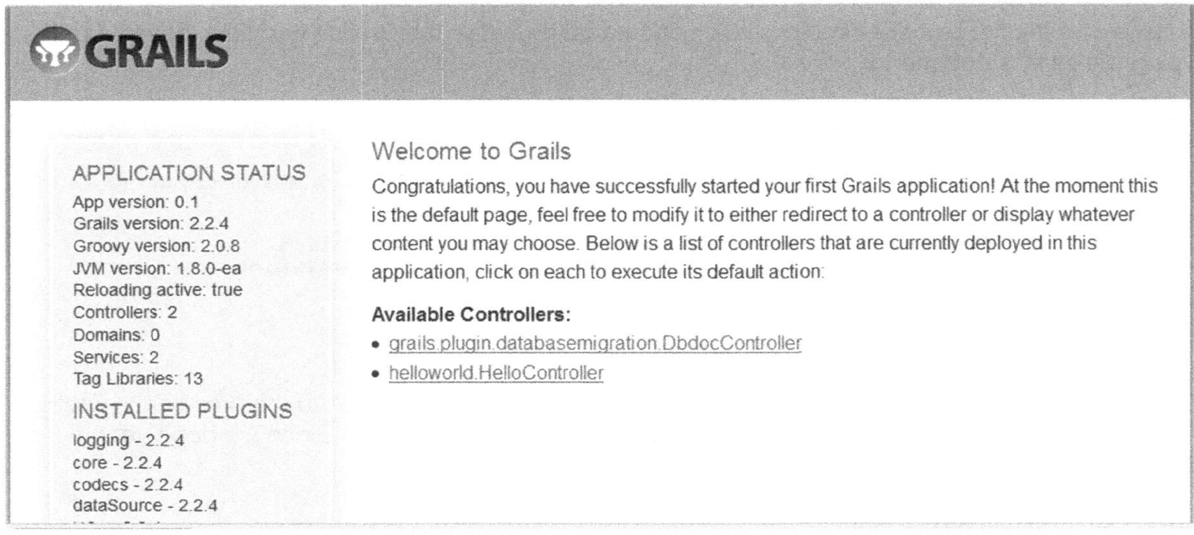
GRAILS
APPLICATION STATUS
App version: 0.1
Grails version: 2.2.4
Groovy version: 2.0.8
JVM version: 1.8.0-ea
Reloading active: true
Controllers: 2
Domains: 0
Services: 2
Tag Libraries: 13
INSTALLED PLUGINS
logging - 2.2.4
core - 2.2.4
codecs - 2.2.4
dataSource - 2.2.4
Welcome to Grails
Congratulations, you have successfully started your first Grails application! At the moment this is the default page, feel free to modify it to either redirect to a controller or display whatever content you may choose. Below is a list of controllers that are currently deployed in this application, click on each to execute its default action:
Available Controllers:
grails.plugin.databasemigration.DbdocController
helloworld.HelloController

***Figure 7-3.** Welcome screen of Grails*

This is the Grails introduction page that is rendered by the `grails-app/view/index.gsp` file. It detects the presence of your controllers and provides links to them. Click the HelloController link to see our custom page containing the text "Hello World." You have your first working Grails application.

> **Note** In Figure 7-3 there is a link to the Dbdoc controller. Clicking this link will produce an error message, as the controller is not implemented. The purpose of the `DbdocController` is to generate static HTML files to view change log information. You can enable it from conf/Config.groovy by setting `dbDocController.enabled = true`

Bookstore Application

In this chapter, you will be learning to leverage the Grails conventions and scaffolding to create a simple but functional version of the bookstore application. This initial version of the application will not be production-ready, however; the objective of this application is to show you how, with scaffolding, you can render a CRUD web application with almost no code other than your domain class code. In addition, Grails will generate a database schema and populate a database with the schema when the application is run.

Creating the Bookstore Application

To create the bookstore application, you need to execute the `create-app` target using an optional project name on the command line, as shown here:

```
>grails create-app bookstore
```

The entire line in the preceding command line is a command, where `create-app` is a target. A target is a specific task that you want Grails to execute.

> **Note** Using the `help` command yields a list of available targets: `>grails help`.

If you don't supply the project name when using `create-app`, you will be prompted for one.

After the `create-app` target has run, you have a new directory matching the name of your project. This is the root of your new project, and you must make all subsequent Grails command-line calls from within this directory. It's a good idea to use the `cd` command to get into the directory now so you don't forget. Within the new project directory, you will find a structure matching the directory structure shown in Figure 7-4.

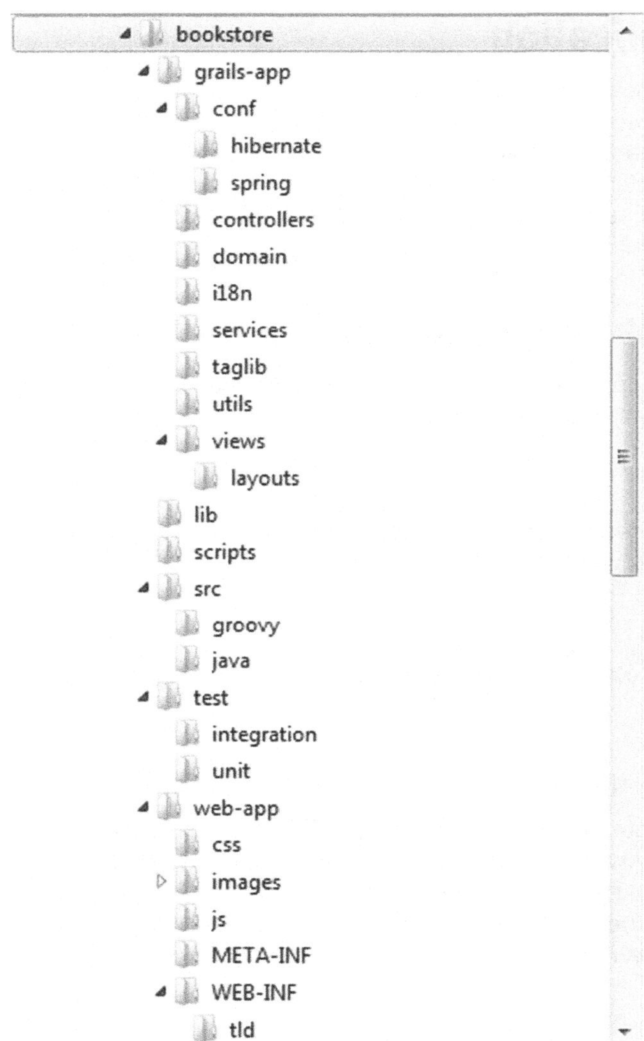

***Figure 7-4.** Directory structure of the bookstore application*

Instead of creating the application from the command line, you can use the IDE of your choice. We recommend the Groovy/GrailsTool Suite (GGTS), which you can download from `www.springsource.org/downloads/sts-ggts`. This book uses the latest version, GGTS 3.0. GGTS provides the best Eclipse-powered development environment for building Groovy and Grails applications. GGTS provides support for the latest versions of Groovy and Grails and comes on top of the latest Eclipse releases. Figure 7-5 shows how to configure Grails in GGTS. Under Preferences, click Grails and then the Add button. In the window Configure Grails Installation, browse for Grails by clicking the Browse button, which opens the Grails Installation directory window. Select your Grails installation directory and click OK.

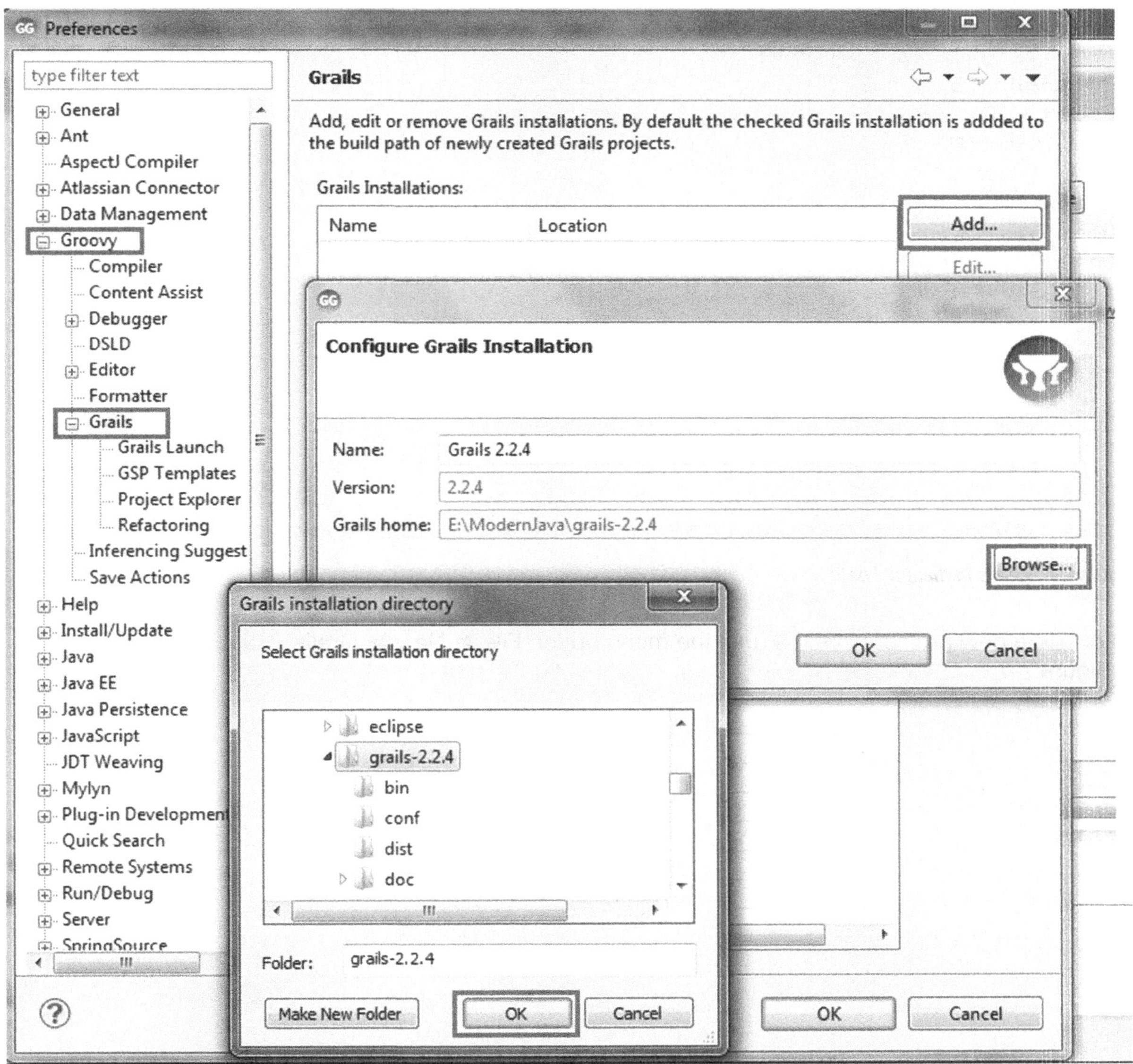

Figure 7-5. Configuring GGTS with Grails

Grails is now added to the build path, as illustrated in Figure 7-6. Click OK. Now the GGTS is configured with Grails, and you can create a Grails project.

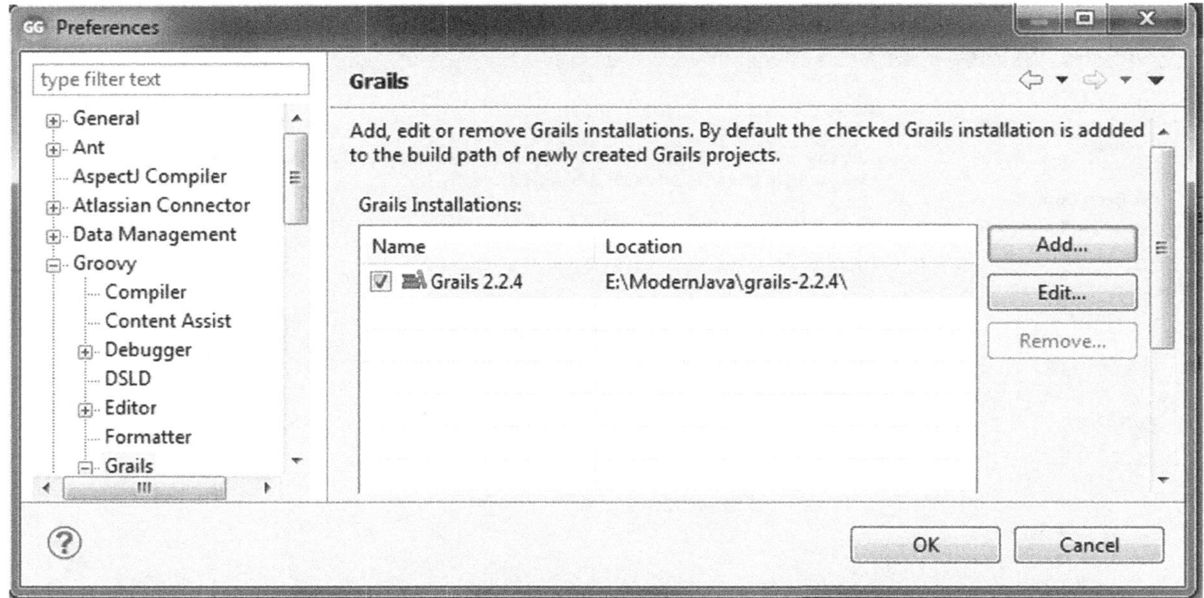

Figure 7-6. Grails in the build path

To create a new project in GGTS, use the menu option File ➤ New ➤ Grails Project, as illustrated in Figure 7-7.

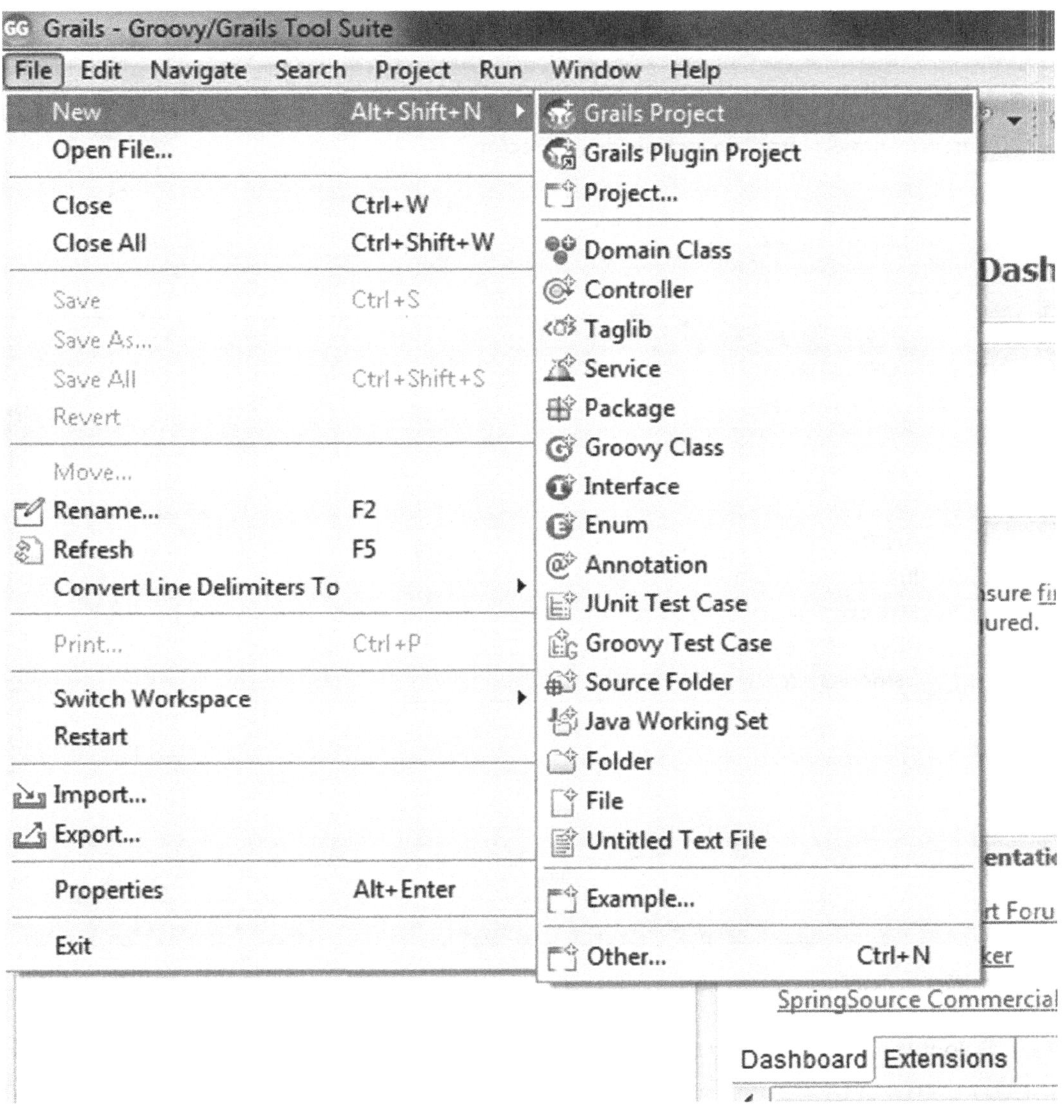

Figure 7-7. Creating a new project

Since you have already created the project from the command line, you can import the created project in GGTS. Select Existing Projects into Workspace in the Import window, as illustrated in Figure 7-8.

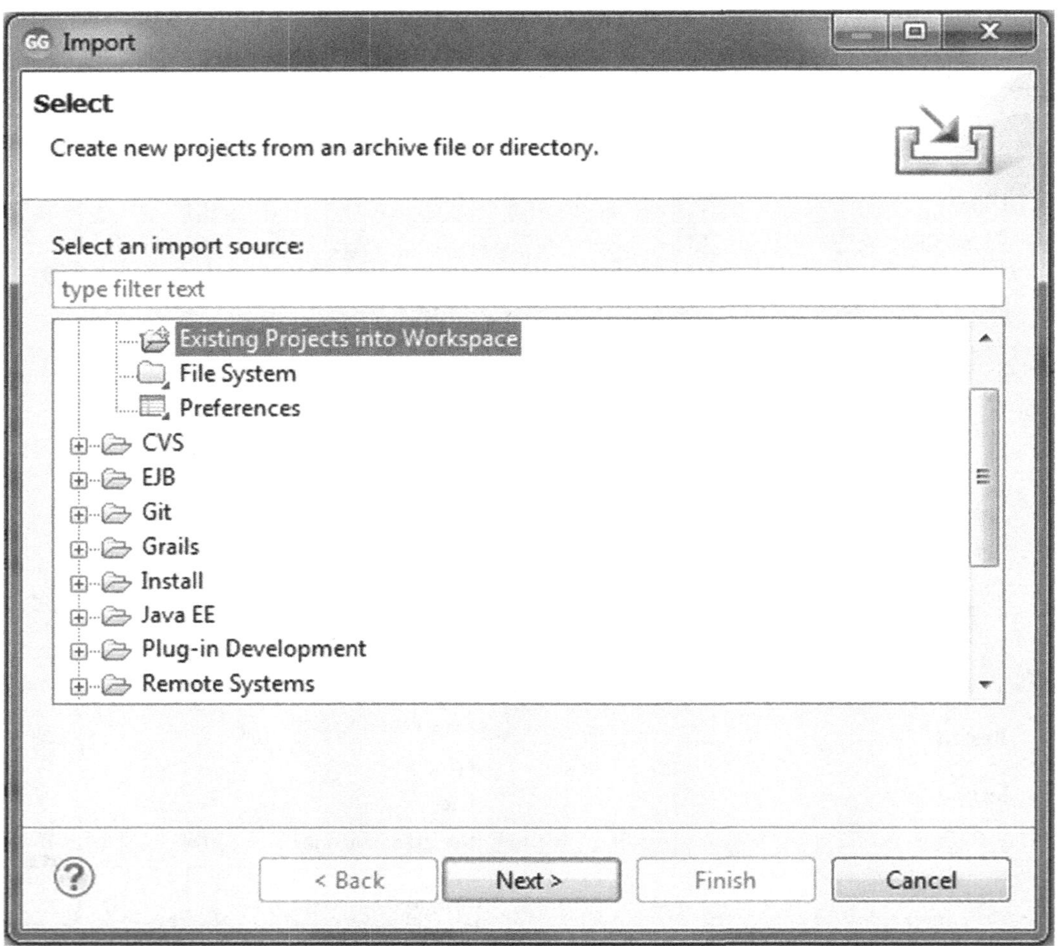

Figure 7-8. Importing an existing project

Click Next. Select the root directory of the project, as illustrated in Figure 7-9.

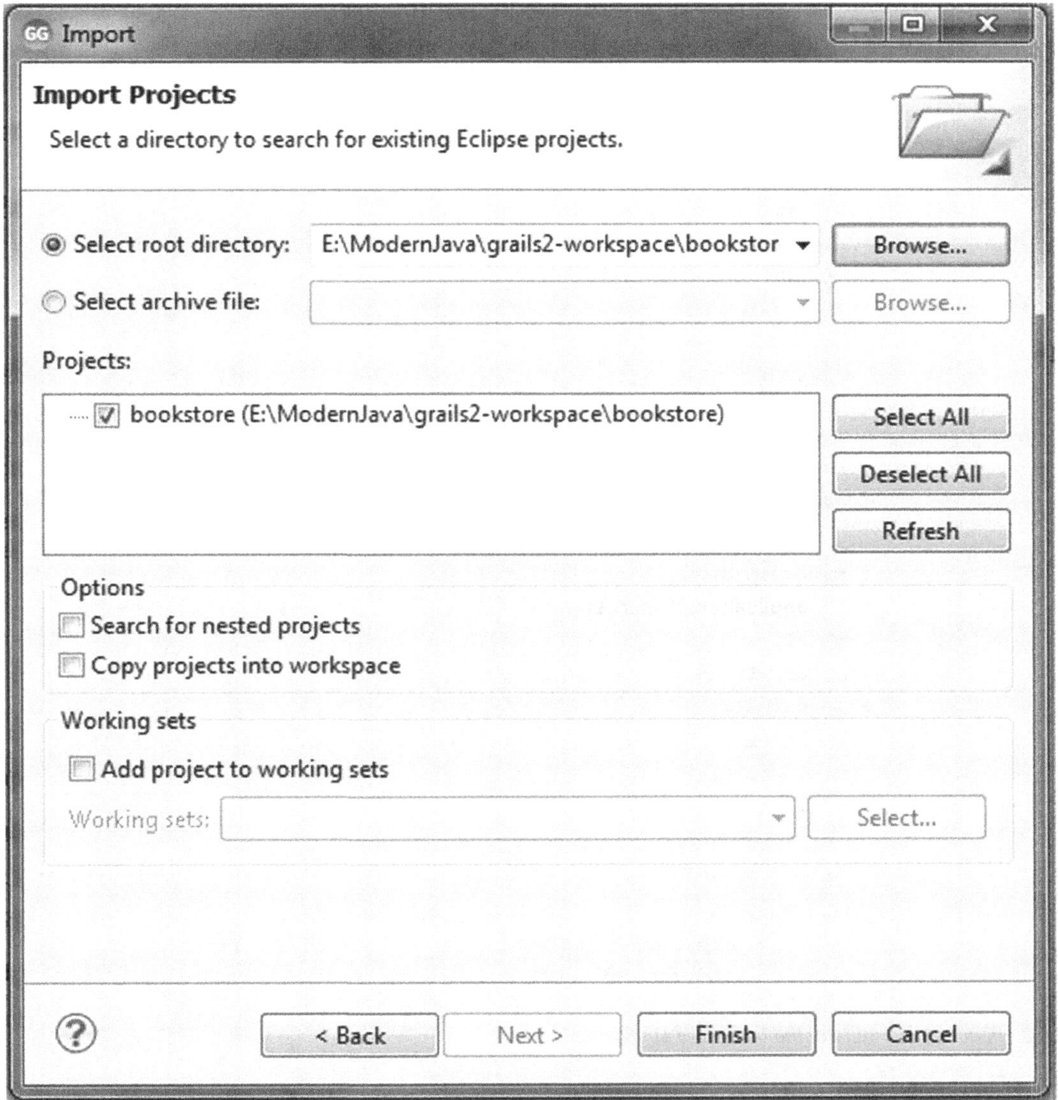

***Figure 7-9.** Selecting a directory to search for existing Eclipse projects*

Click Finish. Figure 7-10 illustrates the directory structure of the bookstore application in GGTS.

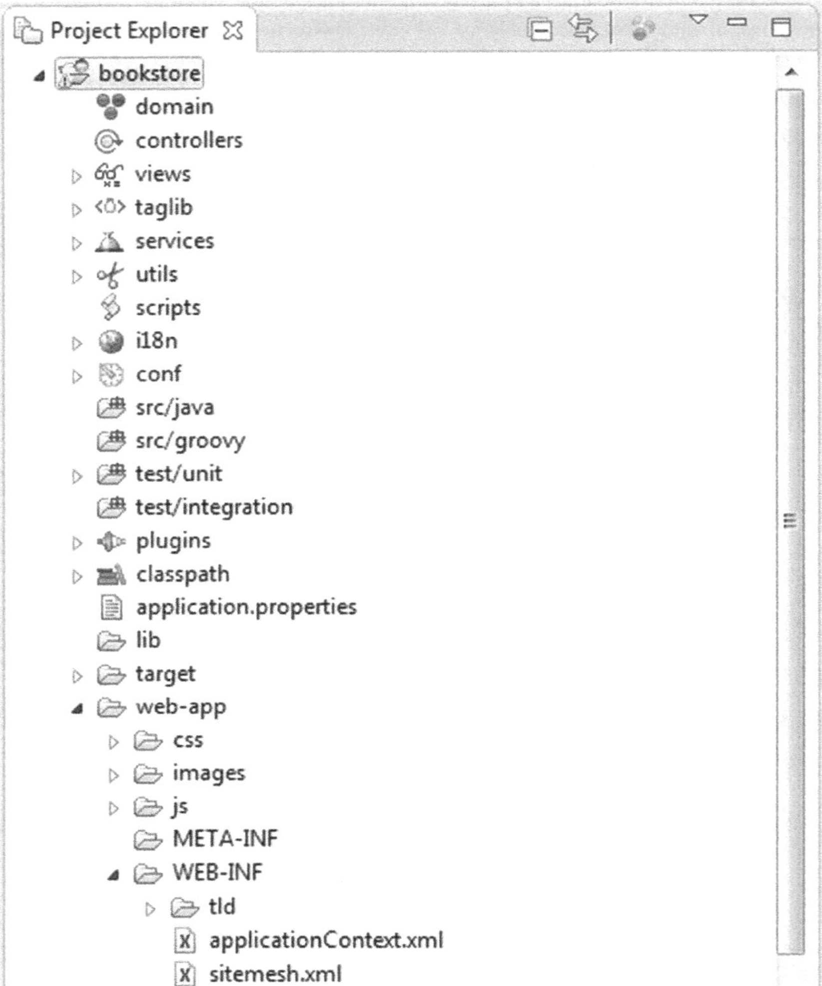

Figure 7-10. Directory structure of the bookstore application

Running the Application

At this point, you have a functional application that you can run and access through a web browser. It does not do much yet, but running it now will enable you to get instant feedback as you add domain and controller classes.

To run a Grails application, execute the `run-app` target from your project root directory, as shown here:

```
> grails run-app
```

The output of executing the `run-app` target is shown here:

```
Server running. Browse to http://localhost:8080/bookstore
```

Accessing the application at the `url http://localhost:8080/bookstore` displays the Welcome screen as illustrated in Figure 7-11.

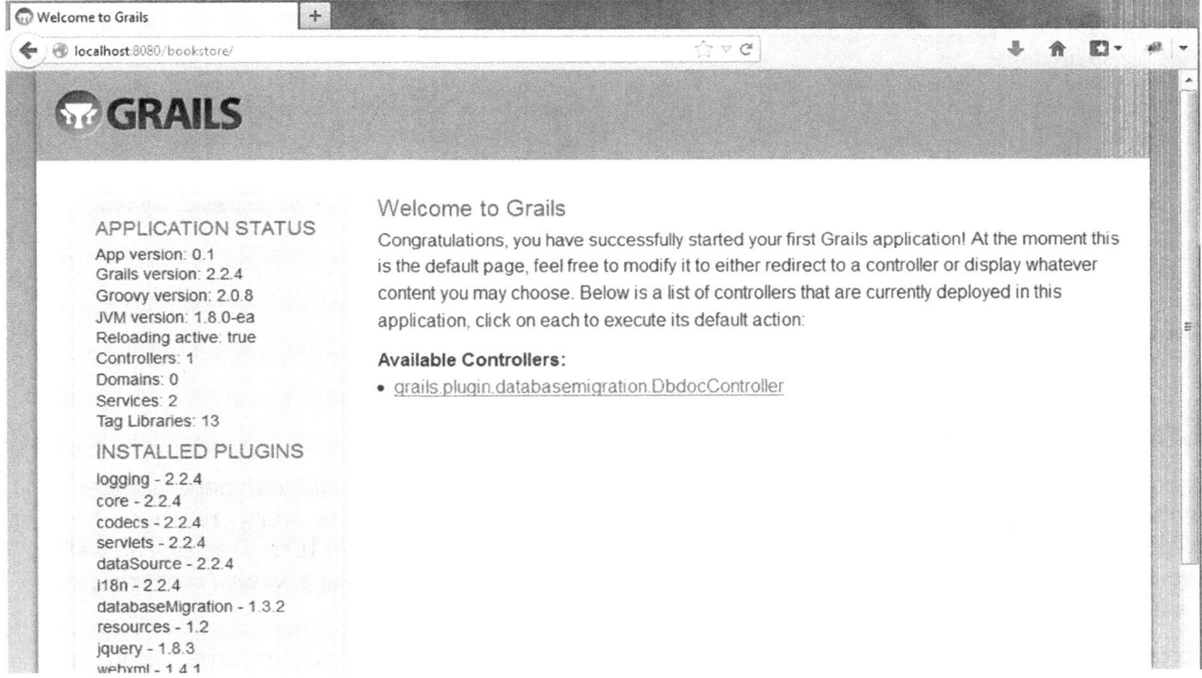

***Figure 7-11.** The Welcome screen of the bookstore application*

To run the application in GGTS, click Grails Command History, as highlighted in Figure 7-12. Type **run-app** in the command window, and hit Enter. Or you can also right-click the project in the IDE and select Run As ➤ Grails (run app).

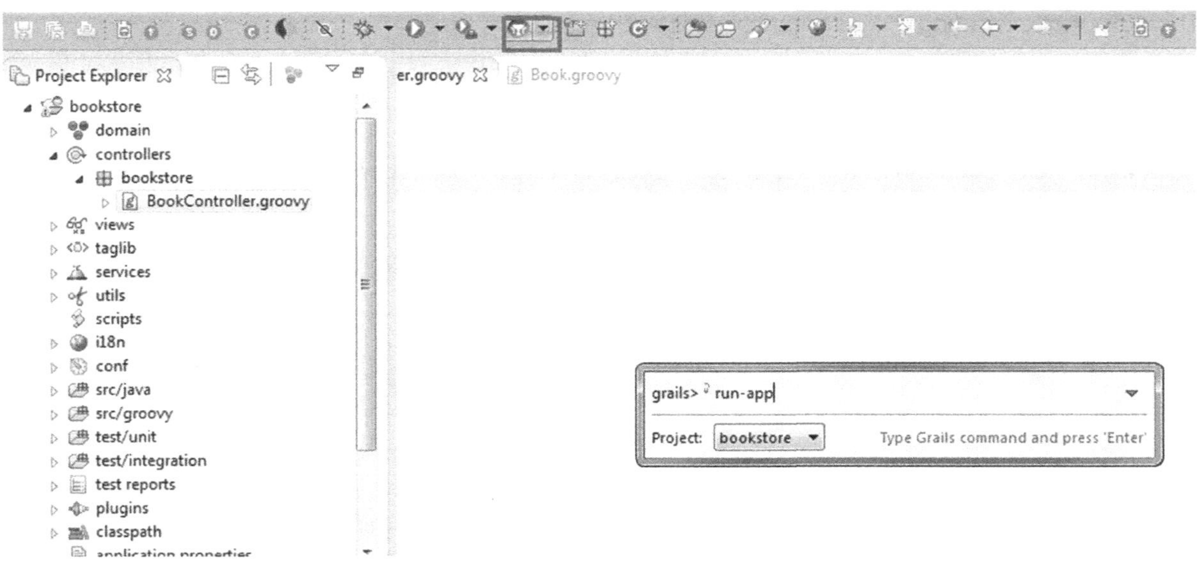

Figure 7-12. Grails command history

Creating the Controller

A controller handles requests and creates or prepares responses. A controller can generate the response directly or delegate to a view. To create a controller class, use the Grails `create-controller` target. This creates a new Grails controller class in the `grails-app/controllers` directory, as well as the unit test for the controller class in `test/unit`. It also creates a `grails-app/views/<controller name>` directory if it doesn't exist already.

To create the `BookController` class, you need to execute the `create-controller` target using an optional class name, as shown here:

```
>grails create-controller book
```

If you don't supply the class name, you are prompted for one. The output of executing the `create-controller` target is shown here:

```
| Created file grails-app/controllers/bookstore/BookController.groovy
| Created file grails-app/views/book
| Created file test/unit/bookstore/BookControllerTests.groovy
```

Notice that when running the `create-controller` with the optional class name, you can leave the class name in lowercase, and Grails will automatically uppercase it for you so that it follows the standard Groovy class naming convention.

To create the controller using GGTS, click the controllers in the bookstore project hierarchy, and then use New ➤ Controller. Type **Book** in the Grails Command Wizard, as shown in Figure 7-13.

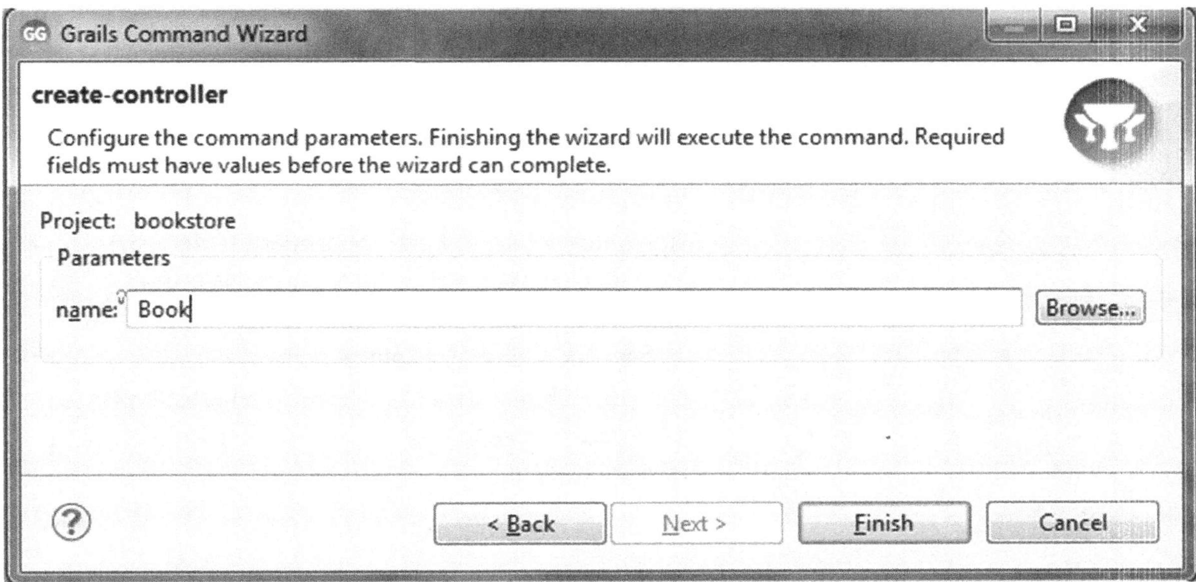

***Figure 7-13.** Creating a controller using GGTS*

Click Finish. GGTS will generate the controller and tests, as illustrated in the following output:

```
Loading Grails 2.2.4
| Environment set to development.....
| Created file grails-app/controllers/bookstore/BookController.groovy
| Created file grails-app/views/book
| Compiling 1 source files.....
| Created file test/unit/bookstore/BookControllerTests.groovy
```

Listing 7-3 illustrates the generated controller.

***Listing 7-3.** BookController Generated by Grails*

```
package bookstore

class BookController {

    def index() {
}
}
```

Now refresh the browser and you can see this controller on the Welcome screen as illustrated in the Figure 7-14.

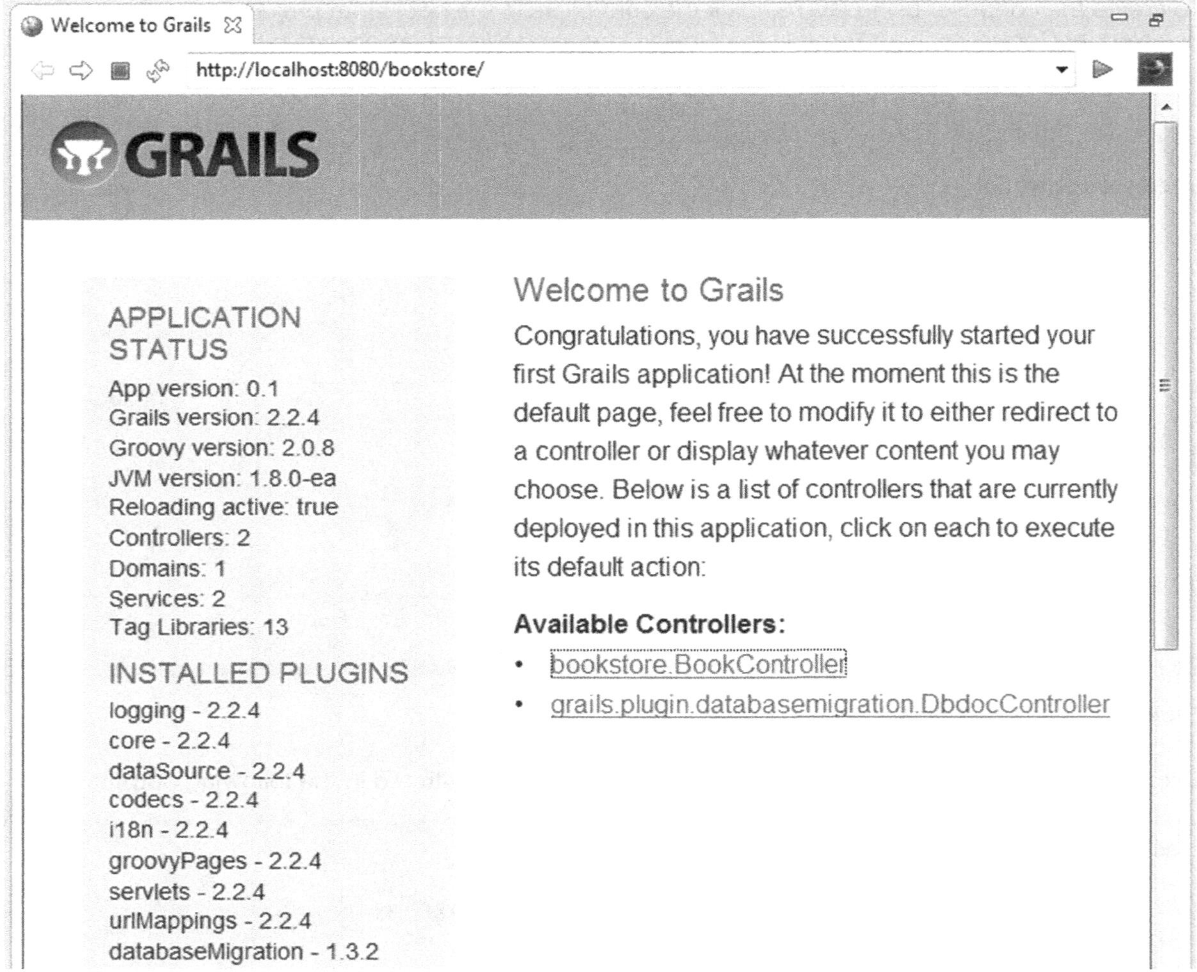

***Figure 7-14.** Welcome screen of the bookstore application*

Modify the code of `index(){}`, as illustrated in Listing 7-4.

***Listing 7-4.** Modifying the Index Action*

```
    def index() {
render "book list"
}
```

Now you can click the BookController link in Figure 7-14, and you will get the simple textual response illustrated in Figure 7-15.

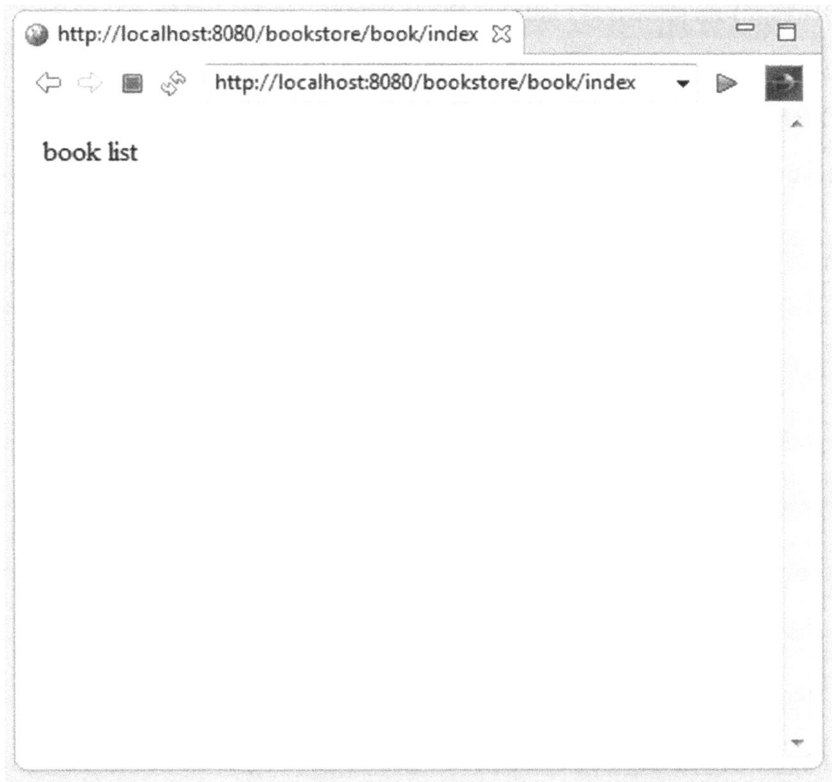

Figure 7-15. Simple textual response

Testing the Controller

Listing 7-5 illustrates the BookControllerTests test generated by Grails.

Listing 7-5. BookControllerTests Generated by Grails

```
package bookstore

import grails.test.mixin.*
import org.junit.*

/**
 * See the API for {@link grails.test.mixin.web.ControllerUnitTestMixin} for usage instructions
 */
@TestFor(BookController)
class BookControllerTests {

void testSomething() {
       fail "Implement me"
}
}
```

Modify testSomething() as shown in Listing 7-6.

Listing 7-6. Adding the Assertion

```
void testSomething() {
controller.index()
assert "book list" == response.text
}
```

Now run the test through the Run as ➤ Grails command (test-app), as illustrated in Figure 7-16.

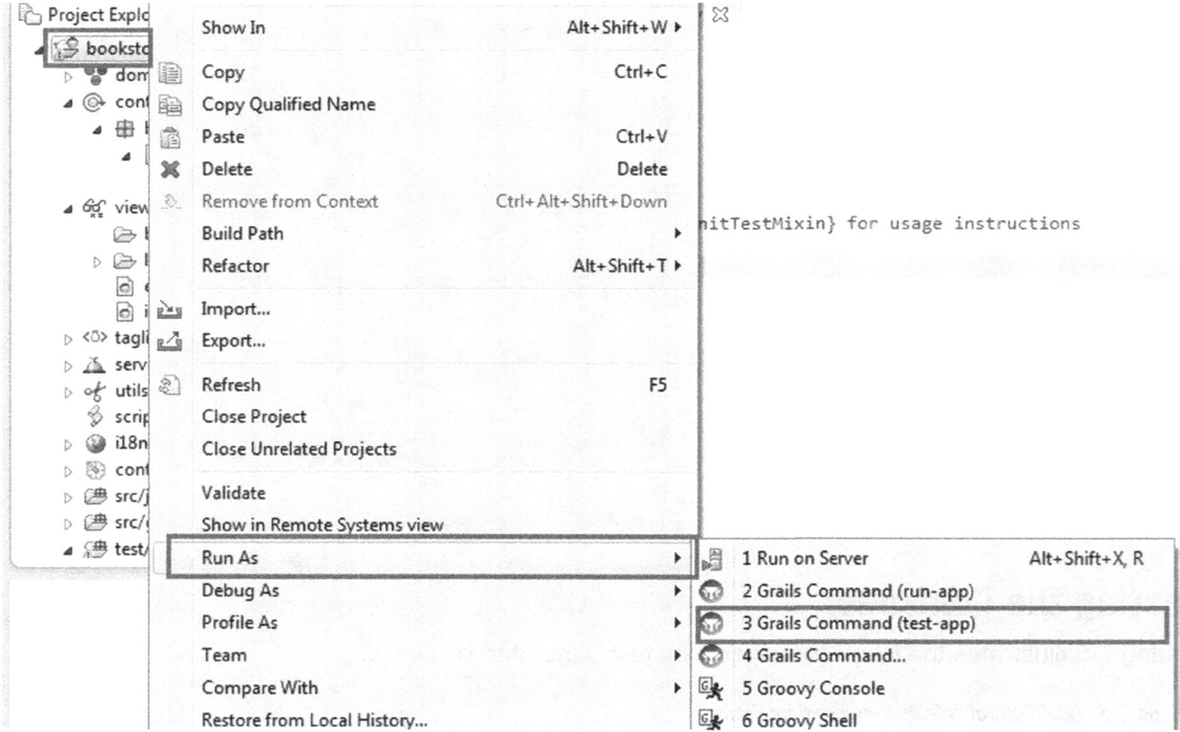

Figure 7-16. The test-app command in Grails

On running the command test-app, Grails runs the test, as shown in the following output:

```
| Loading Grails 2.2.4
| Configuring classpath.
| Environment set to test.....
| Running 1 unit test... 1 of 1
| Completed 1 unit test, 0 failed in 3444ms
| Packaging Grails application.....
| Packaging Grails application.....
| Tests PASSED - view reports in E:\ModernJava\grails2-workspace\bookstore\target\test-reports
```

You can generate the report illustrated in Figure 7-17 from the path shown in the last line of the previous output.

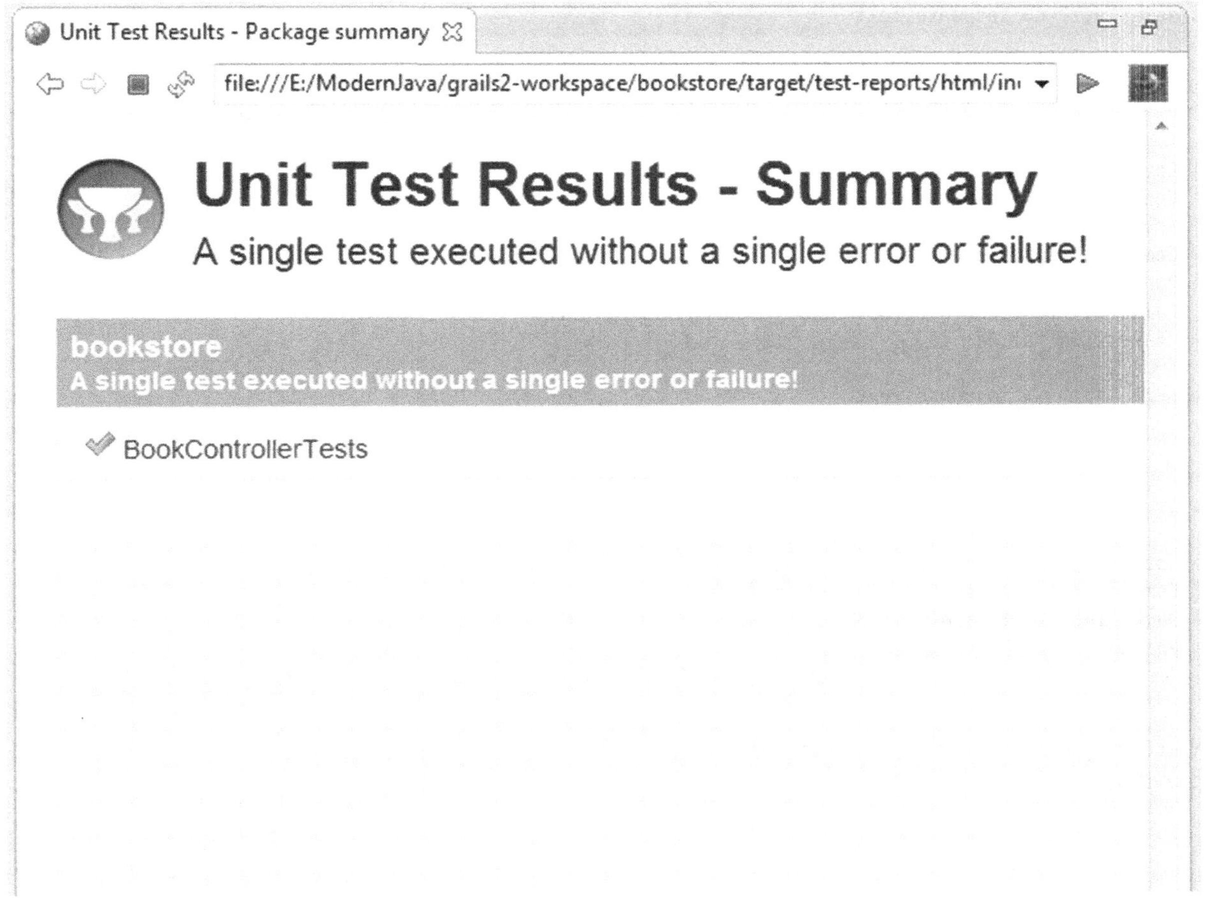

Figure 7-17. Test report: passed test

> **Note** In this way you can augment the unit test for your Controller in the ControllerTests generated by Grails.

The test passed because in Listing 7-6 the assertion made on line 3 was correct. Now replace line 3 in Listing 7-6, as shown here:

```
assert "xyz" == response.text
```

This is an incorrect assertion, because the simple textual response shown in Figure 7-15 is "book list" and not "xyz." So this test should fail. To see how Grails reports the failed test, fail the test by replacing `testSomething()` with Listing 7-7.

Listing 7-7. Replacing the Test with an Incorrect Assertion

```
void testSomething() {
controller.index()
assert "xyz" == response.text
}
```

On running the command `test-app`, Grails runs the test as shown in the following output:

```
| Loading Grails 2.2.4
| Configuring classpath.
| Environment set to test.....
| Compiling 1 source files.
| Running 1 unit test... 1 of 1
| Failure:  testSomething(bookstore.BookControllerTests)
|  Assertion failed:

assert "xyz" == response.text
             |  |        |
             |  |        book list
             |  org.codehaus.groovy.grails.plugins.testing.GrailsMockHttpServletResponse@14cf61d
             false

at bookstore.BookControllerTests.testSomething(BookControllerTests.groovy:16)
| Completed 1 unit test, 1 failed in 3210ms
| Packaging Grails application.....
| Packaging Grails application.....
| Tests FAILED  - view reports in E:\ModernJava\grails2-workspace\bookstore\target\test-reports
```

You can generate the report illustrated in Figure 7-18 from the path shown in the last line of the previous output.

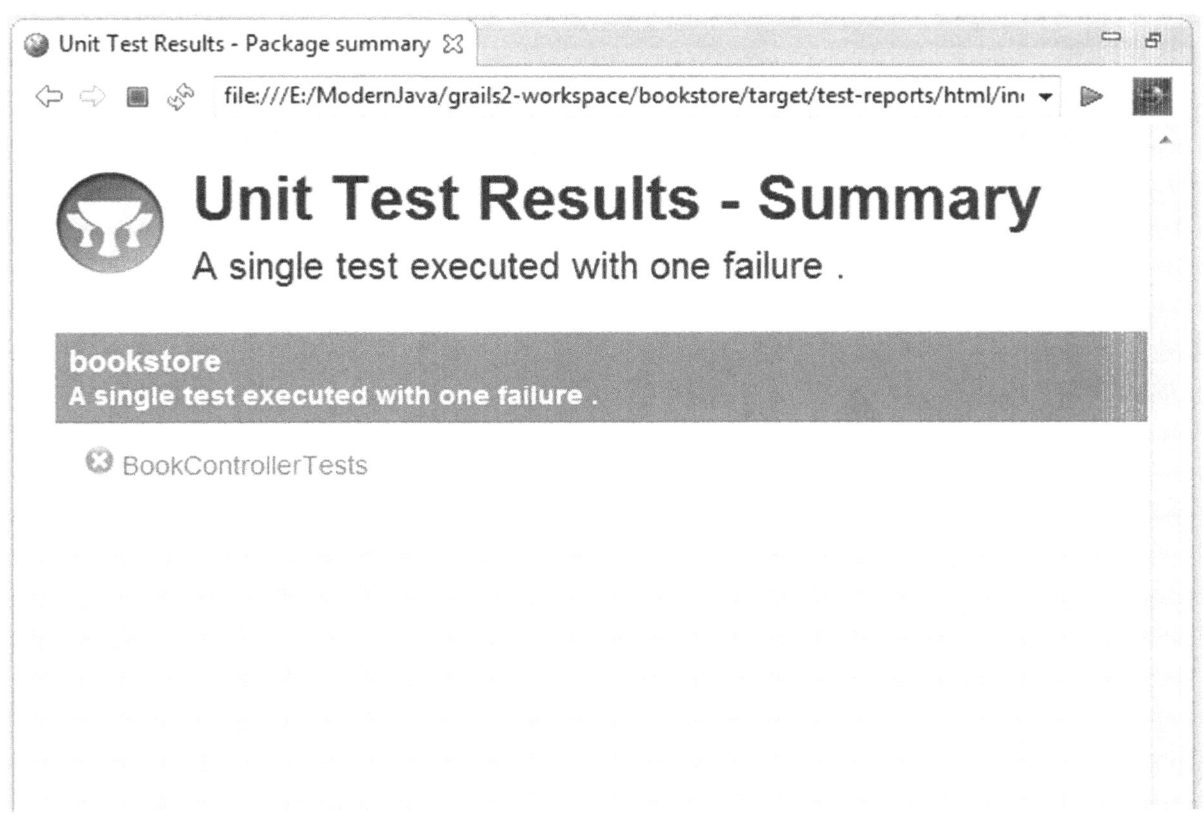

Figure 7-18. Test report: failed test

Creating a Domain Class

At this point, the application we created doesn't really do anything; it just renders a simple textual response. We will move on by creating a domain class. To create a domain class, use the Grails `create-domain-class` target. This creates a new Grails domain class in the `grails-app/domain` directory, as well as a unit test for the domain class in `test/unit`.

To create the `Book` domain class, you need to execute the `create-domain-class` target using an optional class name, as shown here:

```
> grails createdomain-class book
```

If you don't supply the class name, you are prompted for one.

Notice that when running the `create-domain-class` target with the optional class name, you can leave the class name in lowercase, and Grails will automatically uppercase it for you so that it follows the standard Groovy class naming convention.

To create the domain class using GGTS, click "domain" in the project hierarchy and then use New ➤ Domain Class, as illustrated in Figure 7-19.

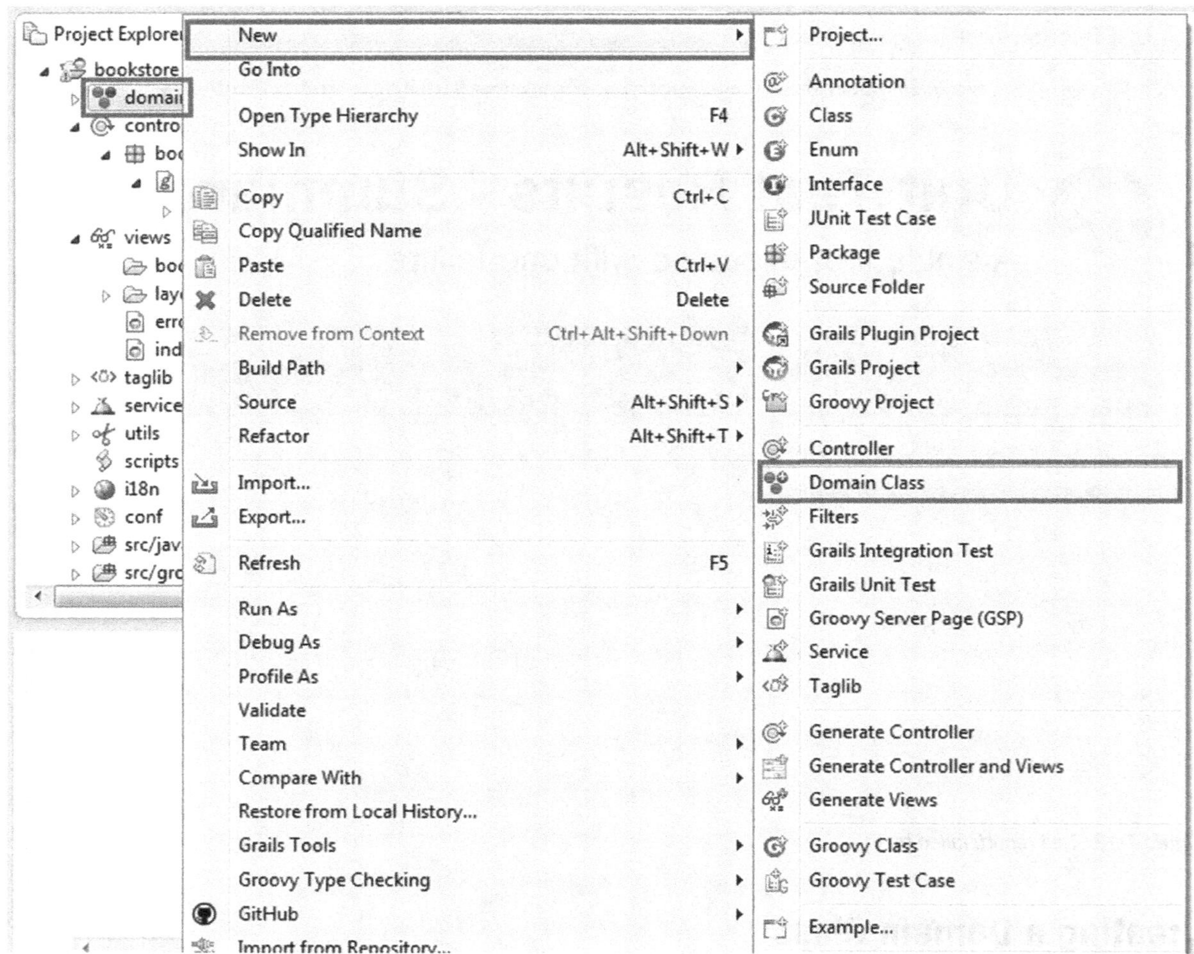

***Figure 7-19.** Creating a domain class using GGTS*

When you click Domain Class in Figure 7-19, the Grails Command Wizard window is displayed, as illustrated in Figure 7-20.

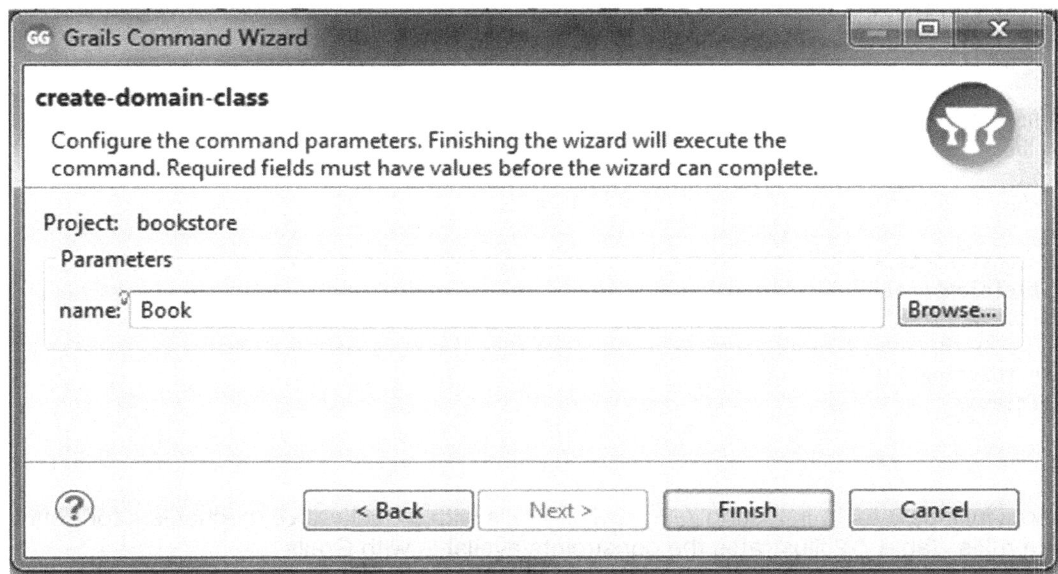

Figure 7-20. Creating a domain class using GGTS

Enter the name of the domain class in the name field and click Finish. Grails creates the Book domain class and BookTests, as shown in the following output:

```
Loading Grails 2.2.4
| Environment set to development.....
| Created file grails-app/domain/bookstore/Book.groovy
| Compiling 1 source files.....
| Created file test/unit/bookstore/BookTests.groovy
```

Listing 7-8 illustrates the Book class generated by Grails.

Listing 7-8. Book Domain Class Generated by Grails

```
package bookstore

class Book {

    static constraints = {
    }
}
```

The Book class in Listing 7-8 is empty. Now you can complete this domain class as illustrated in Listing 7-9.

Listing 7-9. Book Domain Class

```
1.package bookstore
2.
3.class Book {
4.String bookTitle
5.Long price
6.Long isbn
7.
8.static constraints = {
9.bookTitle(blank:false)
10.price(blank:false)
11.}
12.String toString() {
13.bookTitle
14.}
15.}
```

Constraints in lines 8 to 11 in Listing 7-9 provide Grails with a declarative mechanism for defining validation rules. Table 7-2 illustrates the constraints available with Grails.

Table 7-2. Constraints Available with Grails

Constraint	Description
`blank`	Validates that a String value is not blank
`creditCard`	Validates that a String value is a valid credit card number
`email`	Validates that a String value is a valid e-mail address
`inList`	Validates that a value is within a range or collection of constrained values
`matches`	Validates that a String value matches a given regular expression
`max`	Validates that a value does not exceed the given maximum value
`maxSize`	Validates that a value's size does not exceed the given maximum value
`min`	Validates that a value does not fall below the given minimum value
`minSize`	Validates that a value's size does not fall below the given minimum value
`notEqual`	Validates that a property is not equal to the specified value
`nullable`	Allows a property to be set to null; defaults to false
`range`	Uses a Groovy range to ensure that a property's value occurs within a specified range
`scale`	Sets the desired scale for floating-point numbers (i.e., the number of digits to the right of the decimal point)
`size`	Uses a Groovy range to restrict the size of a collection or number or the length of a String
`unique`	Constrains a property as unique at the database level
`url`	Validates that a String value is a valid URL
`validator`	Adds custom validation to a field

Scaffolding

Scaffolding lets you autogenerate a whole application for a given domain class including views and controller actions for CRUD operations. Scaffolding can be either static or dynamic; both types generate the same code. The main difference is that in static scaffolding, the generated code is available to the user before compilation and thus can be easily modified if necessary. In dynamic scaffolding, however, the code is generated in memory at runtime and is not visible to the user. In the section that follows, you will learn about both dynamic and static scaffolding.

Dynamic Scaffolding

As explained earlier, the dynamic scaffolding generates controller actions and views for CRUD applications at runtime. To dynamically scaffold a domain class, you need a controller. You created a controller (`BookController`) in Listing 7-3. To use the dynamic scaffolding, change the `index` action to a `scaffold` property and assign it the domain class, as shown in Listing 7-10. This causes List Page, Create Page, Edit Page, and Show Page views, as well as delete functionality, to be generated for the specified domain class.

Listing 7-10. Dynamic Scaffolding–Enabled BookController

```
package bookstore

class BookController {

    static scaffold = Book
}
```

After changing `BookController` to look like Listing 7-10, execute the `run-app` target.

The output of executing the `run-app` target is shown here:

```
| Loading Grails 2.2.4
| Configuring classpath.
| Environment set to development.....
| Packaging Grails application.....
| Running Grails application
| Server running. Browse to http://localhost:8080/bookstore
```

Click the BookController link on the welcome page.

Clicking the BookController link brings you to the Book List view shown in Figure 7-21.

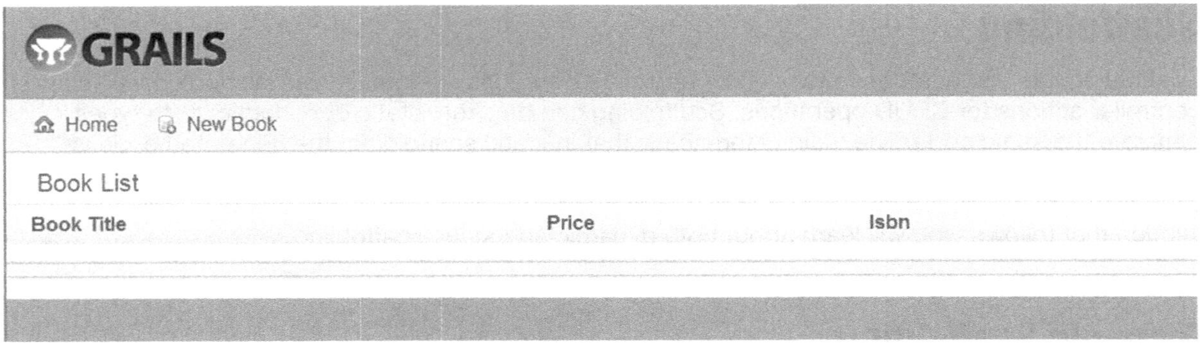

Figure 7-21. Book List view

You can create or add a new book by clicking New Book. Figure 7-22 shows the screen for creating a new book. Figure 7-22 also shows validation in action for which you did not have to write any code. The code for this validation was included in the domain class Book, as illustrated in Listing 7-9 on lines 8 to 11.

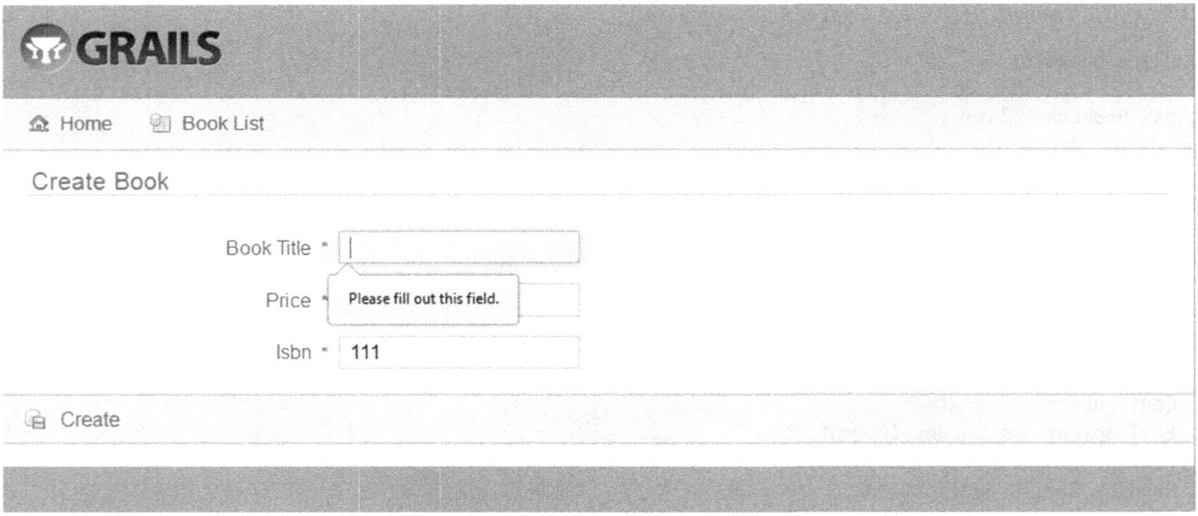

Figure 7-22. Create view with validation in action

Figure 7-23 illustrates creating a new book by fulfilling all validations.

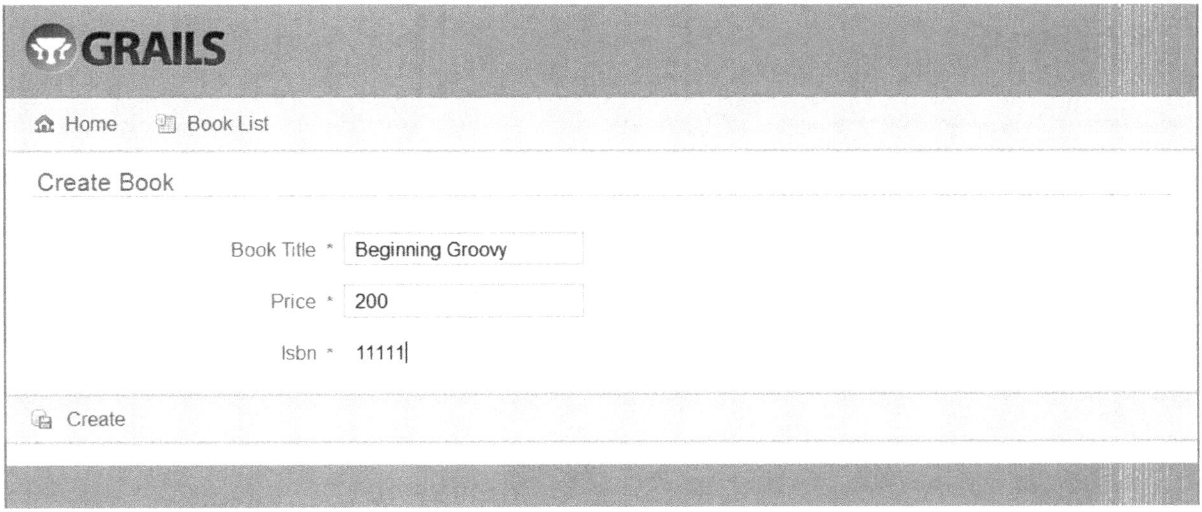

Figure 7-23. Create view

Figure 7-24 illustrates the newly created book.

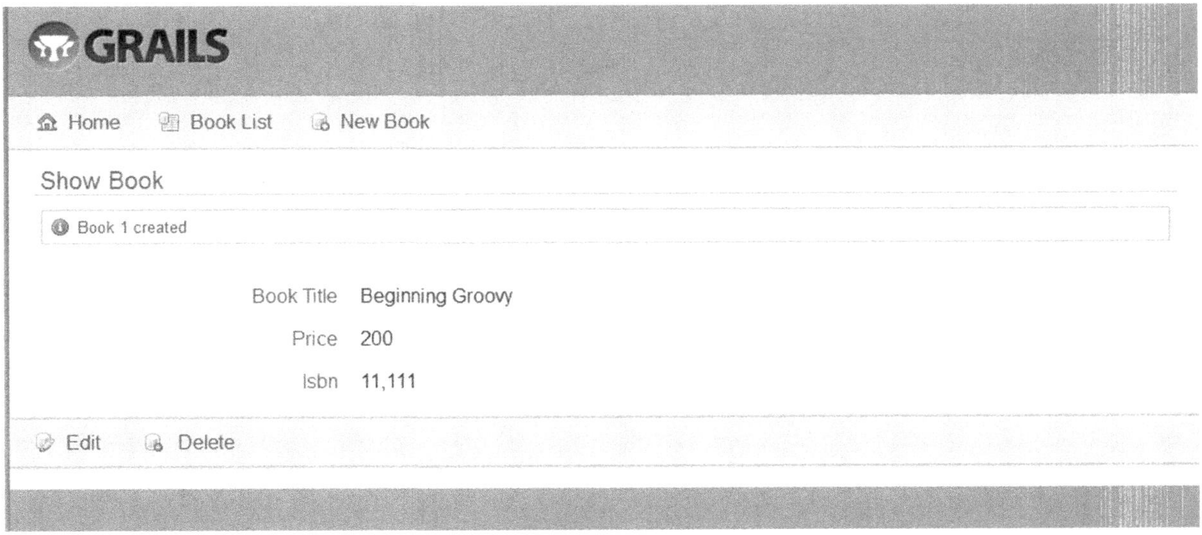

Figure 7-24. Show view

You can edit this newly created book, delete it, or add another book. You can edit the created book by clicking Update. Figure 7-25 illustrates the Edit view.

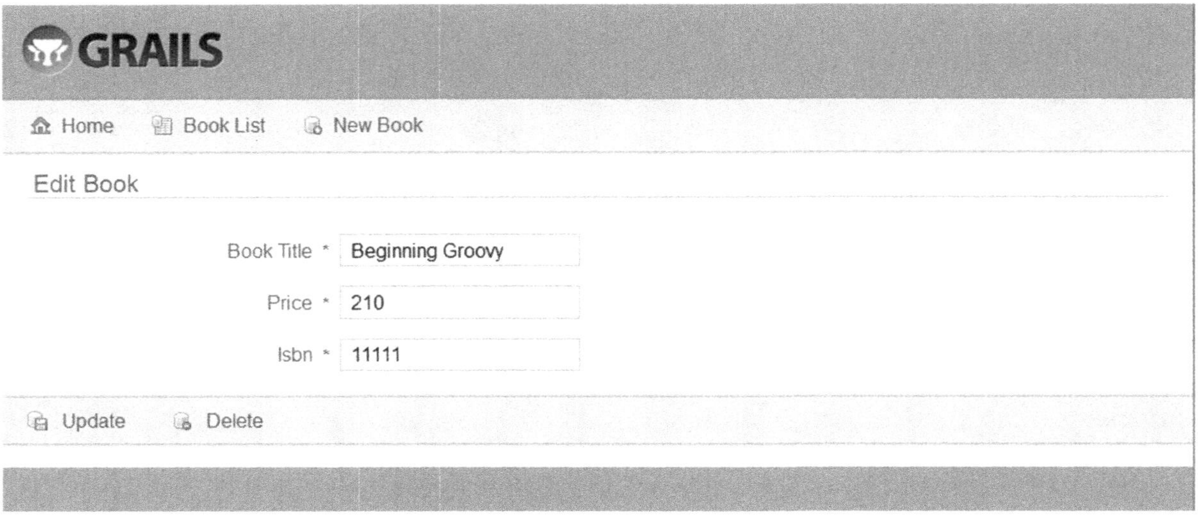

Figure 7-25. Edit view

Figure 7-26 illustrates the updated book.

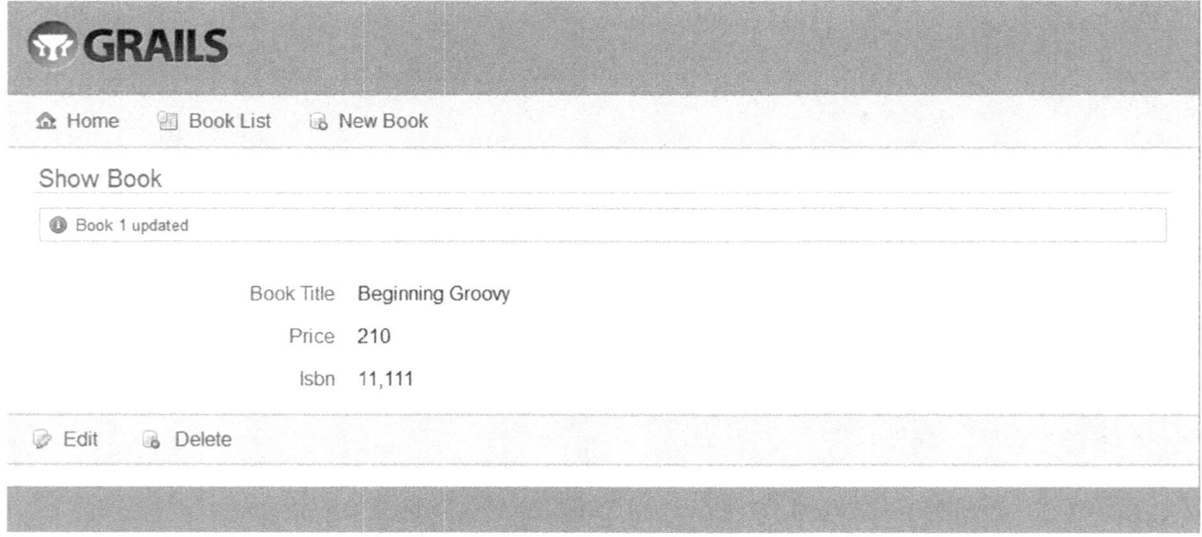

Figure 7-26. Show view with updated message

You can add a new book by clicking New Book. Figure 7-27 illustrates a list of books added in this manner.

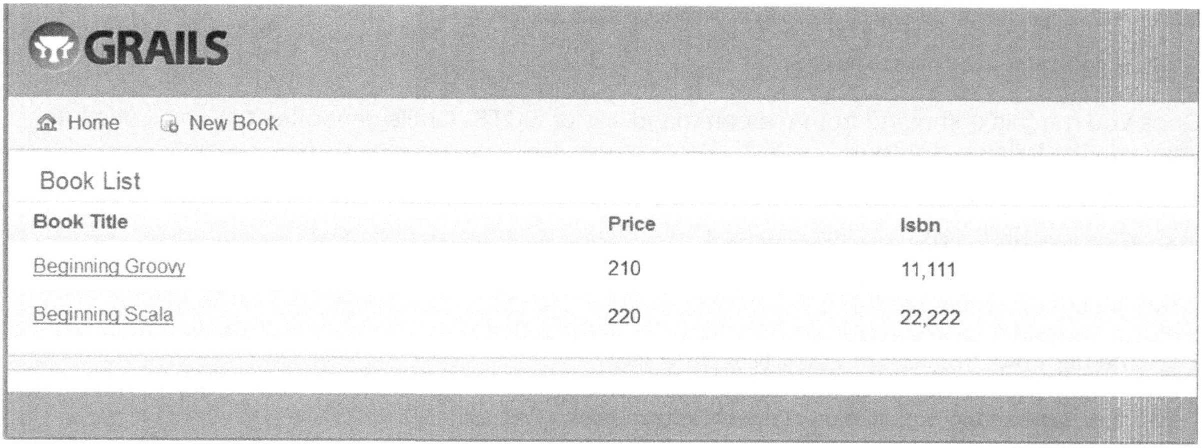

Figure 7-27. List view with list of added books

Static Scaffolding

Static scaffolding provides an excellent learning tool to help you familiarize yourself with the Grails framework and how everything fits together. Now, it is the time to see static scaffolding in action as a learning tool. There is no difference in the domain class for both dynamic and static scaffolding. For quick reference, the Book class is shown in Listing 7-11.

Listing 7-11. Book Domain Class

```
package bookstore

class Book {
String bookTitle
Long price
Long isbn

static constraints = {
bookTitle(blank:false)
price(blank:false)
}
String toString() {
bookTitle
}
}
```

Static scaffolding differs from dynamic scaffolding in the way that views and controllers are generated. The domain class remains the same in both cases. However, in dynamic scaffolding, you need the controller to indicate to Grails that you need the dynamic scaffolding to generate the application for you. If you want Grails to generate the application through static scaffolding, you have to use the command in Listing 7-12.

Listing 7-12. Command for generating the application through static scaffolding

```
>grails generate-all bookstore.Book
```

Once you run this command from the command line or GGTS, Grails generates the application as shown in the following output:

```
Loading Grails 2.2.4
| Configuring classpath.
| Environment set to development.....
| Packaging Grails application.....
| Packaging Grails application.....
| Generating views for domain class bookstore.Book
| Generating controller for domain class bookstore.Book
| Finished generation for domain class bookstore.Book
```

If we run the application now, we will have a complete CRUD application. This `generate-all` command generates one controller (`BookController`) and four views for our domain class `Book` and generates one unit test for our controller, `BookControllerTest`. These files, which give us a complete CRUD application, serve as stubs to which we can add custom code. Let's take a closer look at the code we've generated. We begin with the `BookController` illustrated in Figure 7-28.

```
BookController.groovy

package bookstore

import org.springframework.dao.DataIntegrityViolationException

class BookController {

    static allowedMethods = [save: "POST", update: "POST", delete: "POST"]

    def index() {

    def list(Integer max) {

    def create() {

    def save() {

    def show(Long id) {

    def edit(Long id) {

    def update(Long id, Long version) {

    def delete(Long id) {
}
```

Figure 7-28. BookController

The first thing you will notice in the BookController code illustrated in Figure 7-28 is that a Grails controller is a plain Groovy class that does not extend any class or implement any interface. The next thing you will notice is that the BookController has eight actions.

- Create action
- Delete action
- Edit action
- Index action
- List action
- Save action
- Show action
- Update action

These actions are the closure properties of the controller. All the work in the controller is done in the action. Every closure declared in a controller is an action and can be accessed via a URL that, by default, is mapped to controller actions. The first part of the URL represents the controller name, and the second part of the URL represents the action name. In the sections that follow, you will look deeper into each of these actions, but before that, it is necessary to understand how to exit a controller action. There are three options to properly exit a controller action.

- Calling the render() method
- Calling the redirect() method
- Returning a model or null

In the section that follows, you will look into these three options before probing each of the actions in the BookController shown in Figure 7-28.

Calling the render() Method

The first option to exit a controller action is to call the render() method to render a view or a textual response. For the sake of understanding how render() method works, Listing 7-13 shows a simple Grails controller that, when invoked, greets you.

Listing 7-13. Rendering a Textual Response

```
package chapter5
class HelloController {
def index() {
render 'hello'
}
defshow(){}
def someOtherAction(){}
}
```

As illustrated in Listing 7-13, the controller, when invoked with a request to /hello/index, will execute an index() action defined in the controller, and the index() action will render a textual response, using the render() method. The full URL to invoke the index() action in the HelloController is http://localhost:8080/chapter5/hello/index. As shown in the listing, there can be any number of actions in a controller.

If you specify the view name in the render() method, as shown in Listing 7-14, Grails assumes you mean a view at the location grails-app/views/hello/hello.gsp and renders a view called hello.

Listing 7-14. Rendering a View

```
class HelloController {
...
def show() {
render view: "hello"
}
...
}
```

Calling the redirect() Method

The second option to exit a controller action is to call the redirect( ) method to issue an HTTP redirect to another URL. Grails provides all controllers with a redirect( ) method that accepts a Map as an argument. The Map should contain all the information that Grails needs to carry out the redirect, including the name of the action to redirect to.

In addition, the Map can contain the name of the controller to redirect to. Listing 7-15 shows a standard redirect from the first action to the second action within the same controller.

Listing 7-15. Redirecting to an Action in the Same Controller

```
class HelloController {
def first() {
redirect action: "second"
}
def second() {
...
}
}
```

If the redirect is for an action in another controller, you must specify the name of the other controller. Listing 7-16 demonstrates how to redirect to an action in another controller.

Listing 7-16. Redirecting to an Action in Another Controller

```
class HelloController {
def first() {
redirect action: "second", controller: "other"
}
}
```

In Listing 7-16, the first() action in HelloController redirects to the second() action in the Other Controller.

Returning a Model

The third option to exit a controller action is either to return a model that is a Map containing data, as illustrated in Listing 7-17.

Listing 7-17. Returning the Model

```
class HelloController {
def show() {
    [user: User.get(params.id)]
}
}
```

Grails will attempt to render a view with the same name as the action. It will look for this view in a directory named after the base name of the controller. In Listing 7-17, returning from the `show()` action of the `HelloController` will cause Grails to render the view `/views/hello/show.gsp`.

Now you know how the action of the controller can be called and how it can be exited. Fortified with this knowledge, take a look at Figure 7-28 and let's start investigating each action one by one. First let's get the `allowedMethods` property out of the way.

```
static allowedMethods = [save: "POST", update: "POST", delete: "POST"]
```

The `allowedMethods` property provides a simple declarative syntax to specify which HTTP methods are allowed for your controller actions. By default, all request methods are allowed for all controller actions. The `allowedMethods` property is optional and needs to be defined only if the controller has actions that need to be restricted to certain request methods. This property in the `BookController` specifies that only save, update, and delete can be POST methods.

Index Action

The `index()` action is the default action that is called when you navigate to the `BookController`. By default, this action just redirects to the `list()` action using the `redirect()` method explained earlier as illustrated in Listing 7-18.

Listing 7-18. The Index Action of the BookController

```
def index() {
        redirect(action: "list", params: params)
    }
```

The `redirect()` method issues an HTTP redirect to a URL constructed from these parameters. If the action is not specified, the `index()` action will be used. The `params` hold request parameters, if any.

List Action

Listing 7-19 illustrates the `list()` action of the `BookController`.

Listing 7-19. The List Action of the BookController

```
def list(Integer max) {
        params.max = Math.min(max ?: 10, 100)
        [bookInstanceList: Book.list(params), bookInstanceTotal: Book.count()]
    }
```

The first line of the list closure is working with the params property, which is a Map containing all the parameters of the incoming request.

The last line returns a Map with two elements: bookInstanceList and bookInstanceTotal. The bookInstanceList is loaded with a call to Book.list( ). The list( ) is being passed the params Map, from which it will pull any parameters that it can use. The bookInstanceTotal is loaded with Book.count().The use of the bookInstanceTotal will be mentioned in the "List View" section later. The list() action renders the list view using the data in the Map that's returned from this action.

Create Action

Listing 7-20 illustrates the create() action of the BookController.

Listing 7-20. The Create Action of the BookController

```
def create() {
        [bookInstance: new Book(params)]
    }
```

The create() action creates a new Book instance and then assigns the params to bookInstance's property because it will be used later, as explained in the "Save Action" section discussed next in Listing 7-21. Then it returns that instance in a Map with the key of bookInstance. Finally, it renders the create view.

Save Action

Listing 7-21 illustrates the save() action of the BookController.

Listing 7-21. The Save Action of the BookController

```
def save() {
        def bookInstance = new Book(params)
        if (!bookInstance.save(flush: true)) {
            render(view: "create", model: [bookInstance: bookInstance])
            return
        }

        flash.message = message(code: 'default.created.message', args: [message(code: 'book.label',
default: 'Book'), bookInstance.id])
        redirect(action: "show", id: bookInstance.id)
    }
```

If there are errors, the user is redirected to the create() action. For this redirect to the create() action, params was assigned to the bookInstance's property, as mentioned in the create() action earlier in Listing 7-20. If there are no errors, the show view is rendered with the newly created instance.

Show Action

Listing 7-22 illustrates the show() action of the BookController.

Listing 7-22. The Show Action of the BookController

```
def show(Long id) {
        def bookInstance = Book.get(id)
        if (!bookInstance) {
            flash.message = message(code: 'default.not.found.message',
args: [message(code: 'book.label', default: 'Book'), id])
            redirect(action: "list")
            return
        }

        [bookInstance: bookInstance]
    }
```

The show() action expects an id parameter. The first line of the show() action calls the Book.get( ) method to retrieve the Book referred to by the id parameter. If no Book instance exists with the id passed in, an error message is stored in the flash scope, and the user is redirected to the list view.

If a Book instance is found with the id passed in, it is returned in a Map with the key of bookInstance, and the show() action will render the show view.

Edit Action

Listing 7-23 illustrates the edit() action of the BookController.

Listing 7-23. The Edit Action of the BookController

```
def edit(Long id) {
        def bookInstance = Book.get(id)
        if (!bookInstance) {
            flash.message = message(code: 'default.not.found.message', args: [message(code: 'book.
label', default: 'Book'), id])
            redirect(action: "list")
            return
        }

        [bookInstance: bookInstance]
    }
```

The edit() action loads the necessary data that will be used during editing and passes it to the edit view. The edit() action is very much the same as the show() action. The name of the edit() action, edit, is used to render the edit view.

Update Action

The update() action is called when changes from the edit view are submitted. Listing 7-24 illustrates the update() action of the BookController.

Listing 7-24. The Update Action of the BookController

```
def update(Long id, Long version) {
        def bookInstance = Book.get(id)
        if (!bookInstance) {
            flash.message = message(code: 'default.not.found.message',
args: [message(code: 'book.label', default: 'Book'), id])
            redirect(action: "list")
            return
        }

        if (version != null) {
            if (bookInstance.version > version) {
                bookInstance.errors.rejectValue("version", "default.optimistic.locking.failure",
                          [message(code: 'book.label', default: 'Book')] as Object[],
                          "Another user has updated this Book while you were editing")
                render(view: "edit", model: [bookInstance: bookInstance])
                return
            }
        }

        bookInstance.properties = params

        if (!bookInstance.save(flush: true)) {
            render(view: "edit", model: [bookInstance: bookInstance])
            return
        }

        flash.message = message(code: 'default.updated.message', args: [message(code:
'book.label', default: 'Book'), bookInstance.id])
        redirect(action: "show", id: bookInstance.id)
    }
```

The update() action tries to retrieve a Book instance with the id parameter. The id is provided from the edit view. If an instance is found, an optimistic concurrency check is performed. If there are no errors, all the values from the edit view are assigned to the appropriate property of the Book instance, including any necessary data conversion.

```
bookInstance.properties = params
```

If both of those steps are successful, a "success" message is stored in flash, and the user is directed to the show view. If either step fails, a "failure" message is stored in flash, and the user is directed back to the edit view.

Delete Action

The `delete()` action is available, by default, in the edit and show views. Listing 7-25 illustrates the `delete()` action of the `BookController`.

Listing 7-25. The Delete Action of the BookController

```
def delete(Long id) {
     def bookInstance = Book.get(id)
     if (!bookInstance) {
         flash.message = message(code: 'default.not.found.message', args: [message(code:
'book.label', default: 'Book'), id])
         redirect(action: "list")
         return
     }

     try {
         bookInstance.delete(flush: true)
         flash.message = message(code: 'default.deleted.message', args: [message(code:
'book.label', default: 'Book'), id])
         redirect(action: "list")
     }
     catch (DataIntegrityViolationException e) {
         flash.message = message(code: 'default.not.deleted.message',
args: [message(code: 'book.label', default: 'Book'), id])
         redirect(action: "show", id: id)
     }
}
```

The `delete()` action attempts to retrieve a `Book` instance and redirects to the list view if it can't find one. If an instance is found, a try/catch block is entered, where deletion of the instance is tried. If the deletion is successful, a message is stored in `flash` and redirected to the list view. If there is an exception, a different message is stored in `flash` and redirected to the show view.

Now that you have seen all the actions generated in the `BookController` for the `Book` class, let's examine the views generated by static scaffolding for the `Book` class.

Grails Views

Grails uses Groovy Server Pages (GSP) for its view layer. Grails also uses SiteMesh, the page decoration framework, to help with page layout. SiteMesh merges each of the `.gsp` files into a file called `main.gsp` to give a consistent look to all the pages. You will begin the generated views with `main.gsp`, which can be found in `\views\layouts`, followed by the four views generated for the `Book` class: `list.gsp`, `show.gsp`, `create.gsp`, and `edit.gsp`. Listing 7-26 illustrates `main.gsp`.

Listing 7-26. main.gsp

```
<!DOCTYPE html>
<!--[if lt IE 7 ]><html lang="en" class="no-js ie6"><![endif]-->
<!--[if IE 7 ]><html lang="en" class="no-js ie7"><![endif]-->
<!--[if IE 8 ]><html lang="en" class="no-js ie8"><![endif]-->
```

```
5.<!--[if IE 9 ]><html lang="en" class="no-js ie9"><![endif]-->
6.<!--[if (gt IE 9)|!(IE)]><!--><html lang="en" class="no-js"><!--<![endif]-->
7.<head>
8.<meta http-equiv="Content-Type" content="text/html; charset=UTF-8">
9.<meta http-equiv="X-UA-Compatible" content="IE=edge,chrome=1">
10.<title><g:layoutTitle default="Grails"/></title>
11.<meta name="viewport" content="width=device-width, initial-scale=1.0">
12.<link rel="shortcut icon" href="${resource(dir: 'images', file: 'favicon.ico')}"
type="image/x-icon">
13.<link rel="apple-touch-icon" href="${resource(dir: 'images', file: 'apple-touch-icon.png')}">
14.<link rel="apple-touch-icon" sizes="114x114" href="${resource(dir: 'images',
file: 'apple-touch-icon-retina.png')}">
15.<link rel="stylesheet" href="${resource(dir: 'css', file: 'main.css')}" type="text/css">
16.<link rel="stylesheet" href="${resource(dir: 'css', file: 'mobile.css')}" type="text/css">
17.<g:layoutHead/>
18.<r:layoutResources />
19.</head>
20.<body>
21.<div id="grailsLogo" role="banner"><a href="http://grails.org"><img src="${resource(dir:
'images', file: 'grails_logo.png')}" alt="Grails"/></a></div>
22.<g:layoutBody/>
23.<div class="footer" role="contentinfo"></div>
24.<div id="spinner" class="spinner" style="display:none;"><g:message code="spinner.alt"
default="Loading&hellip;"/></div>
25.<g:javascript library="application"/>
26.<r:layoutResources />
27.</body>
28.</html>
```

- *Lines 1 to 6*: The `main.gsp` page starts with `<!doctype html>`. This is an HTML5 doc type. Grails supports HTML5 out of the box.
- *Line 10*: `<g:layoutTitle>` is used in layouts to render the contents of the title tag of the decorated page. The `<g:layoutTitle>` tag substitutes the `<title>` from the view that is being merged and links it in a style sheet and favicon that will be used by all views.
- *Line 17*: The `<g:layoutHead>` tag merges in the contents of the target view's `<head>` section. `<g:layoutHead>` is used in layouts to render the contents of the head tag of the decorated page.
- *Line 22*: `<g:layoutBody>` is used in layouts to output the contents of the body tag of the decorated page. The `<g:layoutBody>` tag merges in the `<body>` contents of the target view.
- *Line 25*: `<g:javascript>` includes JavaScript libraries and scripts and provides a shorthand for inline JavaScript. Specifying a library tells the Ajax tags which JavaScript provider to use.

The List View

The list View is illustrated in Listing 7-27.

Listing 7-27. list.gsp

```
<%@ page import="bookstore.Book" %>
<!DOCTYPE html>
<html>
<head>
<meta name="layout" content="main">
<g:set var="entityName" value="${message(code: 'book.label', default: 'Book')}" />
<title><g:message code="default.list.label" args="[entityName]" /></title>
</head>
<body>
<a href="#list-book" class="skip" tabindex="-1"><g:message code="default.link.skip.label"
default="Skip to content&hellip;"/></a>
<div class="nav" role="navigation">
<ul>
<li><a class="home" href="${createLink(uri: '/')}"><g:message code="default.home.label"/></a></li>
<li><g:link class="create" action="create"><g:message code="default.new.label"
args="[entityName]" /></g:link></li>
</ul>
</div>
<div id="list-book" class="content scaffold-list" role="main">
<h1><g:message code="default.list.label" args="[entityName]" /></h1>
<g:if test="${flash.message}">
<div class="message" role="status">${flash.message}</div>
</g:if>
<table>
<thead>
<tr>
<g:sortableColumn property="bookTitle" title="${message(code: 'book.bookTitle.label',
default: 'Book Title')}" />
<g:sortableColumn property="price" title="${message(code: 'book.price.label', default: 'Price')}" />
<g:sortableColumn property="isbn" title="${message(code: 'book.isbn.label', default: 'Isbn')}" />
</tr>
</thead>
<tbody>
<g:each in="${bookInstanceList}" status="i" var="bookInstance">
<tr class="${(i % 2) == 0 ? 'even' : 'odd'}">
<td><g:link action="show" id="${bookInstance.id}">${fieldValue(bean: bookInstance,
field: "bookTitle")}</g:link></td>
```

```
40.<td>${fieldValue(bean: bookInstance, field: "price")}</td>
41.
42.<td>${fieldValue(bean: bookInstance, field: "isbn")}</td>
43.
44.</tr>
45.</g:each>
46.</tbody>
47.</table>
48.<div class="pagination">
49.<g:paginate total="${bookInstanceTotal}" />
50.</div>
51.</div>
52.</body>
53.</html>
```

- *Line 14*: The `<g:link>` tag creates a link to the `create` action of the `BookController`.
- *Line 19*: The `<g:if>` tag checks for the existence of `flash.message` that was stored in the action and, if found, displays it.
- *Lines 26 to 31*: The `<g:sortableColumn>` tag is used to provide sorting on our list view.
- *Lines 35 to 45*: The `<g:each>` tag iterates over the `bookInstanceList`. Each item in the list is assigned to the `bookInstance` variable. The body of the `<g:each>` tag fills in the table row with the properties of the `bookInstance`. In the line `<tr class="${(i % 2) == 0 ? 'even' : 'odd'}">`, a Groovy expression is used to determine the style class of the `<tr>`, and the `fieldValue( )` method is used to render the value of each `Book` property.
- *Line 49*: The `<g:paginate>` tag displays the pagination controls if there are enough elements in the list view. The `bookInstanceTotal` is used from Listing 7-19, as mentioned earlier.

The Create View

The create view is illustrated in Listing 7-28.

Listing 7-28. create.gsp

```
<%@ page import="bookstore.Book" %>
<!DOCTYPE html>
<html>
<head>
<meta name="layout" content="main">
<g:set var="entityName" value="${message(code: 'book.label', default: 'Book')}" />
<title><g:message code="default.create.label" args="[entityName]" /></title>
</head>
<body>
<a href="#create-book" class="skip" tabindex="-1"><g:message code="default.link.skip.label"
default="Skip to content&hellip;"/></a>
```

```
11.<div class="nav" role="navigation">
12.<ul>
13.<li><a class="home" href="${createLink(uri: '/')}"><g:message code="default.home.label"/></a></li>
14.<li><g:link class="list" action="list"><g:message code="default.list.label" args="[entityName]" />
</g:link></li>
15.</ul>
16.</div>
17.<div id="create-book" class="content scaffold-create" role="main">
18.<h1><g:message code="default.create.label" args="[entityName]" /></h1>
19.<g:if test="${flash.message}">
20.<div class="message" role="status">${flash.message}</div>
21.</g:if>
22.<g:hasErrors bean="${bookInstance}">
23.<ul class="errors" role="alert">
24.<g:eachError bean="${bookInstance}" var="error">
25.<li <g:if test="${error in org.springframework.validation.FieldError}">data-field-id=
"${error.field}"</g:if>><g:message error="${error}"/></li>
26.</g:eachError>
27.</ul>
28.</g:hasErrors>
29.<g:form action="save" >
30.<fieldset class="form">
31.<g:render template="form"/>
32.</fieldset>
33.<fieldset class="buttons">
34.<g:submitButton name="create" class="save" value="${message(code:
'default.button.create.label', default: 'Create')}" />
35.</fieldset>
36.</g:form>
37.</div>
38.</body>
39.</html>
```

- *Lines 22 to 28*: The `<g:hasErrors>` tag examines the `Book` instance assigned to its bean attribute and renders its body if errors are found.
- *Line 29 to 36*: The `<g:form>` tag sets up an HTML form. This tag has an action that will result in the URL to submit the form to.
- *Line 31*: `<g:render >` applies a built-in or user-defined Groovy template against a model so that templates can be shared and reused. The template in this case is called `form` and is located in the `views` directory as `_form.gsp`. The leading underline denotes that the `.gsp` file is a template.

The Show View

The show view is illustrated in Listing 7-29.

Listing 7-29. show.gsp

```
<%@ page import="bookstore.Book" %>
<!DOCTYPE html>
<html>
<head>
<meta name="layout" content="main">
<g:set var="entityName" value="${message(code: 'book.label', default: 'Book')}" />
<title><g:message code="default.show.label" args="[entityName]" /></title>
</head>
<body>
<a href="#show-book" class="skip" tabindex="-1"><g:message code="default.link.skip.label" default="Skip to content&hellip;"/></a>
<div class="nav" role="navigation">
<ul>
<li><a class="home" href="${createLink(uri: '/')}"><g:message code="default.home.label"/></a></li>
<li><g:link class="list" action="list"><g:message code="default.list.label" args="[entityName]" /></g:link></li>
<li><g:link class="create" action="create"><g:message code="default.new.label" args="[entityName]" /></g:link></li>
</ul>
</div>
<div id="show-book" class="content scaffold-show" role="main">
<h1><g:message code="default.show.label" args="[entityName]" /></h1>
<g:if test="${flash.message}">
<div class="message" role="status">${flash.message}</div>
</g:if>
<ol class="property-list book">

<g:if test="${bookInstance?.bookTitle}">
<li class="fieldcontain">
<span id="bookTitle-label" class="property-label"><g:message code="book.bookTitle.label" default="Book Title" /></span>

<span class="property-value" aria-labelledby="bookTitle-label"><g:fieldValue bean="${bookInstance}" field="bookTitle"/></span>

</li>
</g:if>

<g:if test="${bookInstance?.price}">
<li class="fieldcontain">
<span id="price-label" class="property-label"><g:message code="book.price.label" default="Price" /></span>

<span class="property-value" aria-labelledby="price-label"><g:fieldValue bean="${bookInstance}" field="price"/></span>

</li>
</g:if>

```

```
43.<g:if test="${bookInstance?.isbn}">
44.<li class="fieldcontain">
45.<span id="isbn-label" class="property-label"><g:message code="book.isbn.label"
default="Isbn" /></span>
46.
47.<span class="property-value" aria-labelledby="isbn-label"><g:fieldValue bean="${bookInstance}"
field="isbn"/></span>
48.
49.</li>
50.</g:if>
51.
52.</ol>
53.<g:form>
54.<fieldset class="buttons">
55.<g:hiddenField name="id" value="${bookInstance?.id}" />
56.<g:link class="edit" action="edit" id="${bookInstance?.id}"><g:message
code="default.button.edit.label" default="Edit" /></g:link>
57.<g:actionSubmit class="delete" action="delete" value="${message(code:
'default.button.delete.label', default: 'Delete')}" onclick="return
confirm('${message(code: 'default.button.delete.confirm.message', default: 'Are you sure?')}');" />
58.</fieldset>
59.</g:form>
60.</div>
61.</body>
62.</html>
```

- *Lines 55 to 56*: The ? after the bookInstance reference is a safe navigation operator. When this expression is evaluated and if bookInstance is null, the whole expression evaluates to null, and no exception is thrown.
- *Line 57*: The <g:actionSubmit> tag generates a submit button that maps to a specific action, which lets you have multiple submit buttons in a single form. JavaScript event handlers can be added using the same parameter names as in HTML.

The Edit View

The edit view is illustrated in Listing 7-30.

Listing 7-30. edit.gsp

```
<%@ page import="bookstore.Book" %>
<!DOCTYPE html>
<html>
<head>
<meta name="layout" content="main">
<g:set var="entityName" value="${message(code: 'book.label', default: 'Book')}" />
<title><g:message code="default.edit.label" args="[entityName]" /></title>
</head>
```

```
9.<body>
10.<a href="#edit-book" class="skip" tabindex="-1"><g:message code="default.link.skip.label"
default="Skip to content&hellip;"/></a>
11.<div class="nav" role="navigation">
12.<ul>
13.<li><a class="home" href="${createLink(uri: '/')}"><g:message code="default.home.label"/></a></li>
14.<li><g:link class="list" action="list"><g:message code="default.list.label" args="[entityName]" />
</g:link></li>
15.<li><g:link class="create" action="create"><g:message code="default.new.label"
args="[entityName]" /></g:link></li>
16.</ul>
17.</div>
18.<div id="edit-book" class="content scaffold-edit" role="main">
19.<h1><g:message code="default.edit.label" args="[entityName]" /></h1>
20.<g:if test="${flash.message}">
21.<div class="message" role="status">${flash.message}</div>
22.</g:if>
23.<g:hasErrors bean="${bookInstance}">
24.<ul class="errors" role="alert">
25.<g:eachError bean="${bookInstance}" var="error">
26.<li <g:if test="${error in org.springframework.validation.FieldError}">data-field-id=
"${error.field}"</g:if>><g:message error="${error}"/></li>
27.</g:eachError>
28.</ul>
29.</g:hasErrors>
30.<g:form method="post" >
31.<g:hiddenField name="id" value="${bookInstance?.id}" />
32.<g:hiddenField name="version" value="${bookInstance?.version}" />
33.<fieldset class="form">
34.<g:render template="form"/>
35.</fieldset>
36.<fieldset class="buttons">
37.<g:actionSubmit class="save" action="update" value="${message(code:
'default.button.update.label', default: 'Update')}" />
38.<g:actionSubmit class="delete" action="delete" value="${message(code:
'default.button.delete.label', default: 'Delete')}" formnovalidate="" onclick="return
confirm('${message(code: 'default.button.delete.confirm.message', default: 'Are you sure?')}');" />
39.</fieldset>
40.</g:form>
41.</div>
42.</body>
43.</html>
```

- *Lines 31 to 32*: In Listing 7-24, it was mentioned that the id in the update() action is provided from this edit view. The id comes from the <g:hidden field> tag, as shown in the code.

With this, we have completed all the views generated by static scaffolding for the Book class.

H2 Console

As discussed earlier, Grails enables the H2 database console in development mode (at the URI `/dbconsole`) so that the in-memory database can be easily queried from the browser. To see the dbconsole in action, browse to `http://localhost:8080/bookstore/dbconsole`. The default login parameters should match the default in `grails-app/conf/Datasource.groovy`, as illustrated in Figure 7-29.

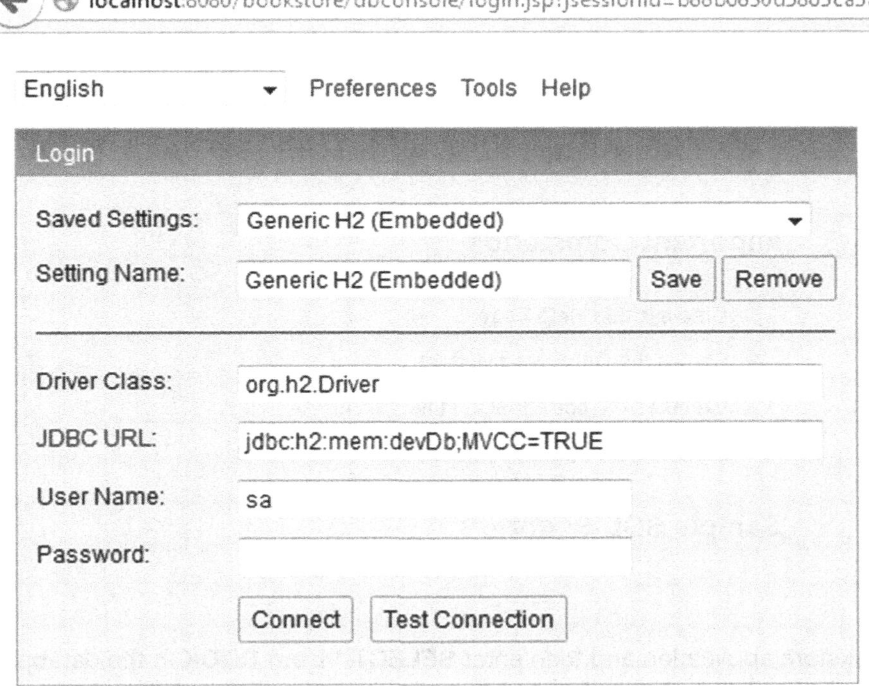

***Figure 7-29.** Login screen of H2*

You can get the user name and password from `Datasource.groovy`. Figure 7-30 illustrates the H2 console.

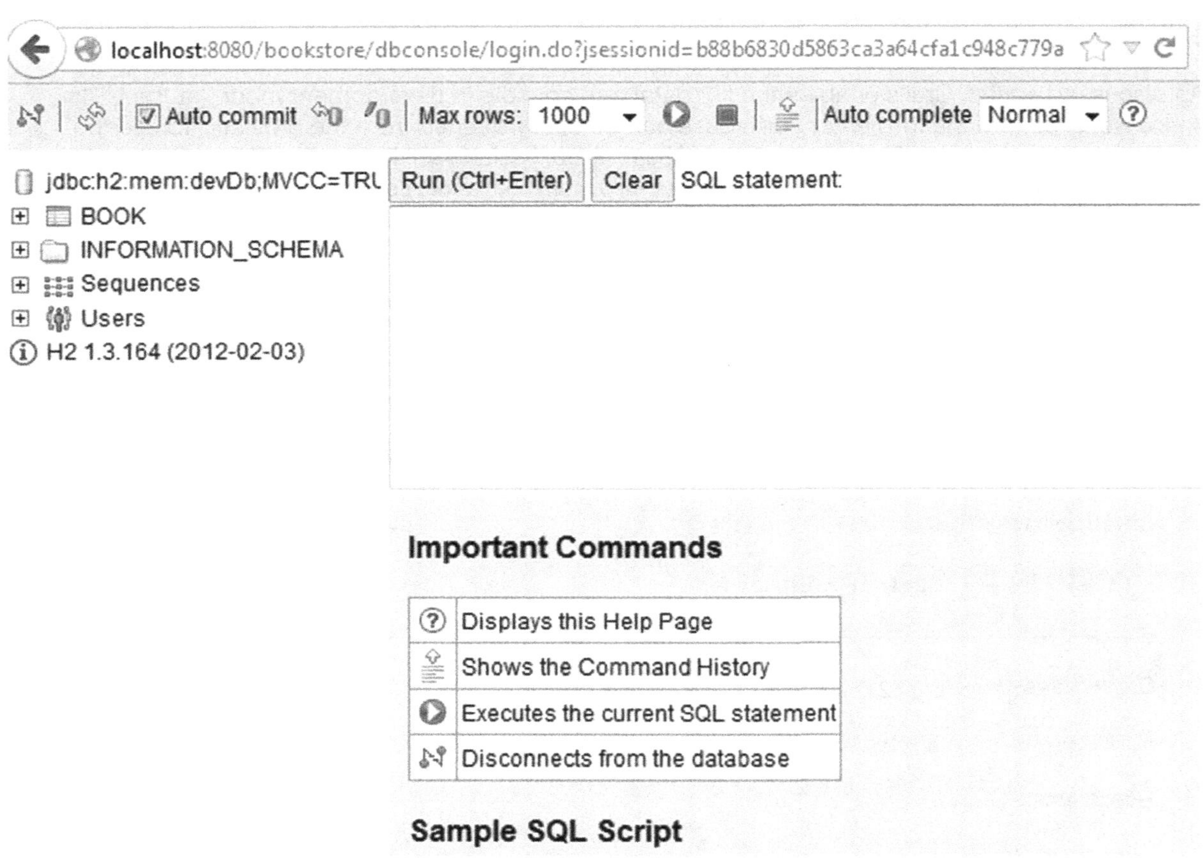

***Figure 7-30.** H2 console*

Now, add a book in our bookstore application and then enter **SELECT * from BOOK** in the database console. The user we created in the application will show up, as illustrated in Figure 7-31.

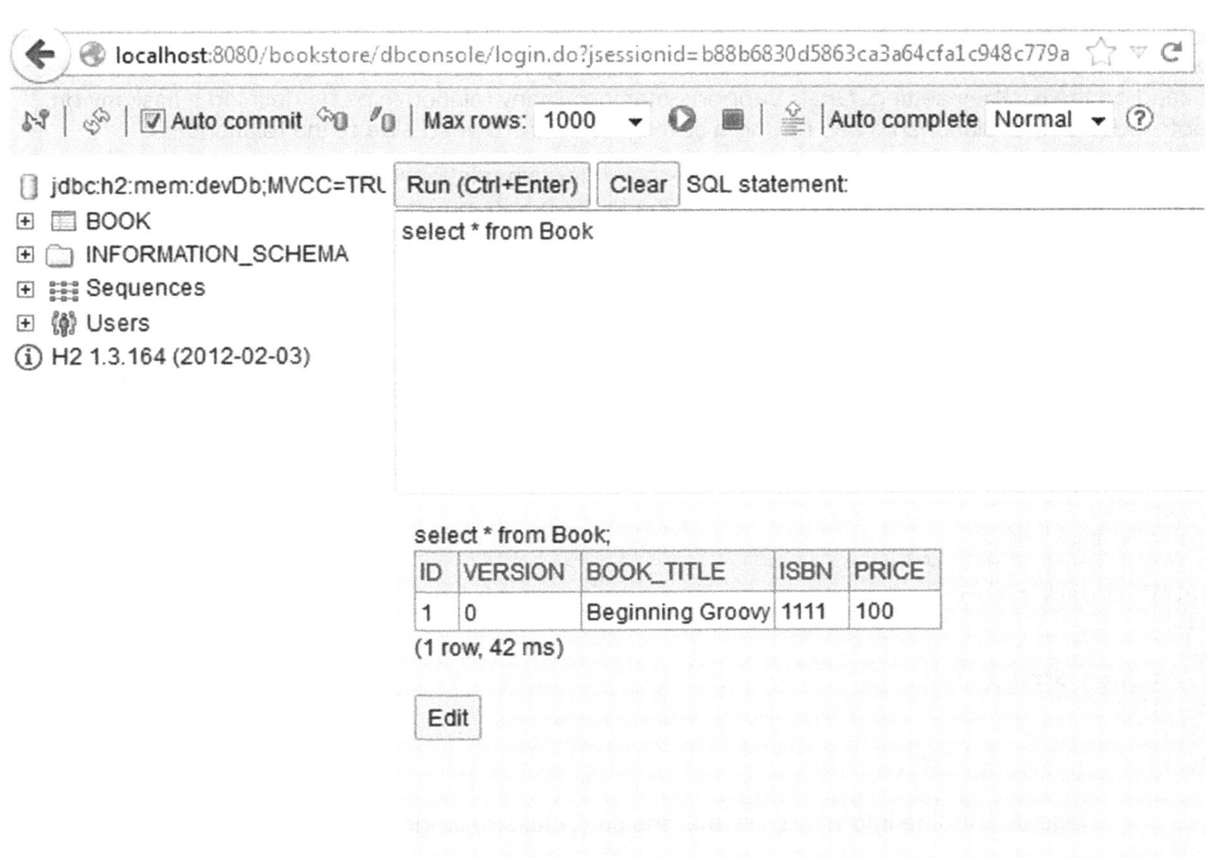

Figure 7-31. Querying the table in H2

Creating Domain Relationships

In an application domain, classes have relationships to one another. The domain relationships define how domain classes interact. Grails provides support for several types of relationships between domain classes. A one-to-many relationship is when one class, `Author`, has many instances of the `Book` class. With Grails you define such a relationship with the `hasMany` setting, as illustrated in Listing 7-31.

Listing 7-31. One-to-Many Relationship Between Author and Book

```
class Author {
    static hasMany = [books: Book]

String name }

class Book {
    String title
}
```

In Listing 7-31 there is a unidirectional one-to-many. Grails will, by default, map this kind of relationship with a join table. Grails will automatically inject a property of type `java.util.Set` into the domain class based on the `hasMany` setting. Grails supports many-to-many relationships by defining a `hasMany` on both sides of the relationship and having a `belongsTo` on the owned side of the relationship.

You will create an application with a many-to-many domain relationship between `Author` and `Book`. You can find the source code for this application in the books project in Chapter 7 of the source code archive that you can download from the Apress website. Listing 7-32 illustrates the `Book` class.

Listing 7-32. Creating a Domain Relationship Between Book and Author

```
1.package books
2.
3.class Book {
4.    static belongsTo = Author
5.    static hasMany = [authors:Author]
6.    String title
7.Long isbn
8.String publisher
9.static constraints = {
10.title(blank:false)
11.}
12.
13.String toString() {
14.title
15.}
16.}
```

- *Line 4*: This line informs Grails that the `Book` class belongs to its owning `Author`.
- *Line 5*: This line inform Grails that the `Book` class has many instances of `Author`.

Listing 7-33 illustrates the Author class.

Listing 7-33. Author class.

```
1.package books
2.
3.class Author {
4.
5.    static hasMany = [books:Book]
6.    String firstName
7.String lastName
8.static constraints = {
9.firstName(blank:false)
10.lastName(blank:false)
11.}
12.String toString() {
13."$lastName, $firstName"
14.}
15.}
```

- *Line 5*: This line tells Grails that an `Author` has many instances of `Book`.

Grails maps a many-to-many relationship using a join table at the database level. The owning side of the relationship, `Author` in this application, takes responsibility for persisting the relationship because Grails uses Hibernate as ORM frameworks and, in Hibernate, only one side of a many-to-many relationship can take responsibility for managing the relationship.

With the relationship between the domain classes created, all you need to do is to create `BookController` and `AuthorController` and set their scaffold property. In the `BookController` you created, replace the `index()` action with the `scaffold` property set to `Book`, as illustrated in Listing 7-34.

Listing 7-34. BookController

```
class BookController {

    static scaffold = Book
}
```

In the `AuthorController`, set the `scaffold` property to `Author`, as illustrated in Listing 7-35.

Listing 7-35. AuthorController

```
class AuthorController {

    static scaffold = Author
}
```

Now you can run the application. The scaffolding will generate the application for you and point you to the URL. Figure 7-32 shows the welcome screen of the application.

GRAILS
APPLICATION STATUS
App version: 0.1
Grails version: 2.2.4
Groovy version: 2.0.8
JVM version: 1.8.0-ea
Reloading active: true
Controllers: 3
Domains: 2
Services: 2
Tag Libraries: 13
INSTALLED PLUGINS
logging - 2.2.4
core - 2.2.4
Welcome to Grails
Congratulations, you have successfully started your first Grails application! At the moment this is the default page, feel free to modify it to either redirect to a controller or display whatever content you may choose. Below is a list of controllers that are currently deployed in this application, click on each to execute its default action:
Available Controllers:
• books.AuthorController
• books.BookController
• grails.plugin.databasemigration.DbdocController

Figure 7-32. Welcome screen of book application

When you click the AuthorController, the Author List screen is displayed, as illustrated in Figure 7-33.

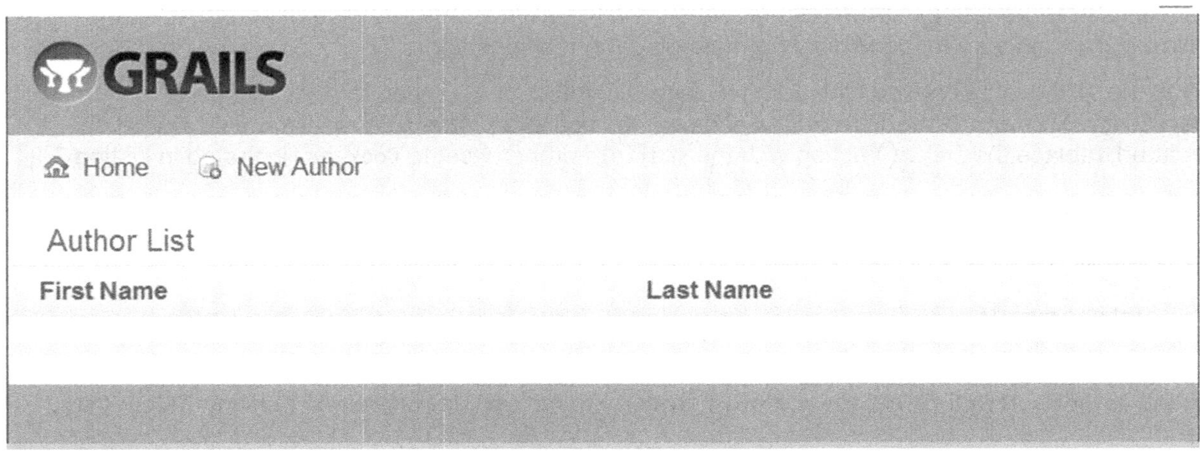

Figure 7-33. Author List screen

In Figure 7-33, you can create a new author by clicking the New Author link. Figure 7-34 illustrates the list of authors thus created.

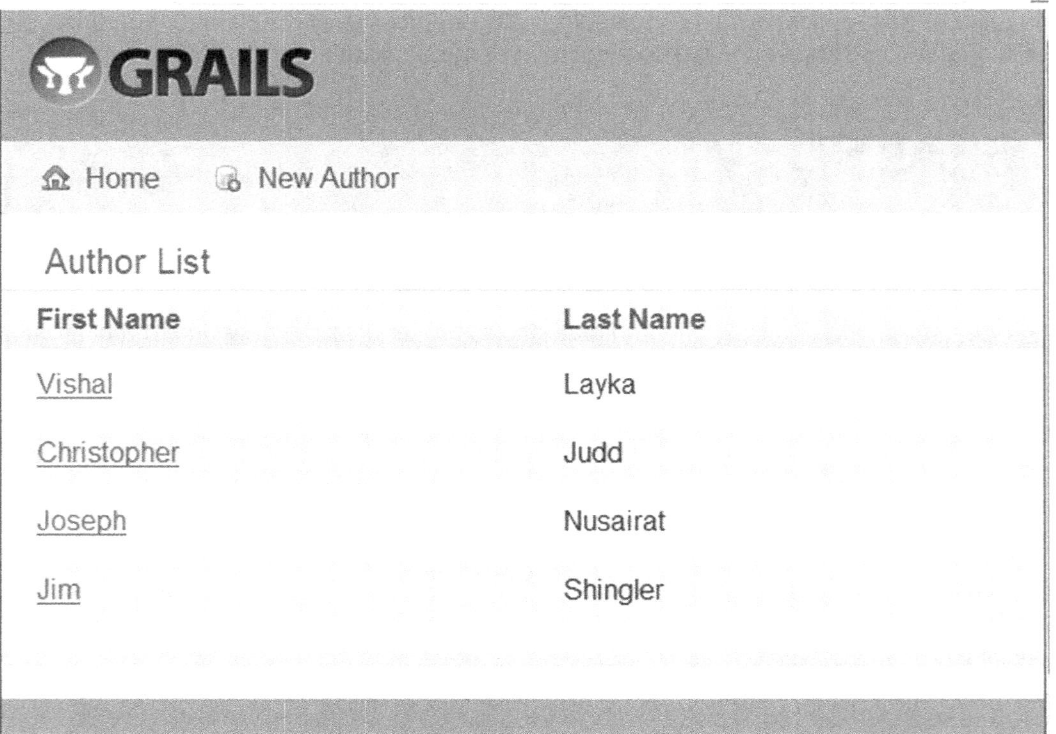

Figure 7-34. List of authors

Now you can view the Book List by clicking the BookController link on the welcome screen, as illustrated in Figure 7-35.

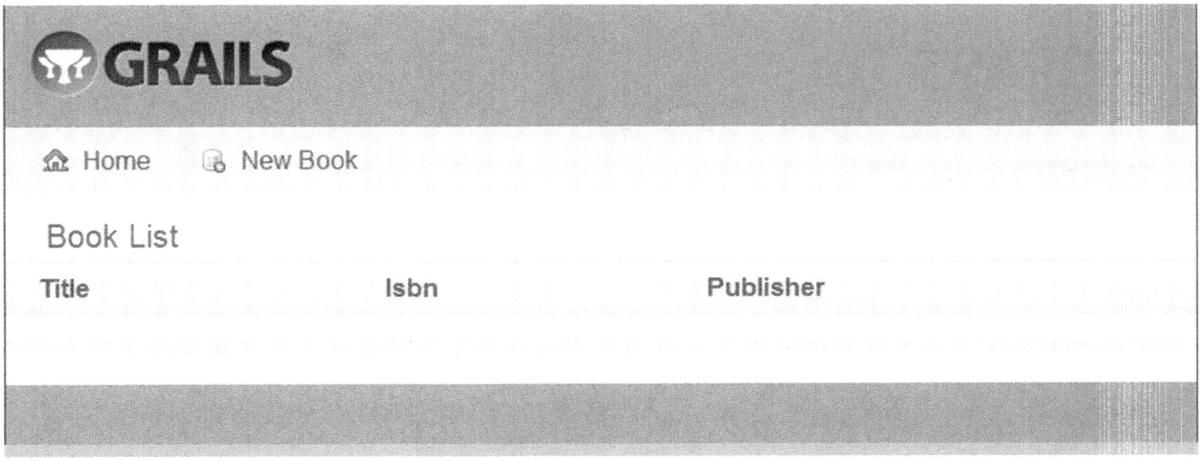

***Figure 7-35.** Book List screen*

You can add a new book by clicking the New Book Link. When you click New Book, a Create Book screen is displayed. If you try to create a book with blank Title and Isbn fields, you will get the validation message illustrated in Figure 7-36. You did not write any constraints for the ISBN in Listing 7-32, but still there is validation on the ISBN field because Grails provides constraints by default for some fields, and ISBN is one of them (as listed in Table 7-2 of this chapter).

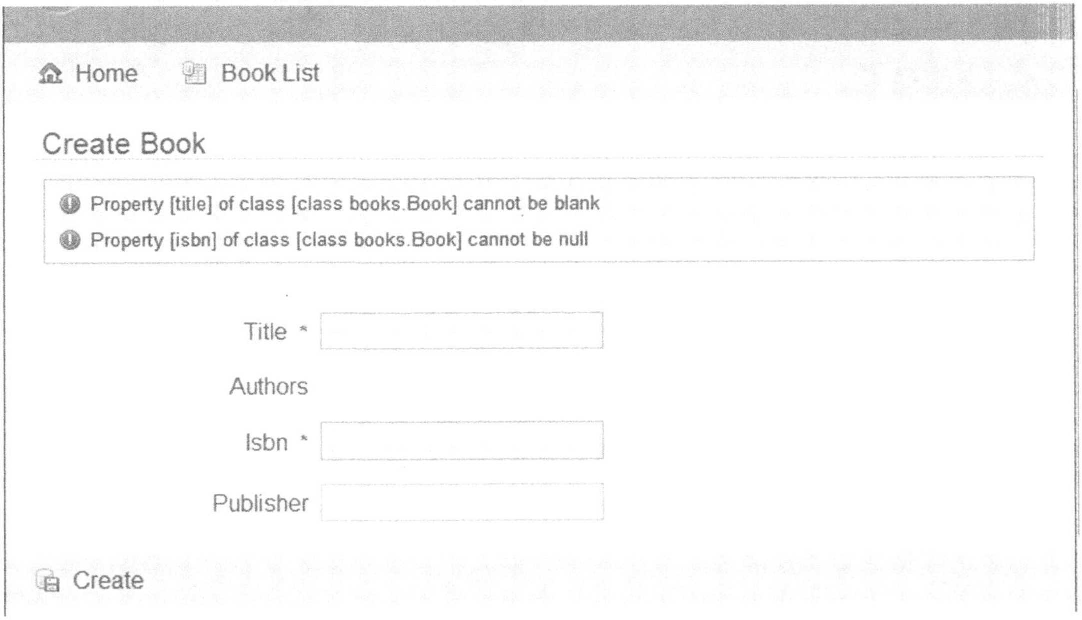

***Figure 7-36.** Validation error*

Now you can create the book by providing values for these fields. Figure 7-37 illustrates the Book List screen with two books created.

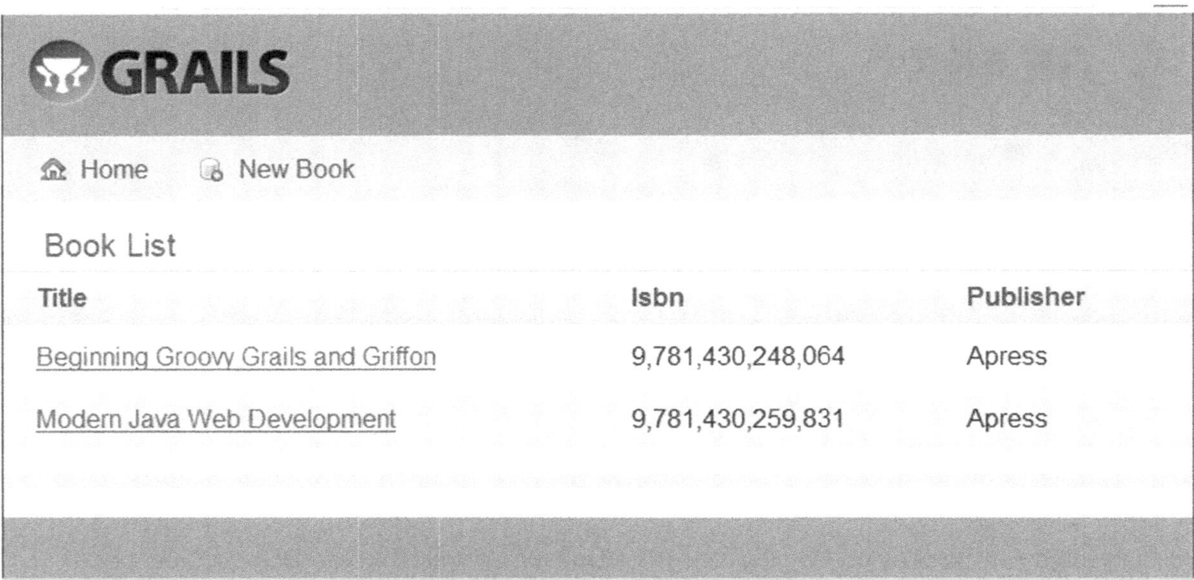

Figure 7-37. Book List screen

Now you can go to the Author List screen and click the Edit button, as illustrated in Figure 7-38.

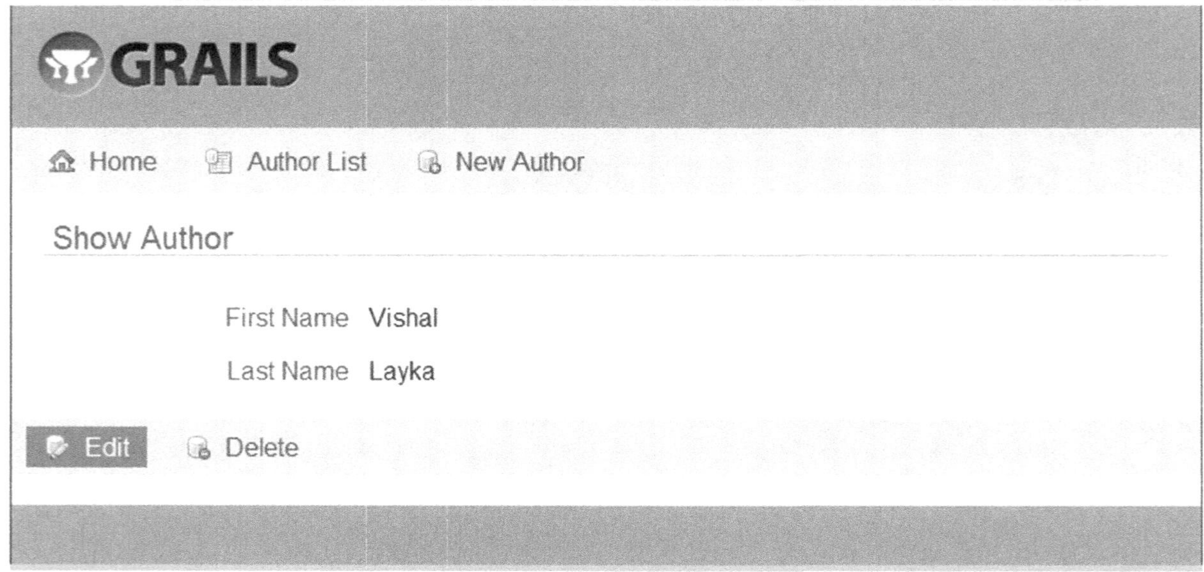

Figure 7-38. Editing the author

When you click the Edit button, you will see that two books are available, as illustrated in Figure 7-39. You can select both books and click the Update button.

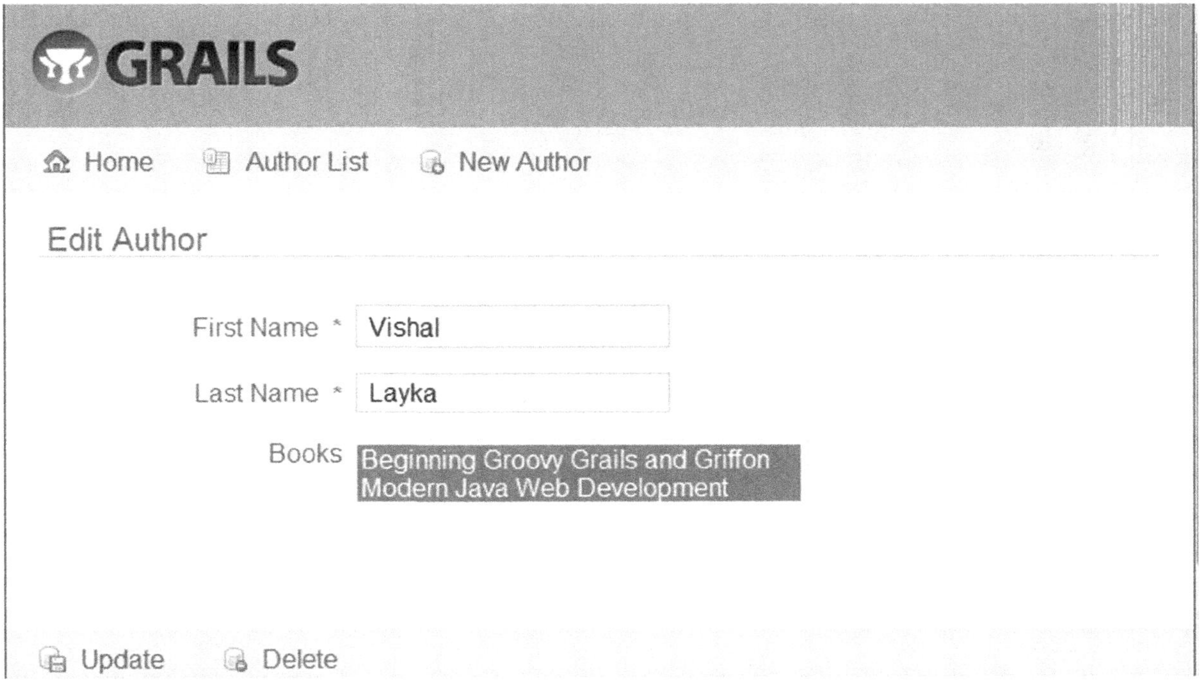

Figure 7-39. Edit Author screen

In this way, you can add the books for all the authors you have created. Now when you go to the Book List screen and click one of the Book Title links, the Show Book screen is displayed with the name of all the authors for that book, as illustrated in Figure 7-40.

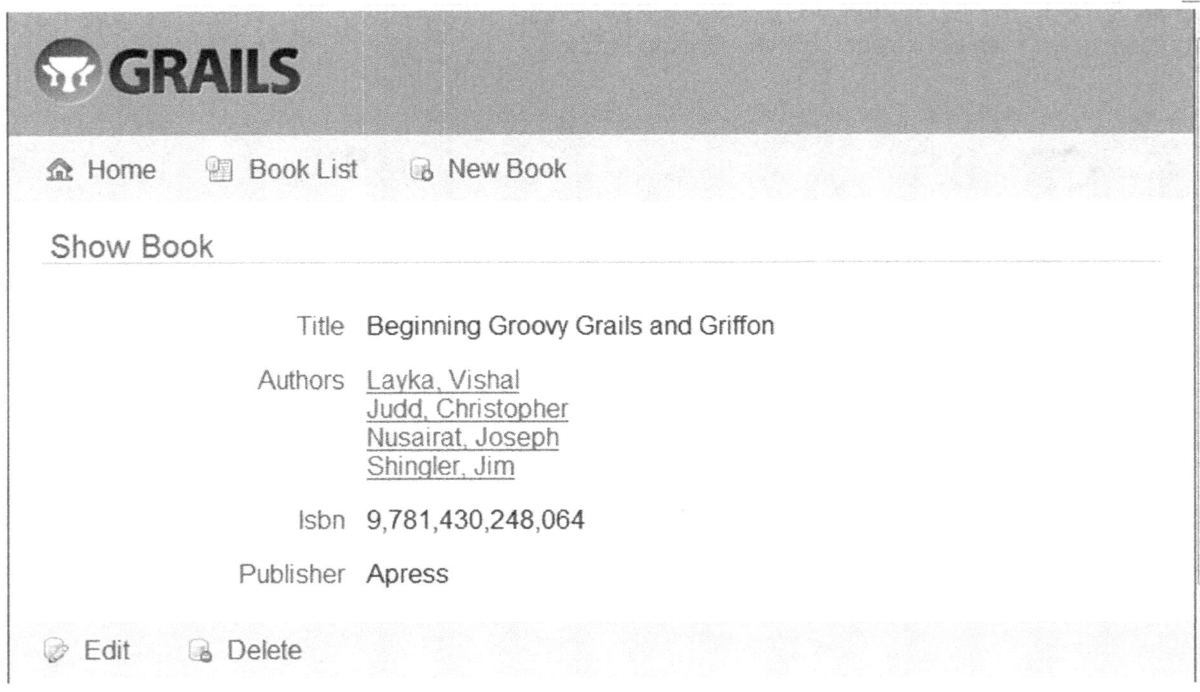

***Figure 7-40.** Show Book screen*

This concludes the chapter, which sketched a brief overview of Grails 2. For more detailed coverage, I recommend *Beginning Groovy, Grails, and Griffon* by Vishal Layka, Christopher M. Judd, Joseph Faisal Nusairat, and Jim Shingler (Apress, 2012), as well as *The Definitive Guide to Grails 2* by Jeff Scott Brown and Graeme Rocher (Apress 2012).

Summary

In this chapter, you learned that Grails is a rapid web development framework that combines the best of Java open source, conventions, the Groovy dynamic language, and the power of the Java platform. You saw how easy it is to develop a fully functional application using Grails scaffolding to do most of the work. You used static scaffolding as a learning tool, generating the controller and views for one domain class (`Book`). Then you navigated through the controller, and saw that all the work in the controller is done in the actions. Then you learned the code for each action responsible for the corresponding view. Finally, you navigated through the views and saw how the views take advantage of the Grails tag libraries to promote a clean separation of concerns.

Chapter 8

Play with Java and Scala

Oh, throw away the worser part of it. And live the purer with the other half.

—William Shakespeare

Java EE continues to evolve in a, sort of, benign continuum. Inspired by frameworks such as Spring, Java EE introduced features such as annotations and dependency injection to address complex tasks like transactions and database connectivity. Java EE 7, the latest edition as of this writing, further reinforces the advancements in the Java Persistence API (JPA) and JAX-RS for REST-based web services, to name just a few. Most of the complexity involved with Java web development will continue to be addressed, in many ways, by commercial or open web frameworks' innovations.

However, the Play 2 web framework meanders off the beaten track. Play 2 is *not* Java EE–centric and is not constrained by Java EE. It is part of the Typesafe stack that provides an alternative to the Java EE stack. Typesafe redefines the layers of modern Java applications formerly defined by Java EE, and in this new demarcation Play constitutes the web layer.

Play is an open source web application framework, written in Scala and Java, and provides out-of-the-box support for the modern Web. Play was built for the needs of modern web and mobile applications, leveraging technologies such as REST, JSON, and Web Sockets, among others.

Play targets the JVM and focuses on enhancing developer productivity by providing features such as convention over configuration, hot code reloading, and errors in the browser. Play implements the MVC architecture by means of a route file that maps HTTP requests to controllers and view templates that represent the result. Play 2 builds upon the functional paradigm by providing native support for the Scala programming language and provides an adapted Java-specific API that formulates a highly reactive web framework.

Features of Play 2

Play 2.0 was released in 2012 in conjunction with the Typesafe stack. Play 2 was built using Scala as the core language, whereas Play 1 used the Java language and provided support for Scala by means of plug-ins. Play 2.2 was released in September 2013. Table 8-1 describes the key features of Play 2.

Table 8-1. Key Features of Play 2

Feature	Description
Asynchronous I/O	Play 2 can service long requests asynchronously as a result of using JBoss Netty[1] as its web server.
Built-in web server	Play 2 provides the JBoss Netty web server out of the box, but Play web applications can also be packaged as WAR files to be distributed to Java EE application servers.
Dependency management	Play 2 provides sbt[2] for dependency management.
Hot reloading	In a Play 2–based application, the code in development mode is checked for updates each time a new request arrives, and any changed files are automatically recompiled; if there is any error, the error is displayed directly in the browser.
In-memory database	Like Grails, Play 2 supports H2 out of the box.
Native Scala support	Play 2 uses Scala natively but is completely interoperable with Java.
ORM	Play 2 provides Ebean[3] as the ORM replacement of JPA to access databases.
Stateless	Play 2 is fully RESTful, and there is no Java EE session per connection.
Templating	Play 2 uses Scala for the template engine.
Testing framework	Play 2 provides a built-in test framework for unit testing and functional testing such as JUnit and Selenium.[4]
Web Sockets	Play 2 implements Web Sockets out of the box to enable a bi-directional connection between a client and the server.

MVC in Play 2

A Play 2 application follows the MVC architectural pattern. In a Play 2 application, the MVC layers are defined in the app directory, each one in a separate package (see Figure 8-1).

[1]http://netty.io/
[2]www.scala-sbt.org/
[3]www.avaje.org/
[4]www.seleniumhq.org/

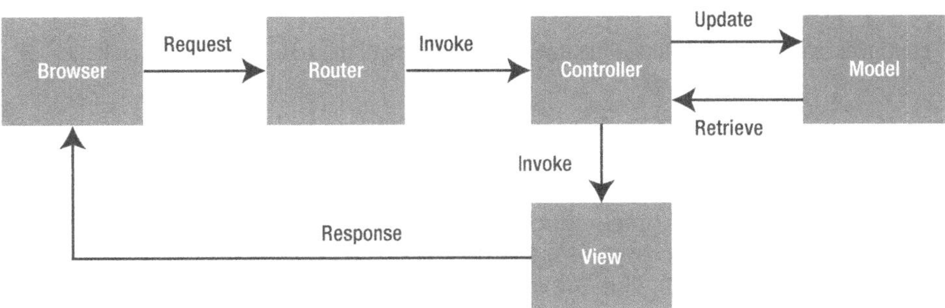

Figure 8-1. MVC in Play 2

The request flow in the MVC architecture illustrated in Figure 8-1 is as follows:

1. An HTTP request is received by the router.
2. The router finds the action defined in the controller to process this request.
3. The controller listens for HTTP requests, extracts relevant data from the requests, and applies changes to the model.
4. The controller renders a template file to generate the view.
5. The result of the action method is then written as an HTTP response.

Router

The main entry point of the web application is the conf/routes file that defines the routes needed by the application. Each route consists of an HTTP method and a URI pattern associated with a call to an action method. Conf/routes is the configuration file used by the built-in component called `Router` that translates each incoming HTTP request to an action call.

> **Note** The HTTP method can be any of the valid methods supported by HTTP (GET, POST, PUT, DELETE, and HEAD).

Controller

In a Java EE–based web application, a *controller* is a Java class that extends the servlet type. Since Play is not Java EE–centric, a controller in Play 2 is a class in Java or an object in Scala that extends the controller type (both in Java and Scala). This controller type is provided in the `play.api.mvc` package. A controller in Play 2 comprises a public, static method called an *action*. An action is basically a method that processes the request parameters and produces a result to be sent to the client. The controller responds to requests, processes them, and invokes changes on the model.

Controllers are, by default, defined in the `controllers` package under the source root—the `app` folder.

> **Note** A controller is a type that extends the controller provided in the `play.api.mvc` package.

Model

The *model* is the domain-specific representation of the information on which the application operates. The most commonly used object for this representation is the JavaBean. However, JavaBeans lead to plenty of boilerplate code. Play 2, like Grails, reduces this boilerplate code by generating the getters and setters for you by means of byte-code enhancement. The model objects may contain persistence artifacts such as JPA annotations, for instance, if they need to be saved into persistent storage.

> **Note** Even if Play 2 uses Ebean for ORM, you can continue to use JPA annotations on your entities.

View

In a Java EE–based web application, the *view* is usually developed using JSP. That is, the view in a Java EE–based web application consists of JSP elements and template text. As Play is not Java EE–centric, the view in Play comprises the template that contains a mix of HTML and Scala code. In Play 1, the templates were based on Groovy, but starting with Play 2, the templates are based on Scala. Using Play 2 you can develop both Java- and Scala-based web applications, and the templates are the same in both of them.

> **Note** In Play 1 the templates were based on Groovy, but starting with Play 2, the templates are based on Scala.

Getting Started with Play

To run the Play framework, you need JDK 6 or newer. You can download Play 2 from here: `www.playframework.com/download`. Play 2 is available in two distributions: standard and Typesafe Activator.

Download the latest stand-alone Play distribution, extract the archive to a location of your choice, and update the `Path` environment variable by adding/editing the `Path` variable in the Environment Variables dialog with the path to the Play installation, as illustrated in Figure 8-2.

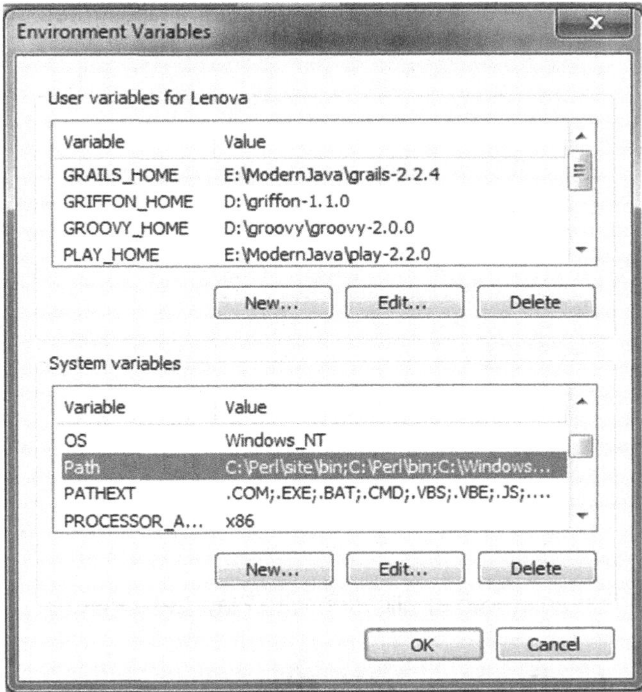

***Figure 8-2.** Adding/editing the path variable*

Now enter the following command in the command-line tool to check whether the Play environment has been correctly set up:

```
> play
```

You should see the output on the console, as illustrated in Figure 8-3, if Play is correctly installed.

```
E:\ModernJava\play2-workspace>play

play 2.2.0 built with Scala 2.10.2 (running Java 1.8.0-ea), http://www.playframe
work.com

This is not a play application!

Use `play new` to create a new Play application in the current directory,
or go to an existing application and launch the development console using `play`
.

You can also browse the complete documentation at http://www.playframework.com.

E:\ModernJava\play2-workspace>_
```

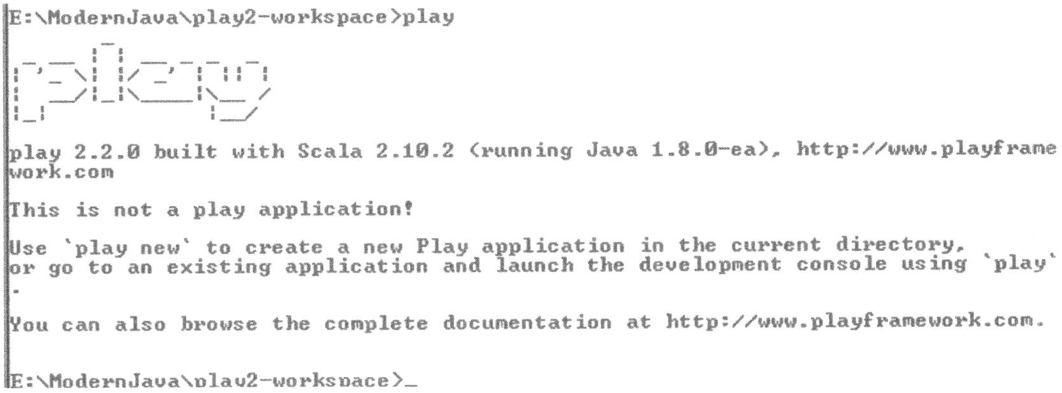

***Figure 8-3.** Verifying whether Play 2 is correctly installed*

You can also get some help by executing the help command, as illustrated in Figure 8-4.

```
> play help
```

```
E:\ModernJava\play2-workspace>play help
       _
 _ __ | | __ _ _  _
| '_ \| |/ _' | || |
|  __/|_|\____|\__ /
|_|            |__/

play 2.2.0 built with Scala 2.10.2 (running Java 1.8.0-ea), http://www.playframe
work.com
Welcome to Play 2.2.0!

These commands are available:
-----------------------------
license             Display licensing informations.
new [directory]     Create a new Play application in the specified directory.

You can also browse the complete documentation at http://www.playframework.com.

E:\ModernJava\play2-workspace>_
```

Figure 8-4. Help in Play 2

Now you can create your first Java web application with Play. Let's Play!

Hello World Java Application with Play

To create a new application, you just have to use the play command-line tool with the parameter new followed by the name of the new application, in this case helloworld, as illustrated in Figure 8-5.

```
E:\ModernJava\play2-workspace>play new helloworld
       _
 _ __ | | __ _ _  _
| '_ \| |/ _' | || |
|  __/|_|\____|\__ /
|_|            |__/

play 2.2.0 built with Scala 2.10.2 (running Java 1.8.0-ea), http://www.playframe
work.com

The new application will be created in E:\ModernJava\play2-workspace\helloworld

What is the application name? [helloworld]
>
```

Figure 8-5. Creating the helloworld application

Play 2 will ask you to specify whether your application is a Scala or Java application, as illustrated in Figure 8-6.

```
Which template do you want to use for this new application?

  1             - Create a simple Scala application
  2             - Create a simple Java application

>
```

Figure 8-6. Specifying whether the application is a Scala or Java application

You have to specify 2 because you want to create a Java application. Specifying 2 creates the source files and the structure of the application for the Java language, as illustrated in Figure 8-7.

```
E:\ModernJava\play2-workspace>play new helloworld
       _
 _ __ | | __ _ _  _
| '_ \| |/ _' | || |
|  __/|_|\____|\__ /
|_|            |__/

play 2.2.0 built with Scala 2.10.2 (running Java 1.8.0-ea), http://www.playframe
work.com

The new application will be created in E:\ModernJava\play2-workspace\helloworld

What is the application name? [helloworld]
> helloworld

Which template do you want to use for this new application?

  1             - Create a simple Scala application
  2             - Create a simple Java application

> 2
OK, application helloworld is created.

Have fun!

E:\ModernJava\play2-workspace>
```

Figure 8-7. Creation of the helloworld project

You can run the application using the run command from the helloworld directory. To do this, enter the Play console, as illustrated in Figure 8-8.

```
> cd helloworld
>play
```

```
E:\ModernJava\play2-workspace\helloworld>play
[info] Loading project definition from E:\ModernJava\play2-workspace\helloworld\
project
[info] Set current project to helloworld (in build file:/E:/ModernJava/play2-wor
kspace/helloworld/)
       _
 _ __ | | __ _ _  _
| '_ \| |/ _' | || |
|  __/|_|\____|\__ /
|_|            |__/

play 2.2.0 built with Scala 2.10.2 (running Java 1.8.0-ea), http://www.playframe
work.com

> Type "help play" or "license" for more information.
> Type "exit" or use Ctrl+D to leave this console.

[helloworld] $
```

Figure 8-8. Entering the Play console

Now type run. This will start the server that will run your application.

```
$ run
```

The output on the console is shown here:

```
[helloworld] $ run
[info] Updating {file:/E:/ModernJava/play2-workspace/helloworld/}helloworld...
[info] Resolving org.scala-lang#scala-library;2.10.2 ...
[info] Resolving com.typesafe.play#play-java-jdbc_2.10;2.2.0 ...
  [info] Resolving com.typesafe.play#play-jdbc_2.10;2.2.0 ...
  [info] Resolving com.typesafe.play#play_2.10;2.2.0 ...
..............................................
  [info] Resolving org.fusesource.jansi#jansi;1.4 ...
[info] Done updating.
--- (Running the application from SBT, auto-reloading is enabled) ---
[info] play - Listening for HTTP on /0:0:0:0:0:0:0:0:9000
(Server started, use Ctrl+D to stop and go back to the console...)
```

As you can see, the console says that it has started the application, and an HTTP server is listening for HTTP requests on the port 9000. You can now send a request to this server by going to the URL `http://localhost:9000/`. Upon requesting the server, a welcome screen is displayed, as illustrated in Figure 8-9.

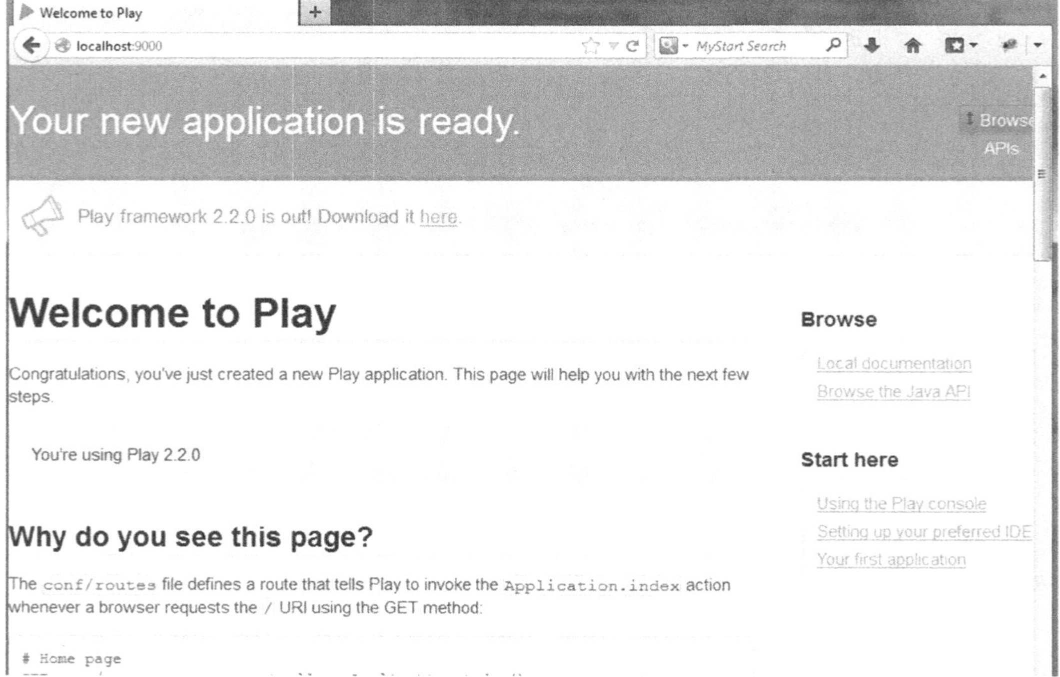

Figure 8-9. Default welcome page of the Play 2 framework

Figure 8-9 illustrates the default Play 2 welcome page. The default welcome page of the application is a great source of information for a beginner, and it is recommended that you read it.

The `run` command creates the structure of the application inside the `helloworld` directory. The structure is illustrated in Figure 8-10.

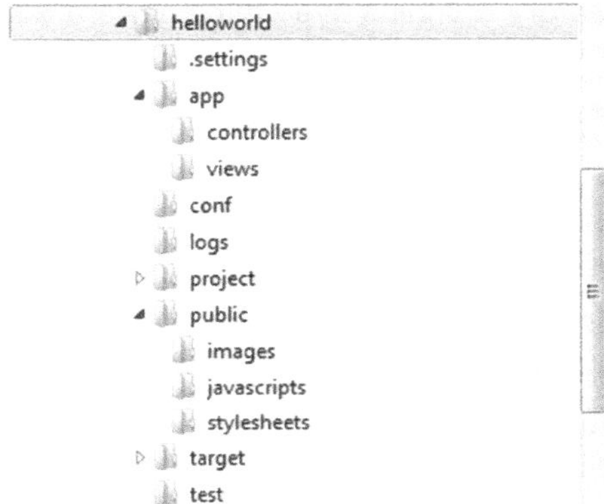

***Figure 8-10.** The directory structure of the helloworld application*

Each folder in Figure 8-10 is described here:

- `app`: This is the root of all the server-side source files such as Java and Scala source code, templates, and compiled assets' sources. At creation, only two subfolders will be created: `controllers` and `views` for the controller and view components, respectively, of the MVC architectural pattern. You can add the directory `app/models` for the model component of the MVC. There is also an optional directory called `app/assets` for compiled assets such as LESS[5] sources and CoffeeScript[6] sources.
- `conf`: The `conf` directory contains the application's configuration files meant to configure the application itself, external services, and so on. There are two main configuration files:

  `application.conf`: The main configuration file for the application, which contains standard configuration parameters

  `routes`: The routes definition file
- `project`: The project folder is meant to contain all of the necessary files to configure the Scala build tool SBT.[7]
- `public`: This directory contains three standard subdirectories for images, CSS style sheets, and JavaScript files.

[5]http://lesscss.org/
[6]http://jashkenas.github.io/coffee-script/
[7]www.scala-sbt.org/

> **Note** Resources stored in the `public` directory are static assets that will be served directly by the web server.

- `target`: The target directory contains everything generated by the build system such as the following:

  `classes`: This contains all the compiled classes (from both Java and Scala sources).

  `classes_managed`: This contains only the classes that are managed by the framework (such as the classes generated by the router or the template system).

  `resource_managed`: This contains generated resources, typically compiled assets such as LESS CSS and CoffeeScript compilation results.

  `src_managed`: This contains generated sources, such as the Scala sources generated by the template system.
- `test`: This last folder will contain all the test files along with some samples provided by the framework.

Now that you have seen the directory structure of the application, you will learn how the default welcome page is displayed when you test the URL: `http://localhost:9000`.

Each row in the conf/routes file is a route that defines how to access server components using HTTP. If you see the generated routes file in the conf/routes file, you will see this first route:

```
GET        /        controllers.Application.index()
```

This route is composed of three parts:

- `GET`: This is the first part in the route (row) that contains the HTTP method used in the request.
- /: This is the second part in the route that contains a relative path.
- `controllers.Application.index()`: This is the third part in the route that contains the action to be invoked.

These three parts in the route inform Play 2 that when the web server receives a GET request for the / path, it must call `controllers.Application.index()`, which calls the index method in the `Application` class that resides in the `controllers` package.

Now you will see what the `controllers.Application.index` method looks like. For that, you need to open the `app/controllers/Application.java` source file. This file is illustrated in Listing 8-1.

Listing 8-1. Application Controller

```
package controllers;

import play.*;
import play.mvc.*;
```

```
5.
6.     import views.html.*;
7.
8.     public class Application extends Controller {
9.
10.      public static Result index() {
11.        return ok(index.render("Your new application is ready."));
12.      }
13.
14.    }
```

- *Line 8*: The `Application` controller class extends `play.mvc.Controller`.
- *Line 10*: The `public static index()` action returns a `Result`. All action methods return a `Result`. The `Result` represents the HTTP response to be sent back to the browser.
- *Line 11*: Here, the action returns a 200 OK response with an HTML response body. The HTML content is provided by a template. An action always returns an HTTP response, which is represented in Play 2 by the `Result` type. The `Result` type must be a valid HTTP response, so it must include a valid HTTP status code. OK sets it to 200.The `render()` method references a template file in Play 2.

The template is defined in the `app/views/index.scala.html` source file. This file is illustrated in Listing 8-2.

***Listing 8-2.** index.scala.html*

```
1.    @(message: String)
2.
3.    @main("Welcome to Play") {
4.
5.        @play20.welcome(message, style = "Java")
6.
7.    }
```

- *Line 1*: The Scala statement starts with the special `@` character. The first line defines the function signature. Here it takes a single String parameter.
  A template is like a function, and thus it needs parameters, which are declared at the top of the template file.
- *Line 3*: This line invokes a function named `main` with one string argument.
- *Lines 3 to 7*: These lines comprise the main function block.
- *Line 5*: Line 5 uses a function called `welcome`, provided by Play 2. This function renders the default welcome HTML page, which is in the file named `main.scala.html` also located in `apps/views` folder.
- *Line 5*: The `welcome` function has an extra parameter `style` that informs the template that this is a Java-based application, and then this `style` parameter is used by the welcome template to show links to documentation.

Configuring Eclipse for Java

Play 2 provides you with the possibility to use the Eclipse IDE. For this you need to ask Play 2 to generate the Eclipse project configuration. You can do this by invoking Eclipse in the Play console, as illustrated in Figure 8-11.

```
[helloworld] $ eclipse
[info] About to create Eclipse project files for your project(s).
[info] Compiling 4 Scala sources and 2 Java sources to E:\ModernJava\play2-works
pace\helloworld\target\scala-2.10\classes...
[info] Successfully created Eclipse project files for project(s):
[info] helloworld
[helloworld] $
```

***Figure 8-11.** Generating the project for Eclipse*

Now you can launch Eclipse, as illustrated in Figure 8-11, and import the project into it, as illustrated in Figure 8-12.

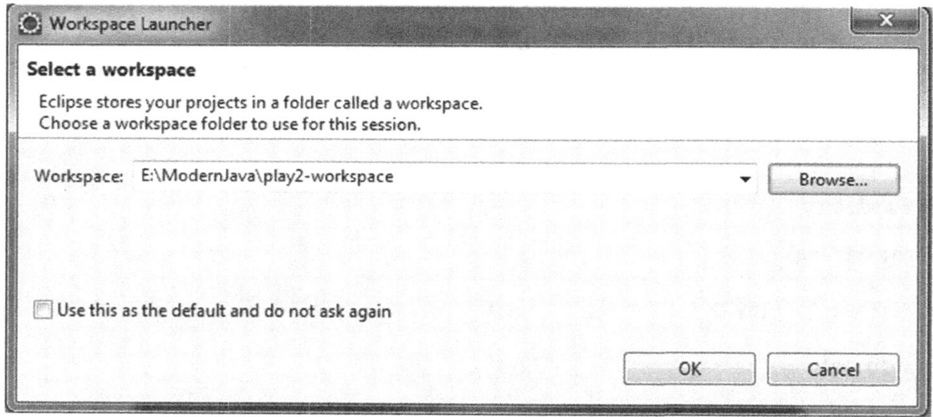

***Figure 8-12.** Selecting a workspace*

For importing the project, select File ➤ Import, select General ➤ Existing Projects into Workspace, and click Next, as illustrated in Figure 8-13.

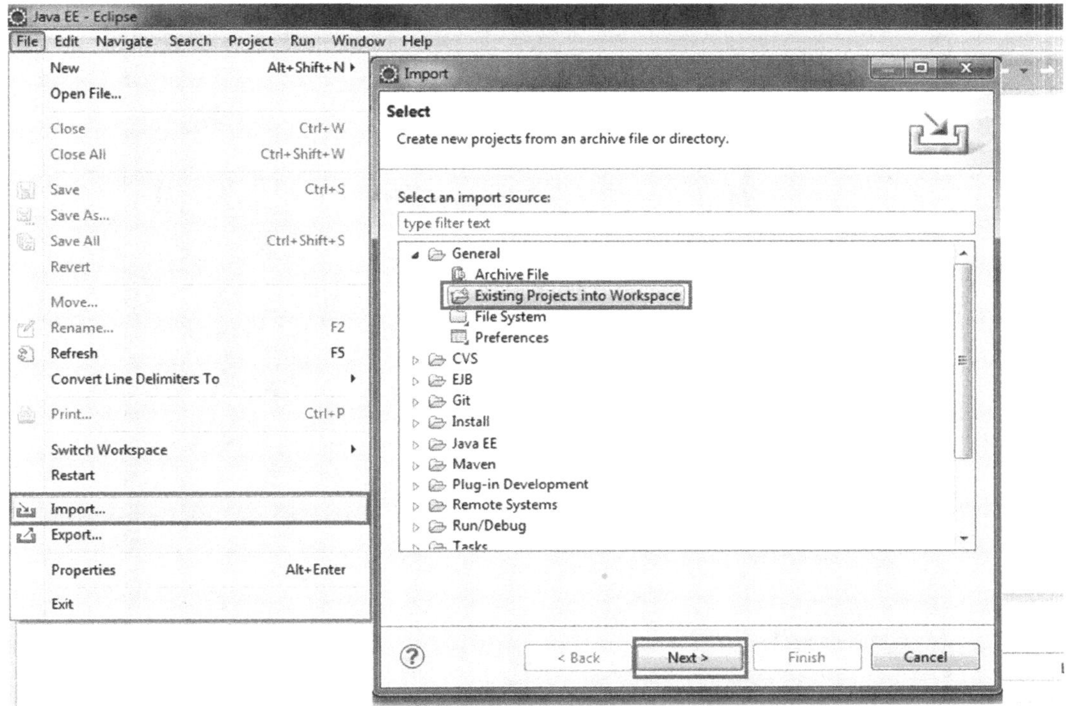

Figure 8-13. Importing the project

Now browse your filesystem, select the project folder `helloworld`, click OK, and then click Finish, as illustrated in Figure 8-14.

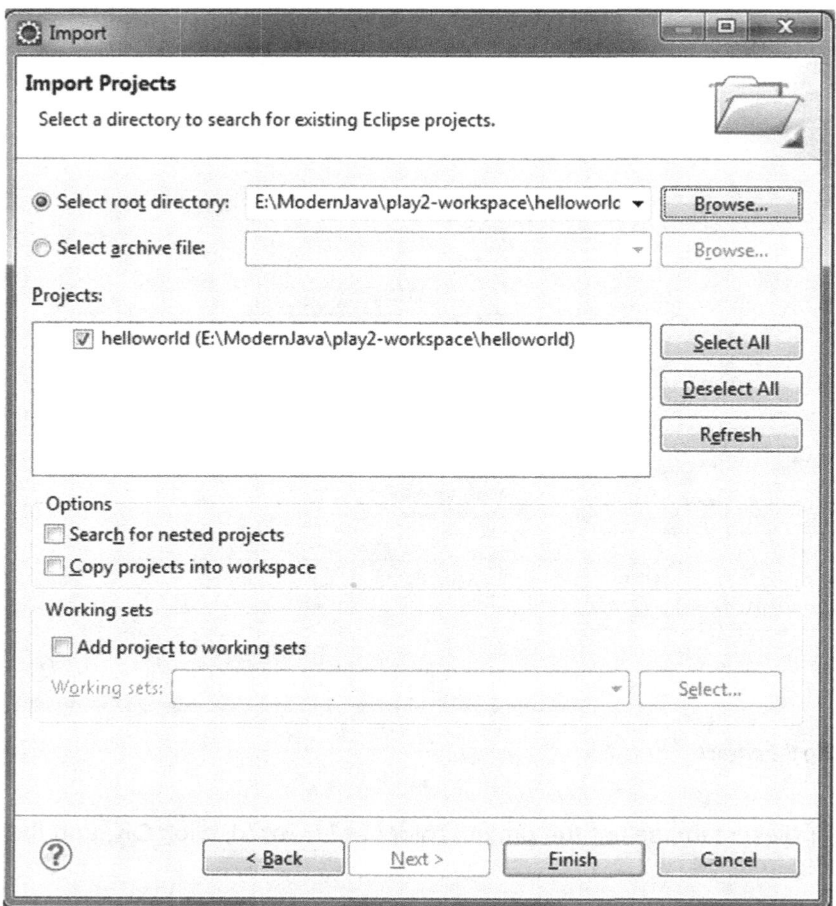

Figure 8-14. Selecting the root directory

All the files necessary to configure an Eclipse project are generated. You saw how to create a project and import it into your development environment. Now you will modify the application. In `Application.java`, change the content of the response in the `index` action, as illustrated in Listing 8-3.

Listing 8-3. Modifying the Index Action

```
public static Result index() {
  return ok("Hello world");
}
```

The `index` action will now respond with "Hello world," as illustrated in Figure 8-15.

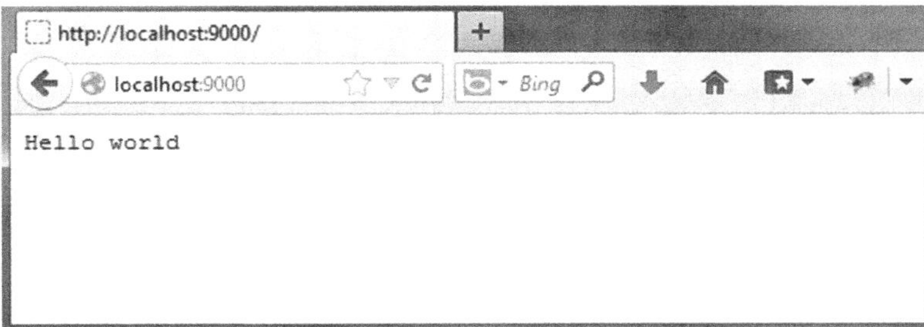

Figure 8-15. "Hello world"

Play 2 provides some sample applications in the `samples` folder in `play-2.2.0\samples\java\`. You can run the helloworld application, as illustrated in Figure 8-16.

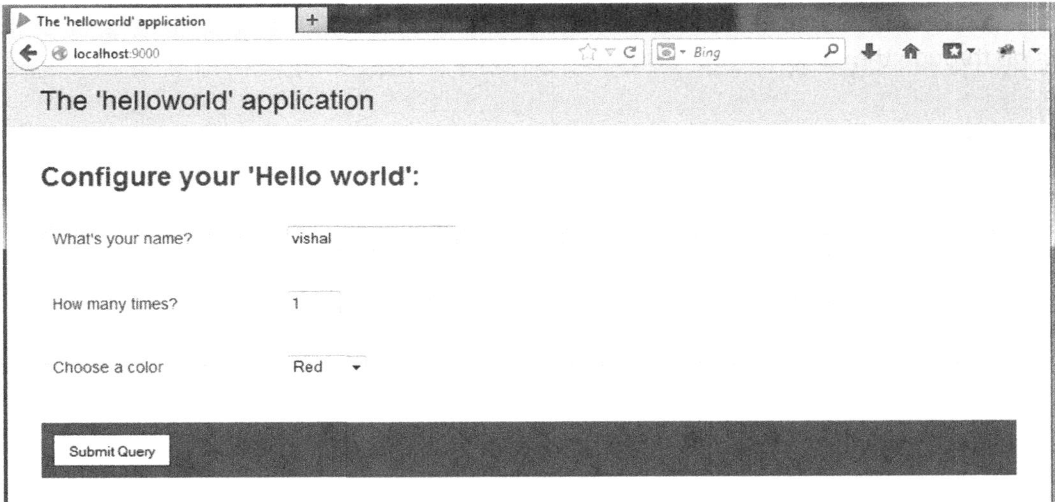

Figure 8-16. The sample helloworld application provided by Play 2

When you click Submit Query, the user's name is displayed based on the selection, as illustrated in Figure 8-17.

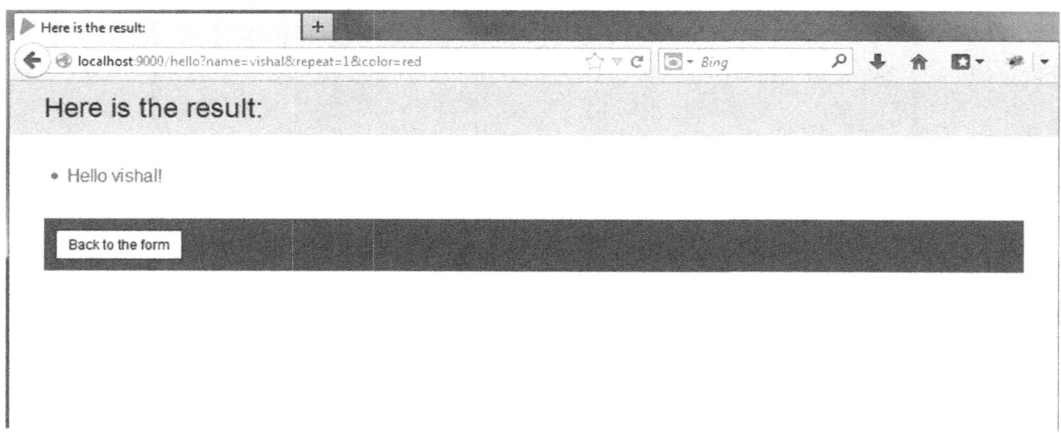

Figure 8-17. Running the sample helloworld application

You can go through the code on your own and improve the application.

Helloworld Scala Application with Play 2

As mentioned earlier, Play 2 allows you to create both Java- and Scala-based web applications. The procedure for generating a Scala-based application is the same as generating the Java application. You can create a `helloworld-scala` application as illustrated in Figure 8-18.

```
E:\ModernJava\play2-workspace>play new helloworld-scala
       _
 _ __ | | __ _ _  _
| '_ \| |/ _' | || |
|  __/|_|\____|\__ /
|_|            |__/

play 2.2.0 built with Scala 2.10.2 (running Java 1.8.0-ea), http://www.playframe
work.com

The new application will be created in E:\ModernJava\play2-workspace\helloworld-
scala

What is the application name? [helloworld-scala]
> helloworld-scala

Which template do you want to use for this new application?

  1             - Create a simple Scala application
  2             - Create a simple Java application

> 1
OK, application helloworld-scala is created.

Have fun!

E:\ModernJava\play2-workspace>_
```

Figure 8-18. Creating the helloworld-scala application

Now you can run the `helloworld-scala` project using the `run` command from the Play console, as illustrated in Figure 8-19.

```
E:\ModernJava\play2-workspace\helloworld-scala>play
Java HotSpot(TM) Client VM warning: ignoring option MaxPermSize=256M; support wa
s removed in 8.0
[info] Loading project definition from E:\ModernJava\play2-workspace\helloworld-
scala\project
[info] Set current project to helloworld-scala (in build file:/E:/ModernJava/pla
y2-workspace/helloworld-scala/)
       _
 _ __ | | __ _ _  _
| '_ \| |/ _' | || |
|  __/|_|\____|\__ /
|_|            |__/

play 2.2.0 built with Scala 2.10.2 (running Java 1.8.0-ea), http://www.playframe
work.com

> Type "help play" or "license" for more information.
> Type "exit" or use Ctrl+D to leave this console.

[helloworld-scala] $ _
```

***Figure 8-19.** Play console for helloworld-scala application*

Now you will look at the controller generated by Play 2 for `helloworld-scala` (see Listing 8-4). You can find the controller in `helloworld-scala\app\controllers`.

Listing 8-4. Application Controller in Scala

```
1.     package controllers
2.
3.     import play.api._
4.     import play.api.mvc._
5.
6.     object Application extends Controller {
7.
8.       def index = Action {
9.         Ok(views.html.index("Your new application is ready."))
10.      }
11.
12.    }
```

- *Line 6*: As you can see on line 6, in Java `controller` is a class, but in Scala the controller is an object.
- *Line 8*: As you can see on line 8, in Java `action` is a static method, but in Scala an action is a function (an object's method).
- *Line 9*: The return type and keyword are missing if you compare this to the Java controller.
- *Line 9*: Scala uses a structure called `Action`, which is a block of code executor.

Now that you have seen the controller in Scala, which differs from a Java controller syntactically, it is time to see the template in `helloworld-scala` (see Listing 8-5), which you can find in `helloworld-scala\app\views`.

Listing 8-5. Template in helloworld-scala

```
1.    @(message: String)
2.
3.    @main("Welcome to Play") {
4.
5.        @play20.welcome(message)
6.
7.    }
```

As you can notice, the template in `helloworld` and `helloworld-scala` are the same except for line 5. The Scala version is not initializing the `style` argument because its default value is Scala.

Configuring Eclipse for Scala

You can use the Scala IDE for Scala-based applications. The Scala IDE is an Eclipse plug-in, and you can install this plug-in by selecting Help ➤ Install New Software. In the "Work with" field, enter the path for the plug-in (`http://scala-ide.org/download/current.html`), as shown in Figure 8-20. You can also find detailed instructions for configuring Eclipse for Scala at `http://scala-ide.org/documentation.html`.

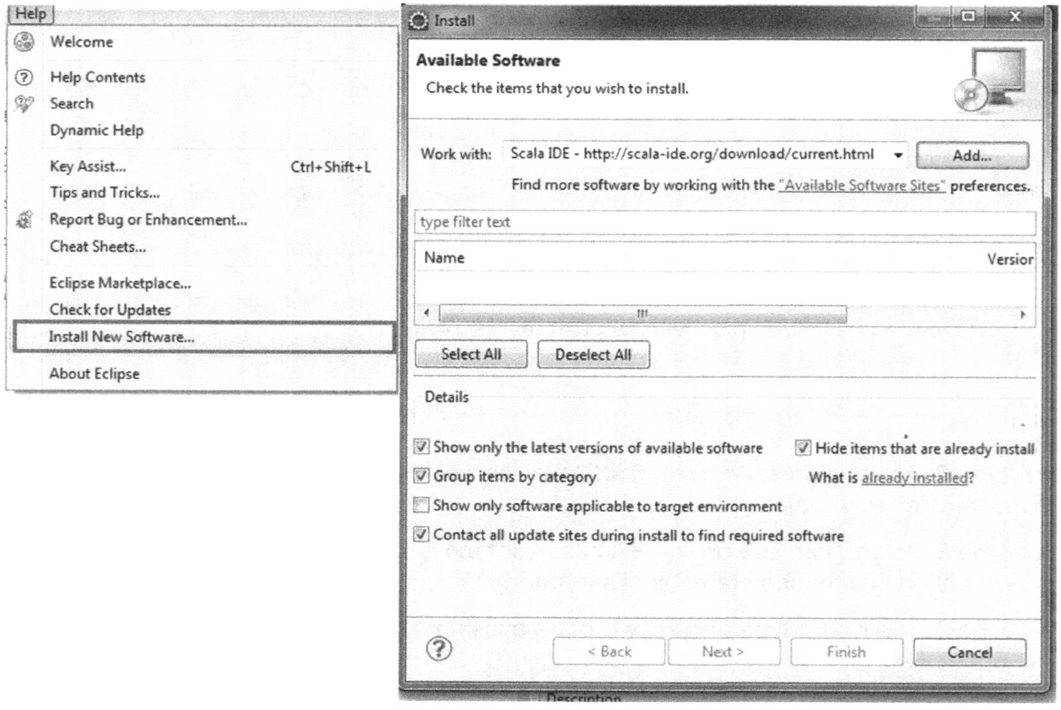

Figure 8-20. Installing the Eclipse plug-in for the Scala IDE

To import the project, you can just repeat the same steps you performed earlier when generating the project configuration for Eclipse in the helloworld Java application.

Now you can modify the `index` action in the application controller to display "Hello world," as shown in Listing 8-6.

Listing 8-6. Modifying the Index Action to Display "Hello world"

```
def index = Action {
    Ok("Hello world")
  }
```

A Basic CRUD Play 2 Java Application

In this section, you will learn to write a simple CRUD application that allows you to create, view, edit, and delete books. For these operations, you need actions and URLs to invoke these actions. The code for this application is available in a downloadable archive on the Apress web site.

Defining the Routes

The first step is to define routes for these operations in the `conf/routes` file, as illustrated in Listing 8-7.

Listing 8-7. Edit the Conf/Routes File

```
1.    # Home page
2.    GET     /                     controllers.Application.index()
3.
4.    # Books
5.    GET     /books                controllers.Application.books()
6.    POST    /books                controllers.Application.newBook()
7.    POST    /books/:id/delete     controllers.Application.deleteBook(id: Long)
```

- *Line 5*: In line 5 you create a route to list all books.
- *Line 6*: In line 6 you create a route to handle book creation.
- *Line 7*: In line 7 you create a route to handle deletion. The route to handle book deletion defines a variable argument ID in the URL path. This value is then passed to the `deleteBook` action.

Now if you refresh your browser, you will see that Play 2 cannot compile your routes file, as illustrated in Figure 8-21.

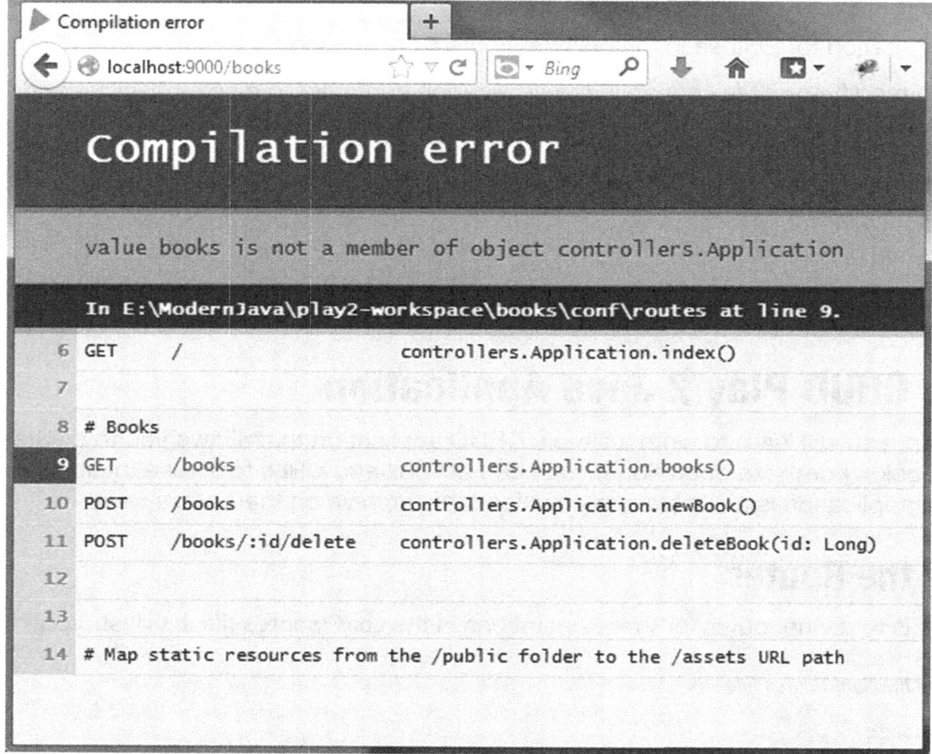

***Figure 8-21.** Routes file compilation error*

Play cannot compile your routes file because it references actions that don't exist. The next step is to add these actions to the `Application.java` file.

Creating the Controller and Actions

In this section, you will create the actions, as illustrated in Listing 8-8.

***Listing 8-8.** Application Controller in the Books Application*

```
public class Application extends Controller {

  public static Result index() {
    return ok(index.render("Your new application is ready."));
  }

  public static Result books() {
    return TODO;
  }

```

```
11.     public static Result newBook() {
12.       return TODO;
13.     }
14.
15.     public static Result deleteBook(Long id) {
16.       return TODO;
17.     }
18.
19.   }
```

- *Lines 7, 11, and 15*: These lines show the actions that were specified in the routes file in Listing 8-7.
- *Lines 8, 12, and 16*: A built-in result TODO is used that returns "Not implemented" response 503. This result tells Play 2 that the action implementations will be provided later. When you access the application via `http://localhost:9000/books`, you see the result displayed in Figure 8-22.

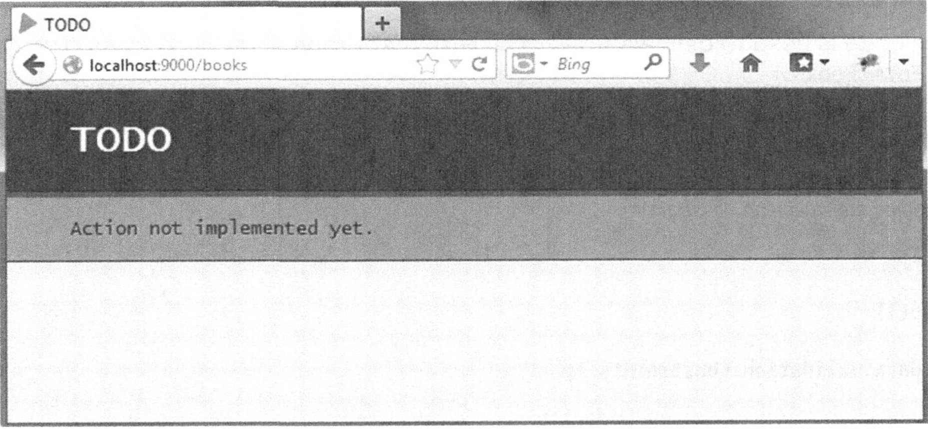

***Figure 8-22.** Built-in TODO result in Play 2*

Creating the Model

The next step is to define the model Book that can be stored in a relational database. For this, create a class in the `app/models/Book.java` file, as illustrated in the Listing 8-9.

***Listing 8-9.** Book.java*

```
package models;
import java.util.*;
public class Book {
  public Long id;
  public String label;
  public static List<Book> all() {
    return new ArrayList<Book>();
```

```
 8.     }
 9.     public static void create(Book book) {
10.     }
11.     public static void delete(Long id) {
12.     }
13.   }
```

- *Lines 6 to 12*: You create static methods to manage CRUD operations on Book. Later you will implement these operations to store the books in a relational database.

The Form and the View Template

A Form object encapsulates an HTML form definition, including validation constraints. To create a form for the Book class, you need to add the following to your application controller:

```
static  Form<Book>  bookForm = Form.form(Book.class);
```

The previous code is used to define a play.data.Form that wraps an existing class. The type of bookForm is Form<Book>.

You can add a constraint to the Book type using JSR-303 annotations. Listing 8-10 illustrates how to make the label field required.

Listing 8-10. Adding the Validation Constraint

```
package models;

import java.util.*;

import play.data.validation.Constraints.*;

public class Book {

  public Long id;

  @Required
  public String label;

  ...
```

Now you need to modify the view template to display the screen for creating the book and listing all the books.

Templates are compiled as standard Scala functions. If you create a views/Application/index.scala.html template file, Scala will generate a views.html.Application.index class that has a render() method. Listing 8-11 shows a simple template.

Listing 8-11. Simple Template

```
@(books: List[Book])
 <ul>
@for(book <- books) {
  <li>@book.getTitle()</li>
}
</ul>
```

You can then call this from any Java code like you would normally call a method on a class.

```
Content html = views.html.Application.index.render(books);
```

Listing 8-12 illustrates the code for the `index.scala.html` template that you will find in the `app/views` folder.

Listing 8-12. index.scala.html

```
@(books: List[Book], bookForm: Form[Book])

@import helper._

@main("books") {

<h1>@books.size() book(s)</h1>

<ul>
        @for(book <- books) {
<li>
                @book.label

                @form(routes.Application.deleteBook(book.id)) {
<input type="submit" value="Delete">
                }
</li>
        }
</ul>

<h2>Add a new book</h2>

    @form(routes.Application.newBook()) {

        @inputText(bookForm("label"))

<input type="submit" value="Create">

    }

}
```

In Listing 8-12, the template takes two parameters. @content is a parameter that represents valid HTML to be written in the body of the document. The type of content is Html, which is the Scala structure that can be written as HTML when invoked by the template. The imported helper._ provides the form creation helpers—that is, the form function that creates the HTML <form> with filled action and method attributes, and the inputText function that creates the HTML input given as a form field.

> **Note** The play.data package contains several helpers to handle HTTP form data submission and validation.

Now you can implement the books() action, as illustrated in Listing 8-13.

Listing 8-13. Implementing the Books Action

```
public static Result books() {
    return ok(
    views.html.index.render(Book.all(), bookForm)
  );
}
```

The books() action renders a 200 OK result filled with the HTML, which is rendered by the index.scala.html template called with the books list and the bookForm form.

You can now try to access http://localhost:9000/books in your browser (see Figure 8-23).

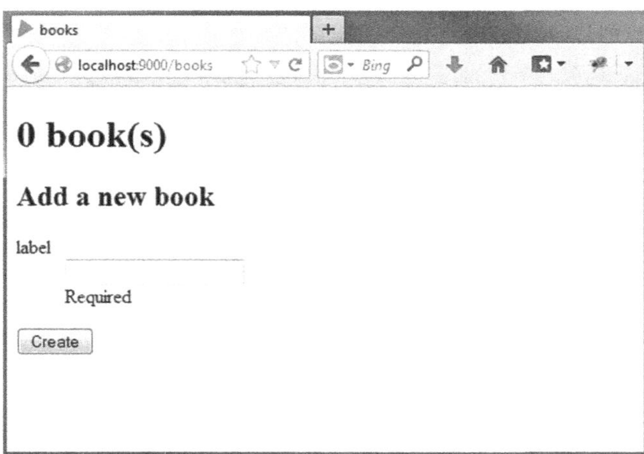

***Figure 8-23.** Displaying the book creation form*

If you submit the book creation form, you will still get the TODO page. You need to implement the newBook() action to be able to create the book. Listing 8-14 illustrates the implementation of the newBook() action.

Listing 8-14. Implementation of the newBook() Action

```
1.    public static Result newBook() {
2.        Form<Book> filledForm = bookForm.bindFromRequest();
3.      if(filledForm.hasErrors()) {
4.        return badRequest(
5.          views.html.index.render(Book.all(), filledForm)
6.        );
7.      } else {
8.        Book.create(filledForm.get());
9.        return redirect(routes.Application.books());
10.     }
11.   }
```

- *Line 2*: We use `bindFromRequest` to create a new form filled with the request data.
- *Lines 3 to 7*: If there are any errors in the form, we redisplay it (here we use 400 "Bad Request" instead of 200 "OK").
- *Lines 7 to 10*: If there are no errors, we create the book and then redirect to the books list.

Accessing the Database

Play 2 supports an object-relational mapping (ORM), Ebean, out of the box to fill the gap between the domain model and the relational database, as illustrated in Figure 8-24. The other popular options that offer ORM for Java are Hibernate and the Java Persistence API, which is standardized by Oracle.

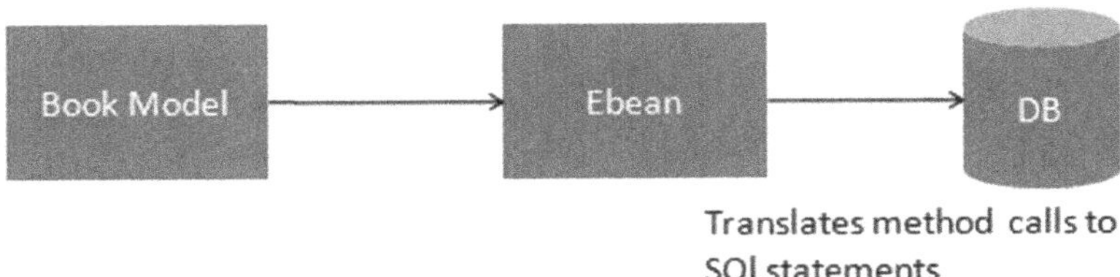

***Figure 8-24.** Using Ebean to query the database*

Like any other ORM, Ebean aims to facilitate the usage of a model when dealing with relational databases by implementing finders based on the model's properties. You will use H2, a lightweight DBMS that comes bundled with Play 2. Play's configuration contains default settings for using H2 and Ebean, but they're commented out. So, open the file `conf/application.conf` in your application's directory, and find and uncomment the following lines to enable the database in your application:

```
db.default.driver=org.h2.Driver
db.default.url="jdbc:h2:mem:play"
```

You will use Ebean to query the database. So, you'll have to enable it in the `application.conf` file as well:

```
ebean.default="models.*"
```

This will create an Ebean server connected to the default data source, managing all entities found in the `models` package.

Now it's time to transform your `Book` class to a valid Ebean entity. You can do this by making the `Book` class extend the `play.db.ebean.Model` superclass to have access to Play's built-in Ebean helper, as illustrated in Listing 8-15.

Listing 8-15. Transforming the Book Class to a Valid Ebean Entity

```
1.   package models;
2.
3.   import java.util.*;
4.   import play.db.ebean.*;
5.   import play.data.validation.Constraints.*;
6.
7.   import javax.persistence.*;
8.
9.   @Entity
10.  public class Book extends Model {
11.    @Id
12.    public Long id;
13.    @Required
14.    public String label;
15.
16.  public static Finder<Long,Book> find = new Finder(
17.      Long.class, Book.class
18.    );
19.
20.
21.  public static List<Book> all() {
22.    return find.all();
23.  }
24.
25.  public static void create(Book book) {
26.    book.save();
27.  }
28.  public static void update(Long id, Book book) {
29.      book.update(id);
30.  }
31.
32.  public static void delete(Long id) {
33.    find.ref(id).delete();
34.  }
35.
36.
37.  }
```

- *Line 13*: Line 13 adds the persistence annotation.
- *Lines 16 to 18*: These lines create a finder helper called `find` to initiate queries.
- *Lines 21 to 34*: These lines implement the CRUD operations. For instance, when you call the `create()` action, Ebean translates the `save()` method call into one or more SQL `INSERT` statements that store a new record in a database table using SQL.

Now when you test the URL `http://localhost:9000/`, you will see the page shown in Figure 8-25.

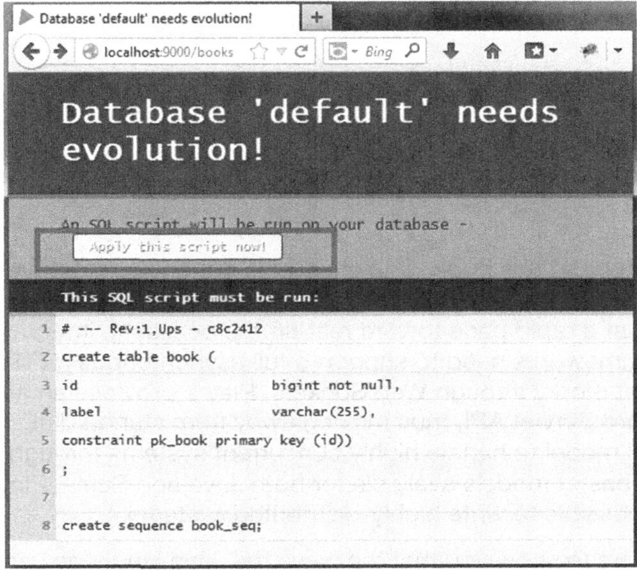

Figure 8-25. Applying a script on the default database

When you defined the database connection to connect to the H2 database, it did not automatically create the schema, in other words, the tables and column definitions. To create the schema, Play 2 generates a SQL script and demands to run it: "Apply this script now." Once you run this script by clicking the "Apply this script now" button, you can test the URL `http://localhost:9000/books` and the new book, as illustrated in Figure 8-26.

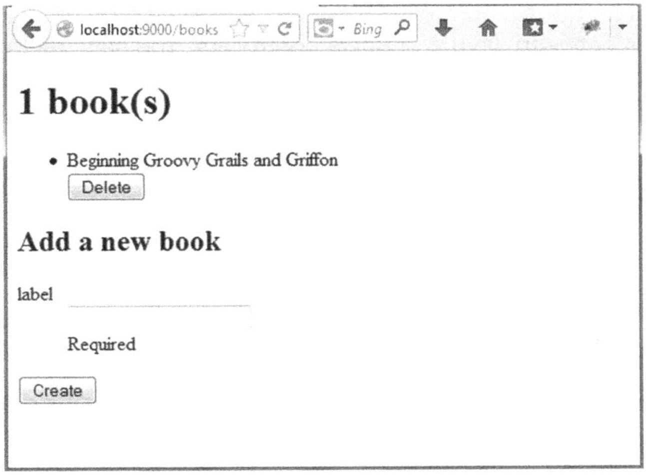

Figure 8-26. Adding a book

Deleting Books

Now that you can create books, you need to be able to delete them. For this you need to implement the deleteBook() action, as illustrated in Listing 8-16.

Listing 8-16. Implementing the Delete Action

```
public static Result deleteBook(Long id) {
  Book.delete(id);
  return redirect(routes.Application.books());
}
```

This concludes the chapter and this book. One chapter is not enough to cover all the features of the Play 2 framework (or any framework, for that matter). Meanwhile, frameworks and the web architecture are evolving at a rapid pace toward real-time processing, integrating more concurrent real-time data, so web frameworks need to support a full asynchronous HTTP programming model and need to use the event model through Web Sockets. Play 2 provides an asynchronous HTTP API instead of the standard Servlet API, thus moving away from standard JEE conventions. Play 2.0 employs the Actor-based model to handle highly concurrent systems through Akka. Akka is the best implementation of Actor-based models available for both Java and Scala. Play 2.0 provides native Akka support making it possible to write highly-distributed systems.

The goals of this book were to show you that the wave the Java language ushered into Web development in late '90s was only a beginning of the Typesafe era that is being transcended today and that the popularity that Java has enjoyed should be accredited to the Java Virtual Machine. It is quite a machine.

Summary

In this chapter, you took a high-level look at the Play 2 framework. You developed a helloworld web application for both Java and Scala, and you learned the basics that are common to all the Play 2 web applications: Java and Scala controllers, actions, and even a bit of views. In addition, you examined the differences between Java and Scala controllers. You saw the best features provided by Play 2, such as compilation on the fly and errors shown on the browser. Then you developed a simple Java-based CRUD web application.

Appendix A

Introduction to Java

One of the fundamental ways in which complexity can be handled is abstraction, which is applied in almost every discipline. For instance, abstract art is art that does not represent or imitate external reality or the objects of nature. As another example, some words are abstract, existing only in the mind, like *truth* or *justice*. In Java, abstraction allows developers to layer complex systems into manageable pieces by using class hierarchies that highlight the essential properties and behaviors of an object, differentiating it from other objects.

Classes and Objects

A *class* is the fundamental building block of object-oriented (OO) programs. Each class generally represents a real-world object. The class is a template for denoting and creating a category of objects, thus modeling an abstraction by defining the properties and behavior of the objects representing that abstraction. A property of an object is defined by a field, which is a variable that can store the value representing that property. The behavior of an object is defined by a method. The fields and methods of a class are known as its *members*. A class definition in Java consists of member declarations (variable declarations and method declarations) and begins with the `class` keyword, as illustrated in Listing A-1.

Listing A-1. A Java Class

```
class ClassA {
// members declarations
}
```

An *object* is an instance of a class. The object is constructed using the class as a blueprint and is a concrete instance of the abstraction that the class represents. An object must be created before it can be used in a program. The process of creating objects from a class is called *instantiation*. When a class is instantiated, a reference value is returned that denotes the created object. A reference value denotes a particular object. An object reference (or, simply, *reference*) is a variable that can store a reference value and provide a handle to an object. The code in Listing A-2 creates an object of `ClassA`. The reference value of this object is stored in the variable `var1`.

Listing A-2. Creating the Object

```
ClassA  var1 = new ClassA();
```

The process of creating objects involves declaring a reference variable to store the reference value of the object and then creating the object using the new keyword followed by initializing the object by a call to a constructor. The concept of constructor is explained later in the appendix. Listing A-3 splits Listing A-2 to show the declaration and creation as separate steps.

Listing A-3. The Declaration and Creation in Separate Steps

```
1.    ClassA  var1 ;
2.    var1 = new ClassA();
```

- Line 1 declares the variable var1. The reference variable var1 can now be used to manipulate the object whose reference value is stored in the reference variable.
- Line 2 creates the object using the new keyword and initialization by calling a constructor ClassA().

Variables

In Java, variables store values of primitive data types and reference values of objects.

Listing A-4 illustrates variable declarations that can store primitive values.

Listing A-4. Variable Declarations

```
int a, b, c;  // a, b and c are integer variables.
boolean flag; // flag is a boolean variable.
int i = 10,   // i is an int variable with initial value 10
```

Variables that store reference values of objects are called *reference variables*. The reference variables specify the type of reference that can be a class, an array, or an interface. Listing A-5 illustrates the reference variable declaration.

Listing A-5. Reference Variable Declarations

```
ClassA  var1 ; // Variable var1 can reference objects of class ClassA.
```

The declaration in the listing A-5 does not create any object of class ClassA; it just creates variable that can store references of objects of ClassA.

Instance Members

Each object created (as illustrated in Listing A-2) has its own copies of the fields defined in its class. The fields of an object are called *instance variables*. The values of the instance variables in an object make up the object's state. The methods of an object define its behavior. These methods are called *instance methods*. Instance variables and instance methods, which belong to objects, are called *instance members* (see Listing A-6) to distinguish them from static members, which belong only to the class.

Listing A-6. The Instance Members

```
1.    class ClassA{
2.    // instance Members
3.    int i ; // instance variable
4.    void methodA(){// instance method
5.    // do something
6.    }
7.    }
```

- In line 3, `i` is an instance variable of type `int`, and `int` is the primitive data type of `i`.
- In line 4, `methodA(){}` is an instance method.

Static Members

Static members, declared with the keyword `static`, are the members that belong only to the class and not to any specific objects of the class. A class can have static variables and static methods. Static variables are initialized when the class is loaded at runtime. Similarly, a class can have static methods that belong to the class and not to any specific objects of the class, as illustrated in Listing A-7.

Listing A-7. Static Members

```
1.    class ClassA{
2.    static int i ;
3.    static void methodA(){
4.    // do something
5.    }
6.    }
```

Unlike instance members, static members in a class can be accessed using the class name, as shown here:

```
ClassA.i           // accessing static variable in Line 2 of Listing A-7

ClassA.methodA(); // accessing static method in Line 3 of Listing A-7
```

Though static members in a class can be accessed via object references, it is considered bad practice to do so.

Method Overloading

Each method has a name and a formal parameter list. The name of the method and its formal parameter list together with the type and the order of the parameter in the parameter list constitute the signature of the method. As long as the method signatures differ, more than one method can have the same method name. Such methods with the same method names and different signatures are called *overloaded methods*, and this phenomenon is called *method overloading*. Thus, overloaded methods are the methods that have the same name but a different parameter list. Listing A-8 shows five implementations of the method methodA.

Listing A-8. Overloaded MethodA( )

```
1.    void methodA{(int a, double b) }
2.    int methodA(int a) { return a; }
3.    int methodA() { return 1; }
4.    long methodA(double a, int b) { return b; }
5.    long methodA(int c, double d) { return a; } //  Not ok.
```

- The first four implementations of method are overloaded correctly, each time with a different parameter list and, therefore, different signatures.
- The declaration on line 5 has the same signature methodA(int, double) as the declaration on line 1. Changing just the return type is not enough to overload a method; the parameter list in the declarations must be different.

> **Note** Only methods declared in the same class and those that are inherited by the class can be overloaded.

Arrays

An *array* is a data structure that is comprised of a fixed number of data elements essentially of the same data type. Any element in the array can be accessed using an index. The first element is always at index 0, and the last element is at index n-1, where *n* is the value of the length field in the array. In Java, arrays are objects where all elements in the array can be of a specific primitive data type or of a specific reference type. Listing A-9 declares references that refer to the array objects.

Listing A-9. Array Declarations

```
int [] intArray;
ClassA[]  classAArray ;
```

The two declarations in Listing A-9 declare intArray and classAArray to be reference variables that can refer to arrays of int values and arrays of ClassA objects. An array can be constructed for a fixed number of elements of a specific type, using the new operator. Given the previous array declarations, the arrays can be constructed as follows:

```
intArray = new int[10];      // array for 10 integers
classAArray = new ClassA[5]; // array of 5 objects of ClassA
```

Constructors

When an object is created using a new operator, the constructors are called to set the initial state of an object. A constructor declaration is comprised of the accessibility modifier followed by the parameter list with the following declarations:

- Modifiers other than an accessibility modifier are not permitted in the constructor header.
- Constructors cannot return a value and, therefore, do not specify a return type, not even void, in the constructor header.
- The constructor name must be the same as the class name.

When no constructors are specified in a class, then an implicit default constructor, that is, an implicit constructor without any parameters, is generated for the class by the compiler that comprises a call to the superclass's constructor. The compiler inserts this call to a superclass's constructor to ensure that the inherited state of the object is initialized. Listing A-10 illustrates a call to an implicit default constructor.

***Listing A-10.** Implicit Default Constructor*

```
class ClassA {
int i;
}
class ClassB {

ClassA var1 = new ClassA(); // (1) Call to implicit default constructor.
}
```

In the listing, the following implicit default constructor is called when a ClassA object is created in ClassB:

```
ClassA() { super(); }
```

In Listing A-11, the class ClassA provides an explicit default constructor at line 4.

***Listing A-11.** Explicit Default Constructor*

```
1.    class ClassA {
2.    int i ;
3.    // Explicit Default Constructor:
4.    ClassA() {
5.    i = 1;
6.    }
7.
8.    }
9.    class ClassB {
10.    // ...
11.    ClassA var1 = new ClassA(); //  Call of explicit default constructor.
12.    }
```

The explicit default constructor ensures that any object created with the object creation expression `new ClassA()`, shown in `ClassB`, will have its field `i` initialized to 1. If a class defines any explicit constructors, then the compiler will not generate the implicit default constructor with a call to the superclass's constructor, and therefore the state of the object will not be set. In such a case, an implementation of the default constructor needs to be provided. In Listing A-12, the class `ClassA` provides only a nondefault constructor at line 4. It is called at line 8 when an object of the class `ClassA` is created with the `new` operator. Any attempt to call the default constructor will be flagged as a compile-time error, as shown on line 11.

Listing A-12. Nondefault Constructor

```
1.    class ClassA {
2.    int i;
3.    // Only non-default Constructor:
4.    ClassA(int i) {
5.    this.i = i;
6.    }
7.    }
8.    class ClassB {
9.    // ...
10.    ClassA var1 = new ClassA(2);
11.    //ClassA var2 = new ClassA(); // Compile-time error.
12.    }
```

Constructors can be overloaded, like methods, and because the names of all the constructors are restricted to be the same as the class's name, the signatures of these constructors can be different only if their parameter lists are different. In Listing A-13, the class `ClassA` provides both an explicit implementation of the default constructor on line 4 and a nondefault constructor on line 8. The nondefault constructor is called when an object of the class `ClassA` is created on line 14 and the default constructor is called on line 15.

Listing A-13. Both Default and Nondefault Constructor

```
1.    class ClassA {
2.    int i;
3.    // Explicit Default Constructor:
4.    ClassA() {
5.    i = 3;
6.    }
7.    // Non-default Constructor:
8.    ClassA(int i) {
9.    this.i = i;
10.    }
11.    }
12.    class ClassB {
13.    // ...
14.    ClassA var1 = new ClassA(4);
15.    ClassA var2 = new ClassA();
16.    }
```

Encapsulation

Encapsulation is the technique to achieve data hiding by preventing the data and the code from being randomly accessed and manipulated by the external code, that is, from the code outside the class. In terms of implementation, encapsulation is achieved by making the fields in a class private and providing access to the fields via public methods. If a field is declared private, it cannot be accessed by anyone outside the class. Listing A-14 illustrates an encapsulated Book class.

Listing A-14. Encapsulation

```
public class Book {
       private String title ;
       public String getTitle() {
        return title;
    }
    public void setTitle(String title) {
        this.title = title;
    }
 }
```

Inheritance

Inheritance is one of the fundamental principles in object-oriented programming. In Java, all classes by default extend the java.lang.Object class. A class can extend another class by using the extends keyword. Java supports single inheritance through *implementation inheritance* in which a class inherits state and behaviors from another class through class extension. Java also supports multiple inheritance in two ways.

- A class can inherit behavior from one or more interfaces by means of implementation.
- An interface can inherit behavior from one or more interfaces through extension.

Figure A-1 presents a UML[1] class diagram that depicts a parent-child relationship between a class, ClassA, and a child class, ClassB. ClassB is a referred to as a *subclass* of ClassA. Note that a line with an arrow is used to depict generalization, in other words, the parent-child relationship.

[1]www.uml.org/

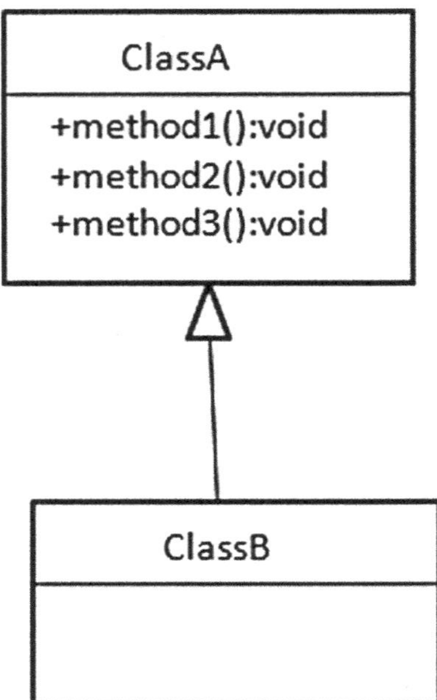

***Figure A-1.** Parent-child relationship. ClassB extends ClassA*

Listing A-15 illustrates how Figure A-1 could be implemented in code. It illustrates implementation inheritance using the keyword extends in line 26.

Listing A-15 . Implementation Inheritance

```
1.    package apress.appendix_A
2.
3.    public class ClassA {
4.
5.        // Instance methods
6.        public void method1() {
7.            System.out.println(" classA - method1");
8.
9.        }
10.
11.        private void method2() {
12.            System.out.println(" classA - method2");
13.
14.        }
15.
16.        // Static methods
17.        public static void method3() {
18.            System.out.println(" classA - method3");
19.
20.        }
21.
22.    }
```

```

package apress.appendix_A;

public class ClassB extends ClassA {


}
```

Listing A-16 is a driver class for testing the inheritance in Listing A-15.

Listing A-16. Testing Inheritance

```
package apress.appendix_A;

public class Test {

    public static void main(String[] args) {
        ClassB var1 = new ClassB();

        var1.method1();
        // var1.method2(); // private method not Inherited

        ClassB.method3();// static method

    }

}
```

Listing A-16 illustrates that even if there are no methods defined in `ClassB`, methods of `ClassA` are available in `ClassB` and can be invoked on the reference variable where the actual object type is of `ClassB`. Line 9 shows that private methods are not inherited.

Here is the output:

```
classA - method1

classA - method3
```

Constructor Chaining

When a subclass is instantiated by invoking one of its constructors, the constructor first calls the no-argument constructor of the superclass. In the superclass, the constructor also calls the constructor of its superclass. This process repeats itself until the constructor of the `java.lang.Object` class is reached. In other words, when you create an object of a subclass, all its superclasses are also instantiated. Listing A-17 illustrates this *constructor chaining*.

Listing A-17. Constructor Chaining

```
package apress.appendix_A;

public class ClassA {

    public ClassA() {

        System.out.println("Class A no-arg constructor");

    }

    public ClassA(String title) {
        System.out.println("Class A constructor");

    }

}

package apress.appendix_A;

public class ClassB extends ClassA {

    public ClassB(String title){
        System.out.println("Class B constructor ");

    }

}

package apress.appendix_A;

public class Test {

    /**
     * @param args
     */
    public static void main(String[] args) {
        ClassB var1 = new ClassB("classB");

    }

}
```

Here is the output:

```
Class A no-arg constructor

Class B constructor
```

The output proves that the constructor of the subclass invokes the base class's no-arg constructor. The Java compiler changed ClassB's constructor to the following:

```
public ClassB(String title) {
 super();
 System.out.println("Class B constructor ");
}
```

The keyword super represents an instance of the direct superclass of the current object. Since super is called from an instance of subclass, super represents an instance of ClassA. You can explicitly call the parent's constructor from a subclass's constructor by using the super keyword, but super must be the first statement in the constructor. Using the super keyword is handy if you want another constructor in the superclass to be invoked.

```
public ClassB(String title) {
 super(title);
 System.out.println("Class B constructor ");
}
```

Polymorphism

Polymorphism is one of the most important principles of OO programming and as such is the heart of OOP. Polymorphism refers to how an object in Java can take on many forms. To understand how polymorphism works in Java, let's look at an example of a class that extends another class (see Figure A-2).

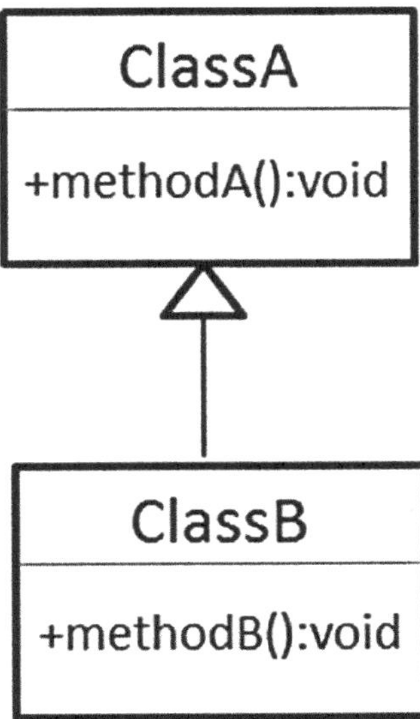

***Figure A-2.** Extending a class*

Figure A-2 shows a superclass-subclass relationship. This relationship allows you to assign an object to a reference variable whose type is different from the object type, as follows:

```
ClassA var1 = new ClassB();
```

This assigns an object of type `ClassB` to a reference variable `var1` whose reference type is `ClassA`. This assignment has different implications at compile time and at runtime. At the compile time, since the type of the `var1` is `ClassA`, the compiler will not allow calling a method on `var1`, which is not in `ClassA`, even if that method is in `ClassB`. Listing A-18 shows the code implementation of Figure A-2.

Listing A-18. Inheritance

```
package apress.appendix_A;
public class ClassA {

    public void methodA() {
        System.out.println("methodA() in ClassA");
    }

}

package apress.appendix_A;

public class ClassB extends ClassA {

    public void methodB() {
        System.out.println("methodB() in ClassB");
    }

}
```

Listing A-19 illustrates the test.

Listing A-19. Driver for Listing A-18

```
package apress.appendix_A;

public class Test {
    public static void main(String[] args) {

        ClassA var1 = new ClassB();
        // var1.methodB(); uncommenting this code will result in compile time
        // error
        var1.methodA();

    }
}
```

On line 2 of Listing A-19, it is not possible to call `methodB()` on `var1` even if `methodB()` is `ClassB`, because the reference type of `var1` is `ClassA` and `ClassA` does not have `methodB()`.

Now let's consider the case where `ClassB` overrides `methodA()` of `ClassA` (see Figure A-3).

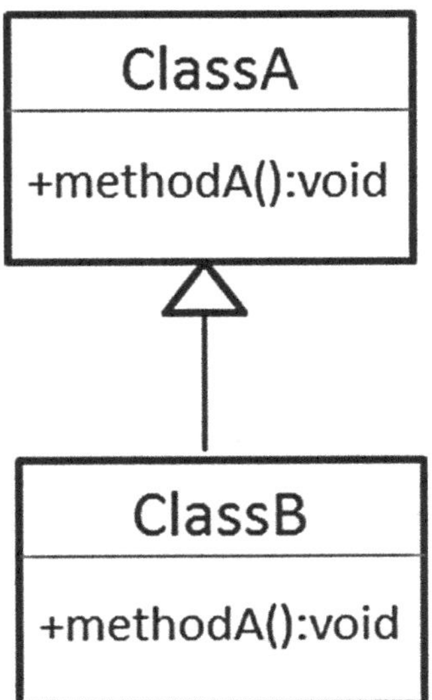

***Figure A-3.** Overriding a method*

Now the code of ClassB looks like that shown in Listing A-20.

***Listing A-20.** Overriding methodA( )*

```
package apress.appendix_A;

public class ClassB extends ClassA {

    public void methodA() {
        System.out.println("methodA() in ClassB");
    }

}
```

Now both ClassA and ClassB have the same method, methodA().

The following assignment:

```
ClassA var1 = new ClassB();
```

confirms that it is possible to call methodA( ) on var1 because ClassA has methodA( ). So, the following test will compile:

```
package apress.appendix_A;

public class Test {
    public static void main(String[] args) {

        ClassA var1 = new ClassB();
        var1.methodA();

    }
}
```

This is, at compile time, the call methodA( ) on var1 will be checked against a reference type of var1, ClassA, by the compiler, and the compiler will allow it because the methodA( ) exists in ClassA.

But what will happen if we run the test; that is, which methodA( ) will be called, methodA( ) in ClassA or methodA( ) in ClassB? When the test is run, it gives the following output:

```
methodA() in ClassB
```

The compiler checked methodA( ) in ClassA but executed methodA( ) in ClassB. This is because at runtime, the JVM verifies, instead of compiles, methodA( ) against the actual object type. The actual object type in the code (ClassA var1 = new ClassB();) is ClassB, while ClassA is a reference type. So, the JVM checks whether the call methodA( ) is in ClassB( ) and calls it. This phenomenon is called *polymorphism*. What will happen if methodA( ) is not in ClassB? To understand this, we implement the code for Figure A-4.

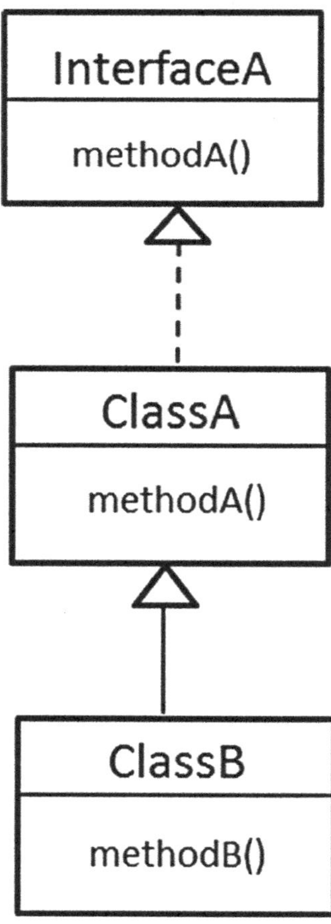

***Figure A-4.** Hierarchy of ClassB*

Figure A-4 shows InterfaceA, just to illustrate that the reference type could be an interface or a class (or abstract class), and the compiler will check the existence of the method against the reference type of any of these in the similar manner. Listing A-21 implements the hierarchy shown in Figure A-4.

Listing A-21. Hierachy of Class B

```
package apress.appendix_A;
public interface InterfaceA {

    public void methodA();


}

package apress.appendix_A;
public class ClassA implements InterfaceA{

    @Override
    public void methodA() {
        System.out.println("methodA() in ClassA");
    }
}

package apress.appendix_A;
public class ClassB extends ClassA {
    public void methodB() {
        System.out.println("methodB() in ClassB");
    }
}
```

In Listing A-21, the call methodA( ) is verified against reference type InterfaceA, and after checking that methodA( ) exists in InterfaceA, the compiler approves the call; that is, there is no compile-time error. Run the test shown in Listing A-22.

Listing A-22. Test Application

```
package apress.appendix_A;
public class Test {
    public static void main(String[] args) {
        InterfaceA var1 = new ClassB();
        var1.methodA();
    }
}
```

You get the following output:

```
methodA() in ClassA
```

The actual object type in line 4 of Listing A-22 is `ClassB`, so at runtime the JVM checks whether `methodA( )` exists in `ClassB`. On not finding `methodA( )` in `ClassB` (because it does not exist in `ClassB`), the JVM checks for the existence of `methodA( )` in the hierarchy of `ClassB`, because the JVM considers the fact that there must be `methodA( )` existing somewhere in the hierarchy of `ClassB`; otherwise, the compiler would not have approved the call. Since `methodA( )` exists in `ClassA`, the JVM executes `methodA( )` in `ClassA` at runtime.

Summary

This appendix introduced you to the basics of Java and object-oriented programming. You learned how classes are the basic building blocks of object-oriented programs and how you can instantiate objects from classes. Next, you were introduced to the three pillars of object-oriented programming: encapsulation, inheritance, and polymorphism.

Appendix B

Introduction to Groovy

Groovy is an agile and dynamic language for the Java Virtual Machine that builds upon the strengths of Java but has additional powerful features inspired by languages such as Python, Ruby, and Smalltalk. It seamlessly integrates with all existing Java classes and libraries and compiles to Java bytecode so you can use it anywhere you can use Java. Groovy provides the ability to statically type check and statically compile your code for robustness and performance and supports domain-specific languages and other compact syntax so your code becomes easy to read and maintain.

Groovy makes modern programming features available to Java developers with almost zero learning curve; increases developer productivity by reducing scaffolding code when developing web, GUI, database, or console applications; and simplifies testing by supporting unit testing and mocking out of the box.

Getting Started

Let's start with a traditional "Hello World" program. But first you need to install Groovy. Groovy comes bundled as a `.zip` file or platform-specific installer for Windows, Ubuntu, and Debian (as well as openSUSE until recent versions). This section explains how to install the zipped version, since it covers the most platforms.

To install Groovy, follow these steps:

1. Download the most recent stable Groovy binary release `.zip` file from `http://groovy.codehaus.org/Download`.
2. Uncompress `groovy-binary-X.X.X.zip` to your chosen location.
3. Set a `GROOVY_HOME` environment variable to the directory in which you uncompressed the `.zip` file.
4. Add the `%GROOVY_HOME%\bin` directory to your system path.

> **Note** Groovy requires Java, so you need to have a version available (while Groovy 1.6 supported JDK 1.4 or greater, for Groovy 1.7 onward, at a minimum JDK 1.5 is needed).

To validate your installation, open a console and type the following:

```
>groovy -v
```

You should see something like this:

```
Groovy Version: 2.0.0 JVM: 1.6.0_31 Vendor: Sun Microsystems Inc. OS: Windows 7
```

Now you can write your first "Hello World" program (see Listing B-1).

Listing B-1. "Hello World" in Java

```
1.  public class HelloWorld {
2.     public static void main( String[] args )
3.  System.out.println("Hello World!");
4.     }
5.  }
```

- *Lines 1 to 2*: The default visibility of methods and fields is public, so you can drop the `public` modifier.
- *Line 2*: Groovy supports dynamic typing, so you can drop type information and the return type `void` on the `main()`.
- *Line 3*: Every Groovy object has at its disposure `println`, which can be seen as a shortcut for `System.out.println`.
- *Line 3*: The semicolon at the end of line is optional, so you can drop that too.

In light of these rules, you can transform Listing B-1 to Listing B-2.

Listing B-2. Transforming "Hello World" Applying Groovy Rules

```
class HelloWorld {
   static main( args ){
println "Hello World!"
   }
}
```

As you can see, Listing B-2 is much more compact. You can write and execute Groovy code in the form of scripts that are also compiled to bytecode. So, you can write the Groovy code illustrated in Listing B-3 for the "Hello World" program.

> **Note** Any Java class/object is also a Groovy class/object.

Listing B-3. Groovy Script for "Hello World"

```
println "Hello World!"
```

You can run Groovy scripts and classes through the command line, GroovyShell, or GroovyConsole.

GroovyShell

GroovyShell is an interactive command-line application (shell) that allows you to create, run, save, and load Groovy scripts and classes. To start GroovyShell, run `groovysh`. Figure B-1 illustrates using GroovyShell to execute a simple script.

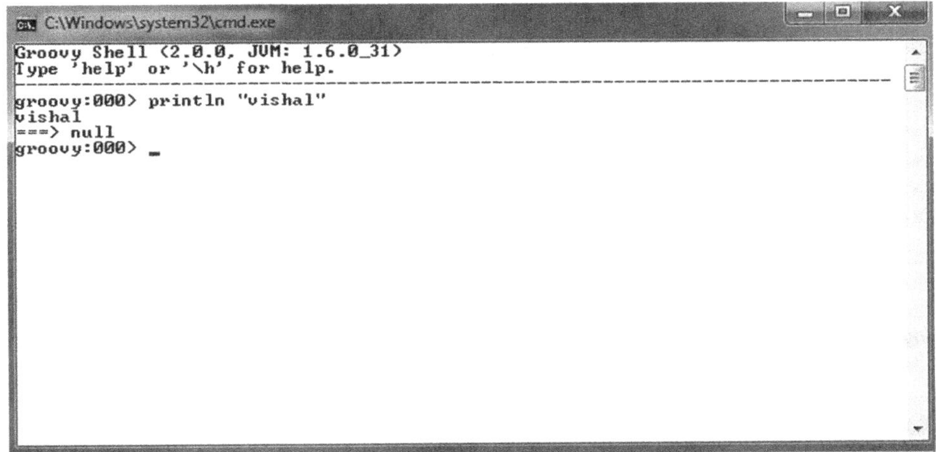

***Figure B-1.** Using GroovyShell*

As you can see, the script prints `vishal`. Then you see `===> null`. As a matter of convention, Groovy always returns the results of methods. In this case, there is no result, so `null` is returned. GroovyShell contains a built-in help facility that you can use to learn more about the shell. To access it, type `help` at the prompt. Figure B-2 shows the help listing.

```
C:\Windows\system32\cmd.exe
Groovy Shell (2.0.0, JVM: 1.6.0_31)
Type 'help' or '\h' for help.
-------------------------------------------------------------------------------
groovy:000> println "vishal"
vishal
===> null
groovy:000> help

For information about Groovy, visit:
    http://groovy.codehaus.org

Available commands:
  help      (\h ) Display this help message
  ?         (\? ) Alias to: help
  exit      (\x ) Exit the shell
  quit      (\q ) Alias to: exit
  import    (\i ) Import a class into the namespace
  display   (\d ) Display the current buffer
  clear     (\c ) Clear the buffer and reset the prompt counter.
  show      (\S ) Show variables, classes or imports
  inspect   (\n ) Inspect a variable or the last result with the GUI object brow
ser
  purge     (\p ) Purge variables, classes, imports or preferences
  edit      (\e ) Edit the current buffer
  load      (\l ) Load a file or URL into the buffer
  .         (\. ) Alias to: load
  save      (\s ) Save the current buffer to a file
  record    (\r ) Record the current session to a file
  history   (\H ) Display, manage and recall edit-line history
  alias     (\a ) Create an alias
  set       (\= ) Set (or list) preferences
  register  (\rc) Registers a new command with the shell

For help on a specific command type:
    help command

groovy:000>
```

Figure B-2. Using GroovyShell help

GroovyConsole

GroovyConsole, shown in Figure B-3, is a graphical version of GroovyShell. It is written using SwingBuilder, a Groovy module that makes building a Swing user interface easier.

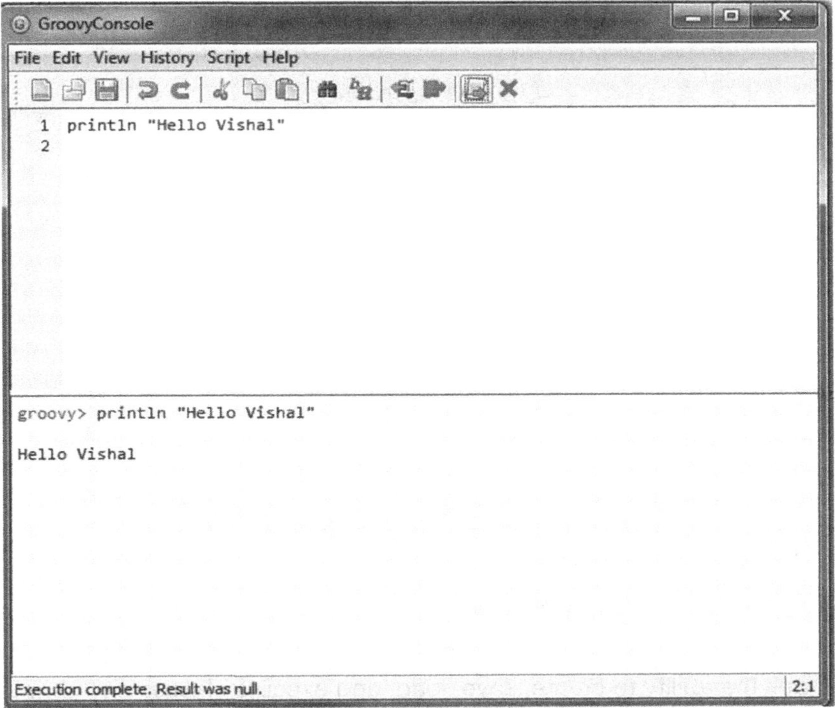

Figure B-3. *GroovyConsole*

Figure B-4 shows GroovyConsole with the output detached. You can start GroovyConsole in a number of ways, depending on your environment and how you installed Groovy. The easiest way is to execute GroovyConsole, which is located in the Groovy `bin` directory.

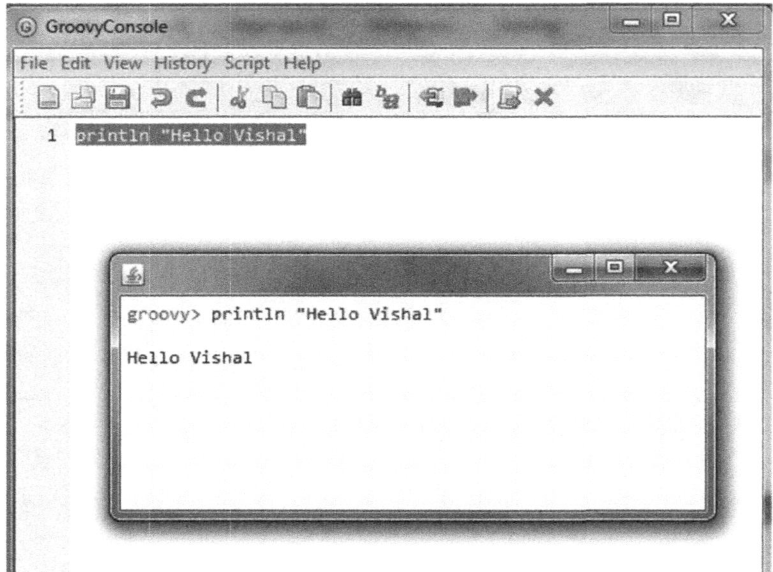

Figure B-4. *Using GroovyConsole with the output detached*

The console provides the ability to create, save, load, and execute classes and scripts. Some of the nice features of the console are undo/redo and the ability to inspect variables. If you have to choose between using GroovyShell and GroovyConsole, I recommend GroovyConsole.You can also define classes in scripts and use them right away, as illustrated in Listing B-4.

Listing B-4. Defining a Class in the Script

```
class HelloWorld {
   def hello( name ){
      "Hello ${name}!"
   }
}
def hw = new HelloWorld()
println hw.hello("Vishal")
```

- The return type of the method `hello` is not of a specific type, so you use the reserved keyword `def`.
- The string `"Hello"` is not a simple `java.lang.String`. It is, in fact, one of the Groovy features: a GString. These types of strings allow string interpolation, as explained in the next section.

Groovy supports two kinds of strings: regular Java strings and GStrings. A string in Groovy is an instance of`java.lang.String` if it is surrounded by single quotes or if it is surrounded by double or triple quotes with no unescaped dollar sign ($).

GStrings

GStrings are an instance of `groovy.lang.GString` and allow placeholders to be included in the text. GStrings are not a subclass of `String` because the `String` class is final and can't be extended. A GString is just like a normal string, but it allows the embedding of variables within it using `${..}`. The curly braces are required only if the embedded variable is a placeholder for an expression. Groovy supports a concept found in many other languages such as Perl and Ruby called *string interpolation*, which is the ability to substitute an expression or variable within a string. If you have experience with Unix shell scripts, Ruby, or Perl, this should look familiar. Java doesn't support string interpolation. You must manually concatenate the values. Listing B-5 is an example of the type of code you need to write in Java, and Listing B-6 shows the same code using a GString.

Listing B-5. Building Strings with Java

```
String name = "Vishal" ;
String helloName = "Hello " + name ;
System.out.println(helloName) ;
```

Listing B-6. String Interpolation in Groovy/GString

```
1.    str1= "Vishal"
2.    str2 = "Hello "
3.    println "$str2$str1"
```

In line 3, curly braces are not used because curly braces are required only if the embedded variable is a placeholder for an expression. When Groovy sees a string defined with double quotes or slashes and an embedded expression, Groovy constructs an `org.codehaus.groovy.runtime.GStringImpl` instead of a `java.lang.String`. When the GString is accessed, the expression is evaluated. Notice that you can include any valid Groovy expression inside the `${}` notation; this includes method calls or variable names.

Groovy supports single-line strings and the strings that span multiple lines. In the sections that follow, you will learn a variety of strings supported in Groovy.

Single-Line Strings

Single-line strings can be single quoted or double quoted. A string enclosed in single quotes is taken literally. Strings defined with single quotes do not interpret the embedded expressions, as illustrated in Listing B-7.

Listing B-7. Single-Quote Strings Do Not Interpret Embedded Expressions

```
name = "vishal"
s1 = 'hello $name'
println s1
Here is the output:
hello $name
```

You can nest a double quote in a single quote, as illustrated in Listing B-8.

Listing B-8. Nested Double Quote in Single Quote

```
s1 = 'hello "vishal"'
println s1
```

Strings defined using double quotes will interpret embedded expressions within the string, as illustrated in Listing B-9.

Listing B-9. Double-Quoted Strings Interpret Embedded Expressions

```
def name = "vishal"
s1 = "hello $name"
println s1
Here is the output:
hello vishal
```

You can nest single quotes in double quotes, as illustrated in Listing B-10.

Listing B-10. Nested Single Quote in Double Quote

```
s1 = "hello 'vishal'"
println s1
Here is the output:
hello 'vishal'
```

Multiline Strings

Groovy supports strings that span multiple lines. A multiline string is defined by using three double quotes or three single quotes. Multiline string support is useful for creating templates or embedded documents (such as XML templates, SQL statements, HTML, and so on). For example, you could use a multiline string and string interpolation to build the body of an e-mail message, as shown in Listing B-11. String interpolation with multiline strings works in the same way as it does with regular strings: multiline strings created with double quotes evaluate expressions, and single-quoted strings don't.

Listing B-11. Using Multiline Strings

```
def name = "Vishal"
def multiLineString = """
Hello, ${name}
This is a multiline string with double quotes
"""
println multiLineString
```

```
Hello, Vishal
This is a multiline string with double quotes
```

Slashy Strings

As mentioned earlier, slashes can be used to define strings. The slashy notation has a nice benefit: additional backslashes are not needed to escape special characters. The only exception is escaping a backslash: \/. The slashy notation can be helpful when creating a regular expression requiring a backslash or a path. Listing B-12 illustrates the difference between using regular quotes and slashes to define a regular expression to match a file system path.

Listing B-12. Using Slashy Strings

```
def quotedString = 'Hello Vishal'
def slashyString = /Hello Vishal/
println slashyString
```

```
Hello Vishal
```

Listing B-12 defines two variables and assigns them to a directory path. The first variable definition, `quotedString`, uses the single-quote notation to define a string. Using the single-quote notation requires that the embedded backslash be escaped using an additional backslash.

Multiline Slashy Strings

Slashy strings can also span multiple lines. This is particularly useful for multiline regexes when using the regex freespacing comment style (see Listing B-13).

Listing B-13. Using Multiline Slashy Strings

```
1.    def name = "vishal"
2.    def path= "c:/groovy"
3.    def multilineSlashy = /
4.    Hello $name
5.    path= $path
6.    dollar = $
7.    path = c:\/groovy
8.    /
9.    println multilineSlashy
```

```
Hello vishal
path= c:/groovy
dollar = $
path = c:/groovy
```

Let's take a look at Listing B-13 in a little more detail.

- Line 1 defines a variable, `name`, and assigns the value `"vishal"` to it.
- Line 2 defines a variable, `path`, and assigns the value `"c:/groovy"` to it.
- Line 3 defines a variable, `multilineSlashy`, and assigns a multiline string to it that includes up to line 8, between the slashes.

- Line 4 has an expression, `$name`, that is evaluated to `vishal`, as shown in the output.
- Line 5 has an expression, `$path`, that is evaluated to `c:/groovy`, as shown in the output.
- Line 6 has a $ sign, but it is not an expression, so it is displayed in the output.
- Line 7 has a slash, which needs to be escaped.

Dollar Slashy Strings

In multiline slashy strings, a slash still needs to be escaped. Moreover, in multiline slashy strings, an unescaped dollar sign that is not an expression results in a `MissingPropertyException`, as illustrated in Listing B-14.

Listing B-14. MissingPropertyException in Multiline Slashy String

```
1.    def name = "vishal"
2.    def path= "c:/groovy"
3.    def multilineSlashy = /
4.    Hello $name
5.    path= $path
6.    dollar = $test
7.    path = c:\/groovy
8.     /
9.    println multilineSlashy
```

```
Caught: groovy.lang.MissingPropertyException: No such property: test for class:
hello
groovy.lang.MissingPropertyException: No such property: test for class: hello
at hello.run(hello.groovy:3)
```

In Listing B-14, there is no such property as `test`; `$test` in line 6 is interpreted as an expression, which results in a `MissingPropertyException`.

Now, let's look at the code in Listing B-15, specifically line 6.

Listing B-15. Unescaped Dollar Sign in Multiline Slashy String

```
1.    def name = "vishal"
2.    def path= "c:/groovy"
3.    def multilineSlashy = /
4.    Hello $name
5.    path= $path
6.    dollar = $ test
7.    path = c:\/groovy
8.     /
9.    println multilineSlashy
```

This time Groovy does not interpret `$ test` in line 6 as an expression because there is an empty space between `$` and `test`, and it renders the output as follows:

```
Hello vishal
path= c:/groovy
dollar = $ test
path = c:/groovy
```

With a dollar slashy string, you are no longer required to escape the slash with a preceding backslash (multiline slashy strings require the slash to be escaped), and you can use `$$` to escape a `$` or use `$/` to escape a slash if needed, as illustrated in Listing B-16.

***Listing B-16.** Using Dollar Slashy String*

```
1.    def name = "vishal"
2.    def path= "c:/groovy"
3.    def dollarSlashy = $/
4.    Hello $name
5.    path = $path
6.    dollar = $$test
7.    path = c:/groovy
8.    /$
9.    println dollarSlashy
```

```
Hello vishal
path= c:/groovy
dollar = $test
path = c:/groovy
```

Let's take a look at Listing B-16 in more detail.

- Line 3 defines a `dollarSlashy` string that includes up to line 8.
- Line 6 has a `$test`, which has caused a `MissingPropertyException` in the case of the multiline slashy string in Listing B-14, which you now escape using a `$`.

Collective Datatypes

Groovy supports a number of different collections, including arrays, lists, maps, ranges, and sets. Let's look at how to create and use each of the collection types.

Arrays

A Groovy array is a sequence of objects, just like a Java array (see Listing B-17).

Listing B-17. Creating and Using Arrays

```
1.    def stringArray = new String[3]
2.    stringArray[0] = "A"
3.    stringArray[1] = "B"
4.    stringArray[2] = "C"
5.    println stringArray
6.    println stringArray[0]
7.    stringArray.each { println it}
8.     println stringArray[-1..-3]
```

- Line 1 creates a string array of size 3.
- Lines 2 to 4 use an index to access the array.
- Line 7 illustrates using the `each()` method to iterate through the array. The `each()` method is used to iterate through and apply the closure on every element.
- Line 8 shows something interesting—it uses a range, which will be discussed shortly, to access the array.

```
[A, B, C]

A

A

B

C

[C, B, A]
```

Lists

A Groovy list is an ordered collection of objects, just as in Java. It is an implementation of the `java.util.List` interface. Listing B-18 illustrates how to create a list and common usages.

Listing B-18. Creating and Using Lists

```
def emptyList = []
def list = ["A"]
list.add "B"
list.add "C"
list.each { println it }
println list[0]
list.set(0, "Vishal")
println list.get(0)
 list.remove 2
 list.each { println it }
```

- On line 1, an empty list is created by assigning a property the value of [].
- Lines 2 to 4 create a list with an item already in it and add items to the list.
- Line 5 iterates over the list, invoking the closure to print out the contents. The each() method provides the ability to iterate over all elements in the list, invoking the closure on each element.
- Lines 6 illustrates how to use an index to access a list. Lists are zero-based.
- Line 7 shows how to use an index to assign position 0 the value "Vishal".
- Line 8 accesses the list using the get() method.

```
A
B
C
A
Vishal
Vishal
B
```

Maps

A Groovy map is an unordered collection of key-value pairs, where the key is unique, just as in Java. It is an implementation of java.util.Map. Listing B-19 illustrates how to create maps and common usages.

Listing B-19. Creating and Using Maps

```
def map = ['a':'Value A', 'b':'Value B ']
println map["a"]
println map."a"
println map.a
println map.getAt("b")
println map.get("b")
println map.get("c", "unknown")
println map
map.d = "Value D"
println map.d
map.put('e', 'Value E')
println map.e
map.putAt 'f', 'Value F'
println map.f
map.each { println "Key: ${it.key}, Value: ${it.value}" }
map.values().each { println it }
```

- Line 1 illustrates how to define a map with multiple entries. When using the square bracket notation, the colon separates the key from the value.
- Lines 2 to 10 show several different techniques for accessing the map.
- Lines 11 to 13 show several different techniques for putting items into the map.

```
Value A
Value A
Value A
Value B
Value B
unknown
[a:Value A, b:Value B , c:unknown]
Value D
Value E
Value F
Key: a, Value: Value A
Key: b, Value: Value B
Key: c, Value: unknown
Key: d, Value: Value D
Key: e, Value: Value E
Key: f, Value: Value F
Value A
Value B
unknown
Value D
Value E
Value F
```

Ranges

A range is a list of sequential values. Logically, you can think of it as 1 through 10 or as a through z. As a matter of fact, the declaration of a range is exactly that: 1..10 or 'a'.'z'. A range is a list of any objects that implement `java.lang.Comparable`. The objects have `next()` and `previous()` methods to facilitate navigating through the range. Listing B-20 illustrates some of the things you can do with ranges.

Listing B-20. Creating and Using Ranges

```
1.    def numRange = 0..9
2.    numRange.each {print it}
3.    println ""
4.    println numRange.contains(5)
5.    def reverseRange = 9..0
6.    reverseRange.each {print it}
7.    def exclusiveRange = 1..<10
8.    println ""
9.    exclusiveRange.each {print it}
10.    def alphabet = 'a'..'z'
11.    println ""
12.    println alphabet.size()
13.    println alphabet[25]
```

- Lines 1, 5, 7, and 10 illustrate how to define ranges.
- Line 1 defines an inclusive range of numbers.
- Line 10 defines an inclusive range of lowercase letters.
- Line 7 defines an exclusive list of numbers. The range results in a range of numbers 1 to 9, excluding 10.
- Line 5 creates a range in reverse order, 9 through 0. Frequently, ranges are used for iterating. In Listing B-20, `each()` was used to iterate over the range. Listing B-21 shows three ways you can use a range to iterate: one in Java and two in Groovy.

```
0123456789

true

9876543210

123456789

26

z
```

Listing B-21. Iterating with Ranges

```
for (i in 0..9) {
println i
}
(0..9).each { i->
println i
}
```

The `each()` method is used to iterate through and apply the closure on every element.

Sets

A Groovy set is an unordered collection of objects, with no duplicates, just as in Java. It is an implementation of `java.util.Set`. By default, unless you specify otherwise, a Groovy set is a `java.util.HashSet`. If you need a set other than a `HashSet`, you can create any type of set by instantiating it, as in `def TreeSet = new TreeSet()`. Listing B-22 illustrates how to create sets and common usages.

Listing B-22. Creating and Using Sets

```
def  set = ["A", "B" ] as Set
set.add "C"
println set
set.each { println it }
set.remove "B"
set.each { println it }
```

```
[A, B, C]
A
B
C
A
C
```

Creating an empty set is similar to creating an empty list. The difference is the addition of the `Set` clause. One of the important differences between a list and a set is that a list provides indexed-based access and a set doesn't.

Methods

Listing B-23 illustrates defining a method in Groovy the Java way, and Listing B-24 shows the same thing but using the Groovy syntax instead.

Listing B-23. Defining a Method the Java Way

```
public String hello(String name) {
return "Hello, " + name;
}
```

Listing B-24. Defining a Method Using the Groovy Idiom

```
def hello(name) {
"Hello, ${name}"
}
```

- The return type and the return statement are not included in the body of the method. Groovy always returns the results of the last expression—in this case, the GString "`Hello, . . .`".
- The access modifier public is not defined. Unless you specify otherwise, Groovy defaults all classes, properties, and methods to public access.

Closures

Functional programming gives you the right foundation to think about concurrency on the basis of underlying principles: *referential transparency*, *higher-order functions*, and *immutable values*. Understanding these key elements is crucial to understanding closures (and other functional features recently introduced in Groovy). Functional programming is built on the premise of pure functions. In mathematics, functions are pure in that they lack side effects. Consider the classic function sin(x): y = sin(x). No matter how many times sin(x) is called, no global or contextual state is modified internally by sin(x). Such a function is pure, free of side effects, and oblivious to the context. This obliviousness to the surrounding context is known as *referential transparency*. If no global state is modified, concurrent invocation of the function is steadfast. In functional programming, functions are first-class citizens, meaning functions can be assigned to variables, functions can be passed to other functions, and functions can be returned as values from other functions. And such functions, which take functions as arguments or return a function, are called *higher-order functions*.

Referential transparency, higher-order functions, and immutable values together make functional programming a better way to write concurrent software. Though functional languages are all about eliminating side effects, a language that never allowed for side effects would be useless. As a matter of fact, introducing side effects is crucial to any language. All functional languages have to provide mechanisms for introducing side effects in a controlled manner because even though functional languages are about pure programming, a language that does not sanction side effects would be useless because input and output are essentially the ramification of side effects.

Understanding Closures

One of the techniques to introduce side effects in a controlled manner is a *closure*. A closure definition in Groovy follows this syntax:

```
{ [closure parameters ->] closure body}
```

where `[closure parameters->]` is an optional comma-delimited list of arguments, and the closure body can be an expression as well as zero or more Groovy statements. The arguments look similar to a method's parameter list, and these arguments may be typed or untyped. A Groovy closure is a block of reusable code within curly braces, `{}`, which can be assigned to a property or a variable or passed as a parameter to a method. A closure is executed only when it is called, not when it is defined. Listing B-25 illustrates this.

Listing B-25. Calling a Closure

```
1.    def closureVar = {println 'Hello world'}
2.    println "closure is not called yet"
3.    println " "
4.    closureVar.call()
```

- Line 1: This line has the closure with no parameters and consists of a single `println` statement. Because there are no parameters, the parameter `List` and the `->` separator are omitted. The closure is referenced by the identifier `closureVar`.
- Line 4: This line uses the explicit mechanism via the `call()` method to invoke the closure. You may also use the implicit nameless invocation approach: `closureVar()`. As shown in the output, the closure prints "Hello world" when it is called in line 4, not when it is defined in line 1.

Here is the output:

```
closure is not called yet
Hello world
```

Listing B-26 illustrates the same closure as in Listing B-25 but with the parameter.

Listing B-26. Closure with Parameter

```
1.    def closureVar = {param -> println "Hello ${param}"}
2.    closureVar.call('world')
3.    closureVar ('implicit world')
```

- *Line 2*: This is an explicit call with the actual argument `'world'`.
- *Line 3*: This is an implicit call with the actual argument `'implicit world'`.

```
Hello world
Hello implicit world
```

As Listing B-27 illustrates, the formal parameters to a closure may be assigned default values.

Listing B-27. Parameters with Default Values

```
1.    def sayHello= {str1, str2= " default world" -> println "${str1} ${str2}" }
2.    sayHello("Hello", "world")
3.    sayHello("Hello")
```

- *Line 1*: The `sayHello` closure takes two parameters, of which one parameter, `str2`, has a default value.
- *Line 3*: Only one actual parameter is provided to the closure, and the default value of the second parameter is used.

Here is the output:

```
Hello world
Hello default world
```

Closures always have a return value. The value may be specified via one or more explicit return statements in the closure body, as illustrated in Listing B-28, or as the value of the last executed statement if `return` is not explicitly specified, as illustrated in Listing B-29.

Listing B-28. Using Return Keyword

```
def sum = {list -> return list.sum()}
assert sum([2,2]) == 4
```

Listing B-29. Return Keyword Optional

```
def sum = {list -> list.sum()}
assert sum([2,2]) == 4
```

To understand closures, you have to understand the concept of free variables. A closure is formed when the body of a function refers to one or more free variables. Free variables are variables that are not local to the function and are not passed as arguments to the function but are defined in the enclosing scope where the function is defined. Thus, closures refer to variables not listed in their parameter list (free variables). They are “bound” to variables within the scope where they are defined. Listing B-30 illustrates this.

Listing B-30. Free Variables

```
def myConst = 5
def incByConst = { num -> num + myConst }
assert  incByConst(10) == 15
```

The runtime “closes over” the free variable (`myConst` in Listing B-30) so that it is available when the function is executed. That is, the compiler creates a closure that envelops the external context of free variables and binds them.

Implicit Variables

Within a Groovy closure, an implicit variable (`it`) is defined that has a special meaning. If only one argument is passed to the closure, the arguments list and the `->` symbol can be omitted, and the closure will have access to `it`, which represents that one argument, illustrated in Listing B-31.

Listing B-31. Using it

```
def closure = {println "Hello ${it}"}
closure.call('world')
```

```
Hello world
```

A closure always has at least one argument, which will be available within the body of the closure via the implicit parameter `it` if no explicit parameters are defined. The developer never has to declare the `it` variable—like the `this` parameter within objects, it is implicitly available. If a closure is invoked with zero arguments, then `it` will be `null`.

Explicit Declaration of Closure

All closures defined in Groovy are essentially derived from the type `Closure`. Because `groovy.lang` is automatically imported, you can refer to `Closure` as a type within your code. This is an explicit declaration of a closure. The advantage of declaring a closure explicitly is that a nonclosure cannot be inadvertently assigned to such a variable. Listing B-32 illustrates how to declare a closure explicitly.

Listing B-32. Explicit Declaration of a Closure

```
Closure closure = { println it }
```

Reusing the Method as a Closure

Groovy provides the method closure operator (`.&`) for reusing the method as a closure. The method closure operator allows the method to be accessed and passed around like a closure. Listing B-33 illustrates this.

Listing B-33. Reusing the Method as a Closure

```
1.    def list = ["A","B","C","D"]
2.    String printElement(String element) {
3.    println element
4.    }
5.    list.each(this.&printElement)
```

Listing B-33 creates a list of names and iterates through the list to print out the names. In line 5, the method closure operator (`.&`) causes the method `printElement` to be accessed as a closure. Here is the output:

```
A
B
C
D
```

Passing a Closure as a Parameter

A closure is an object. You can pass closures around just like any other objects. A common example is iterating over a collection using a closure (see Listing B-34).

Listing B-34. Passing a Closure As a Parameter

```
def list = ["A", "B", "C"]
def x = { println it }
list.each(x)
```

```
A
B
C
```

Specialized Operators

Groovy includes several standard operators found in other programming languages, as well as operators that are specific to Groovy that make it so powerful. In the sections that follow, you will learn the specialized operators in Groovy such as spread, Elvis, safe navigation, field, method closure, and diamond operators.

Spread Operator

The spread operator (`*.`) is a shorthand technique for invoking a method or closure on a collection of objects. Listing B-35 illustrates the usage of the spread operator for iterating over a list.

Listing B-35. Using the Spread Operator

```
1.    def map = [1:"A", 2:"B", 3:"C", 4:"D"]
2.    def keys = [1, 2, 3, 4]
3.    def values = ["A", "B", "C", "D"]
4.    assert map*.key == keys
5.    assert map*.value == values
```

Line 4 and line 5 use the spread operator to access keys and values of the map.

Elvis Operator

The Elvis operator (`?:`) is a shorthand version of the Java ternary operator. For example, `b= a ?: 1` could be interpreted as follows:

```
if(a != 0)
b = a
else
b = 1
```

Listing B-36 illustrates using the Java ternary and Elvis operators in Groovy.

Listing B-36. Using the Elvis Operator

```
def firstName = author.firstName == null ? "unknown" : author.firstName // Java ternary
def firstName2 = author.firstName ?: "unknown" // Groovy Elvis
```

In both cases, if `author.firstName` is null, then `firstName` is set to `unknown`. The `author.firstName` fragment of the Elvis operator example is known as the *expression*. If the expression evaluates to `false` or `null`, then the value after the colon is returned.

Safe Navigation/Dereference Operator

The safe navigation/dereference operator (`?.`) is used to avoid null pointer exceptions. Consider the situation where you have an `Author` object and you want to print the `firstName`. If the `Author` object is `null` when you access the `firstName` property, you will get a `NullPointerException` (see Listing B-37).

Listing B-37. Using the Safe Navigation/Dereference Operator

```
class Author {
String firstName
String lastName
def printFullName = {
println "${firstName} ${lastName}"
}
}
Author author
println author.firstName
```

The code in Listing B-37 throws a `NullPointerException`. In Java, you add a `null` check this way:

```
if (author != null) {
println "Author FirstName = ${author.firstName}"
}
```

Listing B-38 illustrates how to add the `null` check using the safe navigation/dereference operator in Groovy.

Listing B-38. Using the Safe Navigation/Dereference Operator

```
class Author {
String firstName
String lastName
def printFullName = {
println "${firstName} ${lastName}"
}
}
Author author
println "Author FirstName = ${author?.firstName}"
```

Field Operator

Groovy provides a way to bypass the getter and access the underlying field directly. Bypassing the getter and accessing the underlying field is not recommended, however, because it is a violation of encapsulation. Listing B-39 shows an example of using the field operator (`.@`).

Listing B-39. Using the Field Operator

```
class Author {
String name
}
def author = new Author(name: "Vishal")
println author.name
println author.@name
```

```
Vishal

Vishal
```

In this example, the first `println` uses the getter to access `name`, and the second `println` bypasses the getter to access `name` directly.

Method Closure Operator

The method closure operator (`.&`) allows the method to be accessed and passed around like a closure (see Listing B-40).

Listing B-40. Using the Method Closure Operator

```
def list = ["A","B","C"]
list.each { println it }
String printName(String name) {
println name
}
list.each(this.&printName)
```

```
A

B

C

A

B

C
```

This example creates a list of names and iterates through the list to print out the names. A `printName()` method is created that prints the `name` parameter. Lastly and the main point of this example, the list is iterated, executing the `printName()` method as a closure. Using the method closure operator, you are able to expose Java methods as closures.

Diamond Operator

The diamond operator (<>) is introduced in Groovy to avoid the repetition of parameterized types. The parameterized types can be omitted and replaced with pointy brackets, which look like a diamond. Listing B-41 shows a usual verbose way of defining a list.

***Listing B-41.** A Simple Groovy Script: Hello.groovy*

```
List<List<String>> list1 = new ArrayList<List<String>>()
```

Listing B-42 illustrates how to use the diamond operator.

***Listing B-42.** Using the Diamond Operator*

```
List<List<String>> list1 = new ArrayList<>()
```

Summary

This appendix introduced the basics of Groovy. One appendix is not enough to learn any language or technology, but that said, the introduction to Groovy in this appendix is substantial enough to write web applications using Grails. In this appendix, you first learned how to install Groovy; then it showed how to write a "Hello World" program with Groovy. Then you learned how to run Groovy scripts and classes and looked at various strings supported in Groovy. Then the chapter briefly introduced the collective datatypes of Groovy, and you learned what a closure is and how to use it in Groovy. Lastly, you learned how to use specialized operators available in Groovy.

Appendix C

Introduction to Scala

Scala seamlessly integrates object-oriented and functional programming. Scala is a statically typed language that was conceived in 2001 by Martin Odersky, who also wrote the Java reference compiler and coauthored Java generics. Scala compiles to byte code for the Java Virtual Machine (JVM), making it platform independent. That also means that from a Scala program you can use existing Java libraries, and vice versa.

Getting Started with Scala

You can download Scala from `www.scala-lang.org/download/`. This Scala software distribution can be installed on any Unix-like or Windows system. It requires the Java runtime version 1.6 or newer.

```
>scala  -version
```

```
Scala code runner version 2.10.3 -- Copyright 2002-2013, LAMP/EPFL
```

There are three ways to execute Scala code.

- Using the interactive interpreter
- Executing Scala code as a script
- Compiling Scala code

Using the Interactive Interpreter

The Scala interpreter (called a read-evaluate-print loop, or REPL) is the easiest way to execute a single line of Scala code. You can start the interactive interpreter using the Scala command-line tool `scala`, which is located in the `bin` folder in the folder where Scala is installed.

From the command line, enter the following to open the interactive interpreter, shown in Figure C-1.

```
>scala
```

```
Welcome to Scala version 2.10.3 (Java HotSpot(TM) Client VM, Java 1.6.0_05).
Type in expressions to have them evaluated.
Type :help for more information.

scala> _
```

***Figure C-1.** The Scala interactive interpreter*

Using the interactive interpreter you can run your first "Hello world" program by using the println method.

```
scala> println("Hello world");
```

```
Hello world
```

To quit the interpreter, type exit.

```
scala> exit
```

Executing Scala Code as a Script

Another way to execute Scala code is to type it into a text file and save it with the extension .scala. You can then execute that code by typing *filename*.scala. For instance, you can create a file named hello.scala with "Hello world" in it.

```
println("Hello world")
```

To execute it, you specify the file name as a parameter to the Scala command-line tool.

```
>scala  hello.scala
```

Compiling Scala Code

You can also execute Scala code by first compiling it using the scalac command-line tool. Then the code will need to be executed in the context of an application, so you will need to add an object with a main() method (see Listing C-1).

***Listing C-1.** The "Hello world" Program*

```
object HelloWorld {
def main(args: Array[String]) {
println("Hello, world")
   }
}
```

> **Note** The semicolon at the end of a statement is usually optional.

- *Line 1*: The `main()` method is defined in an object, not in a class. Scala has an `object` construct with which you can declare a singleton object. You will learn more about singletons later in this appendix.
- *Line 2*: Scala program processing starts from the `main()` method, which is a mandatory part of every Scala program. The `main()` method is not marked as static. In Scala, everything is an object. The `main()` method is an instance method on a singleton object that is automatically instantiated.
- *Line 2*: There is no return type. Actually, there is `Unit`, which is similar to `void`, but it is inferred by the compiler. You can explicitly specify the return type by putting a colon and the type after the parameters.

```
def main(args: Array[String]) : Unit = {
                     }
```

- *Line 2*: There is no access-level modifier in Scala. You have a `public` modifier in Java in this context, but Scala does not specify the `public` modifier because the default access level is public.
- *Line 2*: Scala uses the `def` keyword to tell the compiler that this is a method.

Save the code in Listing C-1 in a file called `HelloWorld.scala` and compile the code using the following command:

```
>scalac HelloWorld.scala
```

Now run the program using this command:

```
>scala HelloWorld
```

```
Hello, World!
```

> **Note** Java requires you to put a public class in a file named after the class. For example, you should put class `HelloWorld` in file `HelloWorld.java`. In Scala, you can name `.scala` files anything you want, no matter what Scala classes or code you put in them. However, it is recommended you name files after the classes they contain as is done in Java so as to easily locate classes based on file names.

Variables

Scala allows you to decide whether a variable is immutable (read-only) when you declare it. An immutable variable is declared with the keyword `val`. This means it is a variable that cannot be changed. Listing C-2 illustrates creating an immutable variable, and Figure C-2 shows what happens when you try to change it.

Listing C-2. Immutable Variable

```
val immutableVar : String = "Hello"
immutableVar = "Hi"
```

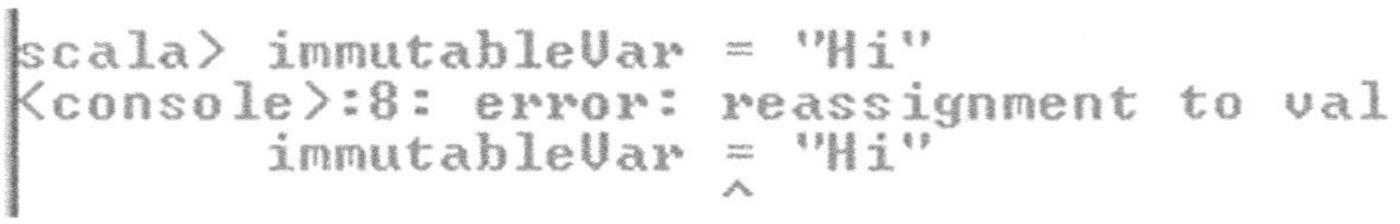

```
scala> immutableVar = "Hi"
<console>:8: error: reassignment to val
       immutableVar = "Hi"
                    ^
```

***Figure C-2.** Error when trying to change val*

Listing C-3 illustrates creating a mutable variable, and Figure C-3 shows it successfully changed.

Listing C-3. Mutable Variable

```
var mutableVar = "Hello"
mutableVar = "Hi"
```

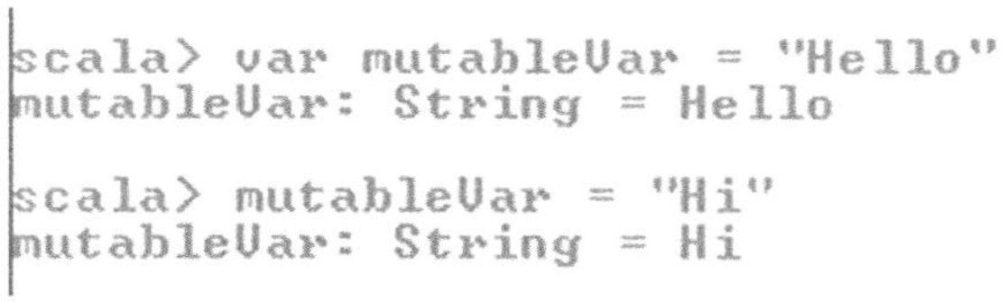

```
scala> var mutableVar = "Hello"
mutableVar: String = Hello

scala> mutableVar = "Hi"
mutableVar: String = Hi
```

***Figure C-3.** var changed successfully*

When you assign an initial value to a variable, the Scala compiler can infer the type of the variable based on the value assigned to it. This is called *type inference*, as illustrated in Listing C-4.

Listing C-4. Type Inference

```
var  var1= 10
var var2 = "Hello world"
```

In Listing C-4, Scala will infer `var1` to be of the `Int` type and `var2` to be of the `String` type variable.

Collections

Scala collections distinguish between mutable and immutable collections. A mutable collection can be updated or extended in place. This means you can change, add, or remove elements of a collection as a side effect. Immutable collections, by contrast, never change. You still have operations that simulate additions, removals, or updates, but those operations will in each case return a new collection and leave the old collection unchanged. Scala has a rich collections library. The most commonly used collections are lists, sets, and maps, which are explained in the following sections. You can find details on Scala's collection library at `http://docs.scala-lang.org/overviews/collections/introduction.html`.

Lists

Lists are immutable, which means the elements of a list cannot be changed by assignment. The type of a list that has elements of type T is written as `List[T]`, as shown here:

```
val numberList: List[Integer] = List(1, 2, 3)
```

Listing C-5 illustrates how to create and use an immutable list.

Listing C-5. Creating an Immutable List

```
val list = List(1, 2, 3, 2, 3)
println (list.head)
println(list.tail)
println(list.length)
println(list.max)
println(list.min)
println(list.sum)
println(list.sorted)
println(list.reverse)
```

```
head    --- 1
tail    --- List(2, 3, 2, 3)
length --- 5
max     --- 3
min     --- 1
sum     --- 11
sorted --- List(1, 2, 2, 3, 3)
reverse--- List(3, 2, 3, 2, 1)
```

Scala defines only an immutable list. However, it also defines some mutable list types, such as `ArrayBuffer`. Listing C-6 illustrates how to create a mutable list.

Listing C-6. Creating a Mutable List

```
import collection.mutable
val list = mutable.ArrayBuffer(1, 2, 3, 2, 3)
assert (list.length  == 5)
```

Sets

A set is a collection that contains no duplicate elements. There are two kinds of sets, the immutable and the mutable. Listing C-7 illustrates how to create an immutable set.

Listing C-7. Creating an Immutable Set

```
val set = Set(1, 2, 3, 2, 3)
println ("head -- "+set.head)
println("tail -- "+set.tail)
println("size -- "+set.size)
println("sum  -- "+set.sum)
```

```
head -- 1
tail -- Set(2, 3)
size -- 3
sum  -- 6
```

By default, Scala uses the immutable set. If you want to use the mutable set, you will have to import `scala.collection.mutable.Set`. Listing C-8 illustrates how to create and use a mutable set.

Listing C-8. Creating a Mutable Set

```
import collection.mutable
val set = mutable.HashSet(1, 2, 3, 2, 3)
assert (set.size == 3)
```

Maps

A Scala map is a collection of key-value pairs. By default, Scala uses the immutable map. If you want to use the mutable map, you'll have to import the `scala.collection.mutable.Map` class explicitly. Listing C-9 illustrates how to create and use an immutable map.

Listing C-9. Creating an Immutable Map

```
val map = Map("1" -> 1, "2" -> 2, "3" -> 3, "2" -> 2, "3" -> 3)

println ("head  -- "+map.head)
println("tail  -- "+map.tail)
println("size  -- "+map.size)
```

```
head  -- (1,1)
tail  -- Map(2 -> 2, 3 -> 3)
size  -- 3
```

Classes

Classes in Scala are declared very much like Java classes. One difference is that Scala classes can have parameters, as illustrated in Listing C-10.

Listing C-10. Scala Class with Parameters

```
class Vehicle (speed : Int){
val mph :Int = speed
    def race() = println("Racing")
}
```

The `Vehicle` class takes one argument, which is the speed of the vehicle. This argument must be passed when creating an instance of class `Vehicle`, as follows: `new Vehicle(100)`. The class contains one method, called `race()`.

Extending a Class

It is possible to override methods inherited from a superclass in Scala, as illustrated in Listing C-11.

Listing C-11. Extending a Scala Class

```
1.    class Car (speed : Int) extends Vehicle(speed) {
2.    override val mph: Int= speed
3.    override  def race() = println("Racing Car")
4.    }
```

- *Line 1*: The `Car` class extends the `Vehicle` class using the keyword `extends`.
- *Lines 2 to 3*: The field `mph` and the method `race()` need to be overridden using the keyword `override`.

Listing C-12 illustrates another class called `Bike` that extends `Vehicle`.

Listing C-12. Extending a Scala Class

```
class Vehicle (speed : Int){
val mph :Int = speed
    def race() = println("Racing")
}
class Car (speed : Int) extends Vehicle(speed) {
override val mph: Int= speed
override  def race() = println("Racing Car")

}
class Bike(speed : Int) extends Vehicle(speed) {
override val mph: Int = speed
override  def race() = println("Racing Bike")

}
```

Save Listing C-12 in the file `vehicle.scala` and compile it using the following:

```
>scalac vehicle.scala
```

Now you can enter the REPL using the `scala` command and create the `vehicle` object, as shown here:

```
scala> val vehicle1 = new Car(200)
```

With this command, Scala creates the `vehicle1` object, as shown here:

```
vehicle1: Car = Car@19a8942
```

Now you can use this `vehicle1` object created by Scala to access the speed of `Car`.

```
scala> vehicle1.mph
```

The Scala REPL emits the speed of `Car`, as shown here:

```
res1: Int = 200
```

In the similar manner, you can execute the `race()` method of `vehicle1`, as shown here:

```
scala>vehicle1.race()
```

The Scala interpreter emits the output, as shown here:

```
Racing Car
```

Now you can create the `Bike` object and access its property and method, as shown here:

```
scala> val vehicle2 = new Bike(100)
```

```
vehicle2: Bike = Bike@b7ad3
```

```
scala>vehicle2.mph
```

```
res4: Int = 100
```

```
scala> vehicle2.race()
```

```
Racing Bike
```

Traits

Say you want to add another class to your vehicle hierarchy. This time you want to add a batmobile. A batmobile can race, glide, and fly. But you cannot add glide and fly methods to the `Vehicle` class because in a nonfictional world, `Car` and `Bike` do not glide or fly. Not yet at least. So, if you want to add `Batmobile` to your vehicle hierarchy, you can use a *trait*. Traits are like interfaces in Java that can also contain code. In Scala, when a class inherits from a trait, it implements the interface of the trait and inherits all the code contained in the trait. Listing C-13 shows flying and gliding traits.

Listing C-13. Scala Traits

```
trait flying {
    def fly() = println("flying")
}

trait gliding {
def gliding() = println("gliding")
}
```

Now you can create the `Batmobile` class that extends `Vehicle` class along with the `flying` and `gliding` traits, as shown in Listing C-14.

Listing C-14. Using Traits

```
Batmobile(speed : Int) extends Vehicle(speed)  with flying with gliding{
override val mph: Int = speed
override  def race() = println("Racing Batmobile")
override def fly() = println("Flying Batmobile")
override def glide() = println("Gliding Batmobile")

}
```

You can now create a batmobile in the REPL, as illustrated here:

```
scala> val vehicle3 = new Batmobile(300)
```

```
vehicle3: Batmobile = Batmobile@374ed5
```

Now you can access the `fly()` method of `Batmobile`, as illustrated here:

```
scala> vehicle3.fly()
```

```
Flying Batmobile
```

Create a list of vehicles, and then you can use the `maxBy()` method provided by the Scala collections library to find the fastest vehicle in the list.

```
scala> val vehicleList = List(vehicle1, vehicle2, vehicle3)
```

```
vehicleList: List[Vehicle] = List(Car@562791, Bike@e80317, Batmobile@374ed5)
```

```
scala> val fastestVehicle = vehicleList.maxBy(_.mph)
```

```
fastestVehicle: Vehicle = Batmobile@374ed5
```

Singleton Objects

Scala does not have static members. Instead, Scala has singleton objects. A singleton object definition looks like a class definition, except instead of the keyword class you use the keyword `object`. A singleton is a class that can have only one instance. Listing C-15 illustrates how to use the singleton object in an application.

Listing C-15. Using a Singleton Object in an Application

```
class Vehicle (speed : Int){
val mph :Int = speed
def race() = println("Racing")
}
class Car (speed : Int) extends Vehicle(speed) {
override val mph: Int= speed
override  def race() = println("Racing Car")
}
 class Bike(speed : Int) extends Vehicle(speed) {
 override val mph: Int = speed
 override  def race() = println("Racing Bike")
 }
 trait flying {
 def fly() = println("flying")
 }
 trait gliding {
 def glide() = println("gliding")
 }
 class Batmobile(speed : Int) extends Vehicle(speed)  with flying with gliding{
 override val mph: Int = speed
 override  def race() = println("Racing Batmobile")
 override def fly() = println("Flying Batmobile")
 override def glide() = println("Gliding Batmobile")
 }
 object Vehicle {
 def main(args: Array[String]) {
 val vehicle1 = new Car(200)
```

```
    val vehicle2 = new Bike(100)
    val vehicle3 = new Batmobile(300)

    val vehicleList = List(vehicle1, vehicle2, vehicle3)
    val fastestVehicle = vehicleList.maxBy(_.mph)

    printVehicle

    def printVehicle{
    println ("speed of Bike : " + vehicle1.mph);
    println ("speed of Car : " + vehicle2.mph);
    println ("speed of Batmobile : " + vehicle3.mph);
    println ("Fastest Vehicle : " + fastestVehicle.mph + " mph");

        }
      }
    }
```

When the previous code is compiled and executed, it produces the following result:

```
>scalac vehicle.scala
>scala Vehicle
```

```
speed of Bike : 200 mph

speed of Car : 100 mph

speed of Batmobile : 300 mph

Fastest Vehicle : 300 mph
```

Summary

This appendix introduced you to the basics of Scala. You learned three ways to interactively execute Scala code as a script and as a compiled program. Then you learned how to use the Scala collections library. Finally, you learned how to use traits and how to use a singleton object in an application.

Index

A

B

C

D

E

F

G

H

I

J, K

P, Q

R

S

T

U

V

W, X, Y, Z